FIRESIDE

The Woman's Day Book of Soft Toys and Dolls

by JOAN RUSSELL

A Fireside Book
Published by Simon and Schuster
New York

3   4   5   6   7   8   9   10   11   12
1   2   3   4   5   6   7   8   9   10 Pbk.

Library of Congress Cataloging in Publication Data

Russell, Joan.
   The Woman's day book of soft toys and dolls.

   (A Fireside book)
   1. Soft toy making. 2. Dollmaking. I. Woman's
day. II. Title.
TT174.3.R87 1980   745.59′24   79-23713
ISBN 0-671-22085-3
ISBN 0-671-25403-0 Pbk.

Acknowledgments

These toy designs have been selected from those appearing through the years in *Woman's Day* magazine. For the happy presentation my toys have received, my special thanks to these special people: Eileen Tighe, for her generosity; Theresa Capuana, for her encouragement and enthusiasm, for which I'm very grateful; Virginia Savage, for attention to every detail in pattern and instruction; and to Ben Calvo, for his excellent photography. Another special thank you to readers of *Woman's Day,* who have sent me many wonderful letters, and to Nora Fennell, whose aid in answering them has been invaluable. For organizing and producing this book, I heartily thank Julie Houston and Dina von Zweck.

Contents

8

Introduction

Where to begin? Perhaps you've seen a pattern for a toy you would like to make for a favorite child. There are then two things to consider—the child and the choice of suitable materials to make the toy.

If the child is an infant then the toy *must* be safe. No dangling buttons, loose snaps or wires. The fabric will most likely be soft or have an interesting texture, but above all it should be very washable. The stuffing must also be easily washed—polyester fiber (soft and fluffy) or foam (a little lumpy). If the toy has an arm or leg just the right size for a small fist to clutch, it will be loved all the more.

If the child is a toddler, the toy should be tough, able to take long leaps down stairs and be dragged through dust and dirt. A scrubbable, closely woven fabric, sewn with double seams, would be the best choice. If you do use buttons or beads for decoration, they must be securely sewn.

Older, more careful children would probably like more detail—buttons and snaps or Velcro fastenings to manage, hats to put on and shoes not to lose. Colorful, sturdy, washable fabrics—perhaps fabrics taken from their own favorite out-grown clothes—would be suitable. They would probably delight in helping to choose colors, kind of face or hair, even perhaps to sew a cape or hat for their new toy friend, using felt, large needle and doubled thread.

An even older girl might like dolls that are carefully dressed and meant to be admired rather than played with every day. This type of doll could be clothed in the prettiest, most impractical of fabrics: old rescued laces, beautiful velvets, soft, thin lining fabrics. A delight for the eye and imagination and great fun for the person putting it together.

Once you've considered the child and determined the kind of materials you'll need, the collecting begins. The five-and-ten offers a lot for the toy maker: remnants of fabric, buttons and laces, bags of polyester fiber for stuffing, knitting yarns and, of course the necessary threads and needles, pins and marking pencils. Socks and terry cloth towels can be made into small animal toys. Chamois cloth can become a beautiful Indian maiden's dress. Tour through all the departments with your mind open to unusual possibilities. (Once, in desperation for a suitable print for an international doll, I found just the right one at the men's cotton shorts counter.) Of course, once you begin collecting bits and pieces, you'll soon need cardboard boxes and an extra closet to store them in.

Finding something that may seem commonplace to someone else but that *you* know will be just the thing to complete your latest toy is part of the fun of making animals and dolls. The rest of the fun is the satisfaction of creating a completely unique toy—one like no other in the world.

Hoping you'll find this joy, too,

JOAN RUSSELL

Construction Techniques

Before you begin to make the toys, read through the general directions below. These simple guidelines apply to nearly all the individual projects; variations are given with specific instructions.

PATTERNS   All the patterns in this book are actual size. To use them, place a piece of tissue paper or clear vinyl over the book page and trace the outlines of the patterns you will need. Label each piece and cut along outer edges. Plan the placement of the patterns on the wrong side of the fabric you are using, being sure to allow 1″ between the pieces for seams. If two pieces are to be cut from the same pattern piece, reverse the pattern to cut the second piece. If the fabric has a nap, such as velveteen, be sure to place the patterns so that the nap runs in the same direction. Pin each pattern in place. With a soft pencil, outline each pattern on the fabric. This outline will be your stitching guideline. Cut out the pattern pieces, *adding a ½″ seam allowance around each one.* (Note: When the dimensions of a piece are given, they include seam allowance. Appliqué pieces require only a ¼″ seam allowance.)

STITCHING   There are two types of hand stitches used in making these toys. First you need a few "fundamental sewing" stitches to sew them and their clothes together. Then embroidery stitches are used for facial features and certain other decorations. Stitches of both types are illustrated below.

Seams can be done by hand, using a closely spaced, small backstitch, reinforced with running stitches. However, machine stitching is recommended for greater strength, using small stitches and a fine (size 11) needle to keep the needle holes small. Reinforce the seams at stuffing openings with double stitching (i.e. sew the seam line twice).

As each seam is done, check for "jogs" or loose stitches and restitch if needed. All uncorrected bumps and jogs will show after you turn and stuff the toy. Trim the seam allowance to ¼″, and clip **V** notches into it on curved edges, and in such places as between fingers and corners or legs.

Turn pieces carefully to the right side. Tiny pieces may need the careful encouragement of a long, blunt crochet hook or knitting needle to turn completely.

STUFFING   Dacron or polyester fiber stuffing is preferred for smoothness, resiliency and washability. Kapok and cotton batting can be used where washing is not necessary, if care is taken to avoid lumps while you stuff.

Fold masking tape over raw cloth edges of openings to reduce fraying and hold edges open for stuffing. Insert *small* bits of stuffing, and push them gently into the corners with a blunt crochet hook. Stuff until pieces are firm and smooth. Remove the tape before sewing. Continue to add the stuffing as you sew the openings closed in order to keep the sewn area as firm as the rest of the toy.

Hand stitching the dolls is usually less strong than machine stitching, but certainly, if you reinforce the seams with a pair of running stitches, there is no reason why it cannot be done. Consider the use of the doll or toy. One that is going to get lots of wear and tear must be strongly constructed, while a doll that will be admired and displayed will naturally require less sturdy construction.

THE STITCHES
For basic doll construction:

Running stitch

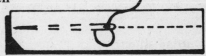

The running stitch is a simple, even hand stitch used for gathering, quilting, tucking and mending. Two parallel rows of the running stitch constitute the "double stitch."

Overcast stitch

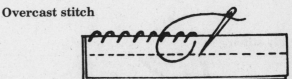

The overcast stitch is used for finishing edges on fabrics that ravel.

Hemstitch

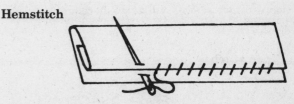

The hemstitch shows on the wrong side but not on the right. Use it for hems and where indicated in the projects.

Basting

The baste stitch is a larger, looser version of the running stitch, used to hold fabric together before final stitching.

Whipstitch

The whipstitch is somewhat similar to the overcast stitch. It is used for basic construction, especially helpful here in attaching body parts and holding them together.

For Embroidery and Appliqué

Outline stitch

This is also called the stem stitch, or crewel stitch. It is used for outlines, stems and any fine lines.

Fly stitch

Use this stitch for borders or for filling in areas. The first and larger loop is tacked into place by a second loop—different sizes will give different effects.

Chain stitch

This is a good stitch for outlines and, worked in even, close rows, it can also be used as a filler.

Satin stitch

The satin stitch is a series of straight stitches, worked close together to fill in an area or to make special shapes.

Couch stitch

In this stitch, you are tacking one or several strands into place with a small, single stitch. This is useful on borders and to outline other shapes.

Blanket stitch

This stitch will cover a seam edge in sewing or in appliqué. Worked in circles, it makes flowers, and it is also used as an outline stitch.

French knot

This stitch is used anywhere the effect of a single dot is necessary. Wind the thread around the needle two or more times before reinserting the needle into the fabric.

Stem stitch

Another name for the stem stitch is the outline stitch.

This is a combination of long and short simple stitches, which is perfect as a filler for special areas and to add texture and strength to your work.

3. Pin or baste your appliqué onto the fabric, and attach it with a running stitch. You can also use an overcast or blanket stitch.

APPLIQUÉ

1. Place your pattern on the fabric and cut around it, remembering to add enough for "seam allowance"—½″ to ¼″

2. Clipping curved edges where necessary to have a flat hem, turn back the "seam allowance" by basting or with an iron.

Noah's Ark

Here are Mr. and Mrs. Noah and all their "two-by-two" animals. Diagrams and building instructions are also included for the pine and plywood ark.

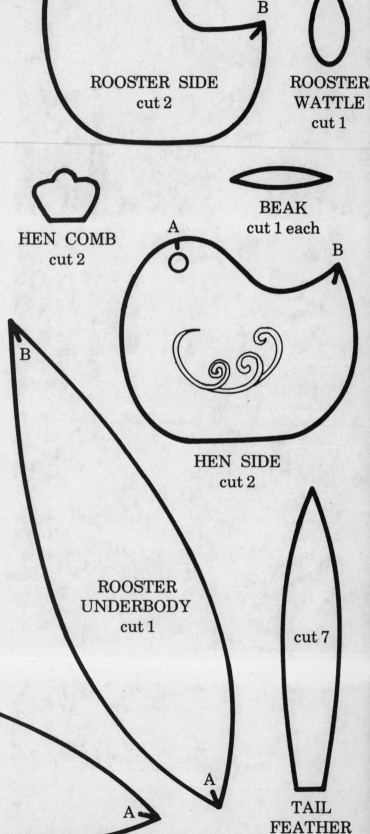

A

A

ROOSTER
COMB
cut 2

B

ROOSTER SIDE
cut 2

ROOSTER
WATTLE
cut 1

BEAK
cut 1 each

HEN COMB
cut 2

A

B

B

HEN SIDE
cut 2

B

ROOSTER
UNDERBODY
cut 1

cut 7

A

B

HEN UNDERBODY
cut 1

A

A

TAIL
FEATHER

Rooster, Hen and Chick

MATERIALS *For all:* 7″ x 8″ piece of cotton—coral color for hen, blue print for rooster; scraps of felt in gold, orange, green, turquoise, navy; coral, gold and green embroidery floss; yellow yarn for chick; 2 black beads; kapok.

ROOSTER Add seam allowances to cotton pieces but omit for felt. Cut blue print sides and underbody; from felt cut gold beak, orange wattle and comb; cut 3 turquoise, 2 navy and 2 green tail feathers.

Seam sides from A to B along back. Matching A's and B's, seam underbody to sides, leaving opening on one lower edge. Trim seams and clip. Turn, stuff, and sew opening. Tack on wattle, beak and comb; outline-stitch green eyes. Sew on tail feathers; curl ends and glue.

HEN Cut from coral cotton and assemble same as Rooster. Tack on turquoise felt eyes, gold beak, orange comb. Outline-stitch gold wings.

CHICK Wind yellow yarn around 2″ cardboard. Slip off; tie center tightly; clip loops to make ball. Sew on yarn strands for tail. Sew on beads for eyes and gold felt bill.

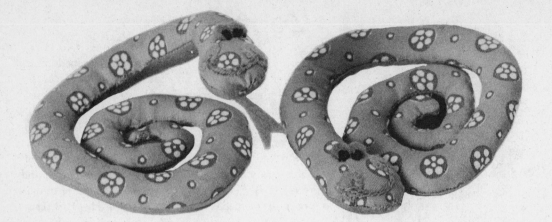

Serpents

MATERIALS *For two:* 5″ x 10″ piece of green cotton; 5″ x 10″ piece of orange-red print; felt scraps in lavender, turquoise and fuchsia; blue and black embroidery floss; 2 pipe cleaners; kapok.

Note: First stitch serpent outline then cut it out as in directions which follow.

FEMALE SERPENT With right sides facing, baste a 5″ square of print over a 5″ square of green. Trace pattern on tracing paper; transfer to print square with carbon paper. With fine machine stitching, sew along pattern, leaving openings at A-A and B-B for turning and stuffing. Seam tip of tail by hand.

Cut carefully between lines of stitching; trim all seams.

Turn carefully to right side, pushing fabric slowly with the eraser end of a slim pencil and pulling it out with a large pin. Press serpent if wrinkled. Stuff lightly; cut pipe cleaner to 4″ length and insert in head end. Sew openings. Cut 2 lavender disks for nostrils, turquoise ovals for eyes and fuchsia tongue. Appliqué disks and outline-stitch mouth with blue floss. Tack on eyes with black floss; sew on tongue.

MALE SERPENT Follow directions for female Serpent but transfer pattern to green square so male coils in opposite direction. Omit tongue.

TONGUE
cut 1

appliqué and embroidery

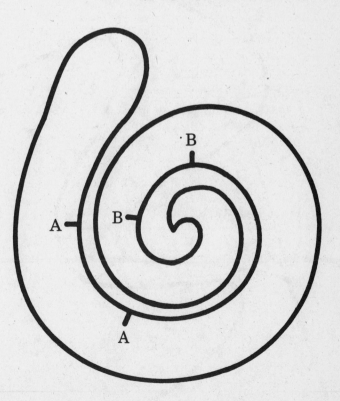

Zebras

MATERIALS *For two:* 36″ striped seersucker, ¼ yard blue for male and ¼ yard green for female; scrap of green jersey; turquoise wool yarn; navy floss; kapok.

Add seam allowances throughout. Following photograph for stripes, cut seersucker sides, underbody and ear pieces for each zebra. Sew darts on underbody. Seam sides from A, around head and back to B. Matching A's, B's and legs, seam underbody to sides, leaving opening on one edge B-C. Trim seams, clip and turn. Stuff firmly and sew opening. Seam ears, leaving opening at D-D. Turn; sew opening. Pleat ears and sew center to head. Appliqué jersey eyes; work navy lashes on female.

For mane, using continuous strands sew 1½″ yarn loops along head and neck seam; for tail, sew center of six 4½″ strands to B.

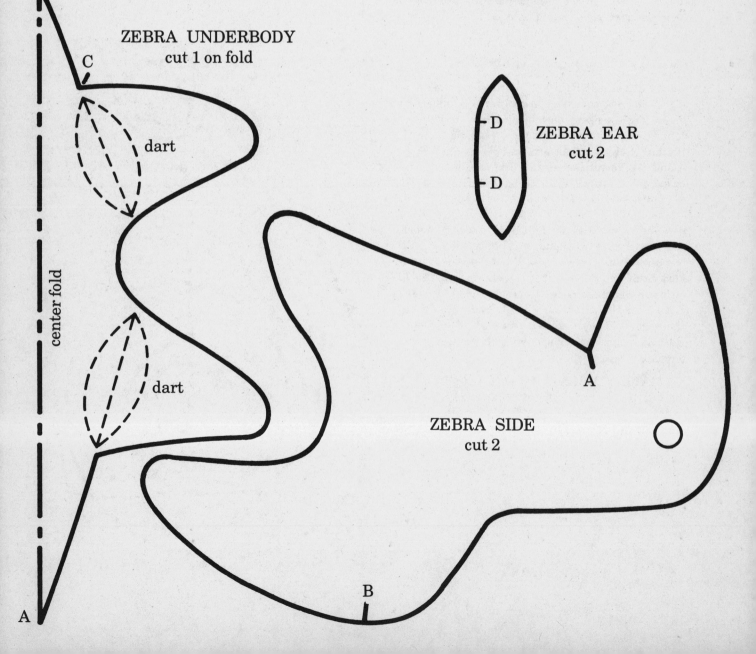

ZEBRA UNDERBODY
cut 1 on fold

center fold

dart

dart

ZEBRA EAR
cut 2

ZEBRA SIDE
cut 2

Owls

MATERIALS *For two:* Scraps of cotton in solid turquoise, powder blue, green, turquoise gingham; turquoise and orange felt; turquoise and powder blue embroidery floss; kapok; cardboard.

Add seam allowances to cotton pieces but omit for felt.

Cut owl body and base from turquoise cotton, eyes from powder blue for one owl, green for the other; cut breast from gingham. Cut turquoise felt pupils and orange beak as in photograph.

Seam body pieces, leaving opening at bottom. Trim seam; turn and stuff. Cut ⅝" cardboard disk; sew fabric base over cardboard at open end.

Appliqué gingham breast, then eyes, to front. Outline eyes with blue floss; work wing tips in fly stitch with turquoise floss. Glue on pupils and beak.

appliqué
and embroidery

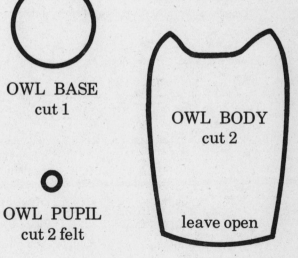

OWL BASE
cut 1

OWL BODY
cut 2

OWL PUPIL
cut 2 felt

leave open

Elephants

MATERIALS *For two:* 36″ cotton, ¼ yard pink broadcloth for female and ¼ yard blue for male; scraps of white and pink-and-white print; gold felt; pink and blue yarn; yellow embroidery floss; kapok.

Add seam allowances throughout except for felt eyes.

FEMALE ELEPHANT Cut pink sides, underbody and ears; cut white tusks, print cheeks and felt eyes.

Seam sides from A, around trunk and back to B. Sew darts in underbody. Seam it to sides, matching A, legs and B, leaving opening on one edge C-D. Trim seams and clip; turn. Stuff firmly and sew opening.

Seam pairs of ears, leaving edges E-F open. Trim seams and turn; fold in raw edges and sew to head.

Seam pairs of tusks, leaving wide end open. Trim, turn and stuff. Turn in raw edges and sew to elephant.

Appliqué eyes and cheeks; outline-stitch toes with yellow floss. For tail, cut three 8″ lengths of yarn; fold in half and tack to B; braid halfway and tie braid.

MALE ELEPHANT Follow patterns and directions for Female Elephant to cut, sew and stuff blue male, omitting cheek appliqué. Sew on eyes and add tail.

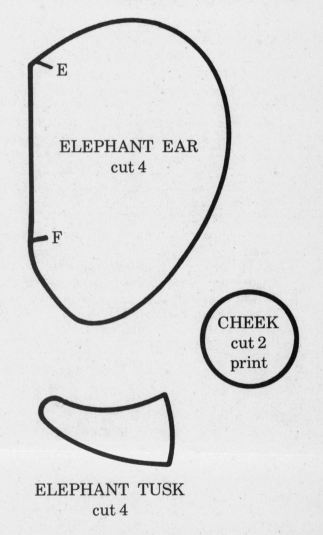

E

F

ELEPHANT EAR
cut 4

CHEEK
cut 2
print

ELEPHANT TUSK
cut 4

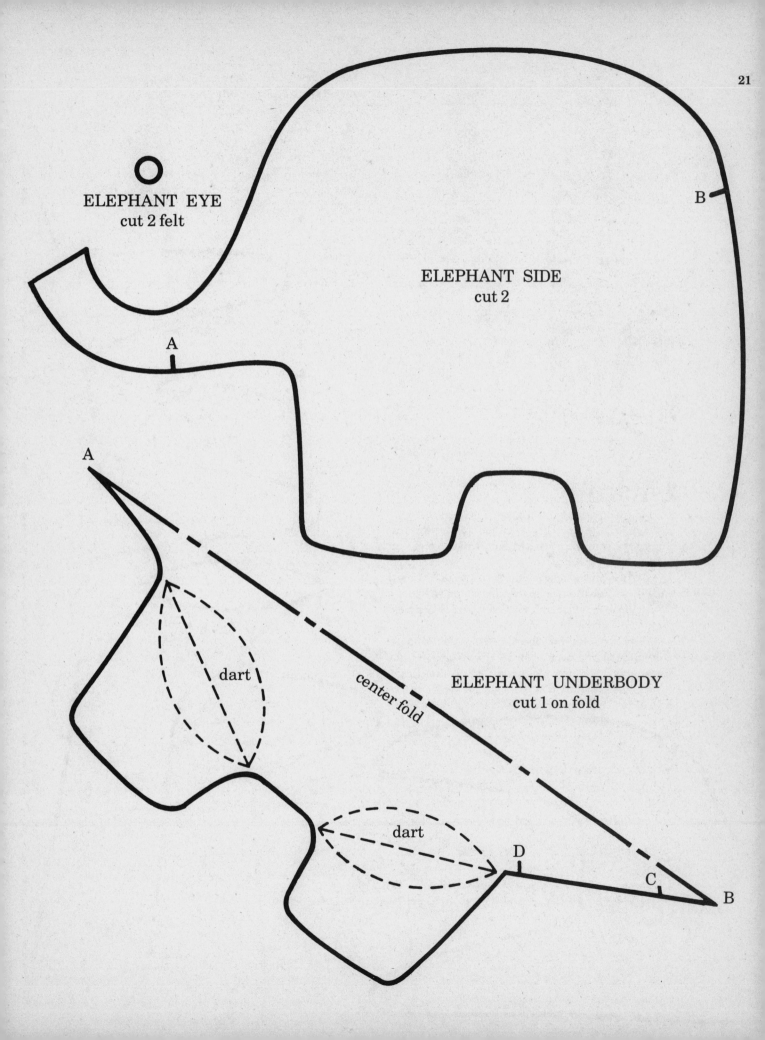

ELEPHANT EYE
cut 2 felt

ELEPHANT SIDE
cut 2

B

A

A

B

dart

center fold

ELEPHANT UNDERBODY
cut 1 on fold

dart

D

C

B

seam underbody to sides. Trim seams and clip at corners; turn. Stuff firmly and sew opening.

Seam two ear pieces, leaving opening. Turn and sew opening. Pleat ear at center and sew to head.

For mane sew ½″ yarn loops close together along center seam, from ears to back; clip loops for short, bushy mane. For tail, sew centers of three 4″ yarn strands to B; braid yarn; tie with thread; clip to 1½″ length. Glue eyes to head; tack horns between ears of male giraffe.

Giraffes

MATERIALS *For two:* ¼ yard 36″ yellow calico; scraps of black and gold felt; 1 ounce of green yarn; kapok.

Add seam allowances to cotton pieces but omit for felt. Cut giraffe underbody, sides and ear pieces from calico; cut eyes from black felt and horns from gold.

Sew darts on underbody. Seam sides from A, around head and back to B, leaving 2″ opening for stuffing on back neck. Matching A's, B's and legs,

GIRAFFE HORN
cut 2 felt

GIRAFFE EYE
cut 2 felt

dart

dart

center fold

GIRAFFE EAR
cut 2

GIRAFFE UNDERBODY
cut 1 on fold

B

A

GIRAFFE SIDE
cut 2

②

①

②

①

①

ASSEMBLY DIAGRAM
Trace and assemble pattern pieces as shown before cutting fabric.

B

A

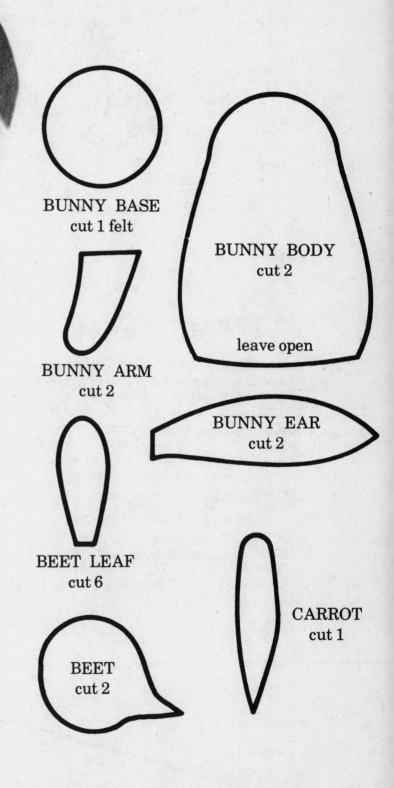

Bunnies with Basket

MATERIALS *For two:* 9″ x 12″ piece of gold felt; scraps of pink, orange and maroon; scrap of blue print cotton; turquoise and green embroidery floss; kapok; cardboard; absorbent cotton.

Add seam allowances only to body pieces.

BUNNIES For each, cut gold felt body, base, arms and ears; cut pink felt nose and orange carrot.

Seam body pieces, leaving bottom open. Trim seam, turn and stuff. Cut 1⅛″ cardboard disk; sew felt base at open end with cardboard inside.

Following photograph, appliqué nose, satin-stitch turquoise eyes and tack on ears. Sew carrot to front of one bunny; add arms and outline paws; couch-stitch green floss leaves. On second bunny, trim carrot to ½″ length and appliqué; work leaves at lower end. Sew arms to sides and tack over carrot; glue on cottontails.

BASKET Use one about 2″ wide and 3″ long; line with excelsior. Adding small seam allowance, cut 4 carrot pieces. Topstitch pairs together, leaving top open; stuff lightly; sew opening; trim seam. Sew strands of green floss to top. Adding small seam allowance, cut beet from maroon felt and leaves from blue print. Seam and stuff beet. Topstitch pairs of leaves; tack to beet.

BUNNY BASE
cut 1 felt

BUNNY BODY
cut 2

leave open

BUNNY ARM
cut 2

BUNNY EAR
cut 2

BEET LEAF
cut 6

CARROT
cut 1

BEET
cut 2

Hippos

MATERIALS *For two:* 36″ cotton, ¼ yard blue for female and ½ yard red print for male; black felt; shocking pink embroidery floss; kapok.

Add seam allowances throughout except to felt eyes. For female, cut sides, underbody and ears from blue; cut print nostrils and felt eyes. For print male, follow photograph for direction of fabric design, cutting underbody from length of goods; cut blue nostrils and felt eyes.

Sew darts on each underbody. Seam sides from A to B along back. Matching A's, B's and legs, seam underbody to sides, leaving an opening on one edge C-D. Trim seams, clip and turn. Stuff firmly and sew opening. Seam ears, leaving opening. Turn; sew to head. Glue on eyes and appliqué nostrils. Using floss, outline-stitch mouths.

ASSEMBLY DIAGRAM

Trace and assemble pattern pieces as shown before cutting fabric.

HIPPO UNDERBODY
cut 1 on fold

A

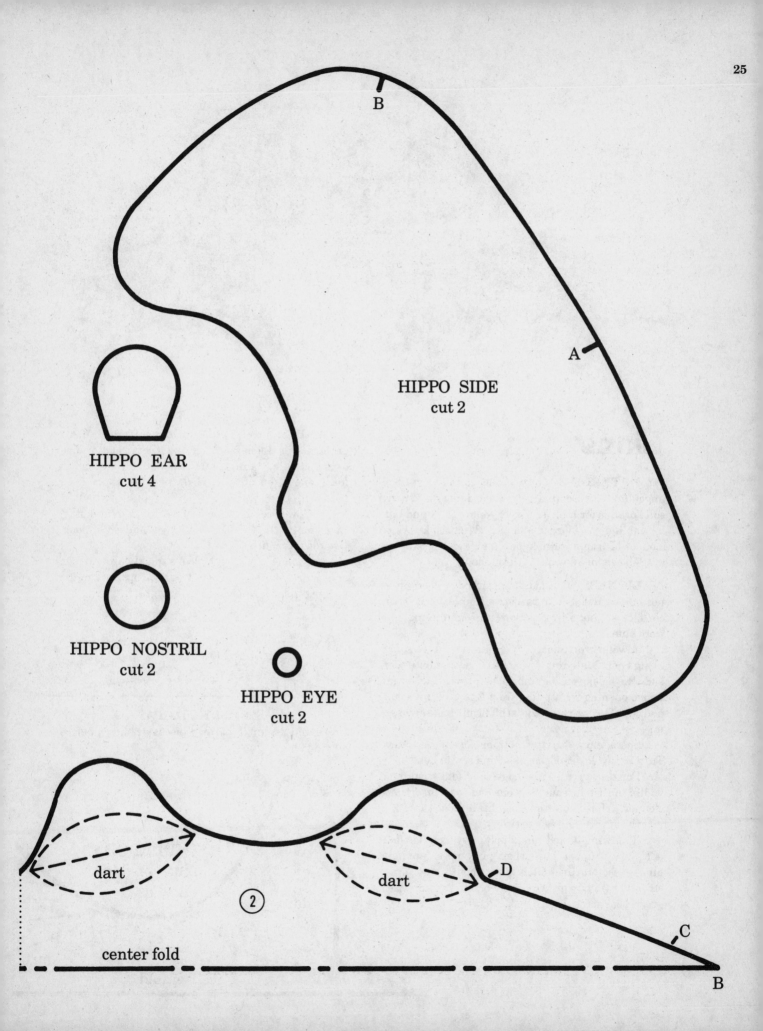

B

A

HIPPO SIDE
cut 2

HIPPO EAR
cut 4

HIPPO NOSTRIL
cut 2

HIPPO EYE
cut 2

dart

dart

D

C

②

center fold

B

Lions

MATERIALS *For both:* 36″ cotton, ¼ yard orange-and-white dotted cotton for Lioness, ¼ yard solid orange for Lion; scraps of yellow, pink and blue for appliqué; red, green and pink floss; black thread; 1 ounce of orange yarn; kapok; 2 pipe cleaners.

Add seam allowances throughout.

LIONESS Cut sides, underbody, ears, upper nose piece and ¾″ x 3″ tail strip from dotted cotton; cut face appliqué from yellow, nose from pink, eyes from blue.

Sew darts on underbody. Seam sides from A to B along back. Matching A's, B's and legs, seam underbody to sides, easing fabric to prevent wrinkles. Leave opening for stuffing from B to C. Trim seams and clip. Turn to right side; stuff firmly and sew opening.

Seam ears, leaving bottoms open, and turn. Turn in raw lower edges, pleat and sew to head.

For tail, turn in raw edges and fold strip to ¼″ width; topstitch seam. Sew one end to B. Insert pipe cleaner, trim it to fit and bend tail. Fold three 2½″ lengths of yarn and sew to tip.

Following dotted line, appliqué yellow for face; add dotted upper nose then pink nose; appliqué blue eyes. Outline-stitch pink mouth and make straight-stitch whiskers with black thread. Work green floss across each eye.

LION Cut orange sides and underbody from patterns for Lioness, reversing them; cut orange ears and ¾″ x 3″ tail strip; cut appliqué the same as for Lioness, but use solid orange for upper nose piece.

Follow directions for Lioness to seam and stuff Lion, make the tail, appliqué face and embroider. Use red for mouth.

For mane, sew 2″ yarn loops thickly around face and across the back of head; trim loops to lengths varying from ¾″ to 1½″, as in photograph.

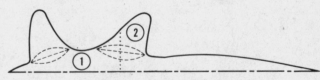

ASSEMBLY DIAGRAM

Trace and assemble pattern pieces as shown before cutting fabric.

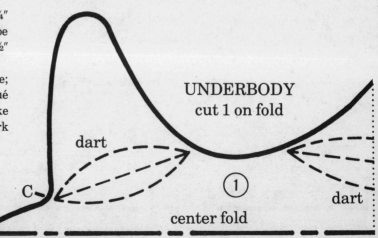

UNDERBODY
cut 1 on fold

dart

C

①

dart

center fold

B

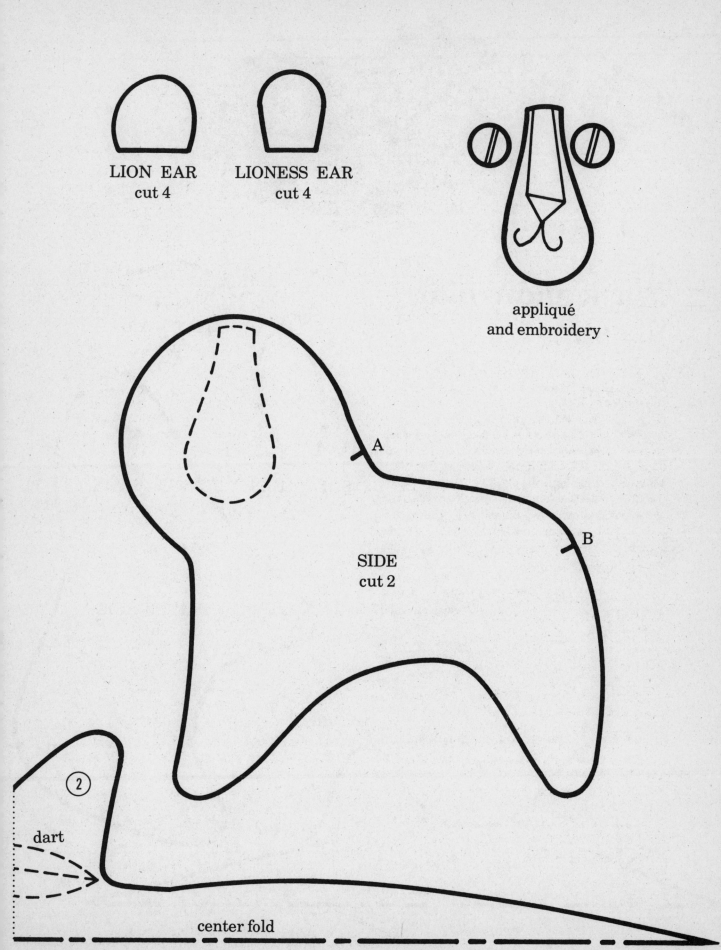

LION EAR
cut 4

LIONESS EAR
cut 4

appliqué
and embroidery

A

B

SIDE
cut 2

② dart

center fold

A

Black and White Sheep

MATERIALS *For two:* ¼ yard 36″ black-and-white-checked lightweight wool; scraps of turquoise and black felt; red embroidery floss; ½ ounce each of heavy black and white yarn; kapok.

Add seam allowances throughout except for felt nose and eyes. Cut sides, underbody, ears and tail from checked wool; cut turquoise felt nose and black felt eyes as in photograph.

Seam sides from A to B along back. Sew darts on underbody. Matching A's, B's and legs, seam underbody to sides, leaving opening for stuffing on one edge B–C. Trim seams and clip. Turn to right side; stuff firmly and sew opening.

Seam pairs of ears and tail, leaving opening; turn. Sew ears to head and tail to B. Appliqué nose and outline-stitch mouth with floss. Fringe eyes and tack in place.

Using a continuous length of thread sew yarn loops ranging from ¼″ to ¾″ in length thickly over body of sheep, as in photograph.

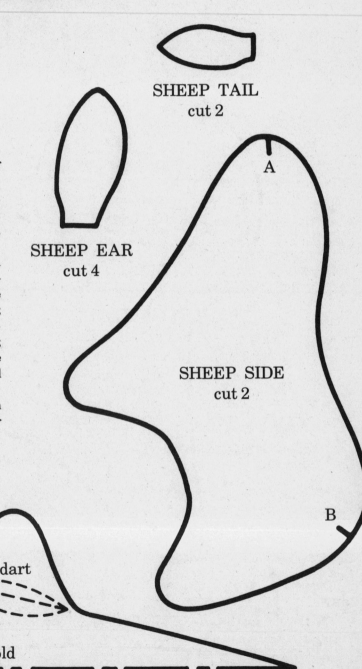

SHEEP TAIL
cut 2

SHEEP EAR
cut 4

SHEEP SIDE
cut 2

SHEEP UNDERBODY
cut 1 on fold

dart

dart

center fold

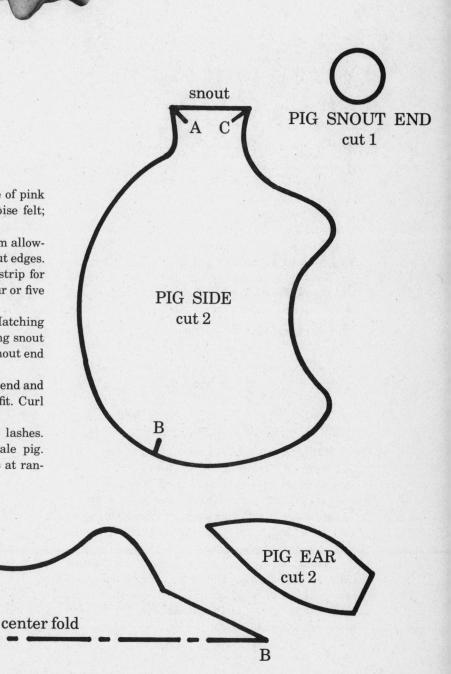

Pigs

MATERIALS *For two:* 9″ x 12″ piece of pink felt; scrap of blue cotton fabric and turquoise felt; blue embroidery floss; pipe cleaner; kapok.

Cut each pig from pink felt, adding seam allowances to sides and underbody except for snout edges. Cut pink felt snout end, ears and ½″ x 2″ strip for tail; cut turquoise eyes. For appliqué cut four or five ½″ and ¾″ blue cotton disks.

Seam sides from A to B along back. Matching B's and C's, seam underbody to sides, leaving snout open. Trim seams and turn. Stuff and sew snout end over opening.

For tail, fold strip lengthwise; seam one end and long edges. Insert pipe cleaner and cut to fit. Curl tail around pencil; sew to B.

Glue felt eyes to male pig; embroider lashes. Work blanket-stitch closed lashes on female pig. Sew ears to each head. Appliqué blue disks at random to pigs.

snout

A   C

PIG SNOUT END
cut 1

PIG SIDE
cut 2

B

PIG UNDERBODY
cut 1 on fold

PIG EAR
cut 2

center fold

C   B

Mr. and Mrs. Noah and Doves

MATERIALS *For all:* 36″ cotton, ¼ yard each of blue-and-white-striped and blue print for Mrs. Noah, solid blue cotton and red print for Mr. Noah; ⅛ yard white cotton for doves; scraps of bright pink, orange and green. Pink and gold felt; purple, white and black embroidery floss; white crochet cotton; kapok; cardboard; 2 buttons.

MRS. NOAH Following photograph for direction of stripes, cut body, base, sleeves and 1″ x 4″ band to appliqué across front. From blue print cut front and back of cloak following dotted lines, omitting opening when cutting the back piece. From pink felt cut face and hands, from pink and orange cotton cut cheeks and nose.

Seam body pieces, leaving bottom open. Trim seams, clip and turn. Stuff firmly. Sew fabric base over cardboard around open edge. Appliqué striped band across front ⅞″ up from lower edge. Sew hands to sleeves; appliqué to front.

Sew face to head; appliqué pink cheeks and orange nose. Make a purple French knot for each eye; following photograph, sew crochet cotton around face for hair.

Seam cloak pieces and turn. Fold under raw edges and blindstitch to figure. Sew buttons to dress front.

MR. NOAH From blue cotton cut body, base and one sleeve; from red print cut 6½″ x 8″ piece for cloak; cut pink felt face and hand; cut pink and orange cheeks and nose.

Following directions for Mrs. Noah, seam body, stuff and add base; sew on face and appliqué cheeks and nose. Work purple straight stitch for each eye, white stitch for eyebrow. Following photograph, sew crochet cotton to face for hair and beard.

Seam sleeve pieces, leaving wrist end open; hem opening and insert hand. Sew lower sleeve edge to body, curving it to hold dove.

For cloak, hem one 8″ edge. Center hemmed edge on head and tack at each side. Pleat fabric, fold under rest of edge to fit and sew to front, curving cloak outward over arm. Fold under lower edge and hem to body.

FEMALE DOVE Cut white cotton sides, gold felt beak and green cotton olive branch. Seam sides, leaving opening at lower edge. Trim seams, turn and stuff; sew opening. Work black eyes and outline-stitch white wings. Tack on beak; sew olive branch to it. Tuck dove in Noah's arm.

MALE DOVE Cut white cotton sides, underbody and tail pieces; cut gold felt beak. Seam sides from A to B along back. Matching A's and B's, seam underbody to sides, leaving opening. Turn; stuff; sew opening. Seam tail pieces, leaving edge C–D open; turn; sew opening. Sew tail to dove. Work black eyes and white wings; tack on beak.

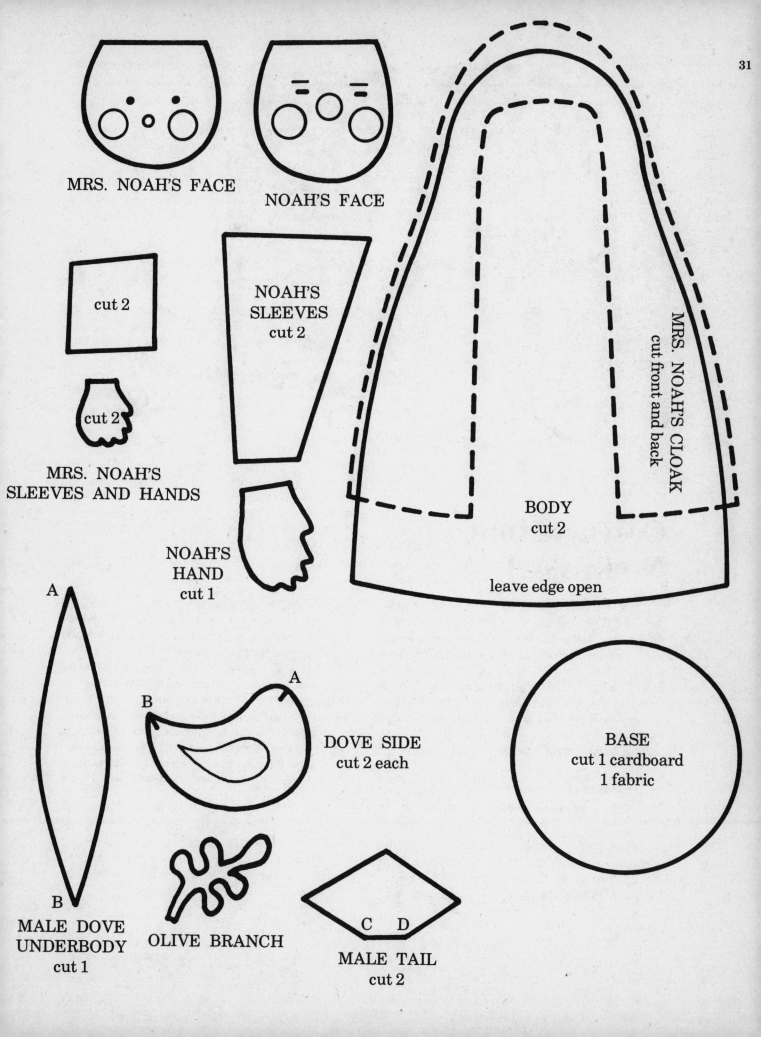

MRS. NOAH'S FACE

NOAH'S FACE

31

cut 2

NOAH'S SLEEVES
cut 2

cut 2

MRS. NOAH'S CLOAK
cut front and back

MRS. NOAH'S
SLEEVES AND HANDS

NOAH'S
HAND
cut 1

BODY
cut 2

leave edge open

A

A

B

B

DOVE SIDE
cut 2 each

BASE
cut 1 cardboard
1 fabric

B

MALE DOVE
UNDERBODY
cut 1

OLIVE BRANCH

C   D

MALE TAIL
cut 2

Constructing Noah's Ark

MATERIALS 6 feet of ¾″ x 9⅝″ pine for lower deck and cleats; 16 feet of ½″ x 5⅝″ pine for upper deck, walls, stall center piece, roof and ramp; scraps of ¼″ plywood for stall crosspieces and ladder sideplates; 2 feet of ¼″ dowel for ladder rungs; white glue; 2″ and 1¼″ finishing nails; screws to fit all hardware; four 1½″-diameter plate-top casters; 18″ of ½″ continuous hinge; four ⅝″ x 1⅝″ decorative hinges for trap door and ramp; wood bead; shellac; alcohol; red and white enamel; 5 feet ¼″ rope for pull cord.

Alternate Materials If you have plywood, it can be substituted for ¾″ and ½″ pine, if desired, and an exterior ply is recommended for outdoor use.

PIECING The decks, two walls, roof parts and ramp are wider than the wood specified. Piece together two boards for necessary width before shaping parts. When cutting boards, slightly increase dimensions to allow for planing edges and squaring off ends. Plane edges to be joined for a tight fit. Apply glue to planed edges; clamp together until dry. Mark with square and cut to exact size.

Follow diagram 1 to cut lower deck and cleats from ¾″ pine; trace diagram 2 on one end of deck to shape prow. Drill ⅜″ holes for pull cord. Follow dotted lines to mark location of deckhouse and casters.

To reinforce the deck, glue and nail two cleats across the underside between markings for casters.

Follow diagram 3 to cut upper deck and walls of deckhouse. Note that there are 3 windows in back wall, but only one—window A—in front wall. To begin cutting windows, drill a ½″ hole in each corner then complete cutting with a coping saw. Trace diagram 4 on right wall to shape arch of door opening.

Follow diagram 5 to cut stall center from ½″ pine, crosspieces from ¼″ plywood; cut ¼″ slots in center piece, ½″ slots in each crosspiece.

Follow diagram 6 for deckhouse assembly. Glue and nail walls together, using 1¼″ nails. Nail upper deck to walls and attach stall center piece. Drill pilot holes from underside of lower deck, 4 each spaced along marking for left and right walls. Drive 2″ nails through deck into deckhouse walls, being careful not to split the ½″ wood. Set crosspieces of stalls into slots so they fit snugly but can be removed by children. Attach casters to lower deck.

Follow diagram 7 to cut roof parts; piece, with filling strip at outer edge of each. Bevel long edges to approximately 30° angle. Cut opening in back part, beveling one 2½″ edge to support trap door when closed. For best fit, trace opening and cut door, beveling one edge to match opening; add bead for handle. Hinge roof parts together, setting the continuous hinge high enough so that front part may be folded back more than halfway. Attach the back roof to left and right walls with 1¼″ finishing nails. Notch for hinges and attach trap door.

Follow diagram 8 to cut the ramp; bevel to fit the floor. Mark location at edge of deck. Notch for hinges and attach. Ramp can be folded up against wall of deckhouse so ark rolls on casters when pulled by children.

Follow diagram 9 to cut ladder. Round ends of sideplates and notch to catch edge of door opening; drill for dowel rungs and glue in place, flush at outer edges.

Sand the ark well. Apply shellac, thinned 50–50 with alcohol, to all surfaces. Finish with two coats of enamel, using red for the roof, trap door, interior of upper story, edges of windows, door, ramp and deck. Paint other parts white, as in photographs.

Insert ends of pull cord in holes drilled through deck; knot at underside and drive a nail through each knot.

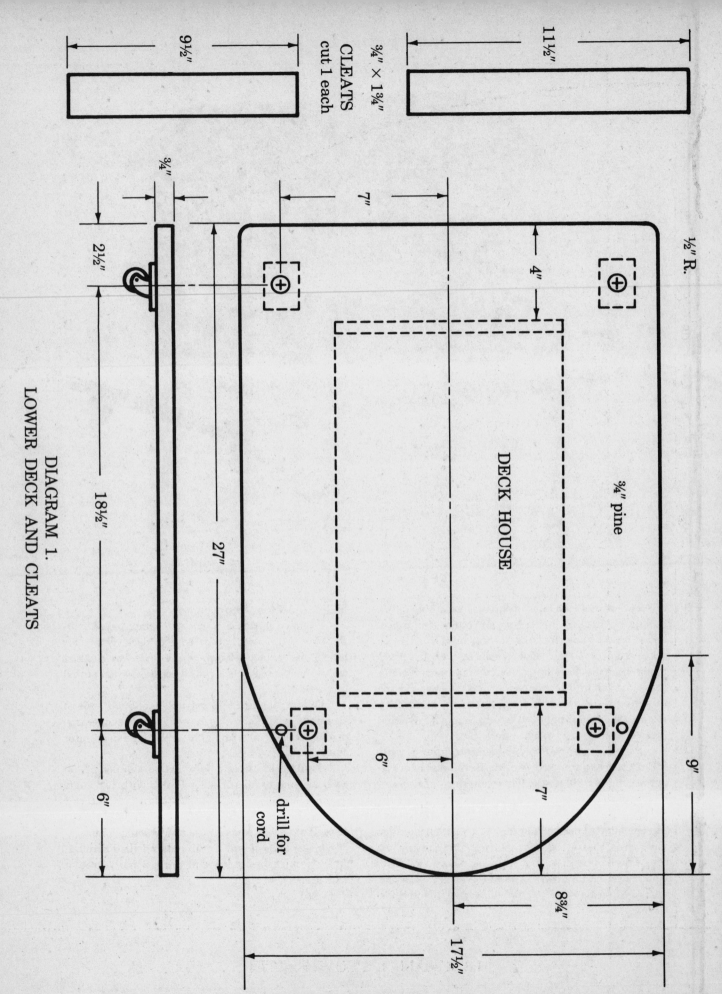

34

CLEATS
cut 1 each

¾" × 1¾"

9½"

11½"

½" R.

¾" pine

DECK HOUSE

DIAGRAM 1.
LOWER DECK AND CLEATS

¾"

2½"

18½"

27"

6"

7"

4"

6"

7"

drill for
cord

9"

8¾"

17½"

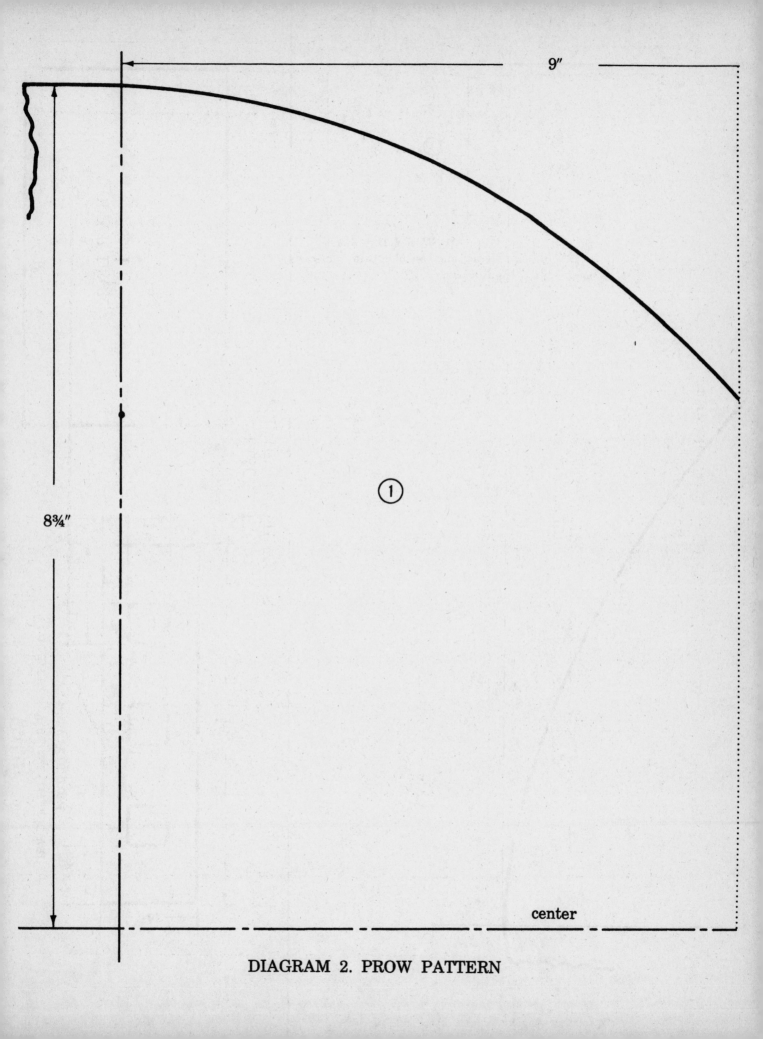

9″

8¾″

①

center

DIAGRAM 2. PROW PATTERN

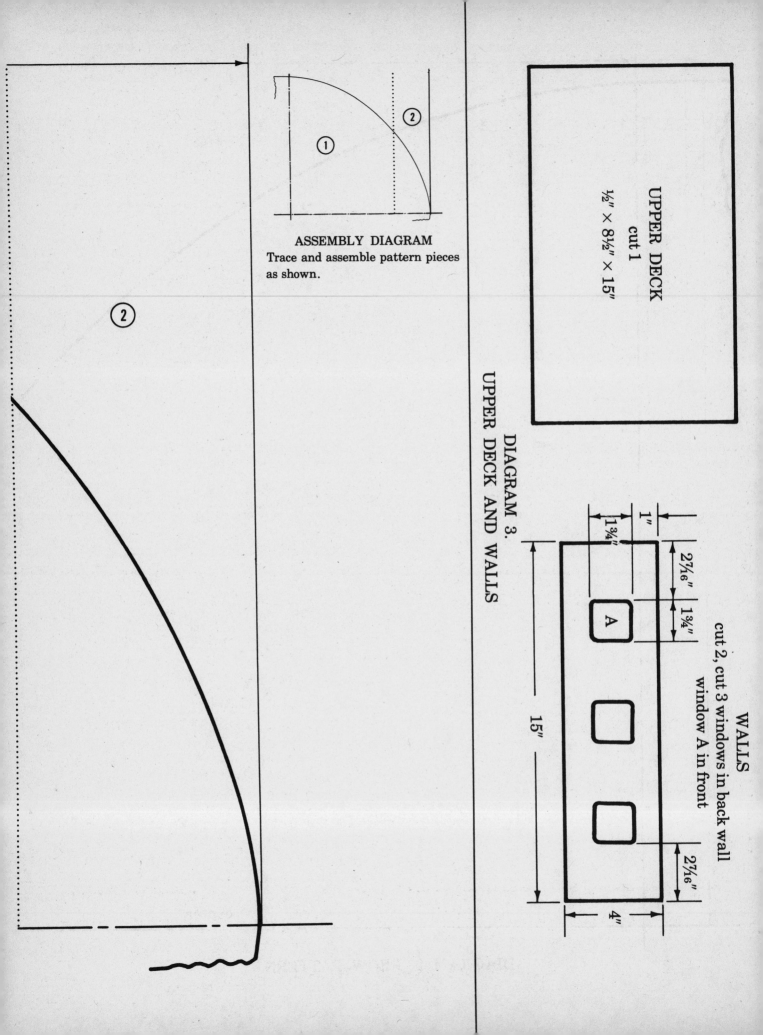

ASSEMBLY DIAGRAM
Trace and assemble pattern pieces as shown.

① ②

②

DIAGRAM 3.
UPPER DECK AND WALLS

UPPER DECK
cut 1
½" × 8½" × 15"

WALLS
cut 2, cut 3 windows in back wall
window A in front

1"
1¾"
2⁷⁄₁₆"
1¾"
A
15"
2⁷⁄₁₆"
4"

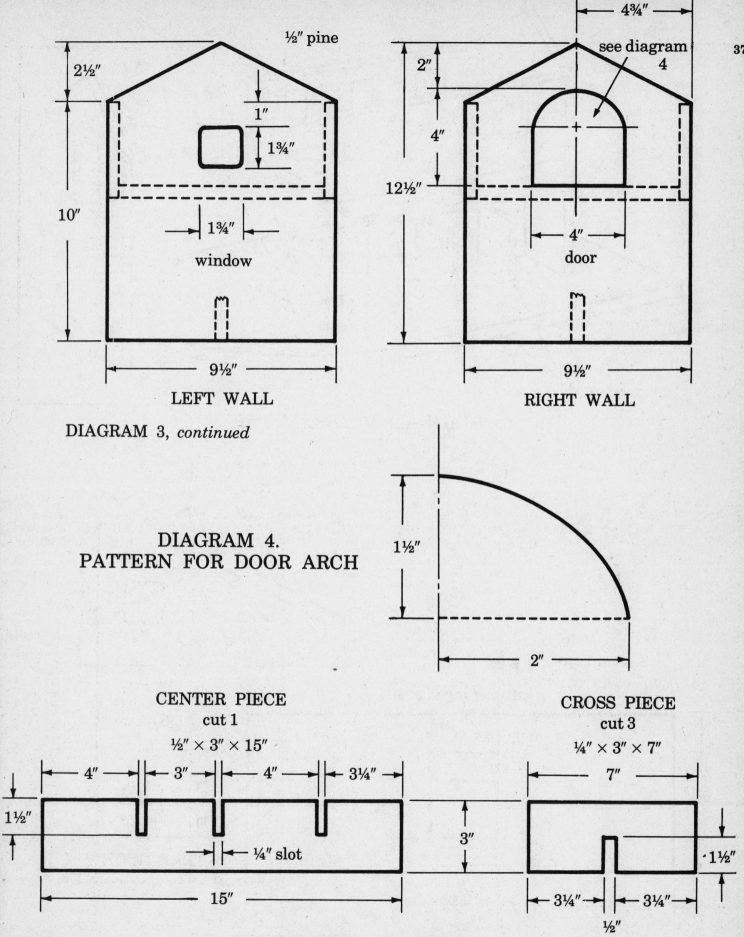

½" pine

2½"

1"

1¾"

10"

1¾"

window

9½"

LEFT WALL

4¾"

see diagram 4

2"

4"

12½"

4"

door

9½"

RIGHT WALL

DIAGRAM 3, *continued*

DIAGRAM 4.
PATTERN FOR DOOR ARCH

1½"

2"

CENTER PIECE
cut 1
½" × 3" × 15"

4"   3"   4"   3¼"

1½"

¼" slot

15"

CROSS PIECE
cut 3
¼" × 3" × 7"

7"

3"

3¼"   3¼"

½"

1½"

DIAGRAM 5. STALLS

38

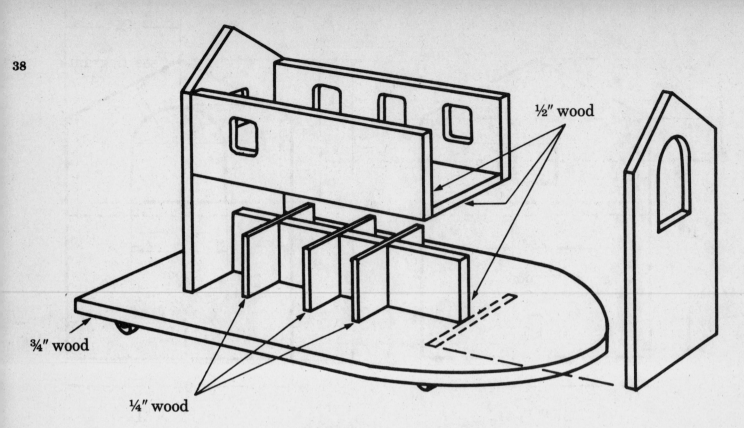

½″ wood

¾″ wood

¼″ wood

DIAGRAM 6. ASSEMBLY

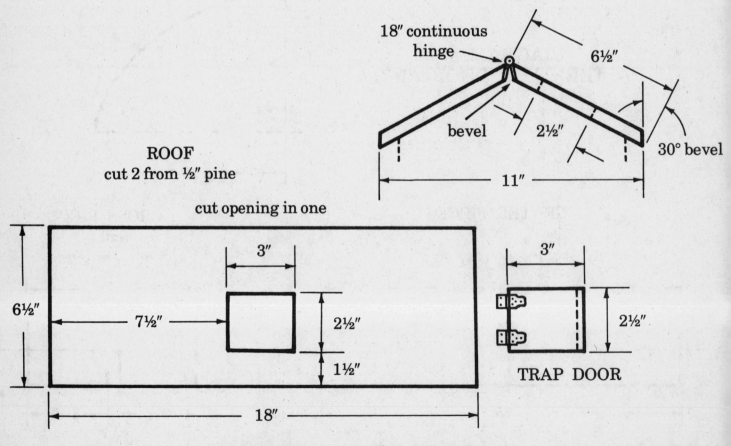

18″ continuous hinge

6½″

bevel

2½″

30° bevel

11″

ROOF
cut 2 from ½″ pine

cut opening in one

6½″

7½″

3″

2½″

1½″

18″

3″

2½″

TRAP DOOR

DIAGRAM 7. ROOF ASSEMBLY

DECK

8" 8"

½"

RAMP
cut 1
½" × 8" × 8"

8"

DECK

8"

bevel

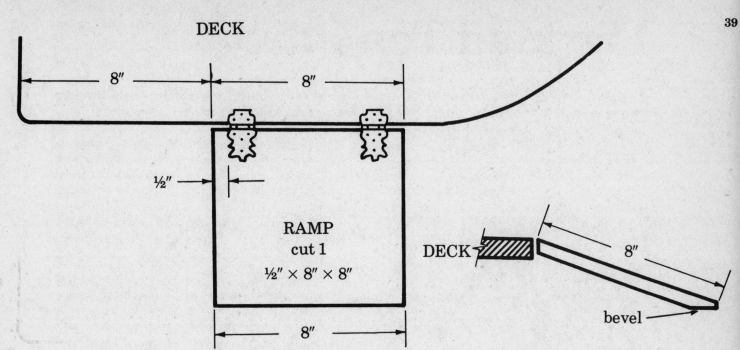

DIAGRAM 8. RAMP ASSEMBLY

RUNG
cut 6

¼" dowel 3½" long

round

upper
deck

SIDEPLATE
cut 2

¼" × ¾" × 8½"

drill
for
dowels

6" approx.

main
deck

3"

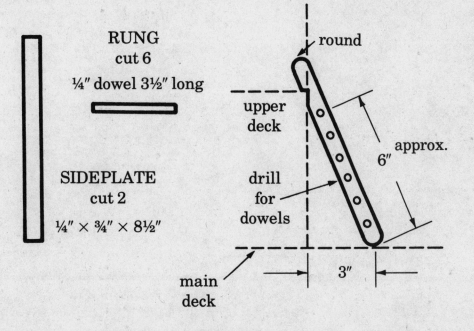

DIAGRAM 9. LADDER ASSEMBLY

The Mad Tea Party

Alice, the March Hare, the Dormouse, the Mad Hatter and the White Rabbit—the famous guests at the merry and mad tea party in Wonderland.

General Directions

PATTERNS AND CUTTING   see Construction Techniques, page 11.

SEWING AND STUFFING Machine-stitch when possible, using small stitches. Stitch twice at necks to reinforce seams, twice around hands so seam allowances can be trimmed very close.

BODY Right sides facing, stitch together fronts along front seam; stitch backs at back seam. Join front to back along sides, matching A's and leaving neck open. Trim seams; clip at curves; turn to right side. Stuff firmly with kapok, using a little at a time.

HEAD Stitch together fronts along front seam, backs along back seam; join at sides, matching B's. Complete same as body.

ARMS AND LEGS   Stitch together two pieces for each; leave top open on arms and legs, except when opening is marked at lower edge. Trim seams; clip at curves. Turn; stuff, poking kapok into small areas with a pencil.

EARS Stitch together two pieces for each, leaving straight edges open. Trim seams; clip; turn.

ASSEMBLING Place head on neck of body, adding more stuffing. Turn in head edges; sew securely. To attach arms to Alice, the Hatter and White Rabbit, turn in top edges, following curve of pattern; sew closed. Using button thread, sew back and forth from top of arms to shoulders, as though attaching a button; keep stitches somewhat long. Wind thread around stitches to form shanks; fasten off.

See individual directions to attach arms or front legs to Dormouse and March Hare, and the alternate method to attach front legs to White Rabbit.

To attach legs to Alice and the Hatter, turn in top edges to fit body; sew closed. Sew securely to body. To attach hind legs to White Rabbit, Hare and Dormouse, turn in lower edges and sew closed. Pin to body so animal sits well; sew securely in place.

To attach animals' ears, turn in open edges and sew closed. Pleat ears and sew to heads, following photographs.

sewing and assembling doll

Alice

MATERIALS 36″ cotton, ¼ yard pink, ½ yard white, ⅜ yard blue; 6″ x 15″ piece of white sailcloth; scraps of turquoise cotton and black felt; 1½ yards narrow lace; bias tape, 2½ yards of white and 1 yard orange; yellow yarn; navy, red, pink and yellow 6-strand floss; snaps and buttons; kapok.

DOLL Following General Directions and 6 patterns, cut legs from white sailcloth and the rest of body from pink cotton. Seam, turn and stuff; outline fingers with stitching. Assemble doll.

For face, follow photograph and appliqué ⅜″ x ½″ turquoise ovals for eyes; with navy floss, satin-stitch pupils. With stem stitch outline yellow brows, pink nose and red mouth; rouge cheeks slightly.

For hair, cut 16″ lengths of yellow yarn. Beginning at top center, ¾″ in front of side seam, fold two lengths in half and sew centers to head. Repeat around face, ending hairline at side seams. Sew parallel rows of strands across head until it is well covered. Pull hair toward back; trim a little.

UNDERPANTS Cut white cotton 6″ x 11″ and a 1″ x 9″ strip for waistband. Stitch a ¼″ hem along an 11″ edge of pants and trim with lace. Seam narrow edges, leaving 1″ for waist opening; hem opening. Pin and fit pants to doll with seam at one side;

pleat top edge and mark 1″-long crotch; remove and stitch; cut excess fabric from crotch. Fold waistband lengthwise, turning in raw edges; stitch to pants, leaving slight overlap; fasten with snap.

PETTICOAT Cut white cotton 7½″ x 36″ (selvages will be at back opening); cut 1″ x 9½″ waistband. Stitch a ⅞″ hem along a 36″ edge of the petticoat. On the right side, take a ¼″ tuck just above the hem. Trim the hem edge with lace, topstitching the lace into place. Press tuck toward hem. Machine-gather top edge and tighten to fit. Fold waistband lengthwise, turning in raw edges, and stitch to gathers, leaving a slight overlap. Fasten with snap.

BLUE DRESS Follow 2 patterns to cut bodice and sleeves; cut 7½″ x 36″ skirt (selvages will be at back opening); cut ⅜″-wide bias strips for sleeve and neck binding.

Cut bodice back open at center; seam back pieces to front at shoulders. Gather sleeves at top armhole edges; stitch to bodice armholes. Gather lower sleeve edges to fit doll's arms loosely; bind sleeves and neck with bias strips. Fit bodice to Alice, pinning hems at back opening, seams at sides and sleeves. Remove and stitch.

On one 36″ skirt edge, stitch a 1″ hem. Fold white tape to ¼″ width; topstitch two bands over hem about ½″ apart. Machine-gather other long edge of skirt and tighten to fit bodice. Right sides facing, seam bodice to skirt. Sew buttons and thread loops to bodice back.

WHITE COTTON PINAFORE Follow 2 patterns to cut pinafore, pockets and linings, adding seam allowance only to neck, lower back and pocket edges. Cut 1″ x 11″ waistband. Seam lining to pinafore at neck, back opening and lower back, taking only a very small seam allowance at center back; turn. Stitch outer edges together to keep layers from shifting; bind with orange tape. Fold waistband to ¼″ width and topstitch edges. Gather pinafore at front waist and back; topstitch waistband to it. Sew buttons and loops to back neck and waistband. Seam pocket pieces, leaving top open; turn; sew opening. Fold orange tape to ⅛″ width and stitch across pockets. Topstitch pockets to pinafore

BLACK FELT SHOES Follow one pattern for cutting. For straps, reinforce felt with a row of stitching; cut very narrow strips from it to fit doll's instep. Stitch shoe seams twice leaving top edge open; trim closely; turn. Put on feet; tack straps to sides.

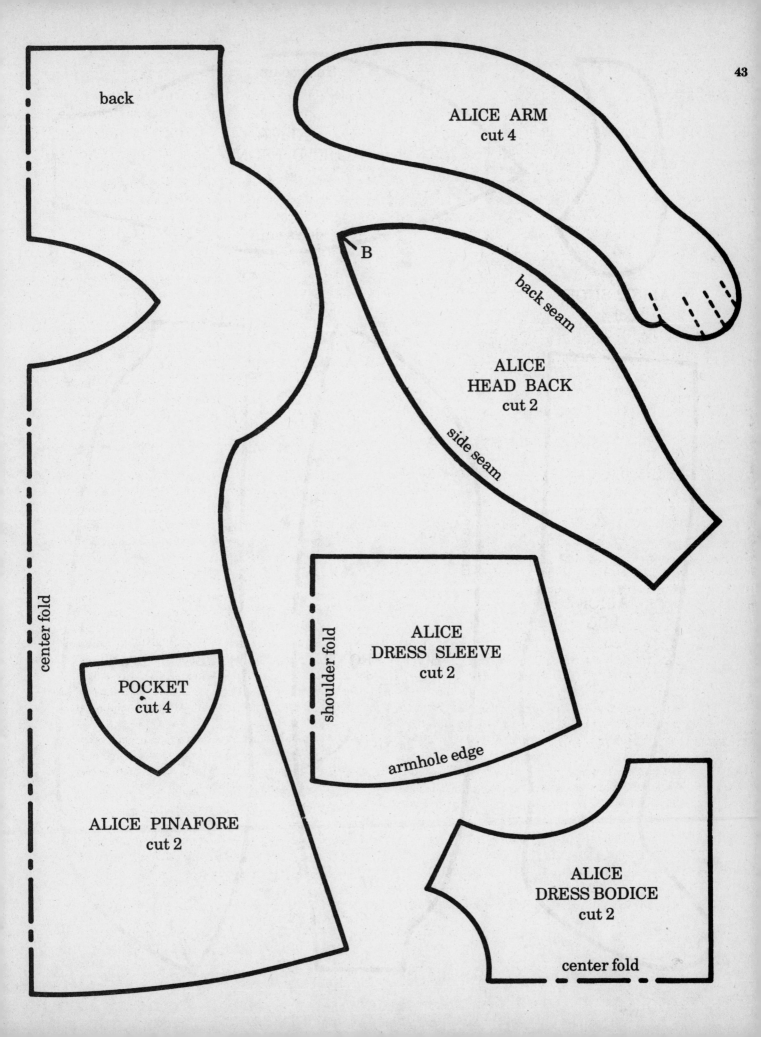

back

ALICE ARM
cut 4

B

back seam

ALICE
HEAD BACK
cut 2

side seam

center fold

POCKET
cut 4

shoulder fold

ALICE
DRESS SLEEVE
cut 2

armhole edge

ALICE PINAFORE
cut 2

ALICE
DRESS BODICE
cut 2

center fold

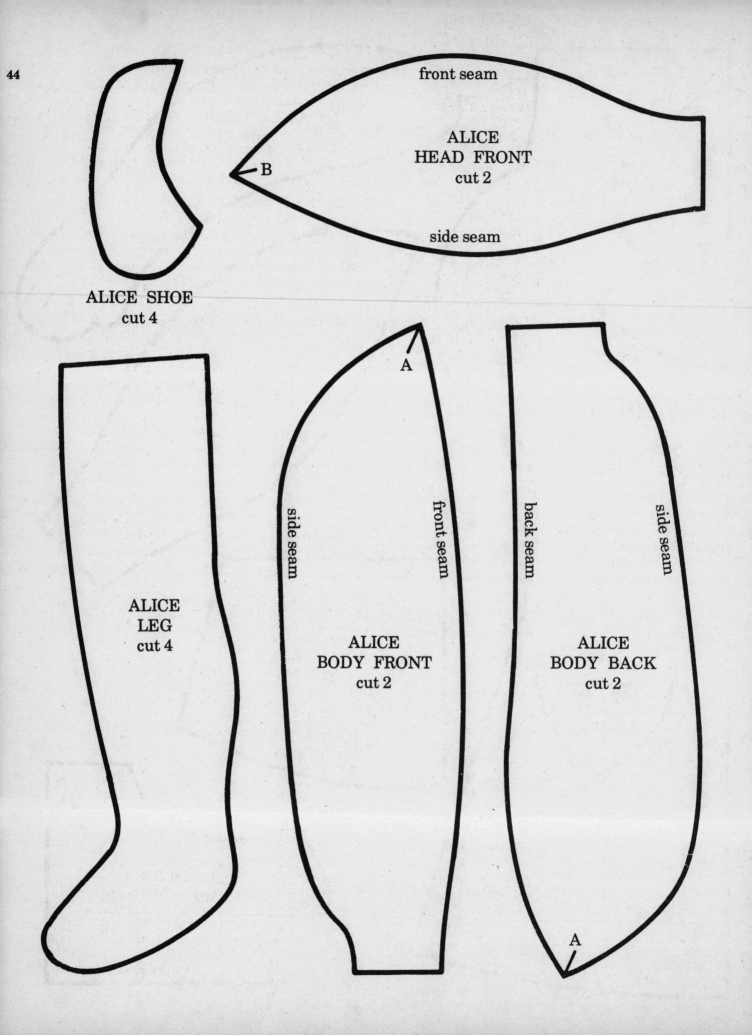

44

ALICE SHOE
cut 4

ALICE
HEAD FRONT
cut 2

front seam

B

side seam

ALICE
LEG
cut 4

ALICE
BODY FRONT
cut 2

side seam

front seam

A

ALICE
BODY BACK
cut 2

back seam

side seam

A

Mad Hatter

MATERIALS 36″ fabric, ¼ yard light pink cotton; 8″ x 12″ piece of blue-striped, ⅛ yard of white, ¼ yard each of turquoise-dotted brown corduroy and solid green jersey, ⅜ yard turquoise velveteen, 4″ x 15″ strip of brown-and-green cotton print; scraps of dark pink, blue and black cotton; scraps of green and gold felt; 1 yard turquoise bias tape; orange yarn; orange and green 6-strand floss; 3 buttons; snap; kapok; white cardboard; masking or other adhesive tape.

DOLL Following General Directions and 6 patterns, cut legs from blue-striped cotton and the rest of body from pink cotton. Seam, stuff and assemble. Stitch together pairs of ears, leaving an opening. Turn; sew to side seams of head.

For face, follow photograph and glue ⅜″ x ½″ blue cotton ovals for eyes and ¼″ black pupils. For nose, cut a small, dark pink circle. Stuff with kapok; gather edges and sew to face. Outline mouth with orange floss, using stem stitch. Rouge cheeks for a hectic flush. For hair, cut 7″ lengths of orange yarn; fold two lengths in half and sew centers to top of head. Repeat, covering head at random with a shock of hair.

WHITE SHIRT Follow 2 patterns to cut collar and shirt. Use left edge to dotted fold line for 4 fronts. Fold cotton and use dotted line to right edge for 2 backs. (Shirt is double and sleeveless.) Seam pairs of fronts at armholes and front opening; seam backs at armholes; turn all. Stitch fronts to backs at shoulders and sides; hem lower edge.

Seam collar pieces, leaving neck edge open; turn. Right sides facing, stitch one layer of collar to outside of shirt; turn up collar; hem to inside. Finish shirt front with buttonholes and buttons. Tack on a green felt bow made from a 1¼″ x 6″ strip.

CORDUROY PANTS Cut two pieces 5″ x 7″. With right sides facing Hatter, pin 7″ side seams to fit and leg inseams 2″ long. Remove and stitch, leaving 1″ open at waistline on one side; hem opening. Cut excess fabric from crotch. Hem waist and legs; turn. Pleat waist to fit, leaving a slight overlap; stitch pleats; fasten with snap.

JERSEY JACKET Follow 5 patterns to cut backs, fronts, sleeves, collar and pocket pieces. Seam 2 front pieces at lower edge and front opening; repeat for remaining 2. Seam 2 back pieces at lower edge. Turn all pieces; stitch fronts to back at shoulders. Seam pairs of sleeves at wrist edges; turn. Right sides facing, stitch sleeves to jacket armholes. Seam jacket sides and sleeves; turn. Following pattern, make an inverted pleat at back of jacket, fitting it to Hatter; topstitch pleat for 1½″. Follow shirt instructions to seam and attach collar. Seam pocket pieces, leaving opening; turn; sew closed. Topstitch to jacket.

GOLD FELT SHOES Follow pattern for cutting. Stitch shoe seams twice, leaving top edge open. Trim close to stitching and turn. Using needle, thread green floss laces through insteps.

VELVETEEN HAT Follow 3 patterns to cut crown top, side and brim pieces, folding fabric once for brim. Also cut cardboard for side, brim and 1⅝″ x 4″ lettered sign.

Seam velveteen side pieces, leaving upper and lower edges free. Stitch top to hat side; turn. On cardboard sides, trim off upper and lower seam allowances; tape sides together at one edge. Roll into a tube and fit inside velveteen; mark overlap on untaped edge then pull out.

Seam velveteen brims at outer edges; turn. Trim cardboard brim and insert. Turn in inner velveteen edges and whip together. Sew bias tape to whipped edge; sew velveteen sides to bias tape. Replace cardboard in crown; join overlap with masking tape. For hatband, fold brown-and-green print strip lengthwise with raw edges at center; fit around hat and tack. Follow photograph to letter the cardboard sign; tuck into hatband.

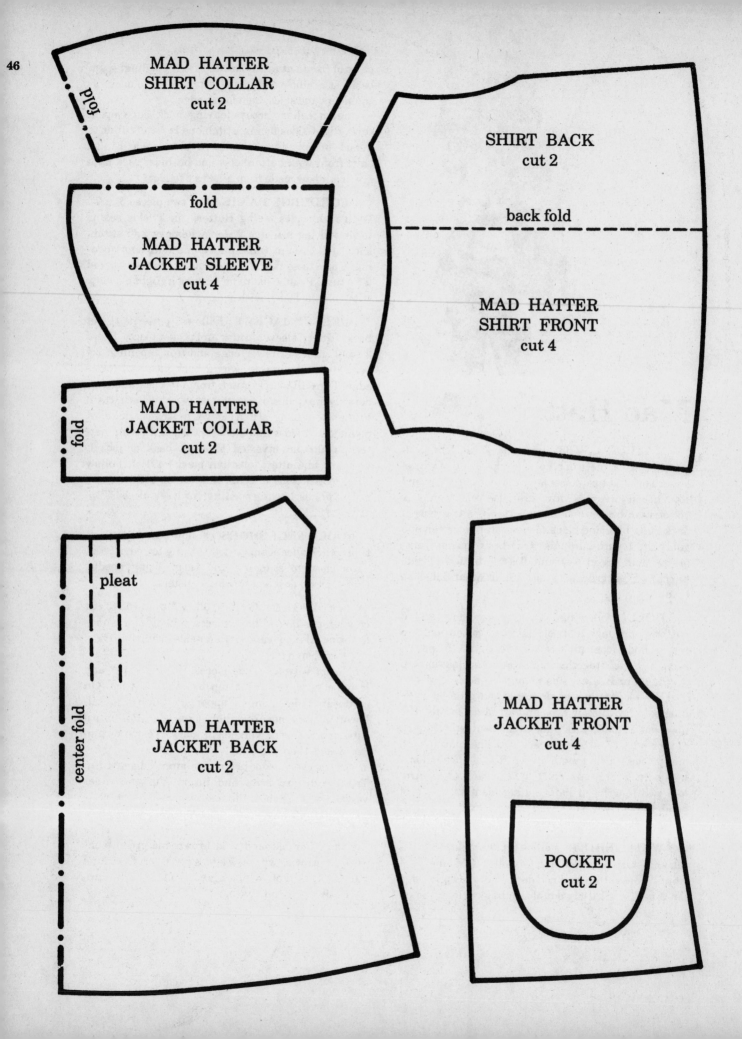

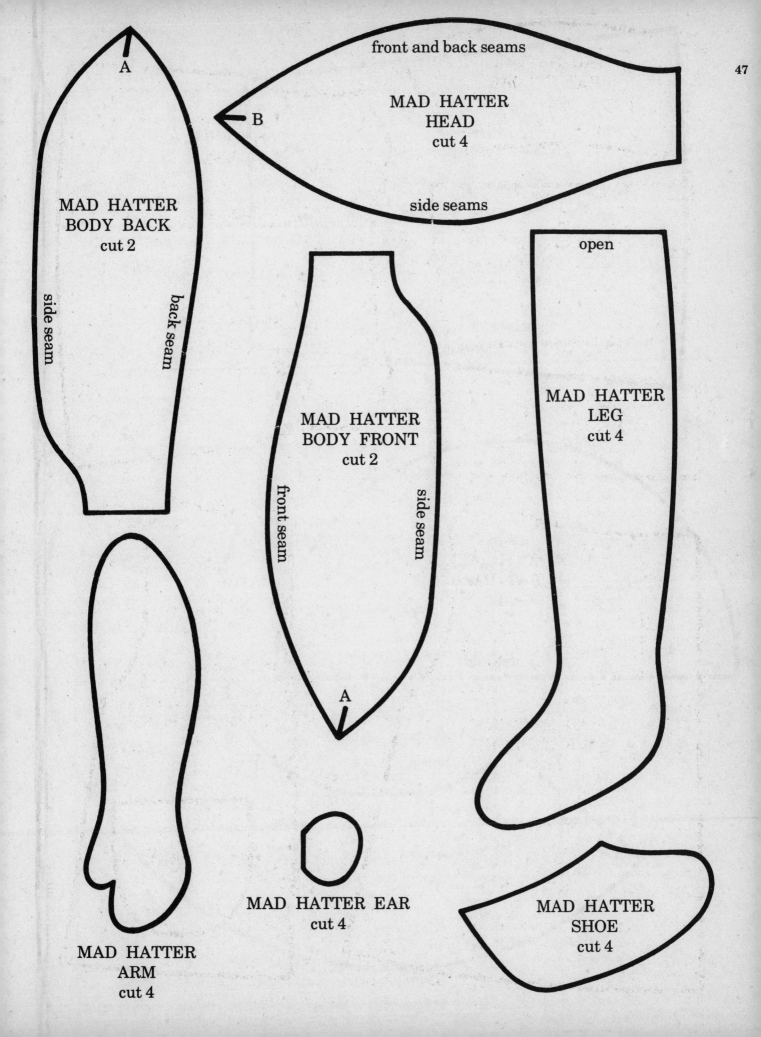

A

front and back seams

**MAD HATTER
HEAD
cut 4**

B

side seams

**MAD HATTER
BODY BACK
cut 2**

side seam

back seam

open

**MAD HATTER
LEG
cut 4**

**MAD HATTER
BODY FRONT
cut 2**

front seam

side seam

A

**MAD HATTER EAR
cut 4**

**MAD HATTER
SHOE
cut 4**

**MAD HATTER
ARM
cut 4**

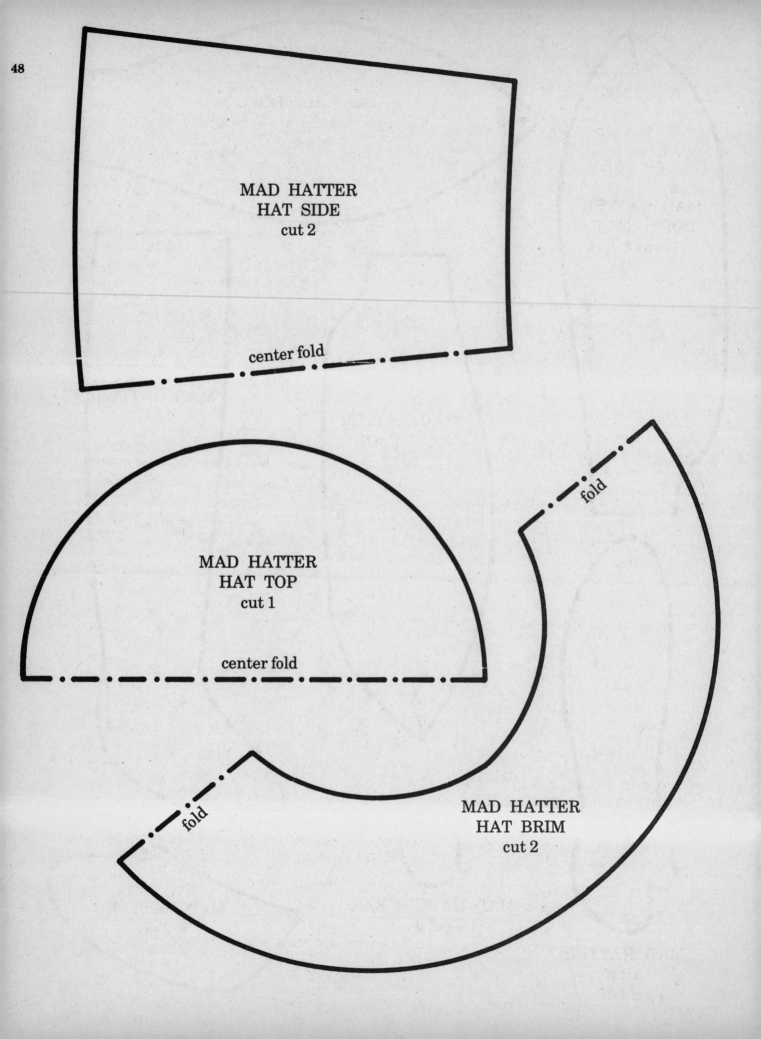

48

MAD HATTER
HAT SIDE
cut 2

center fold

MAD HATTER
HAT TOP
cut 1

center fold

fold

fold

MAD HATTER
HAT BRIM
cut 2

March Hare

MATERIALS 36″ fabric, ⅝ yard orange basketweave wool, ⅜ yard yellow linen, ½ yard pink-and-black cotton print; scrap of blue-dotted cotton; turquoise, black and orange felt; orange yarn; red 6-strand floss; 2 buttons, 2 hooks and eyes; kapok; florist's wire.

HARE Following General Directions and 7 patterns, cut body fronts, backs, head fronts, backs, front legs, hind legs and ears all from orange wool.

Seam, turn and stuff all pieces except ears. Assemble, turning head slightly to one side, as in photograph, when sewing it to body. Pin hind legs to sides so Hare sits well; sew in place. Sew front legs to side seams so they curve upward and outward.

Seam pairs of ears, leaving straight edges open; turn. Bend an 11″ length of florist's wire in half and insert in each ear so it can be partly raised. Turn in raw edges and make pleat; pin ear to head, pushing wire ends into kapok for about ½″. Sew ear in place and bend wire to support it.

For face, cut 1″ x 1¼″ turquoise felt teardrop shapes for eyes and appliqué; glue on ⅝″ black felt pupils. Appliqué a ⅝″ x 1″ orange felt oval for nose; using stem stitch, outline mouth with red floss.

For tail, make a pompon 2″ in diameter by winding orange yarn around a 2″ cardboard; tie yarn, sew to body and clip loops.

YELLOW SHIRT Follow 1 pattern to cut linen shirt; slash center back open on each piece. (Shirt is double and sleeveless.) For collar, cut 2 bias pieces 4″ x 13″; shape one edge to correspond to curve of shirt neckline and round opposite edge.

Seam shirt pieces along back opening and outer edge, leaving neckline open; turn. Hem neckline. Sew 2 buttons down front, hooks and eyes to back opening. Seam collar pieces, leaving neck edge open; turn. Fit collar around Hare's neck; tack raw edge snugly to Hare. Slip shirt over collar and fasten hooks.

For tie, cut a 1½″ x 30″ strip from blue dotted cotton (¼″ seam allowance included). Fold strip lengthwise and turn in raw edges so strip is ½″ wide; topstitch. Tie into a bow around collar.

PINK PRINT JACKET Follow 3 patterns to cut backs, fronts and sleeves. (Jacket body is double.) Seam pairs of fronts together, leaving shoulders, armholes and side seams open; turn. Seam backs in same way and turn. Stitch fronts to back at shoulders. Stitch pairs of sleeves along upper arm seams. Right sides facing, stitch sleeves to jacket armholes. Seam jacket sides and lower edge of sleeves. Following pattern, make an inverted pleat at back of jacket, fitting it to Hare; topstitch pleat for 1½″. Hem sleeve ends.

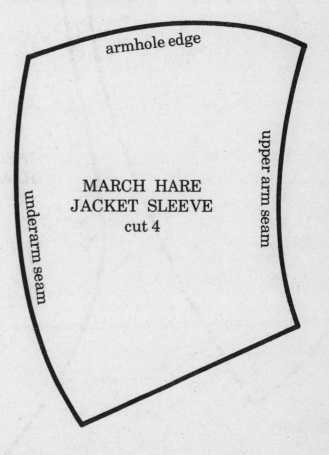

armhole edge

upper arm seam

underarm seam

MARCH HARE
JACKET SLEEVE
cut 4

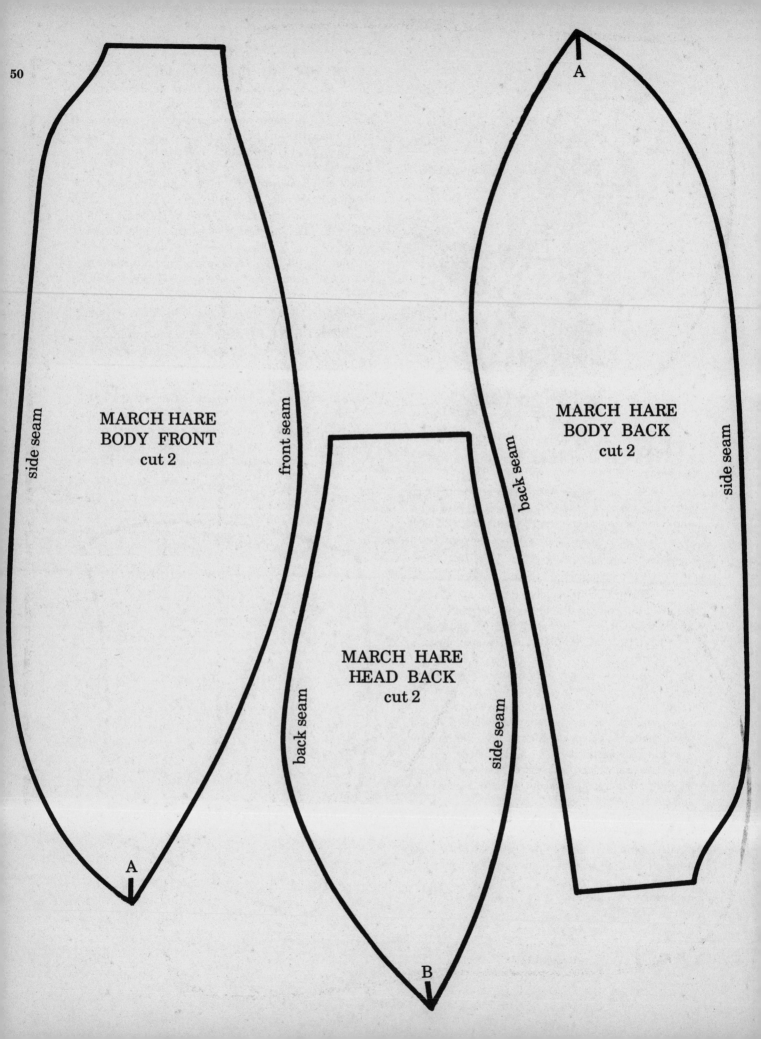

50

MARCH HARE
BODY FRONT
cut 2

side seam

front seam

A

MARCH HARE
HEAD BACK
cut 2

back seam

side seam

B

MARCH HARE
BODY BACK
cut 2

back seam

side seam

A

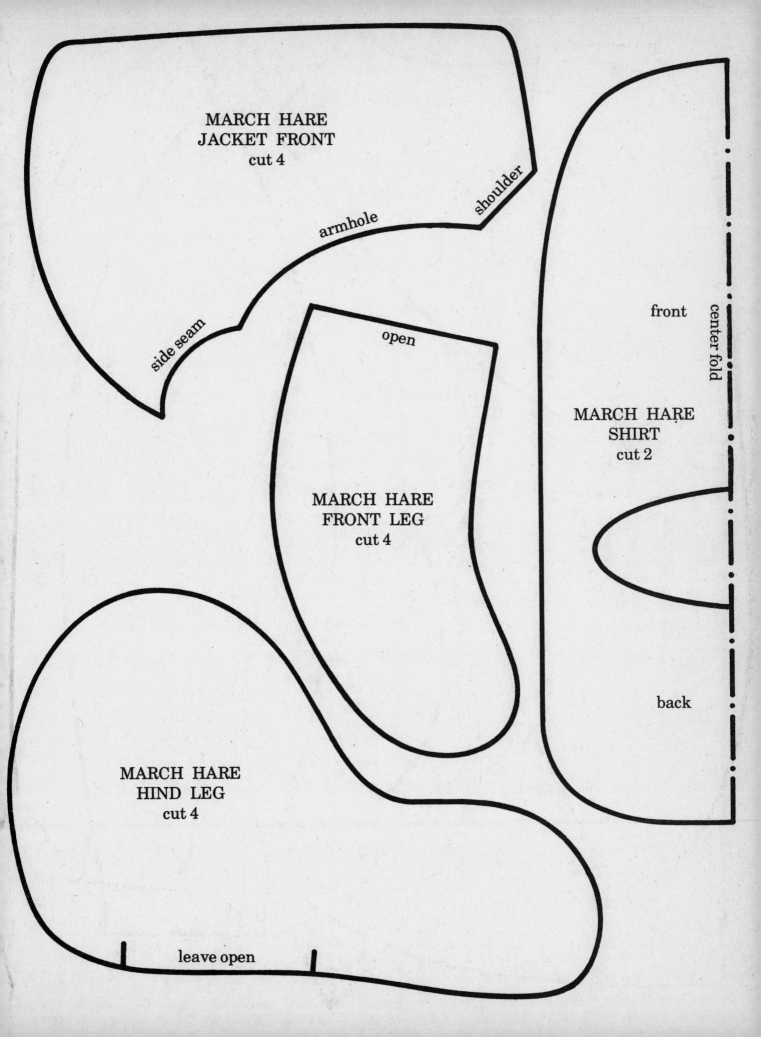

MARCH HARE
JACKET FRONT
cut 4

armhole

shoulder

side seam

open

MARCH HARE
FRONT LEG
cut 4

front

center fold

MARCH HARE
SHIRT
cut 2

back

MARCH HARE
HIND LEG
cut 4

leave open

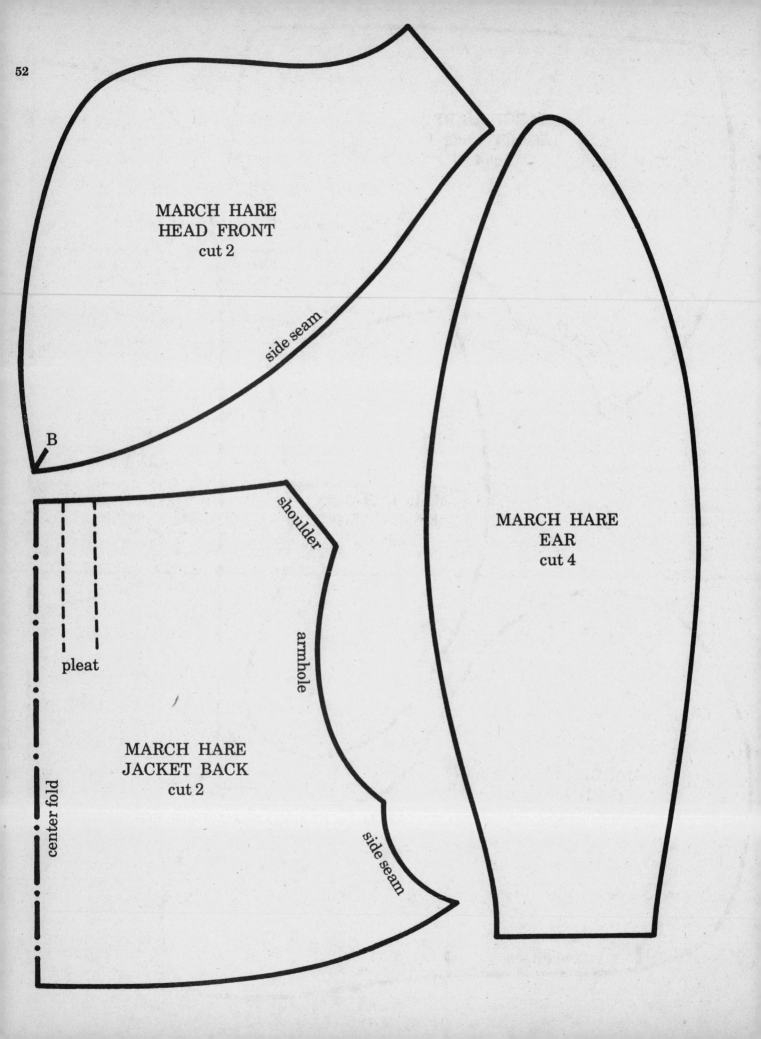

52

MARCH HARE
HEAD FRONT
cut 2

side seam

B

MARCH HARE
EAR
cut 4

shoulder

armhole

pleat

MARCH HARE
JACKET BACK
cut 2

center fold

side seam

Seam each ear to its lining and turn. Sew head to body; pin hind legs to sides so Rabbit sits well; sew in place. Turn in raw edges of ears, pleat slightly and slipstitch to head. Attach front legs as in General Directions if desired, sewing back and forth from top of each leg to shoulder.

Or, to attach movable arms, see diagrams 1 and 2 (p. 131) and directions for Squirrel's arms. (p. 130).

For face, appliqué 1″ x 1¼″ rose-cotton teardrops for eyes and glue on ⅝″ orange felt pupils. Appliqué a ⅞″ heart-shaped pink felt nose; using stem stitch and pink floss, embroider mouth. Track yarn loops 1″ to 1½″ long between ears. For tail, make a thick pompon 2″ in diameter by winding yarn around a 2″ cardboard. Tie yarn, sew to body and clip loops.

BLUE GINGHAM SHIRT   Follow 2 patterns to cut shirt and bias collar, slashing shirt front open down center. (Shirt is double and sleeveless.) Seam shirt pieces along front and outer edges, leaving neckline open; turn shirt; hem neckline. Sew snaps to front. Seam collar pieces, leaving neck edge open; turn. Tack raw edge to Rabbit's neck. Put on shirt and fasten closed.

For bow tie, cut 1¼″ x 9½″ strip to fit around neck, 3″ x 5¾″ piece for bow and 1½″ x 2¼″ bow knot, all from pink-and-olive print. Fold neck strip lengthwise and turn in raw edges so strip is ½″ wide; tack to front. Fold fabric to make 1¼″ x 2¾″ bow; wrap and tack knot around it; attach with a stickpin.

LAVENDER LINEN WAISTCOAT   Follow 2 patterns to cut linen fronts and back and blue gingham lining. Seam lining to back and front pieces, leaving shoulders and sides open; turn. Seam shoulders and sides. Lap one front over the other and sew snaps to underside, gold buttons to outside for decoration.

CHECKED JACKET   Follow 4 patterns to cut back, fronts, sleeves, pockets and checked lining. (Jacket body and pockets are double.) Seam lining to back and fronts, leaving shoulders and sides open; turn. Stitch together shoulders; right sides facing, sew sleeves to armholes. Seam jacket sides and underarms; hem sleeve ends. Seam pairs of pockets, leaving top open; turn and sew opening. Topstitch to jacket.

For watch, cut cardboard to fit the back of brass curtain ring; draw watch face; glue to ring and attach to key chain. For spectacles, mark center of 9″ wire for bridge; bend around ¾″ dowel for each lens frame. Wrap wire ends around bridge once; let extend downward to tuck behind Rabbit's nose.

White Rabbit

MATERIALS   36″ fabric, ½ yard white wool, ⅜ yard blue-and-white gingham, ¼ yard lavender linen, ½ yard cotton checked in brown, gold, turquoise and lavender; 3½″ x 18″ strip of olive-and-pink cotton print; scraps of pale pink and rose cotton, orange and pink felt; pink 6-strand floss; fine white yarn; four 2-hole buttons for movable front legs (optional); 6 gold buttons; 6 snaps; kapok; cardboard, curtain ring and key chain; 9″ length of brass wire.

RABBIT   Following General Directions and 7 patterns, cut body fronts, backs, head fronts, backs, front legs, hind legs and 2 ears from white wool; cut ear linings from pink cotton.

Seam, turn and stuff all pieces except ears.

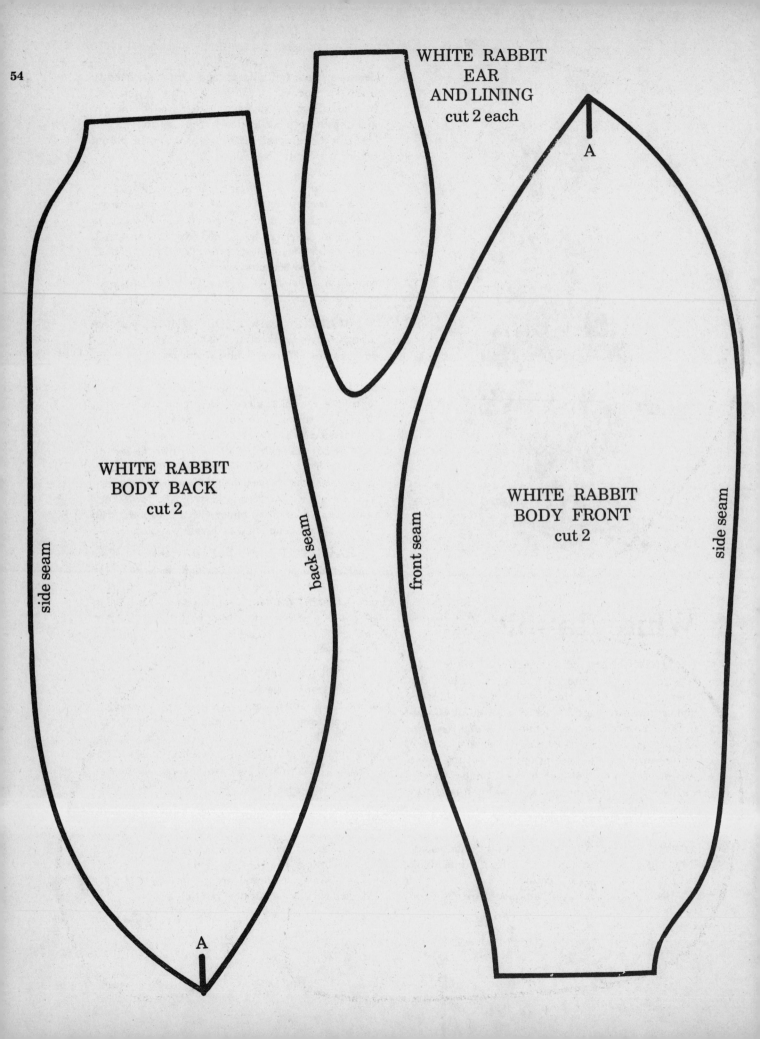

54

WHITE RABBIT
EAR
AND LINING
cut 2 each

WHITE RABBIT
BODY BACK
cut 2

side seam

back seam

front seam

WHITE RABBIT
BODY FRONT
cut 2

side seam

A

A

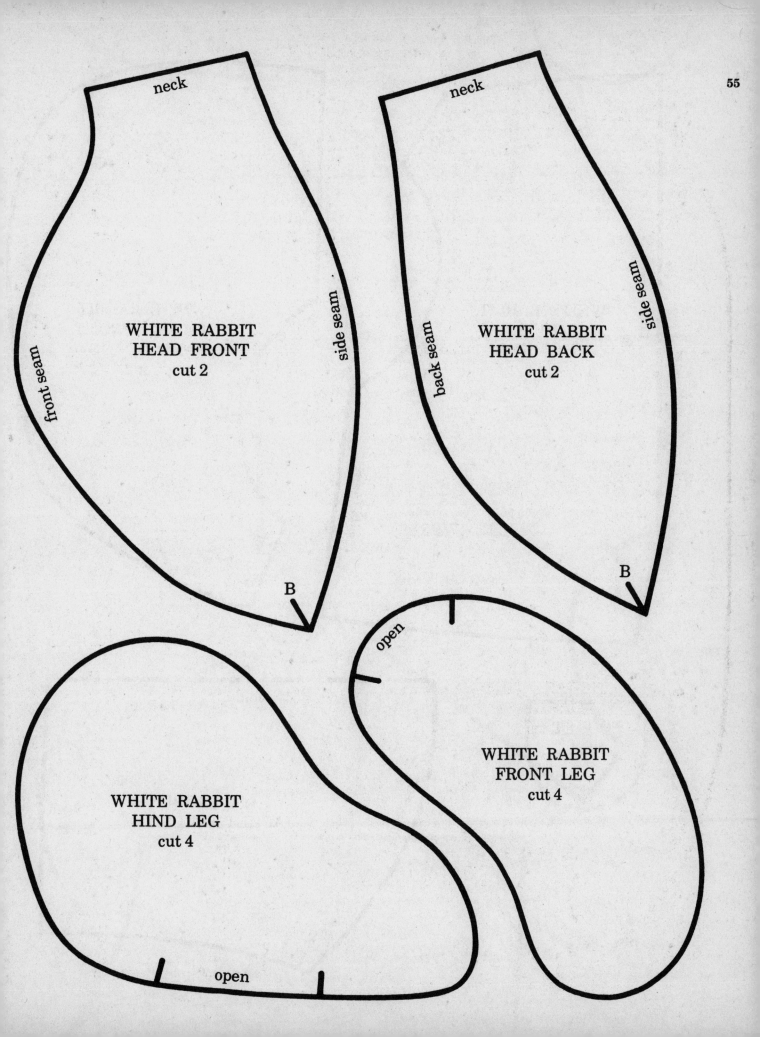

55

neck

WHITE RABBIT
HEAD FRONT
cut 2

front seam

side seam

B

neck

WHITE RABBIT
HEAD BACK
cut 2

back seam

side seam

B

WHITE RABBIT
HIND LEG
cut 4

open

open

WHITE RABBIT
FRONT LEG
cut 4

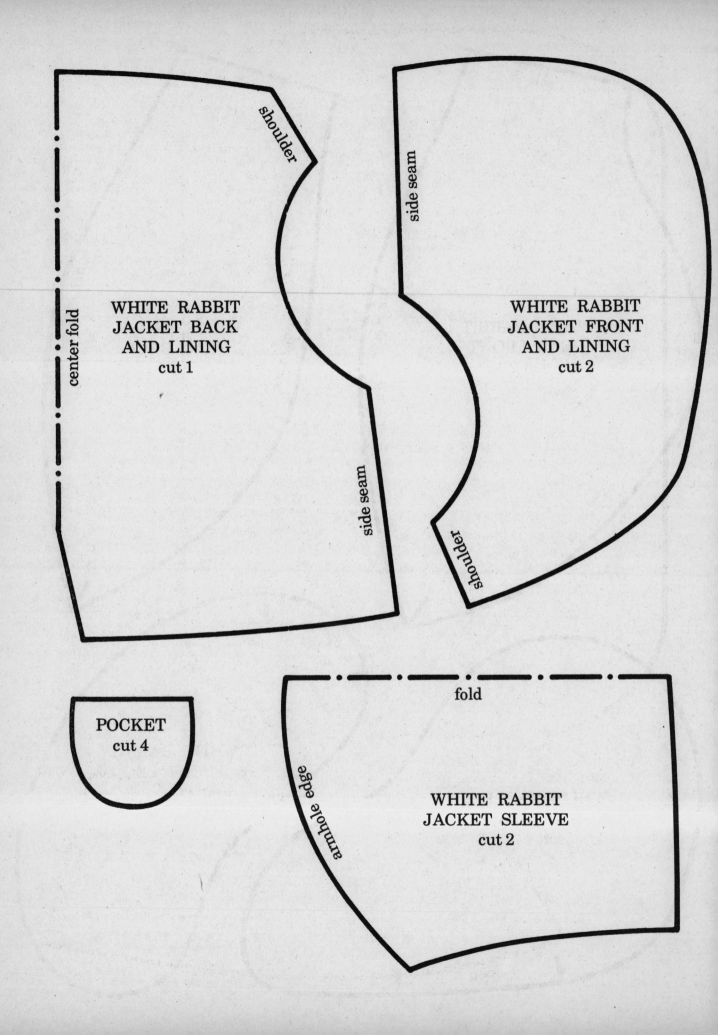

56

shoulder

side seam

center fold

**WHITE RABBIT
JACKET BACK
AND LINING**
cut 1

**WHITE RABBIT
JACKET FRONT
AND LINING**
cut 2

side seam

side seam

shoulder

POCKET
cut 4

fold

armhole edge

**WHITE RABBIT
JACKET SLEEVE**
cut 2

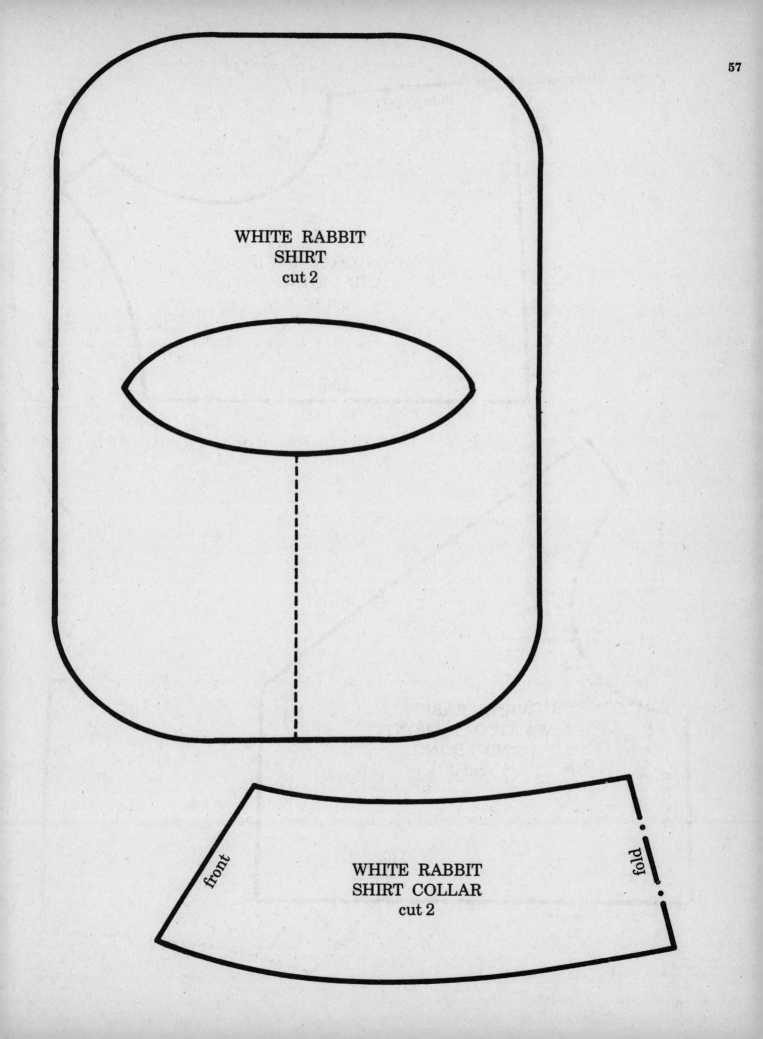

WHITE RABBIT
SHIRT
cut 2

front

fold

WHITE RABBIT
SHIRT COLLAR
cut 2

58

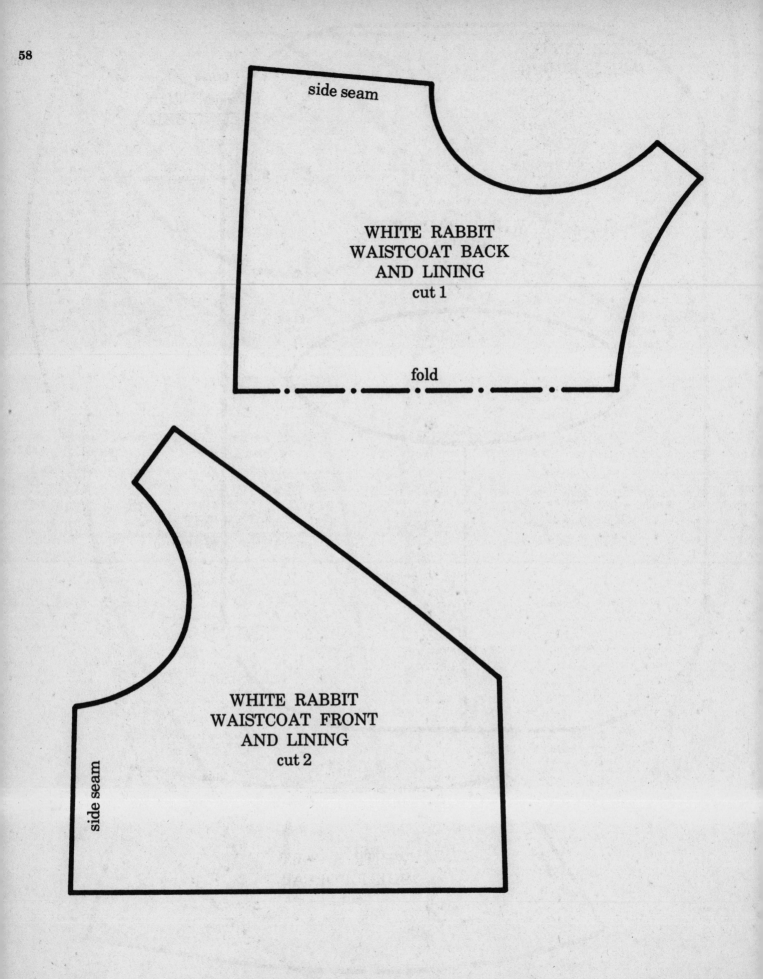

side seam

WHITE RABBIT
WAISTCOAT BACK
AND LINING
cut 1

fold

WHITE RABBIT
WAISTCOAT FRONT
AND LINING
cut 2

side seam

Dormouse

MATERIALS 36″ cotton, ⅜ yard of orange velveteen, ⅛ yard of orange-and-white print; scrap of pink felt; orange yarn; black 6-strand floss; black button thread; kapok for stuffing.

Following General Directions and 6 patterns, cut body fronts, backs, arms, hind legs and 2 ear pieces from velveteen. Place pattern pieces on fabric so nap runs in one direction; note arrows indicating straight of goods. Cut lining for ears and the tail pieces from orange-and-white cotton print.

Stitch together body fronts along front seam; stitch backs along back seam. Matching A's and B's, join front to back along sides, leaving openings for stuffing at one side edge and at center back seam of head. Clip seams and turn. Stuff firmly; sew openings closed.

Stitch together pairs of hind legs, leaving an opening at bottom edge. Clip seams, turn and stuff. Sew opening closed. Pin legs to body sides so Dormouse sits well; sew in place securely.

Stitch together pairs of arms, leaving top edge open. Clip, turn and stuff lightly. Fold in raw edges and stitch. Sew each arm to side seam. Cross arms slightly and tack to front as shown.

Seam tail pieces, leaving an opening. Clip, turn and stuff almost to body end. Hem end closed. Using a needle and orange yarn, cover tail thickly with ½″ loops. Sew tail to back seam.

Stitch a lining to each ear, leaving opening. Clip, turn and sew opening. Pleat ears and sew to head, curving lower edges toward the front.

On face, use black floss and stem stitch to outline closed eyes. Cut a ⅝″ pink felt nose and glue in place. For eyebrows and whiskers, run a long needle and button thread through the head; trim brows to 1″ length, whiskers to 2″ length. Use two threads for brows, six for whiskers.

straight of goods

DORMOUSE
HEAD AND BODY
FRONT
cut 2

B

front seam

side seam

A

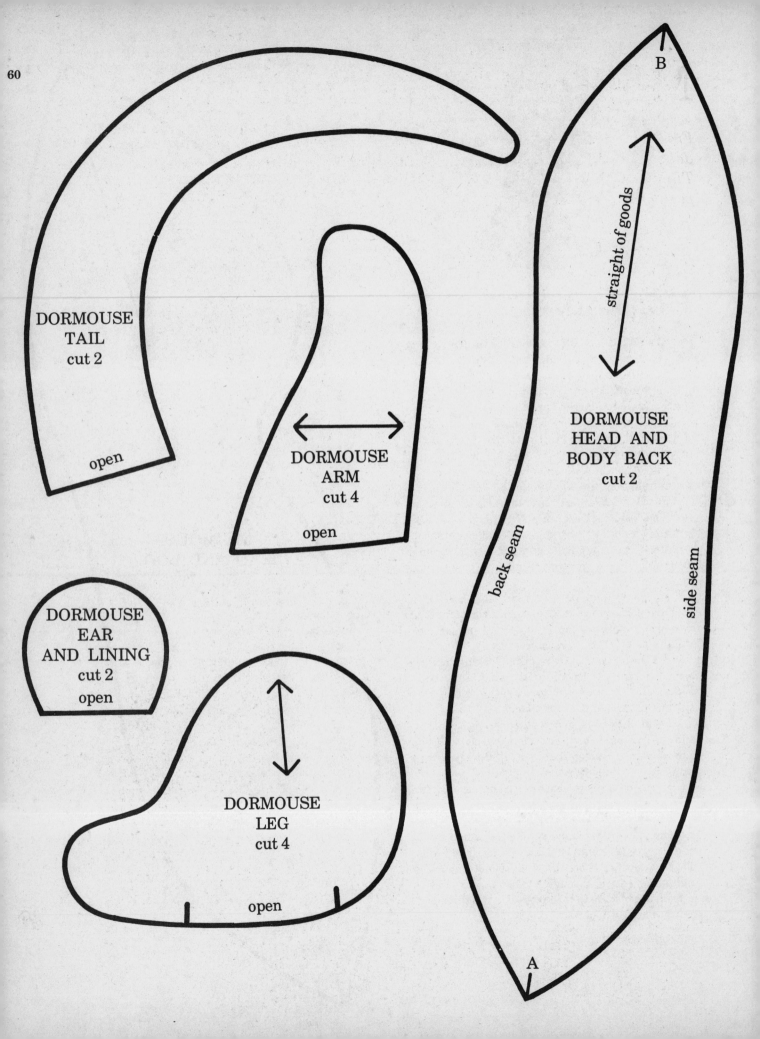

60

DORMOUSE
TAIL
cut 2

open

DORMOUSE
ARM
cut 4

open

DORMOUSE
EAR
AND LINING
cut 2
open

DORMOUSE
LEG
cut 4

open

B

straight of goods

DORMOUSE
HEAD AND
BODY BACK
cut 2

back seam

side seam

A

Mother Goose Dolls

From the pages of the best-loved children's classic come these endearing toys and dolls—Miss Muffet and the spider; Mistress Mary crowned with cockleshells; The Ten O'Clock Scholar sporting his slingshot; Wee Willie Winkie slumbering peacefully; the Fine Lady riding her White Horse to Banbury Cross

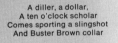

A diller, a dollar,
A ten o'clock scholar
Comes sporting a slingshot
And Buster Brown collar

Mistress Mary is contrary
From cheek to pouty cheek,
With cockleshells
atop her head
And flowers chin-to-feet

After all his running
Through the slumbering town,
Wee Willie Winkie
snores in peace
In cap and flannel gown

Our little Miss Muffet
In gingham and locket
Is quite blissfully unaware—
The spider beside her
(A rogue and conniver)
Would like to spin
webs in her hair

Rings on her fingers
And bells on her toes,
This fine lady rides
a white horse.
Her watering place,
As everyone knows,
Is old Banbury Cross,
of course

MATERIALS *For one doll:* 36" cotton, ½ yard pink, ⅛ yard striped or other fabric for legs (or striped jersey for stockings); embroidery floss for features; yarn for hair; kapok.

Follow 8 patterns. Transfer to wrong side of pink cotton; adding ½" seam allowance, cut pieces, cutting center head on the *bias.* Cut legs from pink fabric or fabric specified to give effect of stockings.

BODY Pin 2 body fronts along front seam, with right sides together; stitch seam. Pin 1 side body back to center body back; stitch side back seam. Repeat with second side body back. Join front bodies to back at side seams, matching A's and necks; double-stitch neck seams to reinforce them. Trim and clip seams; turn to right side.

HEAD To give shaping to chin, make fine running stitches at chin edge of center head; gather evenly to fit chin edge of front neck piece. Right sides facing, pin edges together; baste, easing head edge smoothly. Sew along basting with fine machine stitching; trim seam allowance close to stitching.

With right sides facing, place one side head over center head; pin together from each neck edge to top of head, easing fabric at top. Stitch seam, keeping it especially smooth along cheek; double-stitch neck. Add other side head. Trim seams; turn.

ARMS AND LEGS Pin together 2 pieces for each; sew seam, leaving top open and stitching twice around hand. Trim seam allowances and clip them carefully between thumb and forefinger; turn to right side.

STUFFING AND ASSEMBLY Stuff body and head firmly with kapok, making sure chin and cheeks are full and smooth; stuff hands lightly, arms and legs firmly almost to tops, to allow for movement.

Pin head to body, turning and tilting as specified for some dolls. Stuff neck firmly so head will not wobble. Turn head edges under; sew twice around neck with double thread and small stitches.

Outline fingers on hands with small running stitches; turn in arms at top and sew. Attach as though sewing on a button, using heavy thread to make a long shank from arm to shoulder.

On legs, place seam at center front and back, turn in top edges and sew. Stitch to body about 1" in front of point A.

FEATURES Following photographs and individual directions, embroider with floss. Rouge cheeks lightly with pink chalk or rouge.

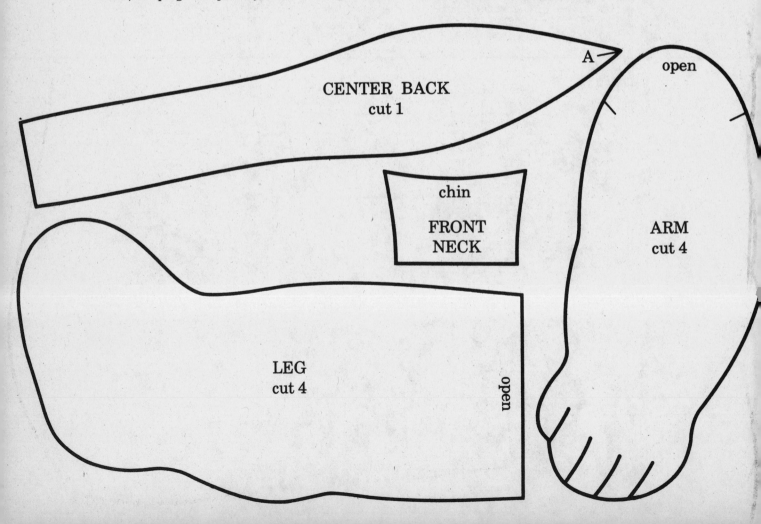

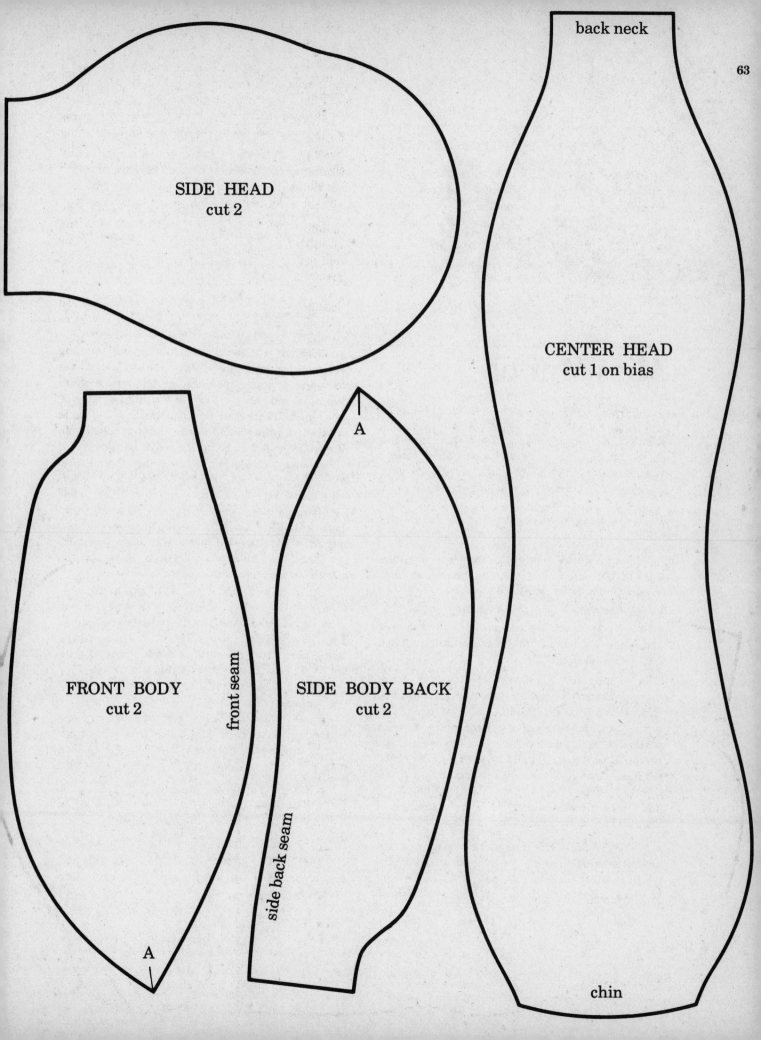

SIDE HEAD
cut 2

back neck

CENTER HEAD
cut 1 on bias

63

A

FRONT BODY
cut 2

front seam

SIDE BODY BACK
cut 2

side back seam

A

chin

Miss Muffet

MATERIALS *Doll:* 36″ cotton, ½ yard pink and ⅛ yard green-and-white-striped denim for legs; kapok; blue, brown, pink and rose embroidery floss; skein of fine brown wool yarn. *Costume:* 36″ cotton, ¼ yard white, ½ yard deep pink for slip, ½ yard dotted pink for dress; scrap of pink felt; ⅜ yard white seam binding; ½ yard lace; ¼ yard elastic; 5 snaps; fabric rosebuds; netting, spangle and child's size chain.

DOLL Follow 8 patterns and General Directions to cut doll from pink cotton and legs from striped denim. Stitch, stuff and assemble.

Features Following photograph and using floss, embroider features. Use satin stitch for blue eyes and blanket stitch for brown lashes. Outline-stitch pink nose and rose mouth.

Hair Drape 16″ to 18″ yarn strands over head, covering it thickly. Sew a center part from front to back. Divide strands at each side into 3 equal sections. Tack middle section to head about 4″ from part; tack back and front sections toward middle. Divide loose strands into 5 or 6 sections. For curls, wind and sew netting around a ¾″ dowel. Wind yarn tightly around netting on dowel, tacking under ends and working toward head. Hold yarn and sew to netting; slip out dowel. Tack blossoms above curls.

PANTALETTES Following 2 patterns and adding seam allowances, cut fronts and backs from white cotton. Stitch fronts together at front seam, stopping at crotch; stitch backs at back seam. Join at

inside legs *only*. Stitch tuck and ¼″ hem at lower edges; trim with lace. Stitch side seams, leaving upper half of one seam open. Hem the opening. Trim and overcast seams; turn. Pleat top edge to fit doll; stitch pleats. Face top with seam binding; add snap.

SLIP Following 2 patterns and adding seam allowances, cut bodice fronts and backs from deep pink cotton; also cut 6½″ x 30″ skirt. Seam 2 bodice backs to each front at shoulders. Right sides together, seam one bodice section to another at back opening, neck and armholes. Trim seams and turn. Pin side seams to fit and stitch.

On skirt, stitch ¾″ hem and a ¼″ tuck; hem skirt ends. Gather top edge to fit bodice. Right sides together, seam to bodice with 2 rows of stitching. Trim seam allowance and overcast. Sew 2 snaps to back opening.

DRESS Following 3 patterns and adding seam allowances, cut bodice fronts, backs and sleeves from dotted pink cotton. Also cut 6″ x 30″ skirt, 1½″ x 60″ and 1½″ x 18″ strips for skirt and neck ruffles, 1″ x 9½″ strip to bind neck.

Seam 2 bodice backs to each front at shoulders. Right sides together, seam one bodice section to another along back opening. Trim seams; turn. Baste layers together around neck and armholes. Gather each sleeve from X to X to fit armhole. Right sides together, seam to armholes. For sleeve casing, turn up lower edge to top dotted line and stitch; run second row of stitching. Pin side and sleeve seams to fit and stitch, leaving casing ends open. Insert elastic, sew and whipstitch openings closed.

On skirt, hem ends and sew ¾″ hem on one long edge. For 60″ ruffle, piece 1½″-wide strips. Right sides together, fold lengthwise and seam 60″ edges. Turn. Gather seam edge to fit skirt; with gathers facing hem, stitch on ruffle and fold down. Gather top edge of skirt to fit bodice. Right sides together, seam skirt to bodice with 2 rows of stitching. Trim seam and overcast.

Make similar ruffle for neck and stitch in place with edges even. Stitch fabric strip over raw edges; turn to inside and hem down. Sew 2 snaps to bodice back.

SHOES Follow low shoe pattern to cut pink felt; cut ⅝″ x 2½″ strips for bows and ¼″-wide strips for knots. Seam shoes and turn. Tack on bows and knots.

LOCKET Cut a tiny heart from a spangle and punch hole for chain. Insert chain and hang around neck.

A diller, a dollar,
A ten o'clock scholar
Comes sporting a slingshot
And Buster Brown collar

Mistress Mary is contrary
From cheek to pouty cheek,
With cockleshells
atop her head
And flowers chin-to-feet

After all his running
Through the slumbering town,
Wee Willie Winkie
snores in peace
In cap and flannel gown

Our little Miss Muffet
In gingham and locket
Is quite blissfully unaware—
The spider beside her
(A rogue and conniver)
Would like to spin
webs in her hair

Rings on her fingers
And bells on her toes,
This fine lady rides
a white horse.
Her watering place,
As everyone knows,
Is old Banbury Cross,
of course

Mother Goose Dolls, page 61.

Ginger Joe and two of the Triplets from
Purrfectly Lovable Cats, page 164.

Frisky Jungle Babies, page 110.

Out of the Forest, Animals to Make, page 123.

Little Women, page 84.

This is Amy. She's a Doll!, **page 235.**

Indian Dolls, page 187.

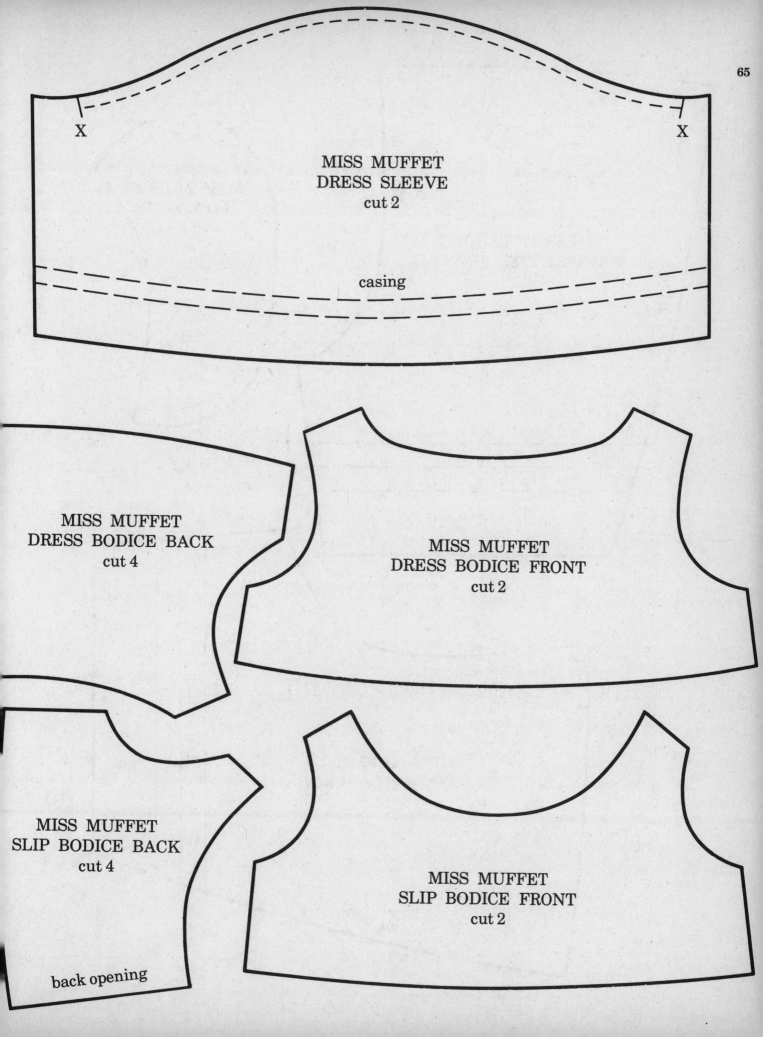

X X

MISS MUFFET
DRESS SLEEVE
cut 2

casing

MISS MUFFET
DRESS BODICE BACK
cut 4

MISS MUFFET
DRESS BODICE FRONT
cut 2

MISS MUFFET
SLIP BODICE BACK
cut 4

MISS MUFFET
SLIP BODICE FRONT
cut 2

back opening

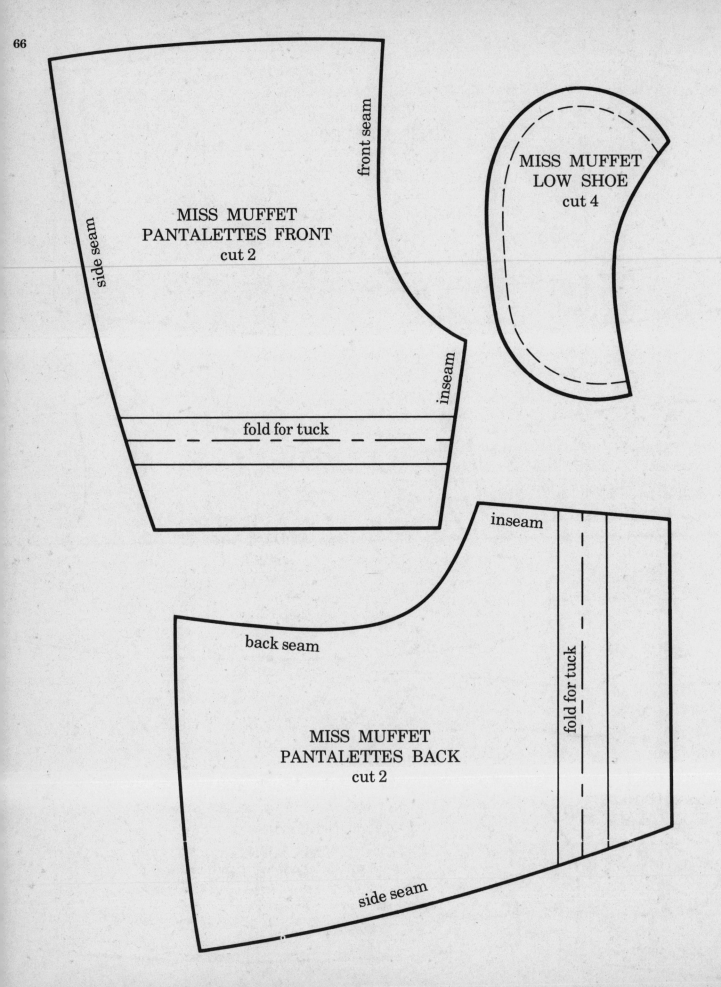

MISS MUFFET
PANTALETTES FRONT
cut 2

front seam

side seam

inseam

fold for tuck

MISS MUFFET
LOW SHOE
cut 4

inseam

back seam

fold for tuck

MISS MUFFET
PANTALETTES BACK
cut 2

side seam

Spider

MATERIALS ¼ yard 36″ blue cotton; 2″ x 9″ strip of yellow print fabric for bow; felt scraps in orange, red, lime, magenta and white; blue embroidery floss; fuzzy yarn scrap; gold bead; kapok; 8 pipe cleaners.

SPIDER Following 2 patterns and adding ¼″ seam allowances, cut spider body and head from blue cotton. Follow remaining 2 patterns to trace (but not cut) outlines for 4 arms and 4 legs on the blue cotton doubled; allow for ¼″ seams. For felt features cut red and lime eyes, magenta nose and white mouth.

Stitch together 2 body pieces, leaving neck open; turn and stuff. Repeat for head. Appliqué features to face. With 2 strands of floss, outline-stitch a toothy grin. Tack yarn tuft to head.

Seam arms and legs through both layers from A, around hand or foot, to B. Cut out and turn to right side. Turn in seam allowances from B to straight ends and topstitch. Stuff hands slightly; insert pipe cleaners in arms and legs, bending to fit; cut off excess.

To assemble spider, turn in neck edge of body. Stack 4 legs, then 4 arms on body; sew securely. Bend up one arm; turn in neck edges of head and sew to body.

WESKIT Follow pattern to cut weskit from orange felt, omitting seam allowance; press back lapels on broken lines. Insert arms and legs through armholes; overlap front edges and tack. Add bead for button. Pleat back to fit and sew.

For bow, fold print strip lengthwise with right side in. Stitch long open edge with ⅛″ seam and turn. Cut off 1½″ for knot strip. Shape ends of long strip, turn in edges and sew. Make a tailored bow, wrap with knot and tack to spider.

lapel

SPIDER WESKIT
cut 1

armhole

lapel

SPIDER HEAD
cut 2

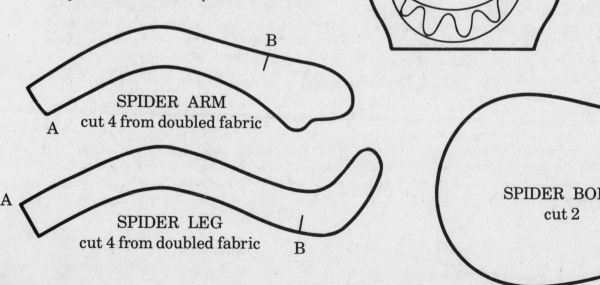

B

SPIDER ARM
cut 4 from doubled fabric

A

A

SPIDER LEG
cut 4 from doubled fabric

B

SPIDER BODY
cut 2

Ten O'Clock Scholar

MATERIALS *Doll:* ½ yard 36″ pink cotton; kapok; green, light brown, pink and red embroidery floss; skein of orange wool yarn. *Costume:* 36″ cotton, ½ yard yellow, ⅛ yard black and 12″ square of white; ⅛ yard striped jersey; 4″ x 18″ piece of green linen; 3½″ x 14″ strip of green taffeta; 2 yards yellow seam binding; ½ yard narrow elastic; ½ yard ¼″ black grosgrain ribbon; ¼″ buckle; 4 round black buttons; 4 small pearl buttons; 3 snaps; forked twig and rubber band for slingshot.

DOLL Follow 8 patterns and General Directions to cut doll from pink cotton. Stitch, stuff and assemble, turning head to one side.

Features Following photograph and using floss, embroider features. Use satin stitch for green eyes, straight stitches and French knots for eyebrows and freckles. Outline-stitch pink nose and mischievous red mouth.

Hair Drape 10″ loops of yarn across top of head; stitch along center top and toward back. Fill in with 2″ loops under top layer so hair has a thick, unruly look. Sew short loops for bangs.

SUIT PANTS Following 2 patterns and adding seam allowances, cut fronts and backs from yellow cotton. Pin and sew 2 fronts along front seam, stopping at crotch; pin and sew backs along back seam; join at inside legs *only.* For casings, turn up lower edges to top dotted lines and hem; run second row of stitching. Pin side seams and stitch, leaving open the casing ends on both seams and the upper half of one seam. Cut elastic to fit doll; insert in casings and sew. Whip casings closed. Hem seam opening. Turn pants; pleat top edges to fit doll and stitch. Face top edge with seam binding; add snap at waist.

JACKET Following 4 patterns and adding seam allowances, cut back, fronts and sleeves from yellow cotton and collar from white. On back, fold fabric to make the box pleat; topstitch on right side for about 2″. With right sides facing, seam fronts to back at shoulders. Gather top of sleeves from X to X to fit armholes; stitch in place. Sew box pleats in sleeves; face wrist edges with binding.

Pin side and sleeve seams to fit doll; stitch seams. Face the neck, front and lower edges with seam binding; topstitch edges. Sew 2 snaps to neck and black buttons to front. Insert ribbon belt in buckle; make ribbon loop for belt keeper.

For collar, seam 2 pieces at ends and outer edge, with right sides facing. Trim and clip seam allowance; turn. Cut a 1″-wide bias strip to fit neckline. Right sides facing, stitch one edge of strip to top side of neckline. Fold strip, turn in raw edges and sew to underside. Tack collar to doll's neck.

For tie, fold taffeta lengthwise; stitch ¼″ seam on one long edge, leaving an opening. Cut off a 2″ length for knot. Shape tie ends and stitch; turn and sew opening. Make bow, wrap with knot strip and tack. Tack tie to doll.

STOCKINGS Follow leg pattern to cut striped jersey, adding narrow seam allowance. Stitch pieces; turn; leave top unfinished.

SHOES Follow high shoe pattern to cut black cotton. Stitch 2 pieces for each shoe; trim seam and turn.

SPATS Following 3 patterns and adding narrow seam allowances, cut inner spats, outer backs and outer fronts from green linen; cut lining from black cotton. Stitch together green pieces at front and back seams; repeat for lining. Right sides together, stitch lining to each spat, leaving an opening for turning. Turn; sew opening. Sew 2 pearl buttons to outer front; tack spat on doll.

Rub pants knees with pencil for dirty effect. For slingshot, wind rubber band on twig and tuck in belt. For school book, cover a 2¼″ x 3″ address book with red self-adhering plastic; glue an antique-type picture to front.

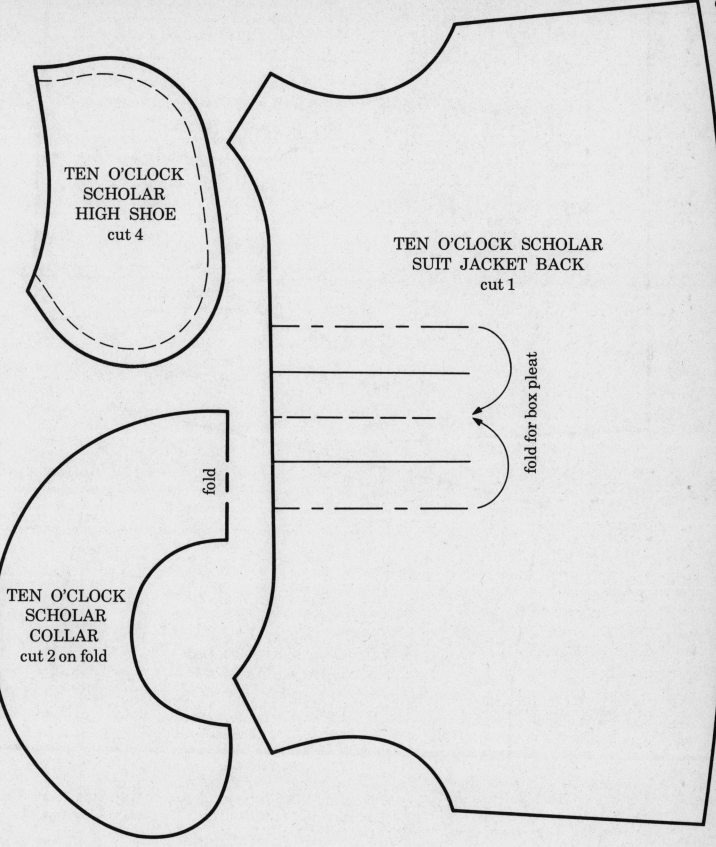

TEN O'CLOCK
SCHOLAR
HIGH SHOE
cut 4

TEN O'CLOCK SCHOLAR
SUIT JACKET BACK
cut 1

fold for box pleat

fold

TEN O'CLOCK
SCHOLAR
COLLAR
cut 2 on fold

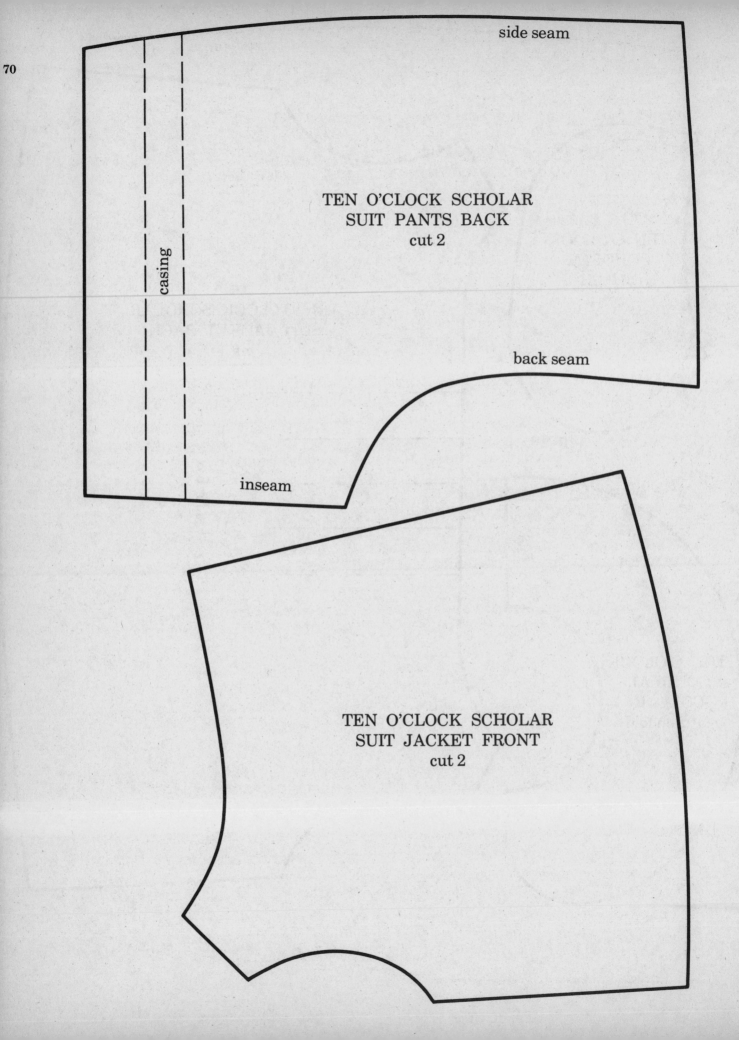

70

side seam

casing

TEN O'CLOCK SCHOLAR
SUIT PANTS BACK
cut 2

back seam

inseam

TEN O'CLOCK SCHOLAR
SUIT JACKET FRONT
cut 2

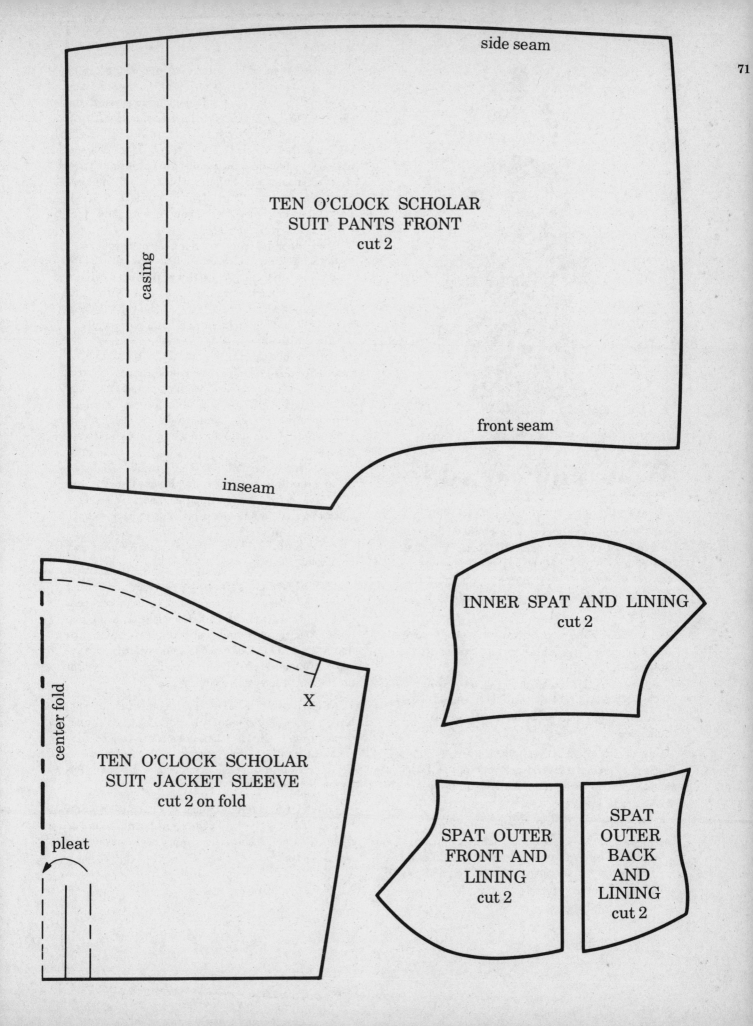

side seam

TEN O'CLOCK SCHOLAR
SUIT PANTS FRONT
cut 2

casing

front seam

inseam

center fold

X

TEN O'CLOCK SCHOLAR
SUIT JACKET SLEEVE
cut 2 on fold

pleat

INNER SPAT AND LINING
cut 2

SPAT OUTER
FRONT AND
LINING
cut 2

SPAT
OUTER
BACK
AND
LINING
cut 2

Wee Willie Winkie

MATERIALS *Doll:* ½ yard 36″ pink cotton; kapok; green, pink and rose embroidery floss; fuzzy brown wool yarn. *Costume:* 36″ fabric, ⅜ yard each red cotton flannel and blue-and-white-striped cotton; 4″ x 14″ strip of orange felt; ¾ yard red seam binding; blue thread; five ½″ pearl buttons; scraps of blue yarns.

DOLL Follow 8 patterns and general Directions to cut doll from pink cotton. Stitch, stuff and assemble.

Features Following photograph and using floss, embroider features. Use straight stitches for green sleepy eyes and rose yawning mouth; outline-stitch pink nose.

Hair Fold 4″ lengths of yarn in half and sew each fold to head. Sew rows around face and back of head, then fill in top until hair has a fuzzy unruly look.

FLANNEL GOWN Following 5 patterns and adding seam allowances, cut front, back, back yoke, sleeves and collar from red flannel. Also cut two 1″ x 4″ cuffs, 1″ x 9½″ strip for front opening and 1″ x 9″ bias strip for neck.

Sew 2 rows of machine stitching along top of back; gather to fit back yoke. Right sides together, sew back to yoke; fold up seam allowance. Right sides together, stitch front to back at shoulders.

Cut front opening from neck to A. With right sides together, stitch 1″ x 9½″ strip to edges of opening with ¼″ seam, making placket extension. Turn strip to inside and finish with ¼″ seam, making placket extension. Turn strip to inside and finish with ¼″ hem. Edge front opening with blue topstitching about ⅜″ from seam.

Sew machine stitching along top of sleeves from X to X; gather to fit armholes. Sew sleeves to armholes with 2 rows of stitching; trim seam allowances. Gather each wrist edge to fit cuff. With right side of cuff facing wrong side of sleeve, stitch in place. Fold cuff to right side, turn in raw edge and topstitch with blue thread.

Stitch collar pieces, right sides together, around outer edge and ends. Trim seam allowance and turn; topstitch with blue thread. With right sides together and raw edges even, stitch collar to neck. Pin bias strip to collar with right sides together; stitch along neck seam. Turn strip to inside at ends and raw edge; sew.

Place gown on doll; pin sleeve and side seams to fit and mark length desired. Remove gown and stitch seams to B; trim seam allowances. With right sides together, stitch seam binding to lower edges; turn to inside and sew.

Sew buttons to one side of front opening and button loops to other side.

NIGHTCAP Following 2 patterns and adding seam allowances, cut 2 cap and 2 band pieces from blue-striped cotton. Right sides together, seam cap pieces; trim seams and turn. Seam band ends; turn and fold. Insert ¼″ of cap in band and turn in raw edges of band; topstitch in place. Tack a 1½″ tassel made from blue yarns to point of cap.

BEDROOM SLIPPERS Following 2 patterns and omitting seam allowances, cut soles and uppers from orange felt. Stitch together two soles for each slipper. Hold sole against doll's foot and pin upper around front of sole from A to A. Remove slipper, stitch, and turn.

CANDLESTICK Glue a spool about 1½″ high to a 2″-diameter jar lid. Glue on a ring hook for handle. Paint bright yellow. Melt wax and attach small candle.

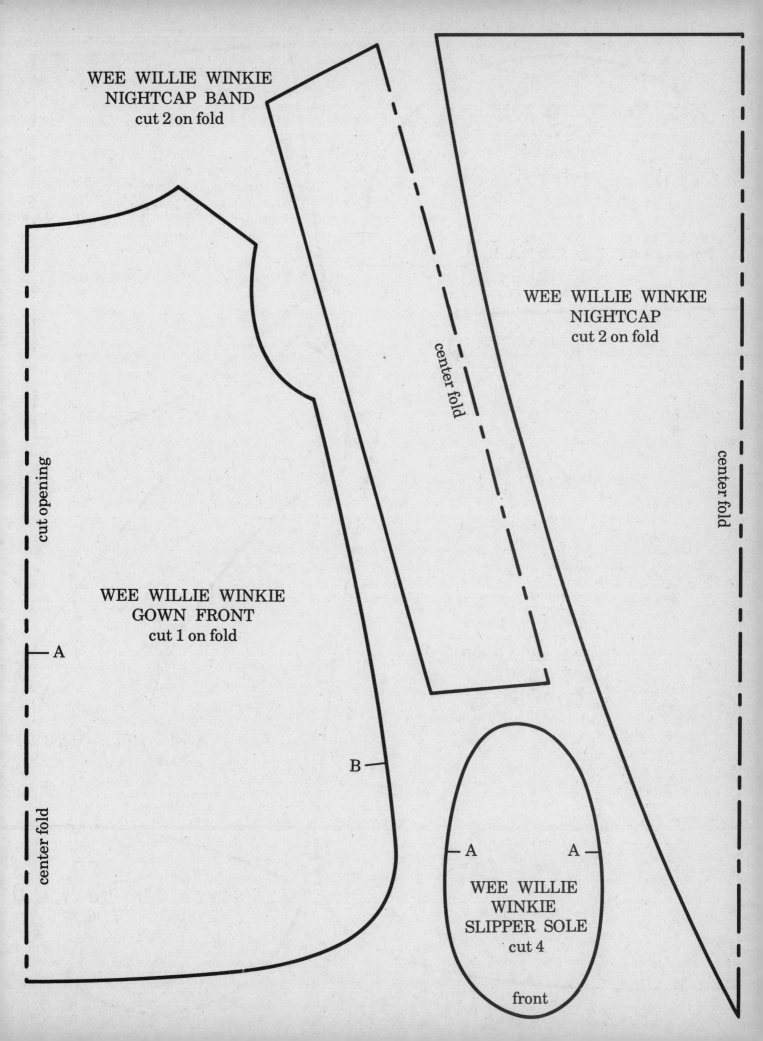

WEE WILLIE WINKIE
NIGHTCAP BAND
cut 2 on fold

WEE WILLIE WINKIE
NIGHTCAP
cut 2 on fold

center fold

center fold

cut opening

A

WEE WILLIE WINKIE
GOWN FRONT
cut 1 on fold

center fold

B

A   A

WEE WILLIE
WINKIE
SLIPPER SOLE

cut 4

front

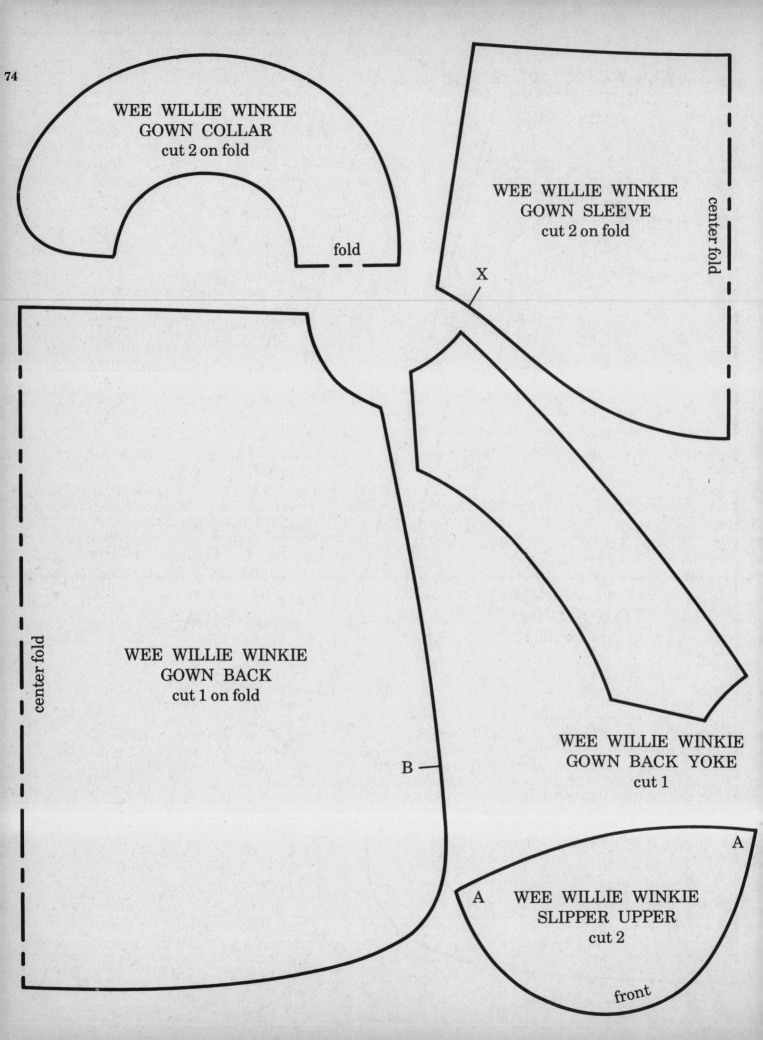

74

WEE WILLIE WINKIE
GOWN COLLAR
cut 2 on fold

fold

WEE WILLIE WINKIE
GOWN SLEEVE
cut 2 on fold

center fold

X

center fold

WEE WILLIE WINKIE
GOWN BACK
cut 1 on fold

B

WEE WILLIE WINKIE
GOWN BACK YOKE
cut 1

A

A

WEE WILLIE WINKIE
SLIPPER UPPER
cut 2

front

A Fine Lady

MATERIALS *Doll:* 36″ cotton, ½ yard pink for body and ⅛ yard yellow for legs; kapok; brown, pink and rose embroidery floss; skein of fine yellow wool yarn. *Costume:* 36″ fabric, ½ yard light blue cotton and ½ yard royal blue cotton velvet; orange felt; ½ yard ¾″ lace; ⅞ yard 1¼″ lace; seam binding, ⅜ yard light blue and 1½ yards royal blue; 5 snaps; cardboard tube; gold paper; glue; 6 small bells; sew-on jewels or rhinestones; pearl bead; necklace.

DOLL Follow 8 patterns and General Directions to cut doll from pink cotton and legs from yellow. Stitch, stuff and assemble, turning head well to one side and tilting it back.

Features Following photograph and using floss, embroider very haughty features. Outline-stitch brown lashes for downcast eyes, pink nose and small rosecolored mouth. Rouge cheeks lightly.

Hair Drape 40″ strands of yarn over head, covering it thickly. Sew a center part from front to back. Divide strands at each side into 3 equal sections. Tack middle section to head about 4″ from part; tack front and then back sections toward middle.

Braid strands tightly; sew braid ends. Coil and sew into a generous ring from front to back, tucking braid ends under.

PANTALETTES Following 2 patterns (page 66) and adding seam allowances, cut fronts and backs from blue cotton; trim ⅛″ from lower edges of legs. Stitch fronts together at front seam, stopping at crotch; stitch backs at back seam. Join at inside legs only. To hem legs, turn under ⅛″ then ¼″ and sew. Stitch tuck; fold up temporarily. Sew narrow lace over hem with upper edge against stitching of tuck; fold down tuck.

Stitch side seams, leaving upper half of one seam open. Hem opening. Trim and overcast seams; turn. Pleat and stitch top edge to fit doll; face top with seam binding and add snap.

SLIP Following 2 slip bodice patterns (page 65) and adding seam allowances, cut 2 fronts and 4 backs from blue cotton; cut 7½″ x 30″ skirt. Seam 2 bodice backs to each front at shoulders. Right sides together, seam one bodice section to another at back opening, neck and armholes; trim seams and turn. Pin side seams to fit and stitch.

On skirt, stitch 1¼″ hem and a ¼″ tuck, with fold line of tuck 1½″ above stitching. Fold tuck up temporarily. Sew wide lace over hem, with upper edge against stitching of tuck; fold down tuck. Hem skirt ends and gather top edge to fit bodice. Right sides together, stitch to bodice with 2 rows of stitching. Trim seam allowance and overcast. Sew 2 snaps to back opening.

DRESS Following 4 patterns and adding seam allowances, cut 2 backs, 2 side fronts, center front and sleeves from velvet. Be sure nap runs in direction indicated for all pieces.

Pin and stitch darts on backs; trim dart seams. Right sides facing, pin and stitch a side front to each side of center front. Join backs to front at shoulders.

On sleeves, sew 2 rows of machine stitching along top edges from X to X; gather to fit armholes. Sew sleeves to armholes with 2 rows of stitching; trim seam allowance. At each wrist edge, fold and pin fabric to center line for a reverse box pleat; topstitch pleat.

Try dress wrong side out on doll wearing slip. Pin sleeve and side seams to fit; remove dress and stitch seams. Trim seam allowance. Cut a ¾″-wide velvet bias strip to fit around neck. With right sides facing, stitch to neck with ⅛″ seam. Fold strip, turn in raw edge and sew to wrong side.

Stitch seam binding to edges of back opening.

turn in edges to overlap and fit doll, leaving space for snaps; sew binding to inside. Trim sleeves and skirt to lengths desired. Stitch seam binding to edges, turn to inside and sew. Add 2 snaps to back opening.

SLIPPERS Follow high shoe pattern (page 69) to cut orange felt. Stitch 2 pieces for each slipper; trim seam allowance and turn. Tack 3 bells to instep.

CROWN Cut a 2¼" length from a cardboard tube 6" in circumference. Follow pattern to cut 6 points. Glue gold paper to inside and outside; trim lower edge with a ¾" gold band. Punch small hole near lower edge so crown can be sewed or pinned to doll's head.

JEWELRY Place a necklace of colored beads on doll. Tack pearl and sew-on jewels to fingers for rings.

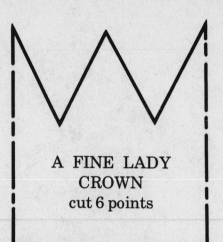

A FINE LADY
CROWN
cut 6 points

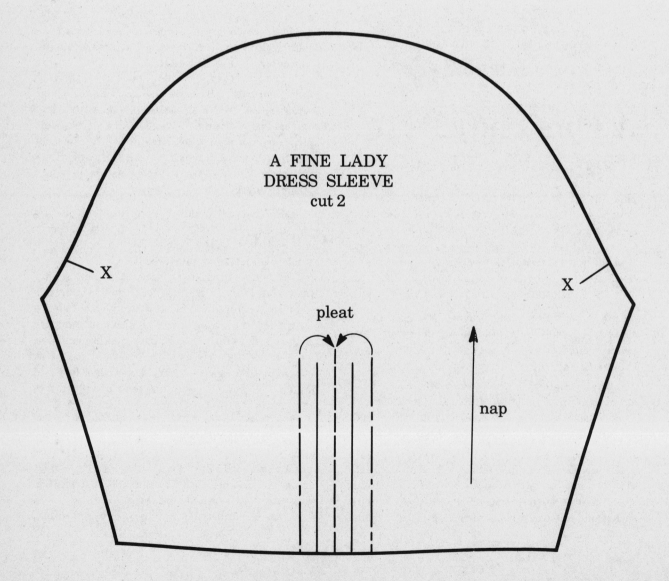

A FINE LADY
DRESS SLEEVE
cut 2

X   X

pleat

nap

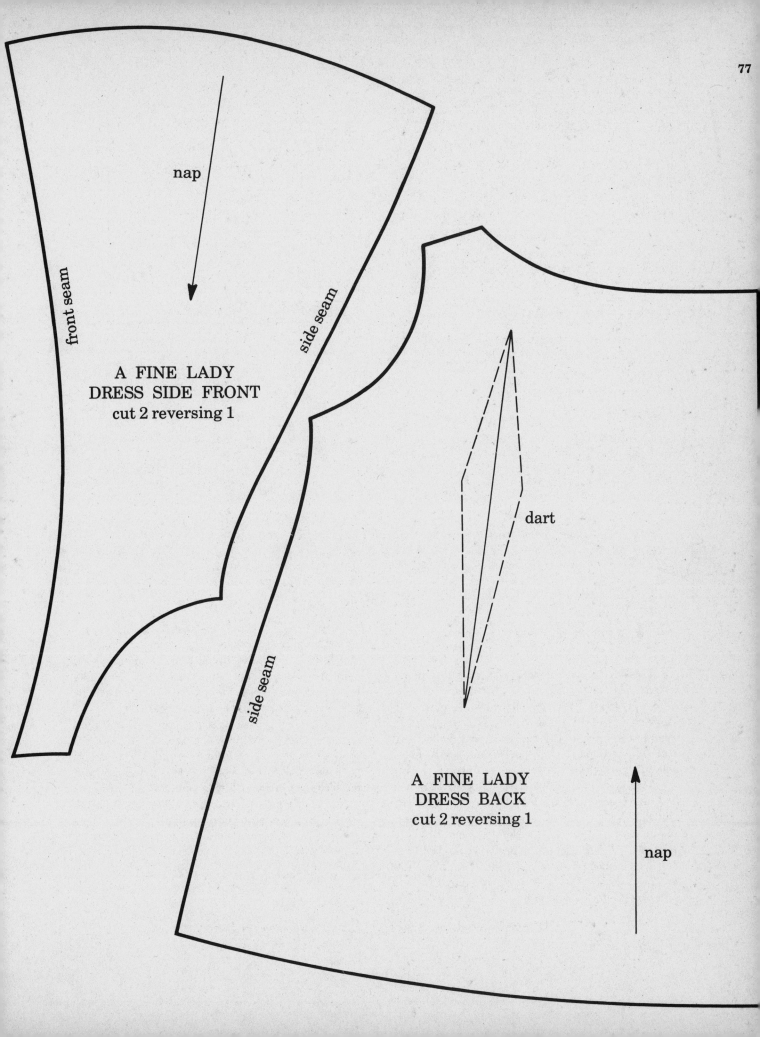

nap

front seam

side seam

A FINE LADY
DRESS SIDE FRONT
cut 2 reversing 1

side seam

dart

A FINE LADY
DRESS BACK
cut 2 reversing 1

nap

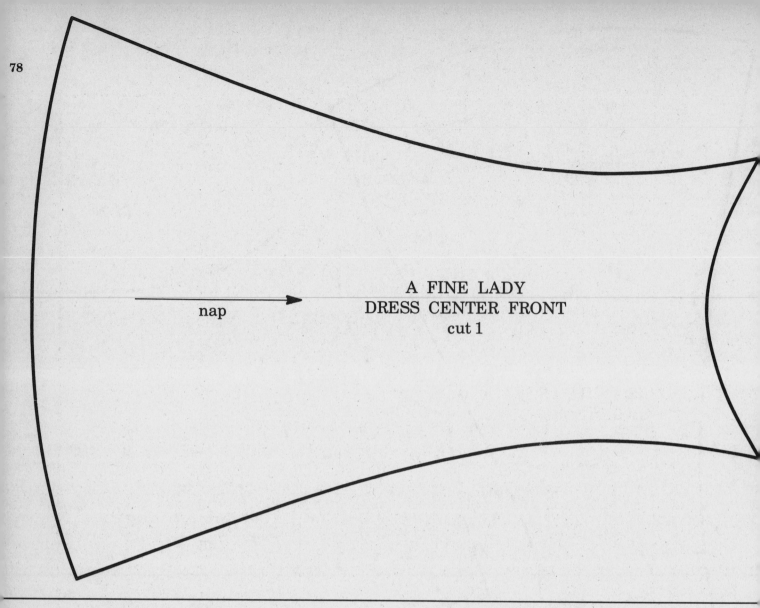

nap →

A FINE LADY
DRESS CENTER FRONT
cut 1

White Horse

MATERIALS 9″ piece of ¾″ x 5½″ pine; 8″ length of 1½″ round; 3″ length of 1″ dowel; 2 feet of ½″ dowel; scrap of ¼″ plywood for neck; four 1¼″-diameter checkers; 4 washers; 4 No. 6 or No. 8 round-head brass screws 1¼″ long; glue; tacks; yellow, red and white enamel; hemp rope; white plastic; black self-adhering plastic; ½ yard of ¼″ ribbon.

Trim pine base to 5″ width and use 8″ length of 1½″ round for body and 3″ length of 1″ dowel for head. Cut four 5½″ lengths of ½″ dowel for legs. Following actual-size diagram and details A and B, mark, then drill through base and partway into body. Insert legs temporarily and trim flush with base. Saw ¼″ plywood neck. Cut ¼″-wide slots on center in head and body to dotted lines.

Paint base yellow, checkers red and horse white, keeping areas to be glued free from enamel.

To assemble, glue legs into base and body. Glue neck into slots in body and head. Then drill pilot holes into sides of base for screws and drill checkers. Screw into place with washers between.

Cut ½″ x 2½″ white plastic strip and point ends for ears. Pleat at center and tack to head. From black plastic cut ⅜″ ovals for eyes and ⅜″-wide bands for hoofs; attach in place. Tack ribbon around head for bridle and make a bow to go over tail. Tack on a 6″ length of rope for mane and glue on a 4½″ length for tail. Ravel rope; add bow.

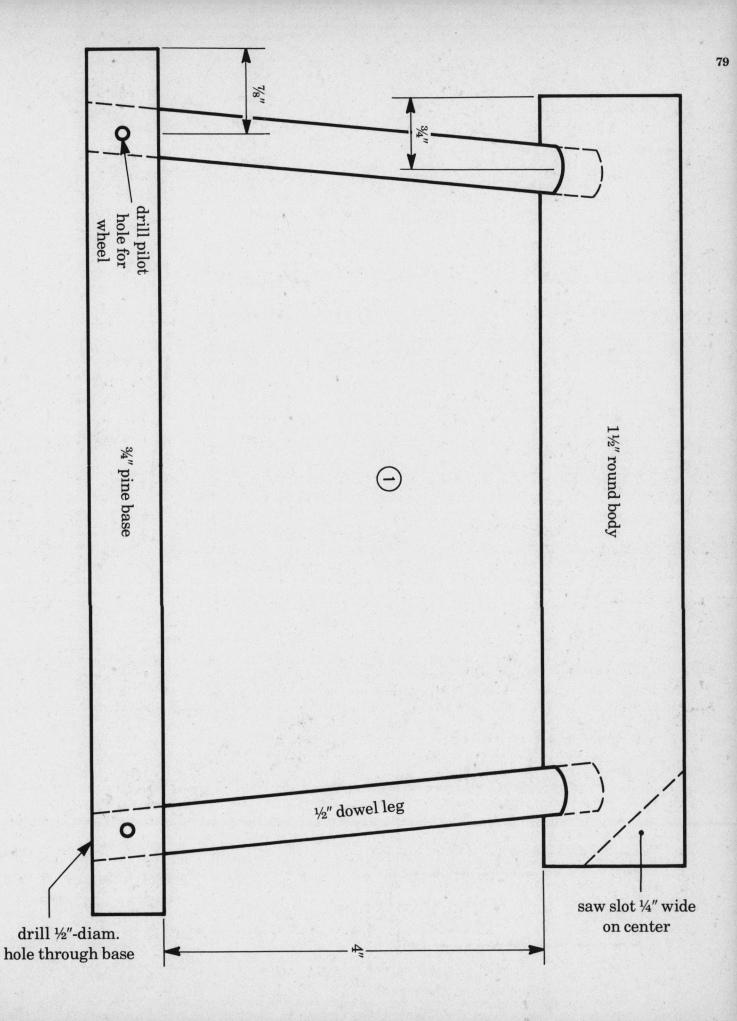

drill pilot hole for wheel

7/8″

3/4″

3/4″ pine base

1

1½″ round body

½″ dowel leg

drill ½″-diam. hole through base

saw slot ¼″ wide on center

4″

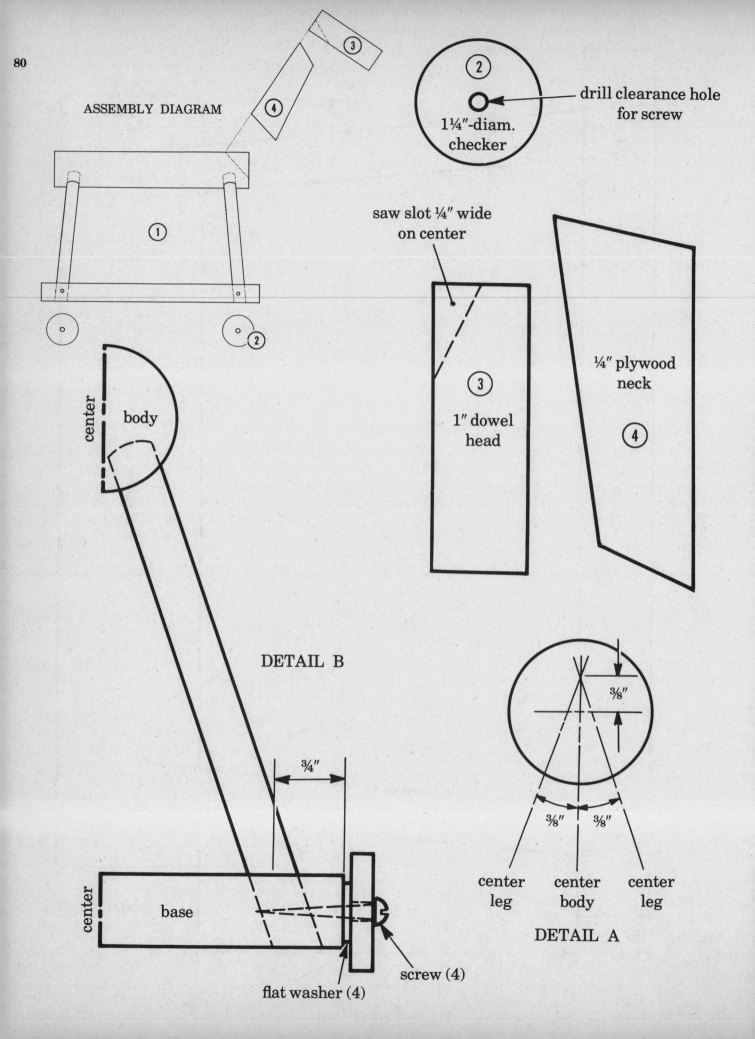

80

ASSEMBLY DIAGRAM

①

②
1¼″-diam.
checker

drill clearance hole
for screw

②

saw slot ¼″ wide
on center

③
1″ dowel
head

¼″ plywood
neck

④

center

body

DETAIL B

¾″

center

base

flat washer (4)

screw (4)

⅜″

⅜″ ⅜″

center
leg

center
body

center
leg

DETAIL A

Mistress Mary

MATERIALS *Doll:* 36″ cotton, ½ yard pink for body and ⅛ yard green for legs; kapok; dark gold, pink and rose embroidery floss; skein of heavy dark gold wool yarn. *Costume:* ¼ yard 36″ green-and-white print cotton for panties; 42″ organdy, ⅜ yard chartreuse, ⅛ yard Kelly green, ½ yard bright pink and ¼ yard yellow; scrap of magenta felt; ⅜ yard green seam binding; ¼ yard narrow elastic; 3 snaps. Plastic foam, 4 seashells, green felt, 3 pipe cleaners and 3 bells, 1 yard ¼″ green ribbon, glue for shell hat.

DOLL Follow 8 patterns and General Directions to cut doll from pink cotton and legs from green. Stitch, stuff and assemble, turning head slightly to one side.

Features Following photograph and using floss, embroider features with a contrary, defiant expression. Work gold eyes in satin stitch, pink nose and rose mouth in outline stitch. Rouge cheeks.

Hair For short curls, wind gold yarn twice around a finger, slip off and tack loops to head with matching thread. Work rows of curls around face and back of head, continuing to top. Tack a curl to forehead.

PANTIES Following 2 pantalette patterns (page 66) and adding seam allowance, cut fronts and backs from green print cotton; trim ⅛″ from lower edges of legs. Also cut two 1½″ x 15″ strips for ruffles.

Stitch fronts together at front seam, stopping at crotch; stitch backs at back seam. Join at inside legs only. To hem legs, turn under ⅛″, then ¼″ and sew. Fold ruffle strips lengthwise, with wrong sides in; gather raw edges to fit legs. Baste each ruffle over leg hem, with gathered edges against fold line of tuck. Fold down tuck, topstitch lower edge, catching ruffle. Stitch side seams, leaving upper half of one seam open. Hem opening. Trim and overcast seams; turn. Pleat and stitch top edge to fit doll; face top with seam binding and add snap.

BASIC DRESS Following 3 patterns for Miss Muffet (page 65) and adding seam allowances, cut bodice, sleeves and 8″ x 34″ skirt from chartreuse organdy. Cut 4″ x 34″ skirt strip from Kelly organdy.

Seam 2 bodice backs to each front at shoulders. Right sides together, seam one bodice section to another along back opening and neck. Trim seams; turn. Baste layers together at armholes.

Gather each sleeve from X to X to fit armhole. Right sides together, stitch to armhole. For sleeve casing, turn up lower edge to top dotted line and stitch; run second row of stitching. Pin sleeve and side seams to fit and stitch, leaving casing ends open. Insert elastic, sew and whipstitch openings closed.

For skirt, fold chartreuse and Kelly strips lengthwise. Turn in long raw edges of Kelly, baste to chartreuse so fold edge of Kelly extends ½″ below fold of chartreuse; stitch in place. Hem ends of skirt and gather top edge to fit bodice. Right sides together, seam skirt to bodice with 2 rows of stitching. Trim seam allowance and overcast. Sew 2 snaps to bodice back.

SCALLOPED RUFFLES From organdy cut 4 pink and 2 yellow 4″ x 42″ strips. Baste together 2 pink strips for bottom ruffle and a pink and a yellow each for middle and top ruffles. Following 3 patterns, mark 15 scallops on bottom ruffle, 17 and 21 scallops on middle and top ruffles. Stitch around scallops and ends of strips; trim seam allowances and clip corners. Turn and press seams. Fold in raw top edges and press; sew 2 rows of machine stitching and gather.

With all pink sides up, sew bottom ruffle to waistline of dress. Alternating scallops, sew middle ruffle around center of bodice and top ruffle to neck.

82

SLIPPERS Follow low shoe pattern (page 66) to cut magenta felt. Follow flower pattern to cut pink organdy. Stitch 2 pieces for each slipper; trim seam allowance and turn. Tack 2 flowers to instep.

COCKLESHELL HAT Cut a 1¼″-diameter disk from ½″ plastic foam. Cut 4 slits for shells in disk wall; insert and glue shells. Glue felt to disk top; punch holes for pipe cleaners and glue. Tack bells to ends. Glue velvet ribbon around disk. Tie remaining ribbon around doll's head; pin hat over it.

cut 4

flower

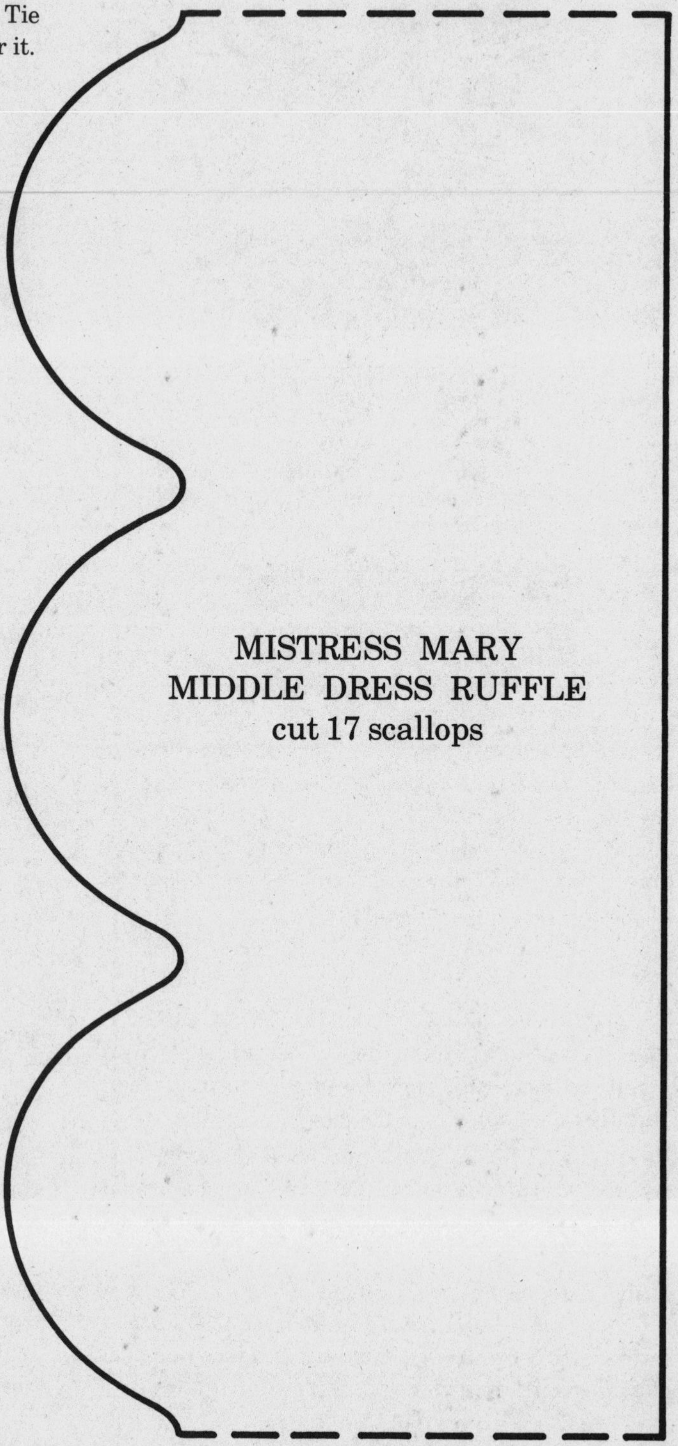

**MISTRESS MARY
MIDDLE DRESS RUFFLE**
cut 17 scallops

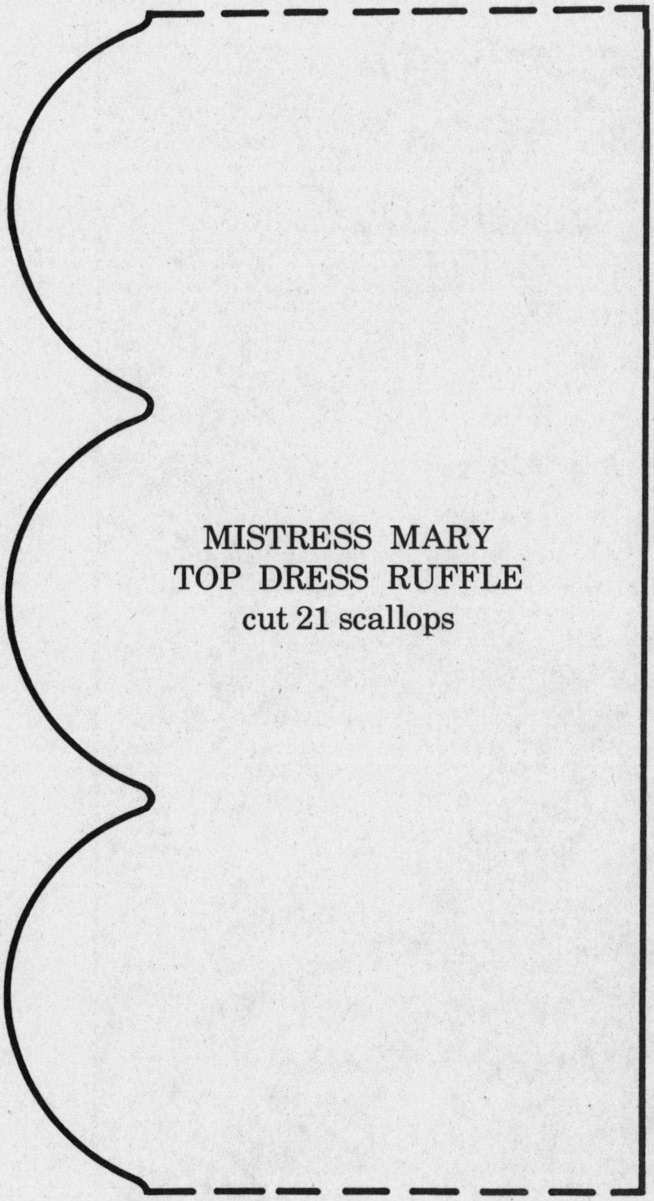

**MISTRESS MARY
TOP DRESS RUFFLE
cut 21 scallops**

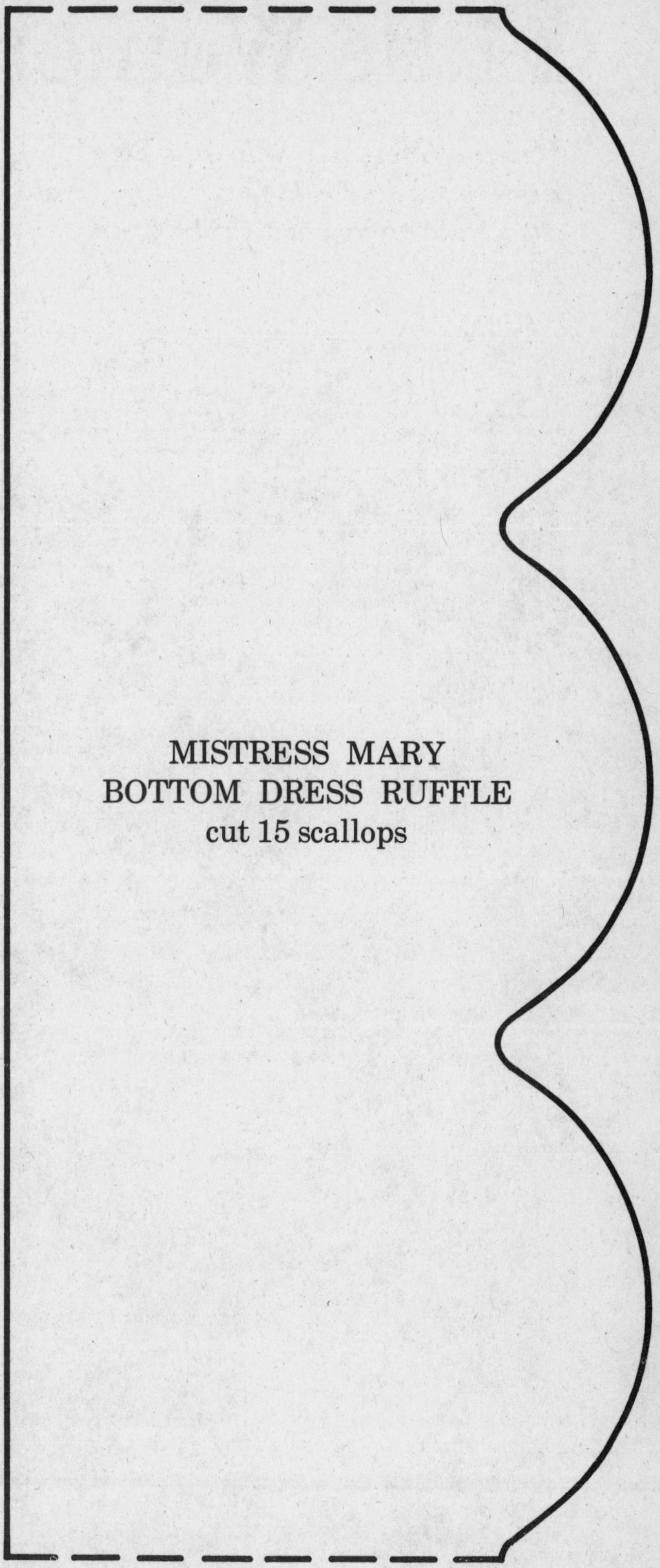

**MISTRESS MARY
BOTTOM DRESS RUFFLE
cut 15 scallops**

Little Women

Here are Meg, Jo, Amy and Beth, complete with period clothes. Included also are dress-up suits for Meg and Jo, a plaid coat for Beth, a wool cape for Amy, plus underwear and a wardrobe trunk for each doll.

General Directions

Your doll will be a treasure if you use very small stitches in machine and hand sewing, pay loving attention to small details and make the clothes from lightweight fabrics with design or texture to fit the size of the doll.

All four dolls are made in the same way, but each has her individual patterns because of differences in size. Meg is 18½″ tall, Jo 20″, Beth and Amy 17½″. They are replicas of dolls of the Civil War period, designed to wear dresses with gathered skirts and long full sleeves. Each arm and leg is made in two parts, then hinged together with strong hand stitches. The upper arm, which is always covered, is left unstuffed.

See Construction Techniques, page 11.

MAKING A DOLL There are 8 pattern pieces for each doll. Cut them from firmly woven cotton.

BODY Pin and sew together two body fronts along center front, from neck to A. Seam two body backs along center back. Join front to back from neck to A. Trim seam allowance; turn. Stuff firmly with kapok or cotton batting.

HEAD Sew together two head fronts along center front, from neck to B; seam two head backs along center back. Join front to back at sides. Trim seams; turn.

Stuff head firmly, paying particular attention to the front center seam and especially to the nose. For a smoother effect, cut a foam rubber disk about the size of a 50-cent piece; trim to an oval. Place this just behind the nose to keep stuffing in place. Complete stuffing the head; sew it to the neck of the body.

If you would like even more molding in the facial contours, cut two more head fronts to be applied as a sort of slipcover to the original face. (This technique also can be used to add a new face to a much-played-with doll.) Sew together these two head fronts along the front seam. Pin to side seams of head, turning in raw edges. To define the face to a greater degree, mark position for eyes and sew from each eye mark to back of head with a long needle and strong thread to make an indentation for eye socket. Pad the nose and cheeks slightly; sew slipcover over first face.

For features and hair, see individual dolls.

LEGS Seam together pairs of upper legs, leaving straight top edge open; turn. Stuff legs almost to top; turn in raw edges. Pin to body just in front of bottom seam, or wherever doll sits best; sew in place, as in sketch.

Seam together pairs of lower legs, leaving opening for stuffing at back seam. Clip ankle seam and turn. Stuff firmly and sew opening. Attach lower leg to knee of upper with ten or twelve hand stitches.

ARMS Seam pairs of lower arms, being especially careful around tips of fingers; leave top edge open. Clip seam allowance at finger tips; turn. Stuff hand lightly, then stitch between fingers to define them. Stuff arm firmly and close top.

Sew each upper arm around top of stuffed lower arm, right sides facing, and turn. Turn in raw edges at side and top, which is about ⅜″ wide. Seam arm and omit stuffing; attach securely to top of shoulder with several hand stitches, as in sketch.

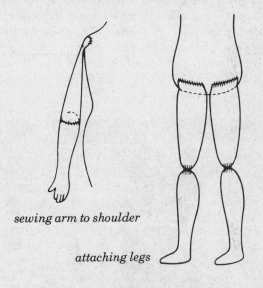

sewing arm to shoulder

attaching legs

UNDERWEAR Fine white cotton such as lawn or nainsook and cottons blended with other fibers can be used. Drawers and petticoats are cut to fit each doll, then pin-fitted and sewed in the following way.

Drawers Cut white cotton wide enough to go easily around doll's hips plus ½″ seam allowances and long enough to fit from waist to below knees plus ½″ allowance for hem and additional allowance for tucks. Cut a band 1″ wide to fit doll's waist and overlap ½″. (See individual instructions for exact measurements.)

Stitch hem, tucks or other trimming across one long edge for bottom. With right side in, stitch together short edges, leaving about 2″ open at top, as

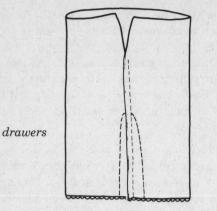

drawers

in sketch. Fit piece on doll with seam at center back; mark inner leg seams and crotch with pins; remove piece. Stitch leg seams. Cut away fabric between legs and trim seams. Hem open back edges.

Place drawers on doll again and fit top edge with tucks or gathers. If legs seem too full, stitch seams at outer edges the length of inner seams. Fold waistband lengthwise, turn in ends and topstitch to drawers, leaving overlap tab at one end. Fasten with snap.

Petticoat Cut white cotton the full width of the material if fabric is lightweight or skirt of dress is full; cut cotton about 22″ wide if fabric is medium weight or dress skirt is slim. Cut cotton long enough to extend from waist to mid-calf for Beth and Amy and almost to ankles for Meg and Jo; add allowance for hem and also for tucks, which give body to the petticoat and help bolster the dress skirt. For a very full skirt, like Amy's, make 2 petticoats. Cut waistband 1″ wide and long enough to fit a doll and overlap ½″. (See individual instructions for exact measurements.)

Hem one long edge and stitch tucks and lace, if desired. Using longest machine stitch, sew other long edge and gather to fit waistband. Fold waistband lengthwise and turn in raw edges; pin to gathered top, turning in raw edges of back opening. Leaving overlap tab, topstitch waistband. Seam back halfway up, then hem open edges. Sew snap to tab.

Stockings Use lower leg of each doll for pattern. Cut stockings from white nylon or rayon tricot for Meg, from white cotton socks or discarded knit underwear for other dolls. Stitch stockings front, foot and back seam. Turn and hem top edge.

SHOES Simple felt slippers are worn by Meg and directions are given with her clothing. Cotton high button boots are worn by the other dolls. Because of their small size, the lower part and spatlike upper part of each boot are made and put on separately. Cut lower part from dull black silk or similar material, following dotted lines on leg pattern. Stitch together 2 pieces; turn and put on foot over stocking.

Follow individual patterns to cut 3 pieces from contrasting fabric for each upper and repeat for lining. (Reverse pattern for second upper.) Sew together pieces for upper at back and instep; repeat for lining. Right sides together, stitch lining to upper, leaving open at edge X–X. Clip seams at scalloped edge; turn; sew opening. Topstitch all around spat. Sew beads for buttons; use 2 snaps to fasten spat over lower part of foot.

DRESSES The directions below give general method for fitting and sewing; individual directions give exact measurements and trimming details.

petticoats and drawers from Amy's wardrobe
are trimmed with tucks and sometimes lace

Bodice Cut a rectangle from fabric and ½"-wide strip for binding neck. Fold rectangle lengthwise then crosswise. Cut a slit up one fold for back (or front) opening; cut a small crosswise slit for neck, as in sketch. Hem back opening; finish neck.

Right sides facing, fit rectangle to doll with edges of opening overlapped and pinned closed. Pin sloping shoulder seams; remove and stitch.

folding fabric for bodice and sleeve

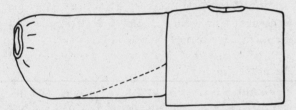

shaping sleeve to fit bodice armhole

Cut rectangles for sleeves and finish wrist edges. Pin sleeves to bodice and fit again, pinning armholes and shaping sleeves, according to individual directions. See sketch. Cut away excess fabric. Stitch sleeves to armholes, then stitch sleeve and side seams.

Skirt Cut a rectangle from fabric. Hem and finish one long edge. Seam together two short edges, leaving opening at top; hem opening. Gather top edge to fit bodice; stitch skirt to bodice.

Meg

MATERIALS *For Doll:* ½ yard shell pink cotton; kapok; scraps of olive green fabric; brown and pink floss; soft brown synthetic switch; ½ yard blue velvet ribbon. *Underwear, suit dickey and cuffs, slippers:* ⅝ yard white cotton; 2½ yards of lace; ¼ yard elastic; scrap of white nylon or rayon tricot (stockings); scraps of lavender felt and seam binding (slippers). *Day dress:* ½ yard olive, orange and pink print, ⅛ yard dark orange cotton; ½ yard lace; 3 pearl buttons. *Apron:* ¼ yard light orange cotton. *Silvery drab suit:* ½ yard light gray cotton, ¼ yard blue plaid for jacket lining; 2½ yards dark gray seam binding; 2 pearl buttons. Scrap of print challis, lining material, floss (handbag).

DOLL Cut doll from pink cotton. Make following General Directions.

Face For eyes, coat underside of olive green fabric with fabric glue to prevent raveling; let dry. Cut two ⅜″ x ⁷⁄₁₆″ ovals; glue in place. With brown floss embroider a straight line over each eye to give effect of eyelashes; with rose floss embroider mouth.

Hair Attach hair after completing wardrobe. Following top view, place switch on head, letting soft waves fall over forehead. Sew to head. Sweep hair back and tack to back of head. Following side view, draw up hair and tack again, letting loose curls cover top of head. Fold velvet ribbon into loops and tack to hair in a curve.

top view of hair   *side view of hair*

UNDERWEAR

Drawers Cut white cotton 9½″ long and 13″ wide, cut waistband 1″ x 10¾″. Finish one 13″ edge with ⅛″ hem and two ⅛″ tucks. Following General Directions, complete.

Petticoat Cut white cotton 10¼″ long and full width of material; cut waistband 1″ x 11¾″. Finish one long edge of petticoat with ½″ hem and two ⅛″ tucks; stitch lace to hem, covering ¼″ of lower edge. Following General Directions complete petticoat.

Stockings Make from white nylon or rayon tricot, following General Directions.

SLIPPERS Follow dotted lines on leg pattern to cut 2 pieces from lavender felt for each slipper, adding narrow seam allowance. Stitch together from instep around to heel; trim seam and turn. Make a tailored bow from matching seam binding and tack on.

PRINT DAY DRESS

Bodice From print cut piece 6″ wide and 7″ long for back and front, 2 sleeves 6½″ wide and 7½″ long, strip ½″ wide to bind neck. From dark orange use pattern to cut scallop trim; also cut ¼″ x 3½″ strips to bind sleeves.

Following General Directions, fold 6″ x 7″ print piece lengthwise then crosswise; cut back opening and 1½″-long slit for neck. Fit neck on doll and round front part. Pin lace down bodice front; stitch in place with ¼″ tuck over it. Hem back opening; bind neck; edge with lace. Pin shoulder seams and stitch.

On each sleeve, gather one 6½″ edge to fit doll's wrist and bind it. Put bodice on doll and pin sleeves in place, making armholes about 4″ around; taper sleeves to fit armholes. Cut away excess fabric; stitch. Pin sides and sleeves; seam.

Seam pairs of scallop trim, leaving opening; turn and sew closed. Pin to bodice, with scalloped edges facing center; topstitch then fold outward.

Skirt Cut print fabric 11½" x 27"; from dark orange use pattern to cut scallop trim. Stitch 1½" hem along one 27" edge of print. Seam scalloped strips together along scallops and ends; turn. Pin strip to right side of skirt with raw edges ½" above top of hem; on wrong side fold hem edge up against raw edge of scallop trim; stitch ½" from fold, catching raw edge of scallops.

Following General Directions, sew back seam and hem opening. Stitch skirt to bodice. Trim front with 3 buttons.

APRON From light orange cotton cut 9" x 12" skirt, 1½" x 24" waistband. Follow pattern to cut 4 pocket pieces. Sew ½" hem along one 12" edge of skirt; add a row of decorative machine stitching to hem and 4 rows above hem.

Seam pairs of pockets, leaving opening; turn, close opening. Topstitch to apron 3½" above lower edge. Hem apron sides; gather top edge to 4½". Fold waistband lengthwise; turn in raw edges and topstitch to gathered top. Hem ties and stitch ends in points.

From white lawn cut a 4½" handkerchief. Hemstitch ⅛" hems and trim with narrow lace.

SILVERY DRAB SUIT

Jacket From gray cotton cut 1 back, 2 fronts, 2 collar pieces and 2 sleeves, following patterns. From blue plaid cotton cut back and 2 fronts of lining.

Seam jacket fronts to back at shoulders; repeat for lining. Sew together collar pieces, leaving straight inner edge open; clip seams and turn. Cut seam binding in half lengthwise; turn in raw edges and topstitch around collar.

With underside of collar facing right side of jacket, baste collar around neck. With right sides facing, pin lining over collar, to jacket front and all lower edges. Stitch lining in place, leaving armholes and sides open; clip seams and turn. Topstitch seam binding to jacket fronts and back.

Sew ⅜" hems at wrist edges of sleeves and topstitch binding ¼" above top of hems. Pin sleeves to armholes and stitch, catching lining. Stitch sleeve seams and sides. Sew 2 gray pearl buttons to jacket front.

Skirt From gray cotton cut piece 11" long and 32½" wide and waistband 1" x 11¾". Make 1½" hem on one long edge of skirt; fold gray seam binding lengthwise and topstitch 1" above hem. Seam short edges, leaving opening at top; hem opening. Gather remaining edge to 10". Fold waistband lengthwise, turn in raw edges; topstitch over gathers, leaving ¼" tab.

Dickey with Jabot and Cuffs Use pattern to cut white cotton dickey; also cut ½"-wide binding strip. For each cuff cut 1¾" x 10" and 2" x 10" strip.

Sew 2 rows of lace up center front of dickey for jabot. Hem back opening and bind neck. Fold dickey at shoulders to fit and seam; hem raw edges.

For pin, glue a pearl to ¾" pin back.

For each cuff, hem one long edge of each strip and sew lace to it. With wrong side of narrow strip facing right side of wide strip, seam long edges; turn; stitch ¼" from fold for casing. Seam strip ends; trim and overcast. Punch hole for elastic, insert in casing so cuff fits doll. Reverse cuff.

Handbag From print challis cut 2 pieces, following pattern; repeat for lining. Seam print pieces, leaving top open; seam lining. Insert lining; turn in top edges. Following dotted lines, run stitching around top and across bottom of bag. With a blunt needle, run floss drawstring twice through top and make tassel at bottom.

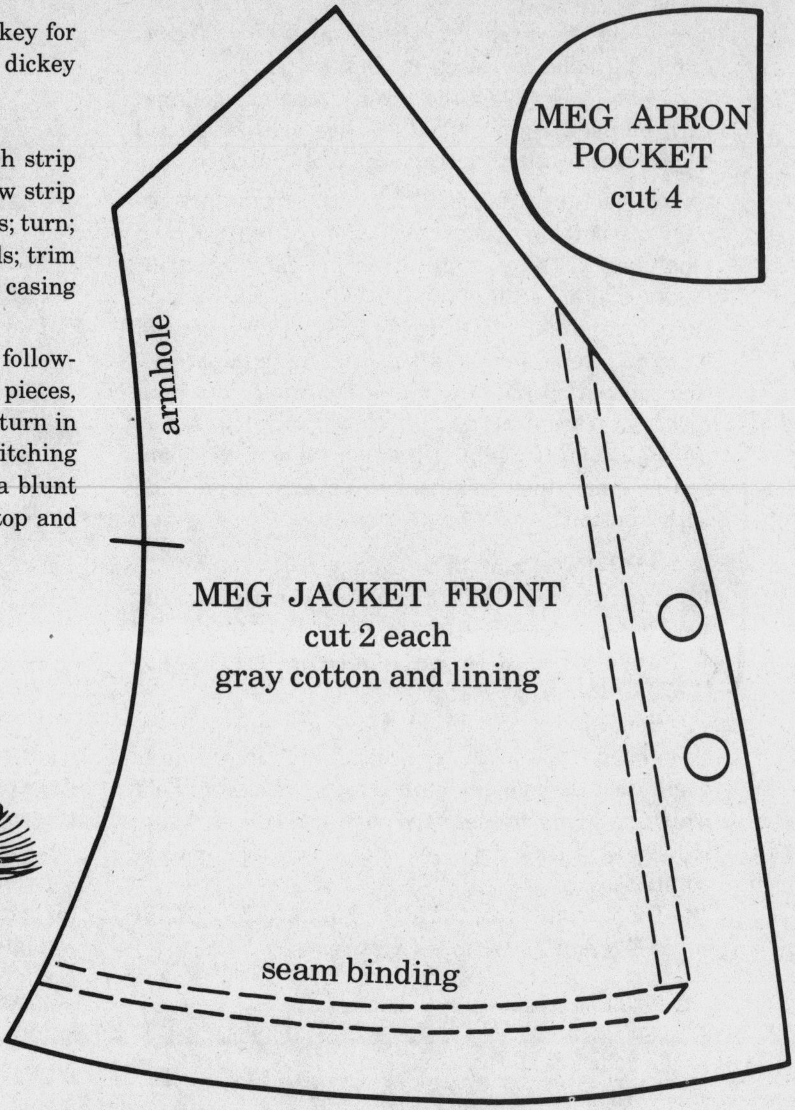

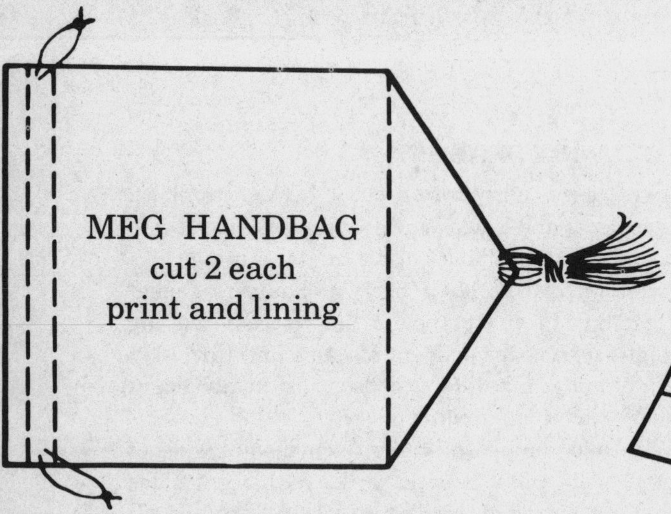

MEG APRON POCKET
cut 4

armhole

MEG JACKET FRONT
cut 2 each
gray cotton and lining

seam binding

MEG HANDBAG
cut 2 each
print and lining

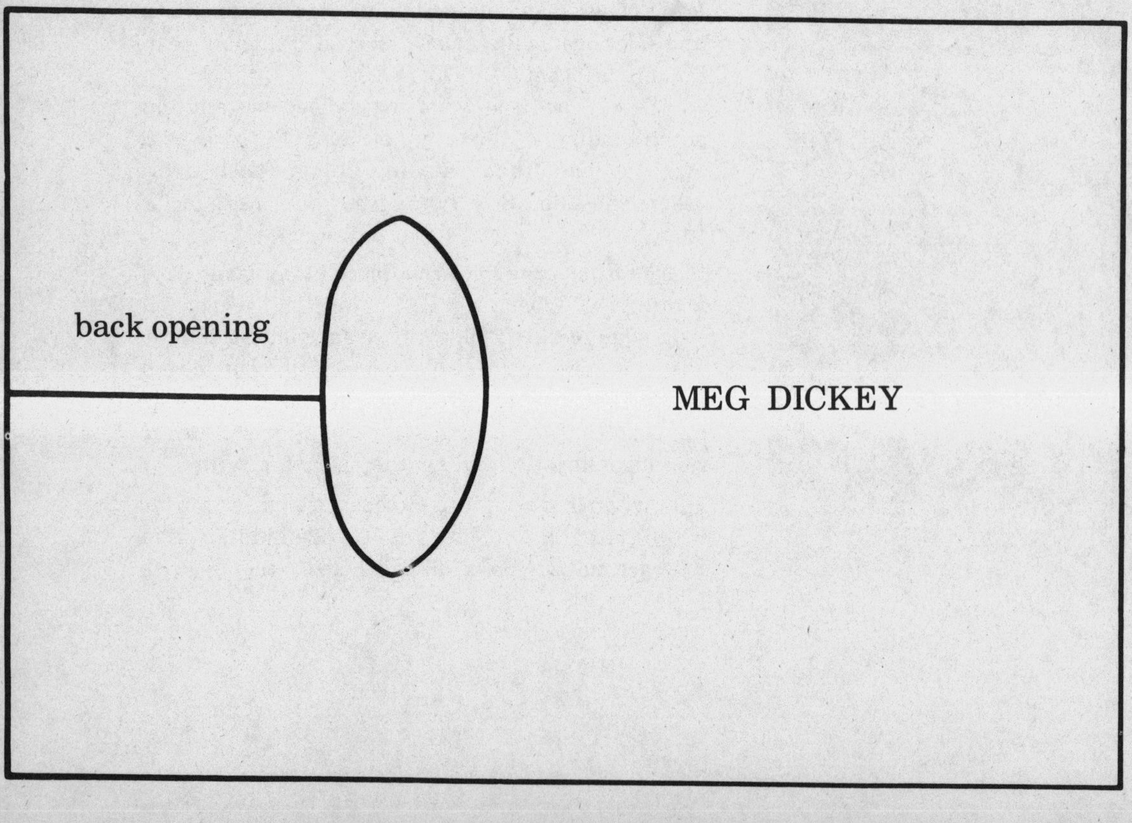

MEG SCALLOP TRIM
FOR DRESS SKIRT

back opening

MEG DICKEY

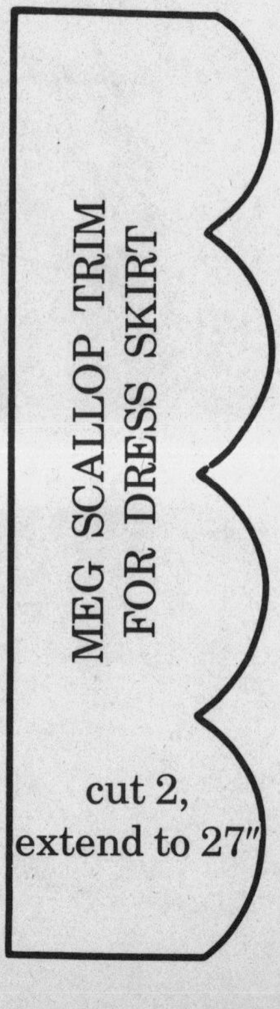

cut 2,
extend to 27"

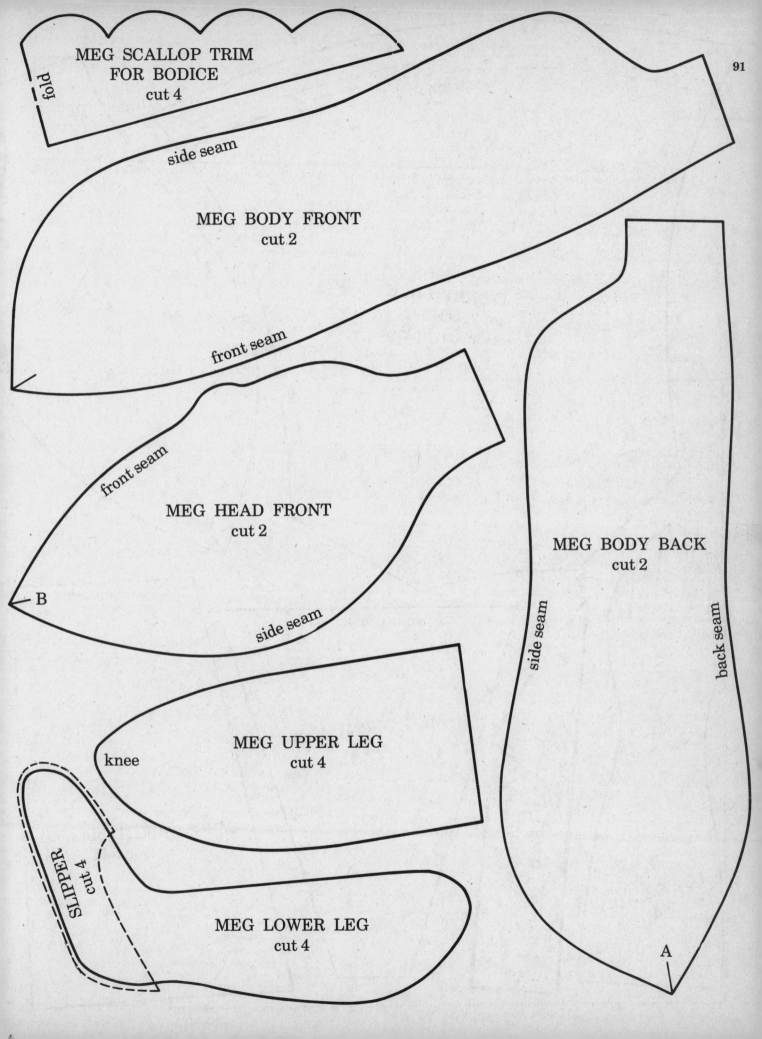

MEG SCALLOP TRIM
FOR BODICE
cut 4

fold

side seam

MEG BODY FRONT
cut 2

front seam

front seam

MEG HEAD FRONT
cut 2

MEG BODY BACK
cut 2

B

side seam

side seam

back seam

MEG UPPER LEG
cut 4

knee

SLIPPER
cut 4

MEG LOWER LEG
cut 4

A

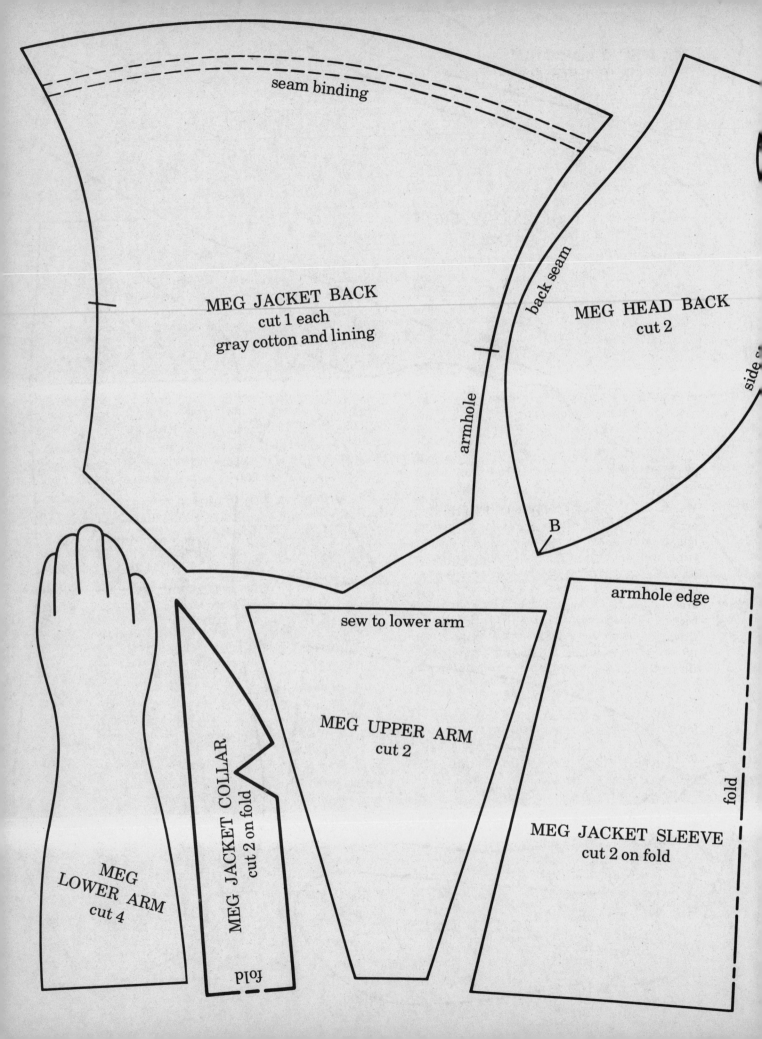

seam binding

MEG JACKET BACK
cut 1 each
gray cotton and lining

back seam

MEG HEAD BACK
cut 2

armhole

side s

B

sew to lower arm

armhole edge

MEG UPPER ARM
cut 2

MEG JACKET COLLAR
cut 2 on fold

MEG JACKET SLEEVE
cut 2 on fold

fold

MEG
LOWER ARM
cut 4

fold

Jo

top view of hair

side view of hair

MATERIALS *For Doll:* ½ yard beige pink cotton; kapok; scraps of olive green fabric; dark brown, light brown and rose floss; auburn synthetic switch; hair net; ½ yard black cotton tape for bow. *Underwear, blouse, boots:* ¾ yard white cotton; ¾ yard lace; 6 pearl buttons; scrap of white sock (stockings); scraps of black silk, brown cotton; 8 black beads (boots). *Day dress:* ⅝ yard red print; ¾ yard narrow white rickrack. *Apron:* ¼ yard gold cotton. *Maroon suit:* ⅝ yard wine cotton; ¼ yard white sateen; black silk thread. *Hat:* Scrap of wine felt; 7″ feather.

DOLL Cut doll from pink cotton. Make following General Directions.

Face Coat underside of olive fabric with glue; let dry. Cut two ⅜″ x 7⁄16″ ovals for eyes; glue in place. With dark brown floss, work a straight line over each for eyelash effect. Stitch light brown eyebrows and rose mouth. Make one stitch above each corner of mouth for dimples.

Hair Attach after completing wardrobe. Following top view, place switch over head and sew along center seam. Following side view, pull hair back and tuck into a snood, made from a hair net. Let curls stray around face; tack black bow to snood.

UNDERWEAR

Chemise Cut white cotton, following pattern. Right sides together, stitch facing to neck and armhole edges of back and front; turn. Hem raw edges of facing to chemise. Seam sides; hem lower edge. Lap shoulder tabs and fasten with snaps.

Drawers Cut white cotton 10½″ long and 14″ wide; cut waistband 1″ x 10½″. Finish one 14″ edge with ⅝″ hem, ¼″ and ⅛″ tucks. Follow General Directions to complete.

Petticoat Cut white cotton 10½″ long and 22″ wide, cut waistband 1″ x 11″. Finish one long edge of petticoat with 1″ hem and two ⅛″ tucks; sew lace to hem. Follow General Directions to complete petticoat.

Stockings Cut from white cotton sock; make as in General Directions.

HIGH BUTTON BOOTS Following patterns, cut lower parts from black silk; cut upper parts from brown cotton and black lining fabric. Make boots as in General Directions; sew on beads for buttons.

TUCKED BLOUSE

Note: This is worn as a guimpe under the day dress and as a blouse with the maroon suit.

From white cotton cut 6″ square for back, two 4½″ x 6″ rectangles for front, strip 1″ x 5¼″ for stand-up collar, two 8½″ x 9″ pieces for sleeves and two 1″ x 4″ strips for cuffs.

Mark one 6″ edge of each front piece for center opening; measure ¾″ in from each edge and stitch five ⅛″ tucks. Turn under ½″ hems at opening and hand sew.

Pin and fit fronts to back at shoulders; seam shoulders. Shape neck and stitch on collar strip.

Gather an 8½″ edge of each sleeve to 2⅞″; fold cuff strip and stitch on, leaving a ¼″ tab. Pin sleeves to blouse, making armholes about 4″ around; taper sleeves to fit armholes. Cut away excess fabric and stitch. Pin side and sleeve seams; stitch.

Close front of blouse with 6 buttons and button loops; fasten cuffs with snaps.

DAY DRESS From red print cut bodice, following pattern; cut ½″-wide strip to face neck, and skirt 12″ long and 36″ wide.

Bodice Cut back opening. Face neck and trim with rickrack. Hem sleeves and add rickrack. Turn in edges of back opening ⅜″ and stitch. Seam sleeves and sides.

Skirt Make 1¼″ hem and ¼″ tuck along one long edge. Seam short edges, leaving opening at top; hem opening. Gather skirt to fit bodice; seam together.

APRON From gold cotton cut 7½″ x 13″ skirt, 1¼″ x 36″ waistband and 2″ x 2½″ pocket.

Make ¼″ hem on one 13″ and two 7½″ edges of skirt; do same to 2″ top of pocket. Run 2 rows of decorative machine stitching around skirt and across pocket top. Turn in pocket edges; sew to skirt from the wrong side. Gather top of skirt to 6½″. Fold waistband lengthwise, turn in raw edges and stitch center to gathered skirt. Seam ends for ties; trim with decorative stitching.

From white cotton cut a 4½″ handerkerchief; hem edges.

MAROON SUIT

Jacket From wine cotton cut 1 back, 2 fronts, 2 collar pieces and 2 sleeves, following patterns; from white sateen cut same pieces except collar.

Following scroll design for jacket fronts, work hand or machine chain stitches with black thread to simulate braid. Work a row of stitches around back, along each sleeve and around one collar piece.

Seam wine fronts to back at shoulders and repeat for lining. Seam collar pieces, leaving inner edge open; clip seams and turn.

With underside of collar facing right side of jacket, baste collar to neck. With right sides facing, pin lining over collar, to front edges and all lower edges. Stitch lining, leaving armholes and sides open; turn.

Seam lining to lower edges of sleeves and turn. Pin lined sleeves to armholes and stitch. Stitch sleeves and jacket sides, sewing wine and lining together; overcast seams.

Skirt From wine fabric cut piece 10¾″ long and 30″ wide; following patterns, cut 4 panel pieces and 2 waistbands, extending waistbands to 11½″ length.

Make 1″ hem on one long edge of skirt; following scroll design, work hand or machine chain stitch with black thread and continue stitching around skirt. Seam short edges, leaving opening at top; hem opening. Gather skirt top to 9½″.

Seam pairs of panels, leaving ends open; turn.

Work black stitching around one waistband piece. Seam together waistbands at top edge and ends; turn. With right sides facing, pin stitched waistband piece to skirt, catching panels between; stitch on wrong side; turn. Fold under raw edges and whip to inside of skirt. Fasten with snap.

PLUMED HAT From wine felt cut a disk about 6″ in diameter for crown and a strip 2½″ x 11½″ for cuff. Place felt disk over the bottom of a glass jar about 3″ in diameter and fasten with a strong rubber band; steam with a steam iron, pulling down edges and shrinking felt to shape of jar. Let dry completely; trim crown to 1″ depth. Fold strip, wrap around crown and over cut edge; sew to inside. Tack plume to cuff.

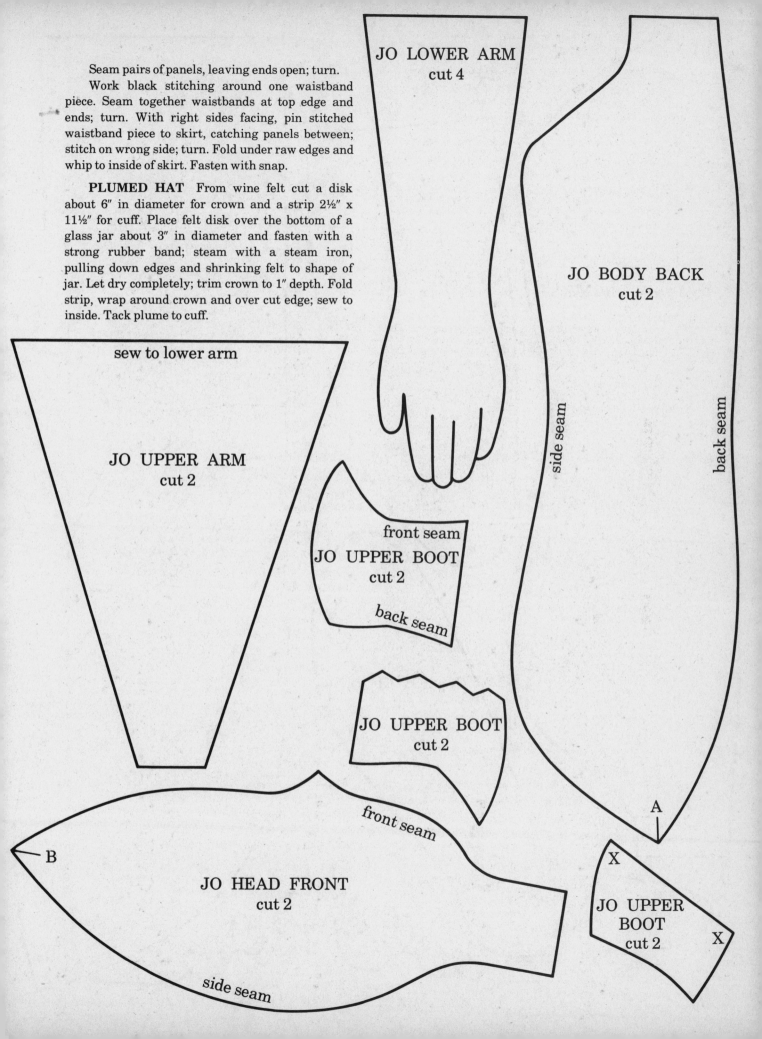

JO LOWER ARM
cut 4

JO BODY BACK
cut 2

side seam

back seam

sew to lower arm

JO UPPER ARM
cut 2

front seam

JO UPPER BOOT
cut 2

back seam

JO UPPER BOOT
cut 2

front seam

JO HEAD FRONT
cut 2

B

side seam

A

X

JO UPPER BOOT
cut 2

X

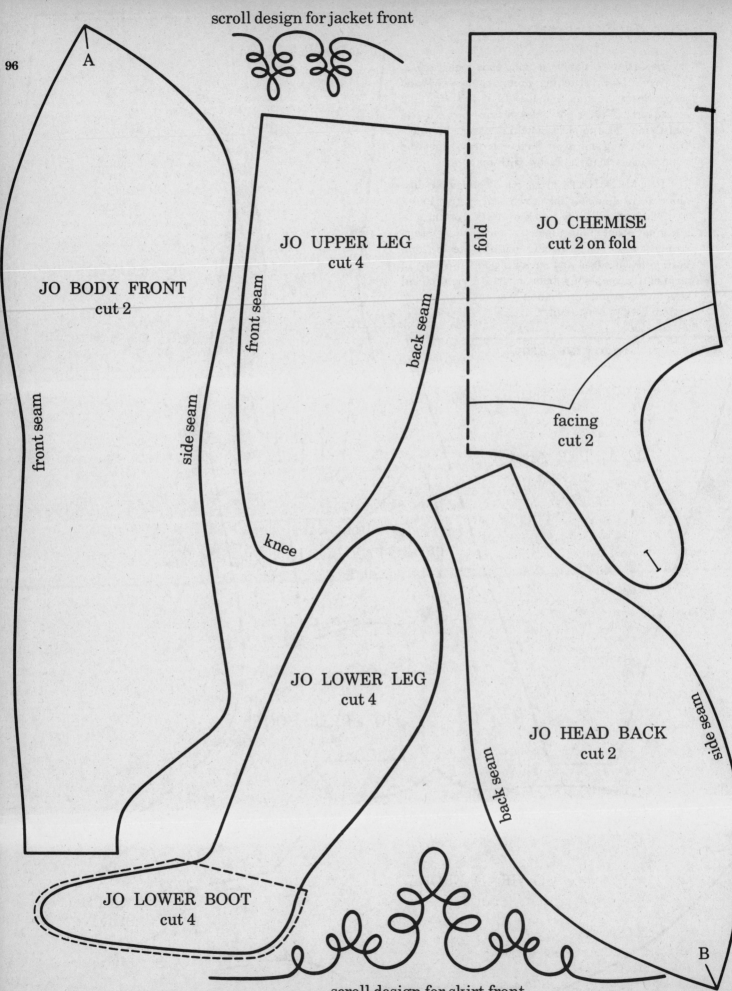

scroll design for jacket front

96

A

JO BODY FRONT
cut 2

front seam

side seam

JO UPPER LEG
cut 4

front seam

back seam

knee

JO LOWER LEG
cut 4

JO LOWER BOOT
cut 4

fold

JO CHEMISE
cut 2 on fold

facing
cut 2

I

JO HEAD BACK
cut 2

back seam

side seam

B

scroll design for skirt front

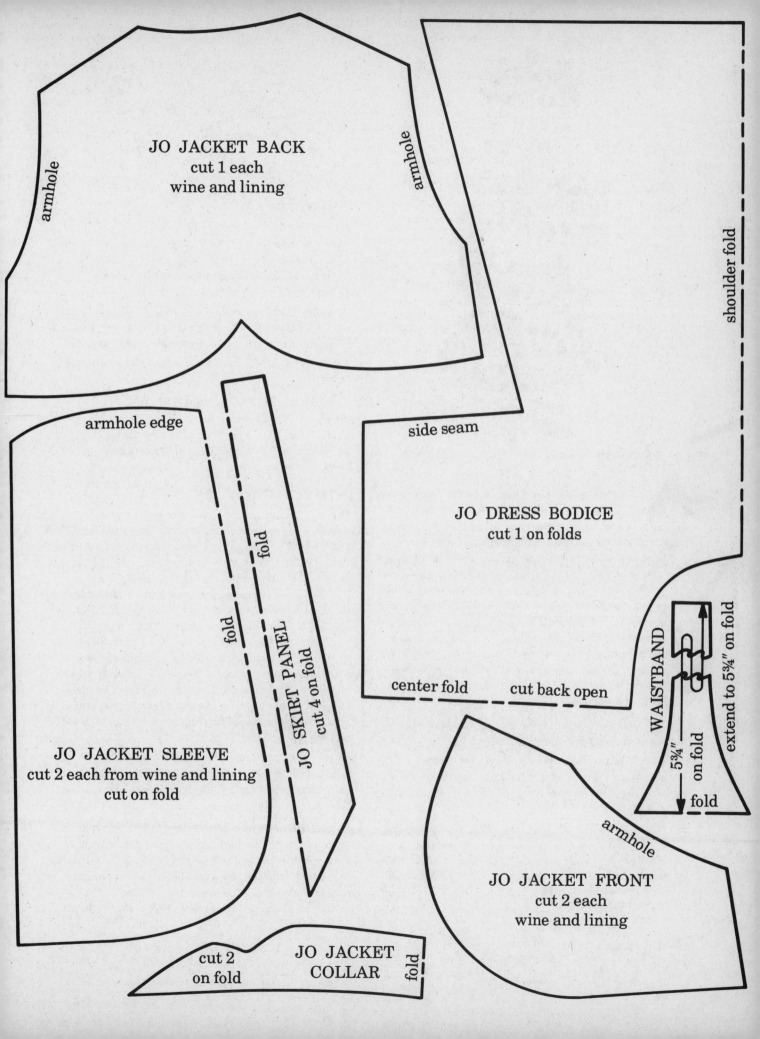

JO JACKET BACK
cut 1 each
wine and lining

armhole

armhole

shoulder fold

armhole edge

side seam

JO DRESS BODICE
cut 1 on folds

fold

fold

fold

JO SKIRT PANEL
cut 4 on fold

center fold

cut back open

WAISTBAND

extend to 5¾" on fold

5¾"

on fold

fold

JO JACKET SLEEVE
cut 2 each from wine and lining
cut on fold

armhole

JO JACKET FRONT
cut 2 each
wine and lining

cut 2
on fold

JO JACKET
COLLAR

fold

top view of hair   *side view of hair*

Beth

MATERIALS *For Doll:* ½ yard beige pink cotton; kapok; light brown, dark brown and rose floss; dark brown synthetic switch; wide rayon shoelace; narrow pink ribbon. *Underwear, boots:* ½ yard white cotton; white cotton sock (stockings); scraps of black silk, brown cotton; 8 black beads (boots). *Day dress:* ½ yard green chambray; 2 yards brown seam binding; scraps of white fabric and narrow lace; pearl button. *Apron:* ⅜ yard green-and-rose print. *Fitted plaid coat;* ½ yard brown-and-green cotton; ¾ yard seam binding; 3 gray pearl buttons. *Nightgown and cap:* ⅝ yard pale green cotton; ¼ yard narrow green ribbon; ½ yard lace; scrap of green floss.

DOLL Cut doll from pink cotton. Make following General Directions.

Face With dark brown floss, embroider half-moons for lowered eyes; with light brown floss work straight lines for eyebrows. Embroider mouth with rose floss.

Hair Attach hair after completing wardrobe. Following top view, place switch on head and sew along center seam. Following side view, tease front hair until it is bouffant around the face and tack to head. Pull rest of hair softly to back and tie with ribbon. Tack shoelace bow to top.

UNDERWEAR

Drawers Cut white cotton 8¾" long and 11½" wide, cut waistband 1" x 10½". Finish one 11½" edge with ½" hem, an ⅛" tuck and lace sewed to hem. Follow General Directions to complete drawers.

Petticoat Cut white cotton 9" long and full width of material; cut waistband 1" x 10¾". Finish one long edge of petticoat with ½" hem and two ⅛" tucks. Follow General Directions to complete petticoat.

Stockings Make from sock; follow General Directions.

HIGH BUTTON BOOTS Following patterns, cut lower parts from black silk; cut upper parts from brown cotton and black lining fabric. Make boots following General Directions; sew on beads for buttons.

DAY DRESS

Bodice From green chambray cut piece 6" wide and 9" long for bodice front and back, 2 sleeves 7" wide and 6¾" long. From brown seam binding cut two 4¼" lengths to trim bodice front, one 5½" and two 3½" lengths to bind neck and sleeves.

Following General Directions, cut bodice, making 2" slit for neck. Fold seam binding and stitch 2 lengths to front; bind neck. Stitch shoulder seams.

On each sleeve, gather one 7" edge to fit wrist and bind it. Put bodice on doll and pin sleeves in place, making armholes about 4" around; taper sleeves to fit armholes. Cut away excess fabric and stitch to armholes. Pin side and sleeve seams; stitch. Sew a white cotton collar, edged with lace, to neck; add button.

Skirt Cut green chambray 10" long and width of fabric. Stitch 1¼" hem then topstitch ½" binding along one long edge. Following General Directions sew skirt to bodice.

APRON

From print fabric follow patterns to cut 2 bodice pieces and pocket; cut 2 skirt pieces 9" long and 16½" wide and 4 tie strips ½" x 8".

Seam bodice pieces at shoulders; cut opening for center back. Hem sides, neck and opening.

Hem skirt sides and sew 1¾" hems at lower

edges. Hem top edge of pocket and sew in place. Gather top edges of skirt to fit bodice; cut opening in back skirt and hem. Topstitch bodice to skirt. Turn in edges of ties, fold and stitch; tack to bodice sides. Sew snaps to back.

FITTED PLAID COAT Keep seam allowances generous for fitting and have doll dressed when you try coat on her.

From brown-and-green plaid cotton, cut 2 side backs, 1 center back, 2 fronts, 2 sleeves, 2 collar pieces and 2 pockets, following patterns which give the straight of goods.

Stitch side backs to center back at side seams. Stitch fronts to back at shoulders. Hem long edges of facing. Right sides together, fold center front edges along dotted line for facing; seam at neckline only.

Stitch together collar pieces, leaving one long edge open; turn. Right sides facing, center and stitch one open edge of collar to neck; turn under other open edge and hand sew to inside neck. Sew collar ends over facing.

On sleeves, fold up cuffs to right side and stitch. Right sides facing, fit and seam sleeves to armholes.

Now fit coat on doll, wrong side out. Seam sleeves and sides. Turn up hem and finish with seam binding.

For pocket, turn in ends; topstitch ends and along fold. Stitch raw edge to coat; turn up pocket and stitch ends. From white cotton cut a 4½" hand-kerchief; hem edges and trim with lace. Tuck in one pocket.

Sew 3 buttons to one front edge of coat and make buttonholes at other.

NIGHTGOWN From pale green cotton cut piece 7½" long, 15" wide for bodice and sleeves, skirt 14" long and 23½" wide. Following General Directions for bodice, fold 7½" x 15" piece lengthwise then crosswise. Cut back opening and 2" slit for neck; round neck slightly. Stitch two ⅛" tucks up center front ⅜" apart. Hem back opening and neck. Gather wrist edges of sleeves to 3½"; bind with narrow green ribbon. Stitch sleeve seams.

On skirt stitch 2½" hem and two ⅛" tucks along one long edge. Seam short edges, leaving opening; hem opening. Gather skirt and stitch to bodice. Gather lace; sew to neck and one edge of opening. Fasten with snaps.

NIGHTCAP From pale green cotton cut two 8½" disks. Seam together, leaving opening. Turn; sew opening. Make casing ½" from edge with 2 rows of stitching. Punch hole; with blunt needle thread floss drawstring through casing.

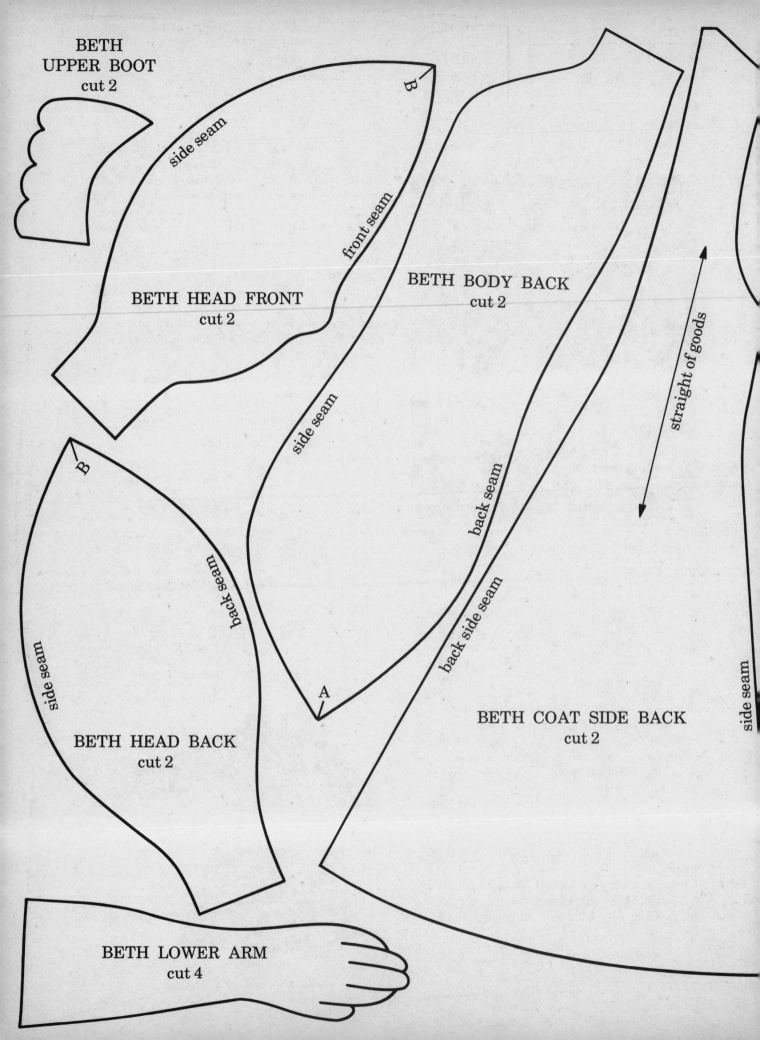

BETH
UPPER BOOT
cut 2

side seam

B

front seam

BETH HEAD FRONT
cut 2

BETH BODY BACK
cut 2

straight of goods

B

back seam

side seam

back seam

back side seam

A

BETH HEAD BACK
cut 2

side seam

BETH COAT SIDE BACK
cut 2

side seam

BETH LOWER ARM
cut 4

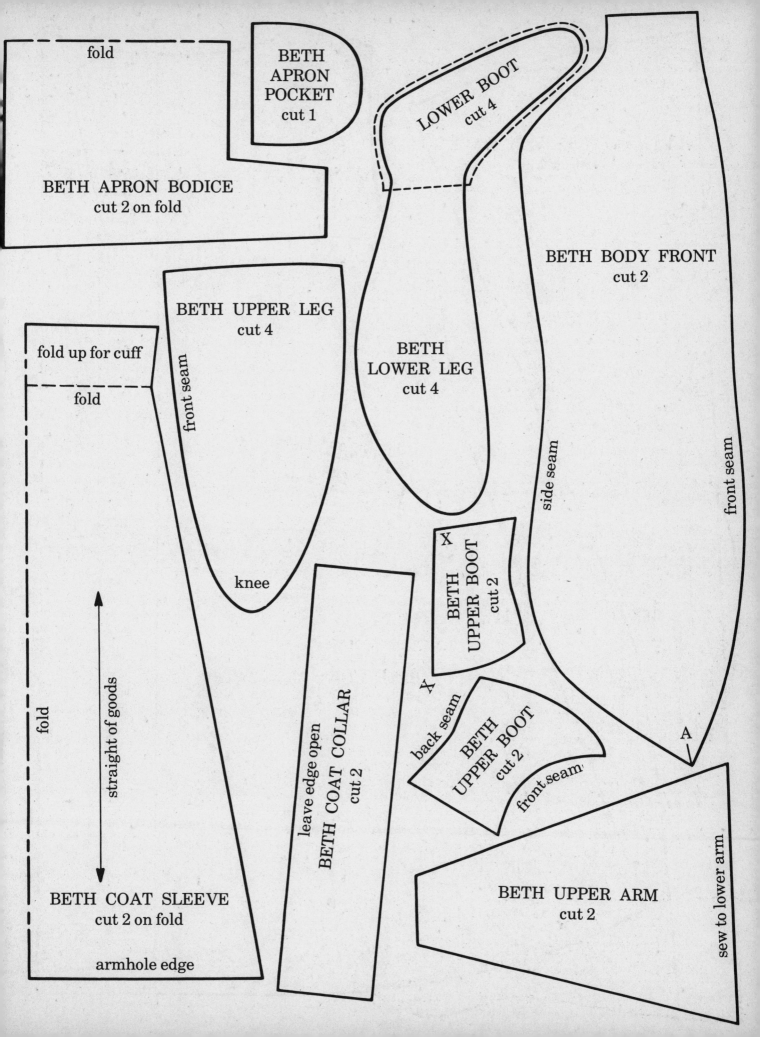

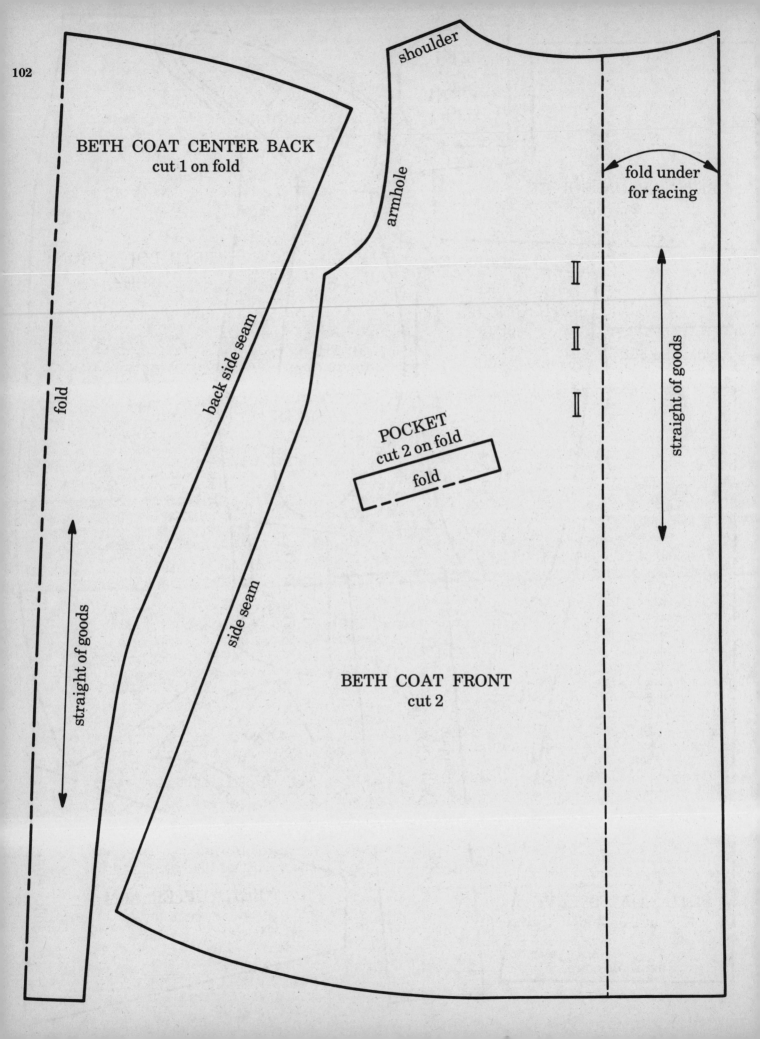

102

BETH COAT CENTER BACK
cut 1 on fold

shoulder

armhole

fold under
for facing

fold

straight of goods

straight of goods

back side seam

side seam

POCKET
cut 2 on fold

fold

BETH COAT FRONT
cut 2

Hair Attach hair after completing wardrobe. Reserve part of switch for side strands. Following top view, sew switch to head. Let hair hang down. Fold and sew strands to temples; following side view, pull back strands and tie with ribbon.

top view of hair　　　　*side view of hair*

UNDERWEAR

Drawers Cut white cotton 8″ long and 12″ wide; cut waistband 1″ x 8½″. Finish one 12″ edge with ½″ hem and two ⅛″ tucks. Follow General Directions to complete.

First Petticoat Cut white cotton 8½″ long and 18½″ wide; cut waistband 1″ x 9″. Finish one 18½″ edge with a 1″ hem, two ¼″ tucks and 2 rows of lace. Follow General Directions to complete petticoat.

Second Petticoat Cut lawn 8½″ long and 36″ wide; cut waistband 1″ x 9½″. Finish a long edge with ¼″ hem, three ⅛″ tucks. Follow General Directions to complete.

STOCKINGS, BOOTS
See patterns and General Directions.

DAY DRESS

Bodice From blue print cut piece 5″ wide and 8″ long for back and front, 2 sleeves 6¼″ long and 6½″ wide, ½″-wide strips to bind neck and sleeves.

Following General Directions, fold 5″ x 8″ piece lengthwise then crosswise; cut back opening and 1¾″ neck slit. On wrong side of front, sew ¼″ tuck so stitches simulate center closing. Hem back and bind neck. Seam shoulders.

Gather one 6½″ edge of each sleeve and bind. Put bodice on doll, pin on sleeves, making armholes 4″ around; taper sleeves. Cut away excess fabric and stitch. Seam sides and sleeves. Sew binding in V shape to front and back.

Skirt Cut print fabric 9¾″ long and 33″ wide. Stitch 2″ hem along one long edge and chartreuse seam binding to top of hem. Following General Directions sew back seam and hem opening. Gather and stitch skirt to bodice.

Tack on a flat bow near waistline. Trim front

Amy

MATERIALS *For Doll:* ½ yard pinkish white cotton; kapok; scrap of bright blue fabric; brown and coral floss; blonde synthetic switch; 12″ strip of narrow green ribbon for hair. *Underwear, boots:* ½ yard lightweight white cotton; ¼ yard white lawn; 1½ yards narrow lace. White cotton sock (stockings); scraps of black silk, green cotton (boots). *Day dress:* ½ yard navy, blue and chartreuse cotton print; 1½ yards chartreuse seam binding; scrap of narrow lace; 3 white pearl buttons; 3 hooks and eyes. *Apron:* ¼ yard chartreuse cotton; turquoise thread. *Cape:* ½ yard each 36″ gold wool and orange cotton; 2 gold buttons. *Bonnet:* Scraps of gold-figured rayon, china silk, cotton edging, cardboard; 2 yards green seam binding. *Nightgown, cap:* ⅝ yard blue printed flannel, ⅜ yard lace; ⅜ yard braid; 1 button.

DOLL Cut doll from pinkish white cotton. Make following General Directions.

Face Use blue fabric for eyes. Coat underside with glue to prevent raveling; let dry. Cut two ¼″ x ⅜″ ovals. Glue in place. With brown floss embroider a straight line over each eye for lashes; embroider coral mouth.

with 3 buttons and neck with lace. Fasten dress with 3 hooks and eyes.

APRON From chartreuse cotton cut 7″ x 13″ skirt and 1″ x 23″ waistband. Stitch ¼″ hem and two ⅛″ tucks to one long edge of skirt, using turquoise thread. Hem sides and gather top to 6½″. Fold waistband lengthwise, turn in raw edges and topstitch with turquoise thread to gathered top. Continue stitching to ends of waistband to seam the ties.

CAPE From gold wool cut upper cape back and 2 fronts, lower cape back and 2 fronts, 1″-wide strip to bind neck, 2 pieces 1½″ x 2½″ for tab; cut orange cotton lining.

Stitch fronts of upper cape to back at sides. Repeat for lower cape and for linings. Right sides facing, seam lining to upper cape, leaving neck open. Turn; topstitch 2 rows of stitches around finished edges. Stitch lining to lower cape, leaving neck and armholes open; turn; hem armholes. Stitch finished edges and design, following dotted lines.

Pin necks together. Right sides facing, stitch binding around outside of neck; fold up and sew to inside. Seam tab pieces, leaving opening; turn and sew closed. Sew tab to one side of neck, snap at other. Add buttons.

BONNET From gold-figured rayon cut 2 crown and 2 brim pieces, following patterns. From silk cut crown lining, from cardboard cut brim stiffening.

Stitch back seam of rayon crown then of lining. Turn rayon; sew gathered edging to lower edge.

Seam rayon brims, leaving inner side open. Sew one edge of brim to rayon crown, other to lining.

Insert cardboard in brim. Sew raw edge of lining to crown. Tack 27″ of seam binding around bonnet, using ends for ties; add bows.

NIGHTGOWN From blue flannel cut nightgown, following pattern and extending it to 14½″. From white cotton (left over from underwear) cut 3″ x 4″ piece to bind neck and ½″-wide strips for sleeves.

Stitch narrow tucks at front and continue tucks along back. Pencil neck and front opening on white cotton piece. Stitch piece to right side of gown along pencil lines. Then cut away excess fabric, slashing front opening; turn binding to inside and sew. Gather sleeve edges to fit wrists and bind.

Seam sleeves and sides. Stitch ½″ hem and two ⅛″ tucks at lower edge. Trim neck with lace; add button and loop.

NIGHTCAP From blue flannel cut 8½″-diameter disk; from white cotton cut lining. Seam flannel and cotton, leaving opening. Turn; close opening. Make casing ½″ from edge. Punch hole; thread braid drawstring through with safety pin.

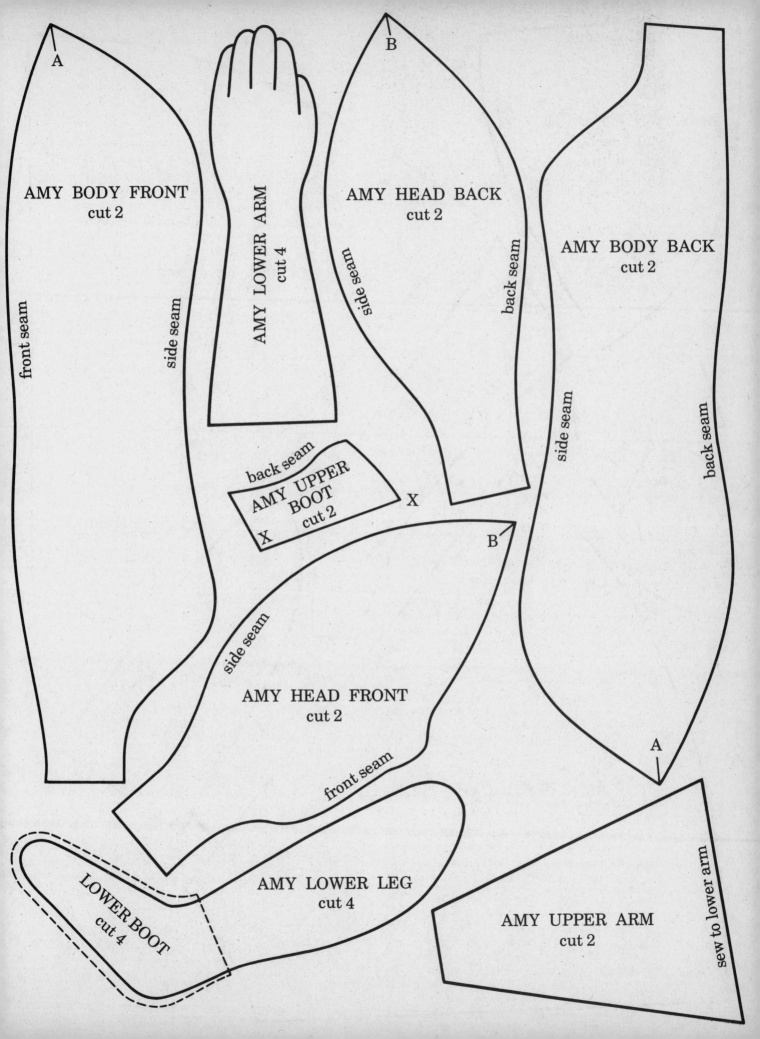

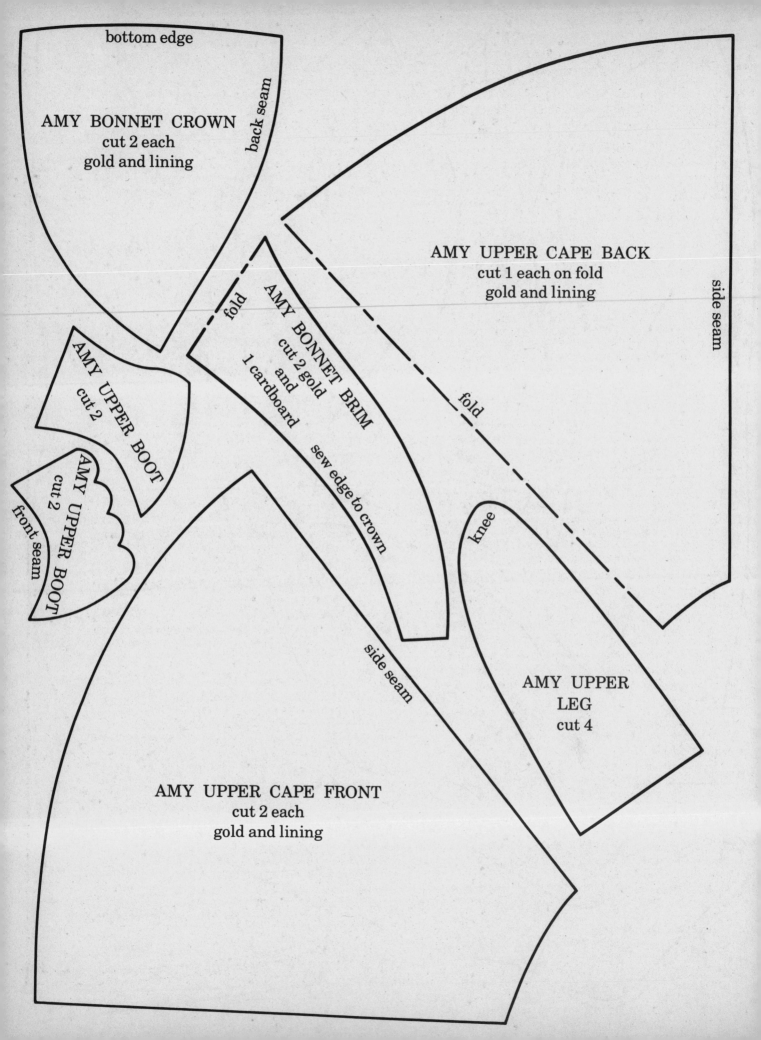

bottom edge

AMY BONNET CROWN
cut 2 each
gold and lining

back seam

AMY UPPER CAPE BACK
cut 1 each on fold
gold and lining

side seam

fold

AMY BONNET BRIM
cut 2 gold
and
1 cardboard

sew edge to crown

fold

AMY UPPER BOOT
cut 2

AMY UPPER BOOT
cut 2

front seam

knee

side seam

AMY UPPER
LEG
cut 4

AMY UPPER CAPE FRONT
cut 2 each
gold and lining

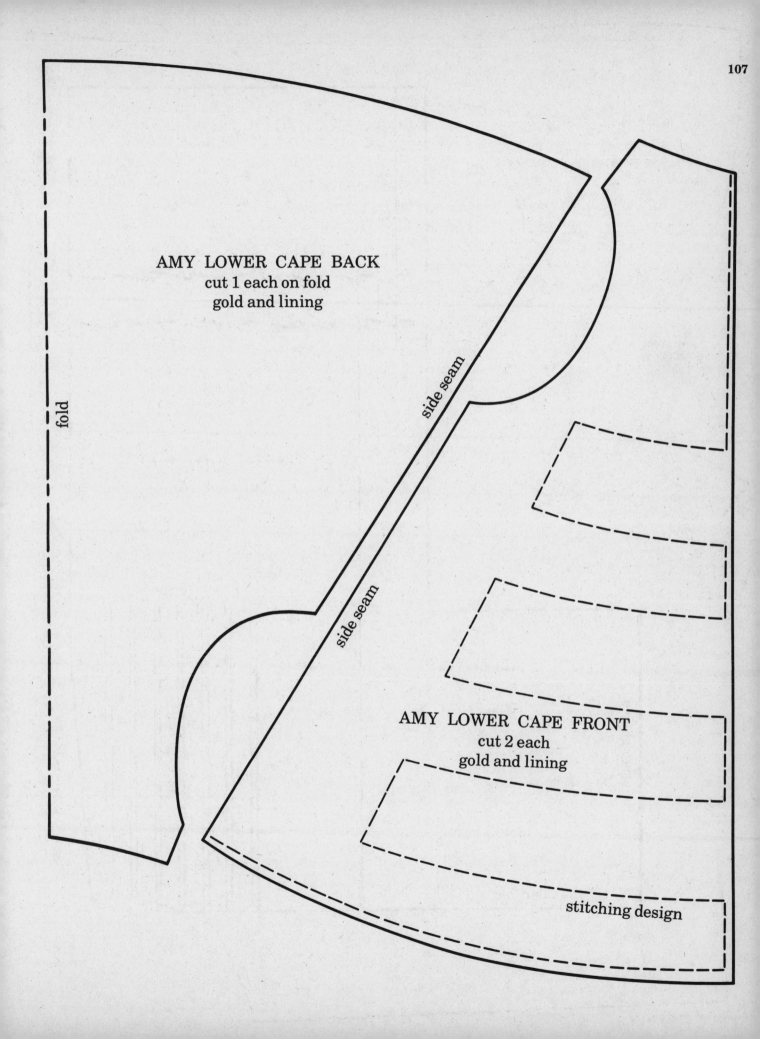

AMY LOWER CAPE BACK
cut 1 each on fold
gold and lining

fold

side seam

side seam

AMY LOWER CAPE FRONT
cut 2 each
gold and lining

stitching design

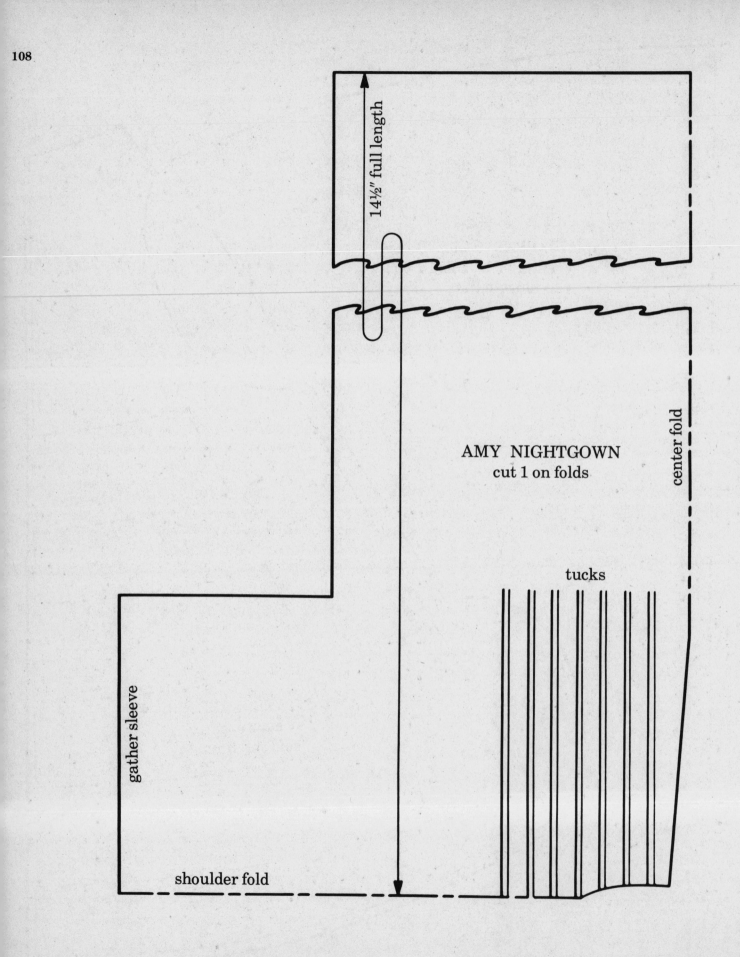

14½" full length

center fold

AMY NIGHTGOWN
cut 1 on folds

tucks

gather sleeve

shoulder fold

Wardrobe Trunks

The four trunks are made in the same way then painted and decorated with a special color scheme for each sister. Meg's trunk is yellow and Beth's is green. Both have marbleized papers in matching colors glued to inner surfaces and outer edges. Amy's trunk is blue, Jo's is crimson, and both are lined and bordered with matching papers printed with gold motifs.

MATERIALS *For one trunk:* wooden card file box 4⅜″ deep, 5¼″ high and 6⅝″ wide; 2″ brass hasp; two 1″-wide watchband buckles and keepers; scrap of felt 2″ x 28″; half an 18″ x 23″ sheet of decorative paper; scraps of gold lace paper or doily; casein glue; enamel.

Paint outside of box and edges of opening; let dry. To line the lid, cut paper to fit each end and a piece to fit center; glue in place. Line box itself in the same way.

For paper border on outside of lid, cut ⅝″-wide strips, mitering corners, to fit. Fold lengthwise and glue along front and back edges then along ends. Glue strips down box corners; let dry. Cut with razor blade where lid and box meet. Add triangles of lace paper at bottom corners.

Attach hasp and its staple to front.

For each felt handle, cut ⅞″ x 3½″ strip and shape ends as in photograph; also cut two ⅜″ x 1½″ strips. Lap these around handle and glue, then glue them to box. Cut felt straps ¾″ x 23″. Punch hole in one end; fold over buckle and through keeper and glue. Attach strap to lower part of box front, to underside and part way up back. Punch hole in second end for buckle prong.

Frisky Jungle Babies

Three delightful animals to stitch and stuff for your own collection or to give with love to the newest member of the crib set.

PATTERNS AND CUTTING See Construction Techniques, page 11.

SEWING AND STITCHERY See Construction Techniques, page 11.

Leopard

MATERIALS ½ yard 36″-wide gold cotton velvet; felt scraps in light green, dark green, orange and yellow; scrap of nonwoven iron-on interfacing; turquoise, orange and green cotton prints; orange 6-strand embroidery floss; heavy white thread for whiskers; two ½″ black buttons; polyester fiber for stuffing; black felt-tipped marker for spots.

Mark 7 patterns on velvet for leopard, reversing them where specified. Cut out pieces. See leaf pattern for collar and cut leaves later.

BODY Pin and stitch two side bodies along back seam, from neck to A. Pin underbody to sides, matching neck, legs and A's; stitch together, leaving neck open. Trim seams, clip at curves and turn.

HEAD Pin and stitch two front pieces along front seam; stitch two back pieces along back seam. Join head pieces along side seams, clip curves and turn.

STUFFING Insert polyester fiber through open necks of body and head, using small bits at a time. Continue until firmly packed.

ASSEMBLY Pin head to body, turning it to one side at a saucy angle. Add more stuffing to neck, if necessary. Turn under raw edges of head and hand sew to body with small stitches. Appliqué velvet nose piece to head center seam, with straight end 2¾″ from front neck seam.

EARS Pin and sew pairs together, leaving straight edges open. Trim seams, clip and turn. Turn in raw edges, cup ears slightly and sew just behind top seam and 1½″ from center seam of head.

TAIL Pin and sew two pieces together, leaving end X open. Trim and clip seam; turn. Stuff; tuck in raw edges and sew to point A.

SPOTS Using felt-tipped marker, follow photograph to draw toes and spots on body and head, ranging in size from ⅛″ to ½″ in diameter.

FACE From felt cut ¾″ green disks for eyes and a small orange triangle for nose. Back the buttons with disks and sew to head; appliqué orange nose. Using three strands of floss, outline-stitch mouth. With a long, thin needle and white thread, take long stitches for whiskers, each anchored with a short stitch on upper lip.

FLOWER COLLAR Omit seam allowances. From felt cut 1″ x 11½″ light green strip; following pattern, cut three dark green and seven light green leaves and three ⅝″ yellow disks. Bond cotton print scraps to interfacing; cut 2″ and 1½″ flowers, six in all. Scallop edges. Fold strip lengthwise and topstitch. Make five flower and leaf arrangements; decorate flowers with felt centers and French knots; sew to collar. Place around leopard's neck and tack ends.

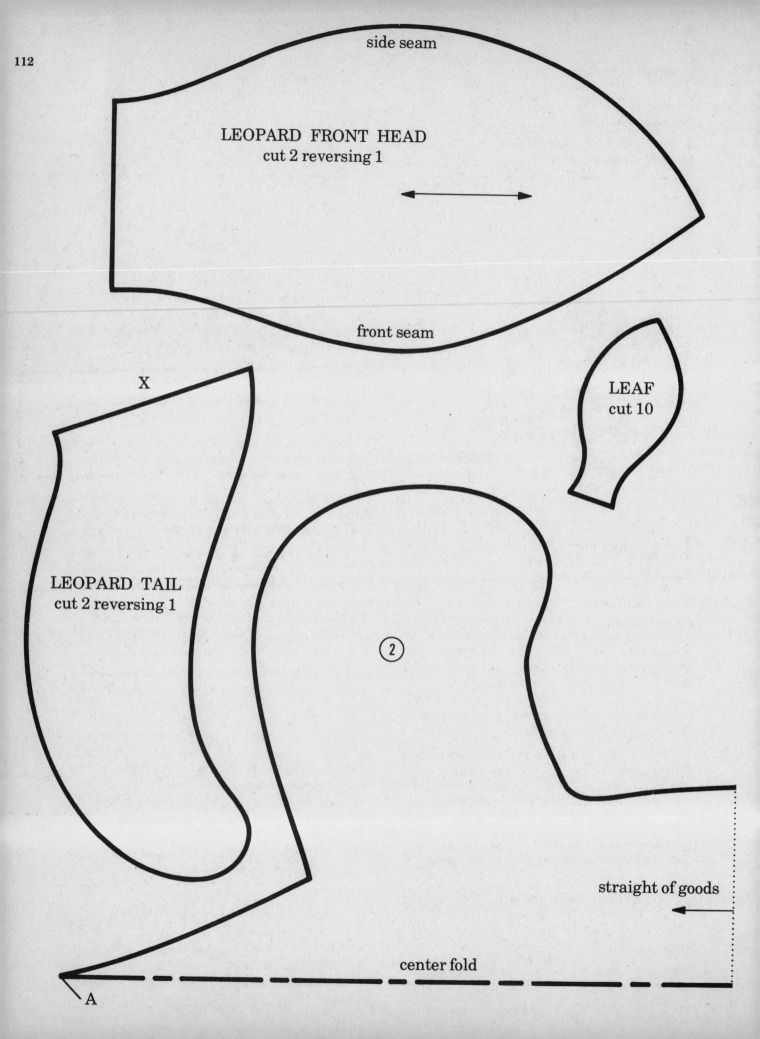

112

side seam

LEOPARD FRONT HEAD
cut 2 reversing 1

front seam

X

LEAF
cut 10

LEOPARD TAIL
cut 2 reversing 1

②

straight of goods

center fold

A

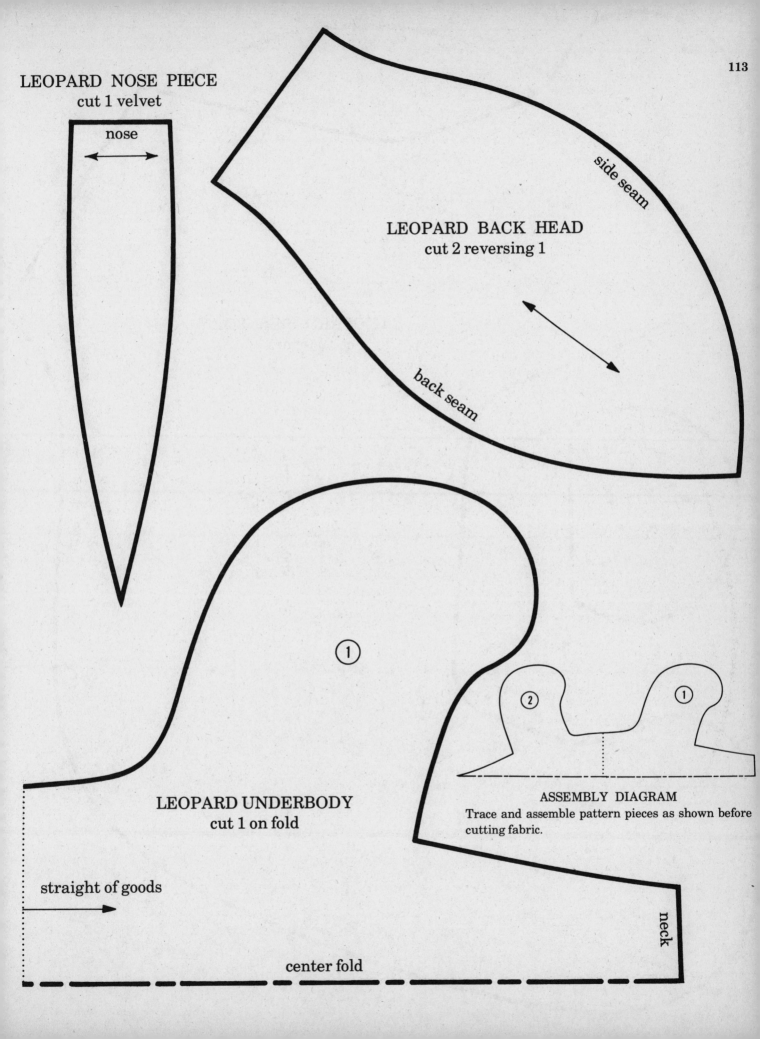

LEOPARD NOSE PIECE
cut 1 velvet

nose

LEOPARD BACK HEAD
cut 2 reversing 1

side seam

back seam

①

LEOPARD UNDERBODY
cut 1 on fold

② ①

ASSEMBLY DIAGRAM
Trace and assemble pattern pieces as shown before cutting fabric.

neck

straight of goods

center fold

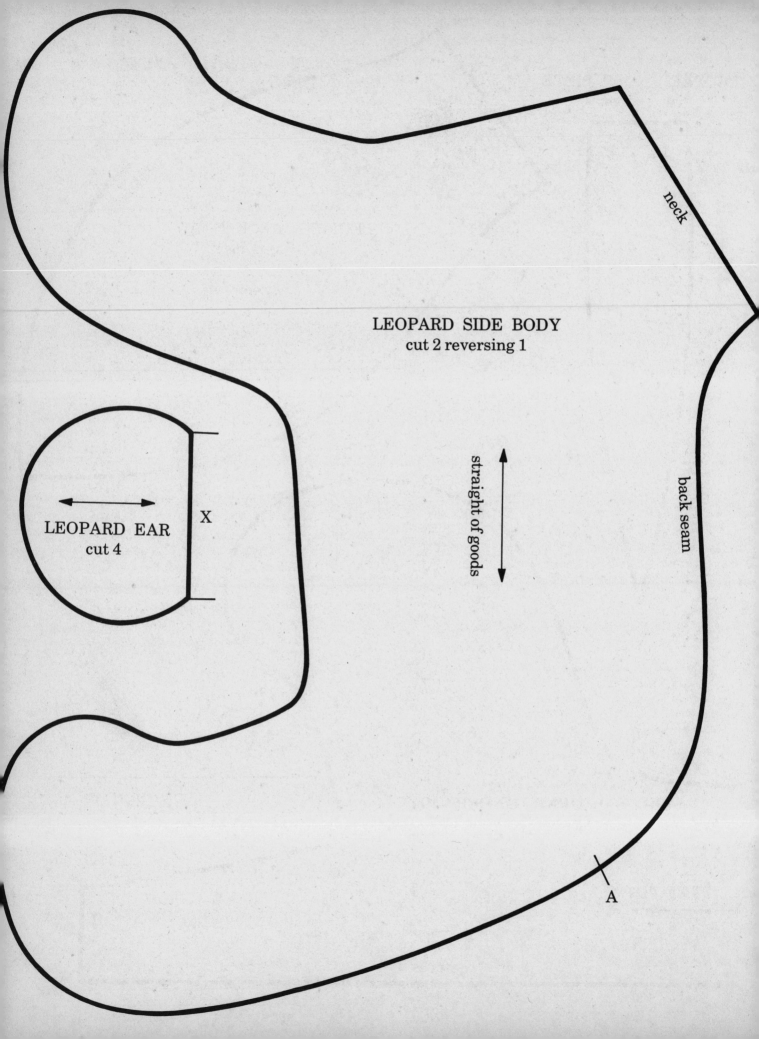

LEOPARD SIDE BODY
cut 2 reversing 1

neck

back seam

straight of goods

LEOPARD EAR
cut 4

X

A

Monkey

The monkey photographed has yellow felt hands and feet. For a completely washable toy, substitute cotton as suggested in note below. Patterns are marked for long openings to facilitate turning edges of heavy toweling; these are later overcast closed.

MATERIALS Orange terry, one 24″ x 46″ bath towel or ½ yard 42″-wide fabric; yellow terry 6″ x 16″ and yellow felt 5″ x 24″. (*Note:* For a completely washable monkey, use ¼ yard of 36″-wide yellow cotton fabric for face, hands and feet.) Scrap of orange felt or cotton for nose; dark orange and light orange 6-strand embroidery floss; two ⁷⁄₁₆″ black buttons; polyester fiber for stuffing.

Mark 8 body patterns on orange terry, reversing them where specified. Mark 4 more patterns on yellow fabrics (or fabric) for face, nose, hands and feet. Cut out pieces.

BODY Pin and stitch two front bodies along front seam; stitch two back bodies along back seam. Join body pieces at side seams, leaving neck open; doublestitch neck seams. Trim seam allowance and turn to right side.

HEAD Pin and stitch two orange front heads along front seam; stitch two back heads along back seam. Join head pieces at side seams, leaving neck open and double-stitching neck seams. Trim and turn to right side.

STUFFING Stuff body and head firmly with polyester fiber.

BODY ASSEMBLY Pin head to neck of body, tipping it slightly. Head will look small at this point, before face and ears are attached. Add stuffing at neck, if necessary; turn under head edge and sew to body.

EARS Pin and sew pairs together, leaving edges X open. Trim, clip and turn. Fold in raw edges; pin and sew ears to side seams.

FACE AND FEATURES Pin yellow face to head, turning under raw edges. Appliqué with matching thread. Stitch together yellow nose pieces along front seam. Trim, turn, stuff lightly and appliqué to face. Sew button eyes and ½″ x ⅞″ orange oval nose to face. Mark with pins or chalk the position of brows and mouth, using three strands of floss, outline-stitch brows and mouth—1 row for brows, 2 rows for mouth.

ARMS AND LEGS Each arm and leg, including hand or foot, is made from four separate pieces. For arms, pin and sew each hand piece to wrist of corresponding arm piece. Trim seam and press open. With right sides together, seam matching arm-hand pieces together, leaving top and part of inner seam open. Trim seam allowance and turn.

Repeat for legs and feet.

Stuff arms and legs lightly, especially at upper ends. Turn in raw edges of inner seams; stuff and sew as you go, using an overcast stitch. Turn in ends and sew to shoulders and lower body, keeping joints flexible. To mark fingers and toes, using matching yellow thread, make small running stitches by hand. To have feet at right angles to legs, bend upward and sew a small tuck across each ankle.

TAIL Pin and sew two pieces together, leaving end and most of inner seam open. Trim seam and turn; stuff lightly. Turn in raw edges of inner seam and sew closed with overcast stitch. Turn in end and sew tail to monkey.

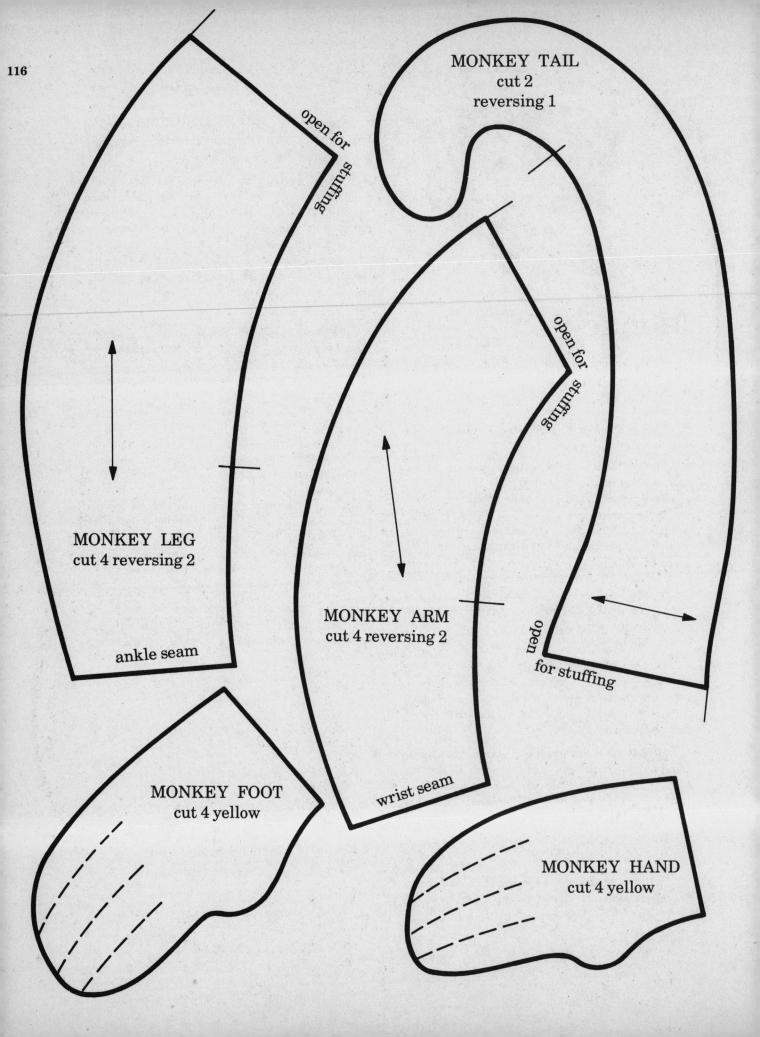

116

MONKEY TAIL
cut 2
reversing 1

open for stuffing

open for stuffing

MONKEY LEG
cut 4 reversing 2

ankle seam

MONKEY ARM
cut 4 reversing 2

open for stuffing

wrist seam

MONKEY FOOT
cut 4 yellow

MONKEY HAND
cut 4 yellow

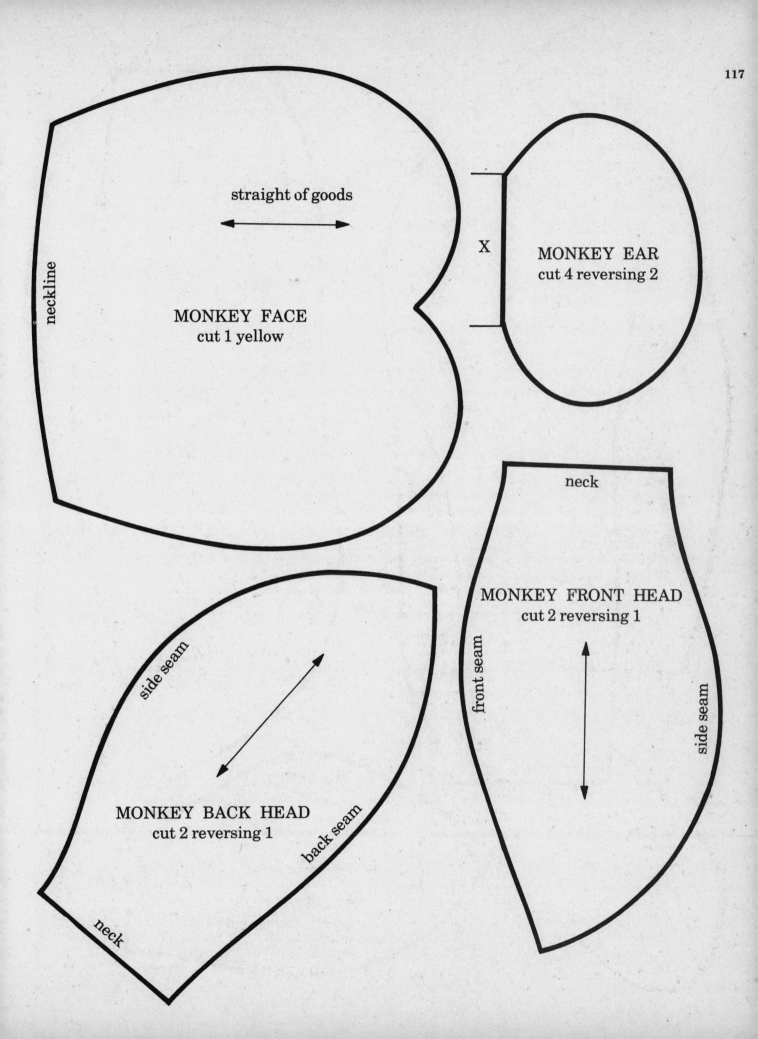

117

straight of goods

neckline

MONKEY FACE
cut 1 yellow

X

MONKEY EAR
cut 4 reversing 2

neck

MONKEY FRONT HEAD
cut 2 reversing 1

front seam

side seam

side seam

MONKEY BACK HEAD
cut 2 reversing 1

back seam

neck

118

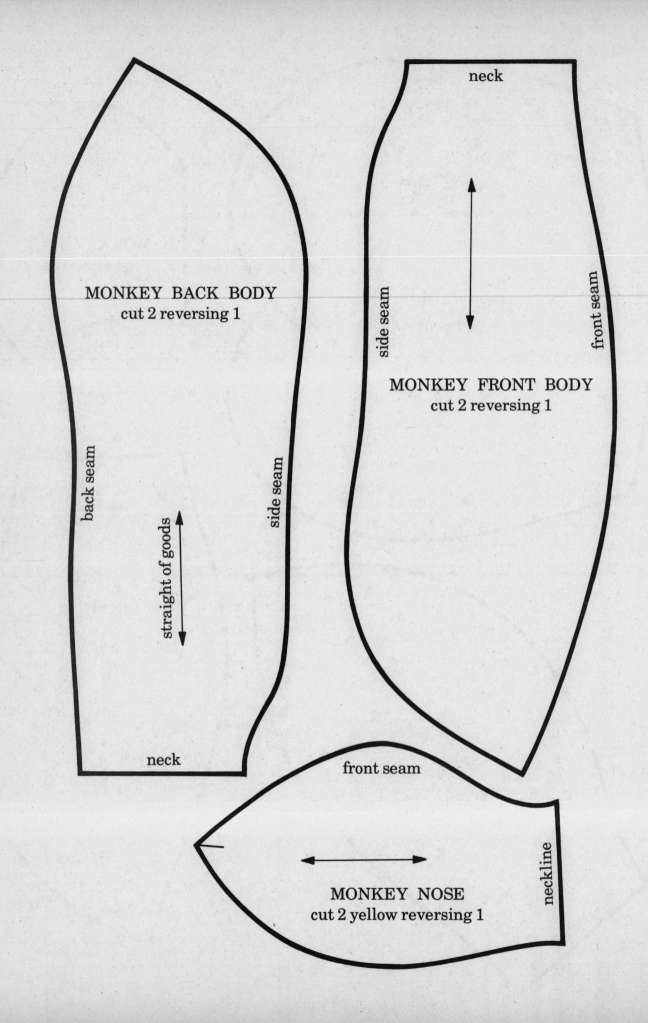

MONKEY BACK BODY
cut 2 reversing 1

back seam

straight of goods

side seam

neck

MONKEY FRONT BODY
cut 2 reversing 1

neck

side seam

front seam

MONKEY NOSE
cut 2 yellow reversing 1

front seam

neckline

Elephant

SIZE   About 10½″ tall.

MATERIALS   ¾ yard 45″-wide brushed blue nylon (or other soft fabric); ⅛ yard 36″-wide yellow calico; scraps orange and green felt and red calico; small green pompon; 2 black buttons or felt for eyes; 1 yard orange yarn; polyester for stuffing.

BODY   Cut underbody and side-body pieces from nylon. Cut 2 ears each from nylon and yellow calico, reversing pattern for one ear of each fabric. Cut yellow calico soles. Cut 1⅝″-diameter circle from nylon for trunk tip.

With right sides facing, stitch side-body pieces from A, along trunk and back to B. With right sides facing, stitch half of underbody to a side body, matching B's, C's, trunk and legs. Do not stitch across bottom of feet or tip of trunk (X). Stitch other half of underbody to other side body in same manner, leaving X's open. Trim seams and clip curves. Turn through one leg (if necessary, open leg seam a bit for ease in turning). Stuff firmly, making legs as stiff as possible. If hind legs tend to splay out, tack top of inner leg to underbody so elephant will stand straight.

Prepare sole pieces by turning seam allowances under, pressing, then clipping to make lie flat; blindstitch to bottoms of legs. Turn in ¼″ around circle for trunk tip and sew to end of trunk.

EARS AND EYES   With right sides facing, stitch a calico ear to a nylon ear, leaving edge X open. Trim and clip seam. Turn. Make another ear. Turn in seams at X and blindstitch to body. Sew felt or button eyes in place (for small child's toy use felt).

TAIL   For tail, cut 1″ x 4½″ piece of yellow calico. Turn under and press ½″ at 1″ ends. Cut six 6″

strands of yarn and place lengthwise along wrong side of calico so they extend about 2″ at one end. Roll calico tightly around them, turn in raw edge and blindstitch. Sew tail to elephant, catching yarn in stitches so strands can't be pulled out.

FLOWER   Cut 3″ circle from orange felt. Cut scallops around edge. From red calico cut and scallop a 2″ circle. Place calico circle on felt circle and pompon on top. Sew all 3 together through center. Cut 1″ x 5″ piece of green felt. Fold in half lengthwise and topstitch. Sew one end to back of flower for stem. Cut 1¼″ x 3½″ rectangle and taper to point at each end for leaf. Wrap end of leaf around stem and tack. Sew flower to trunk.

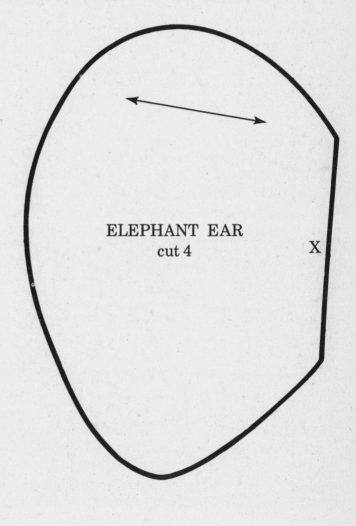

ELEPHANT EAR
cut 4

X

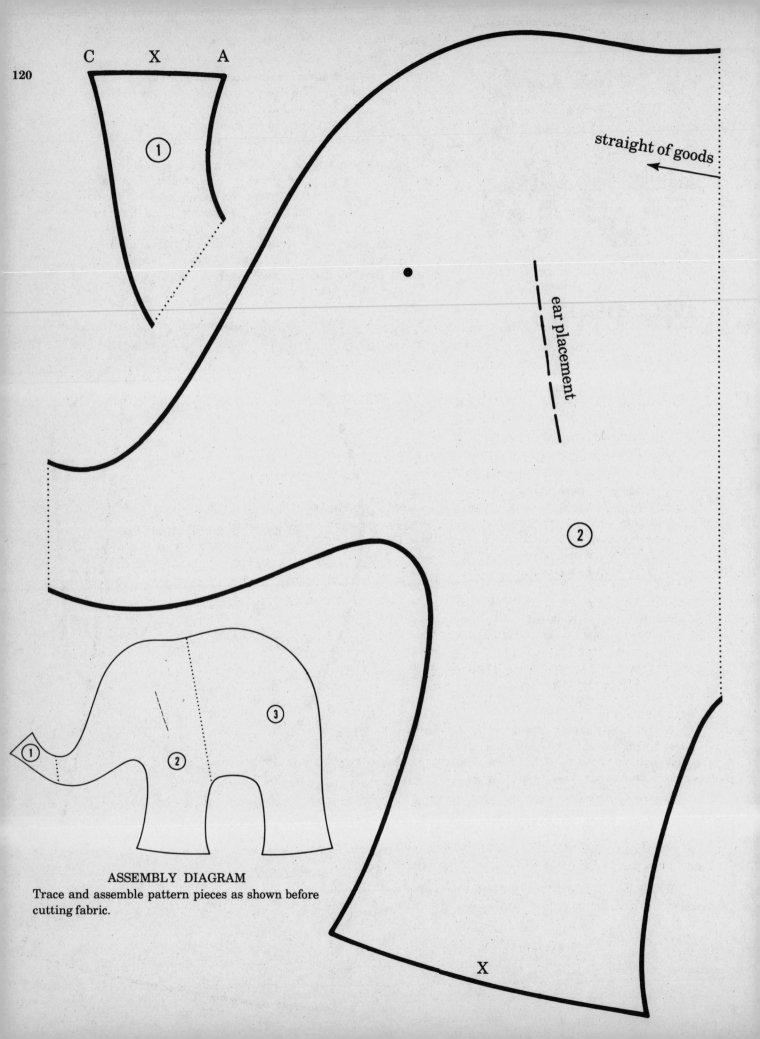

120

C X A

① 1

straight of goods

ear placement

② 2

③ 3

② 2

① 1

X

ASSEMBLY DIAGRAM
Trace and assemble pattern pieces as shown before cutting fabric.

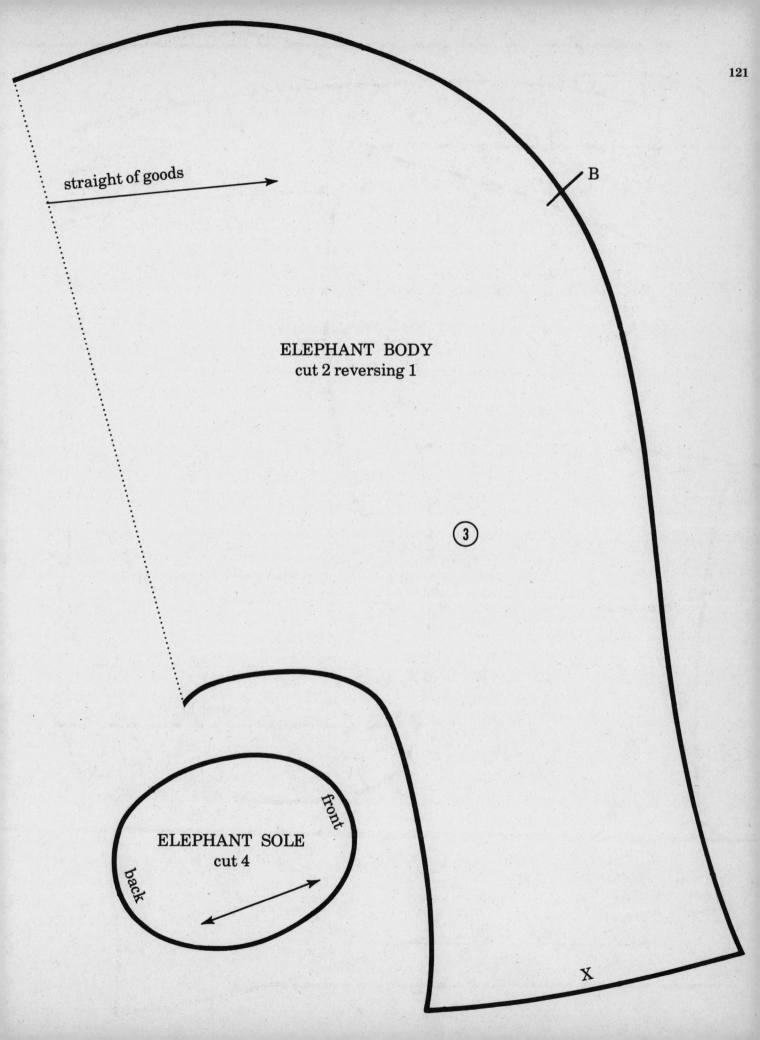

straight of goods

ELEPHANT BODY
cut 2 reversing 1

③

B

ELEPHANT SOLE
cut 4

front

back

X

122

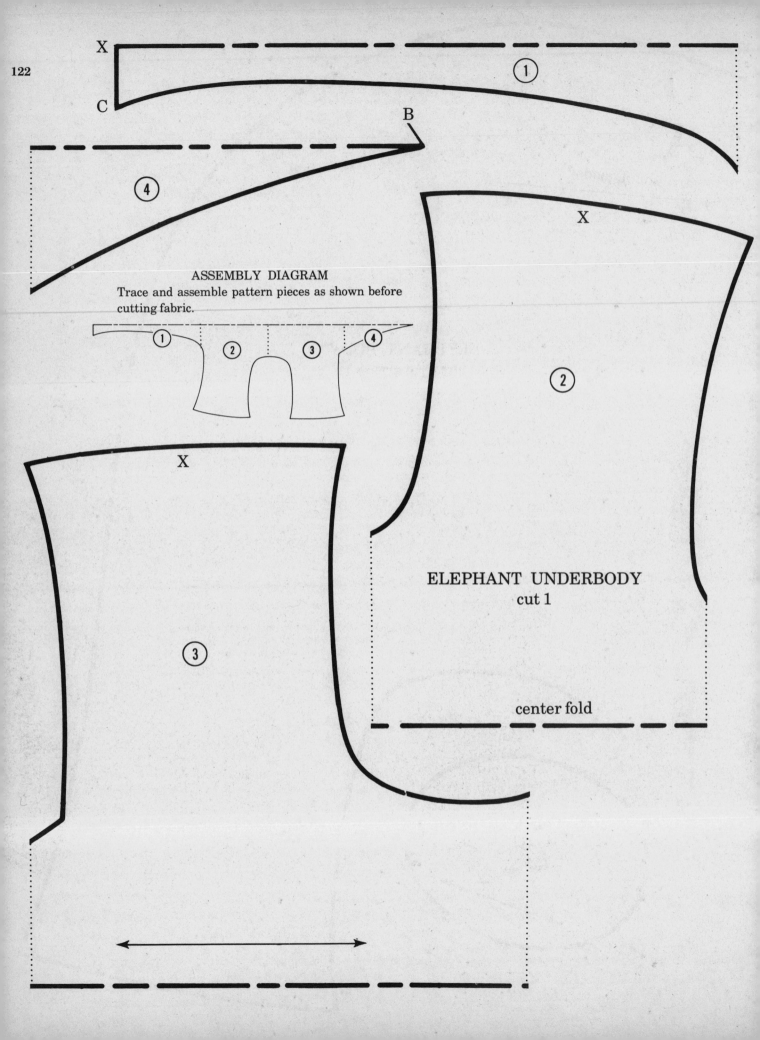

X

C

B

1

4

ASSEMBLY DIAGRAM
Trace and assemble pattern pieces as shown before cutting fabric.

1 2 3 4

X

2

X

3

ELEPHANT UNDERBODY
cut 1

center fold

Out of the Forest, Animals to Make

Here are nine enchanting toys, waiting to come to life for some child you love:
a baby rabbit, tweedy raccoon, frog, velour skunk, a mother rabbit, Christmasy bear,
turtle, squirrel and woolly bear caterpillar.

For pattern cutting, stitching and stuffing, follow the Construction Techniques on page 11.

Turtle

SIZE   About 9″ from head to tail.

MATERIALS   Fabric scraps in following sizes: 11″ x 12″ piece of print dress fabric, 8″ x 9″ of lavender linen, 12″ square of gold-and-brown-striped cotton; ½ yard each of wide red rickrack and purple middy braid; two ¼″ pearl buttons; orange embroidery floss; kapok or Dacron for stuffing.

Trace 6 pattern outlines on paper. Mark on fabrics, reversing patterns for right and wrong sides of material. Add seam allowances when cutting.

BODY   Cut 2 top bodies or shells from print cotton and one bottom body from lavender linen. With right sides together, pin and stitch shell pieces along top seam. Trim seam and put body pieces aside.

LEGS AND TAIL   Cut 8 leg pieces from striped cotton, following photograph for direction of stripes. Right sides together, seam pairs, leaving tops open. Trim seams, turn and stuff firmly about half way up.

Mark tail outline on wrong side of folded striped fabric. Before cutting, stitch seam; cut out tail, trim seam and turn. Stuff lightly.

BODY ASSEMBLY   Pin the four legs and tail to right side of bottom body, following dotted lines; sew in place outside the seam line. With right sides together, place top body over bottom; pin along seam line, leaving opening. Stitch seam slowly; sew again, smoothing out any wriggly sections of seam. Turn to right side; stuff firmly. Sew opening.

HEAD   Cut 2 side heads and center head from striped cotton. Pin and sew together side heads along top seam from neck to A. Pin and sew center head from A back to neck. Trim seam allowance and turn; stuff firmly. Pin head to shell of turtle just above seam; add stuffing if needed. Turn under raw neck edge and sew securely to body. See diagram 1.

Cut a collar strip from striped fabric about 3″ x 5″. Fold in each long edge and wrap around neck of turtle. Sew around base of neck and seam collar ends at front, as in diagram 2.

FEATURES AND TRIM   Sew on two pearl buttons for eyes with green thread. Chain-stitch a smiley mouth with orange floss.

Sew purple braid along lower seam of turtle shell and above neck. Sew red rickrack above braid.

Diagram 1. Pinning head to turtle

Diagram 2. Collar for turtle's neck

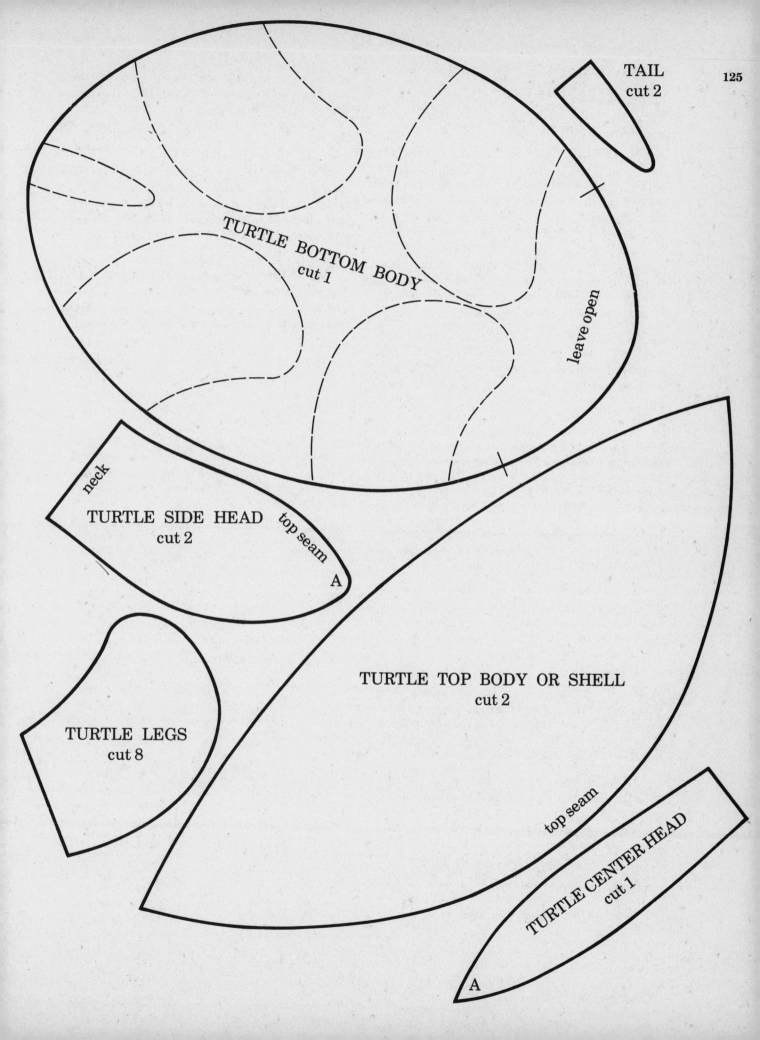

TAIL
cut 2

125

TURTLE BOTTOM BODY
cut 1

leave open

neck

TURTLE SIDE HEAD
cut 2

top seam

A

TURTLE TOP BODY OR SHELL
cut 2

TURTLE LEGS
cut 8

top seam

TURTLE CENTER HEAD
cut 1

A

Skunk

SIZE About 11½" high.

MATERIALS One black sheared, terry cloth hand towel about 16" x 28" and white loop washcloth (or use terry cloth); white nylon mop refill and black wool yarn for tail; green and pink embroidery floss; scrap of pink felt; kapok or Dacron for stuffing; long pipe cleaners; scrap of yellow felt, 2 black satin buttons and 2 green pipe cleaners for flowers.

Trace 8 pattern outlines on paper. Mark on fabrics, using light chalk on black terry; reverse patterns for right and wrong sides of material. Add seam allowances when cutting fabrics.

BODY Cut 2 side bodies, 1 center front body and body base from black terry. With right sides together, pin and sew 2 side bodies along back seam from nose to base edge. Pin center front to sides, starting at nose; sew seam. Trim seam allowances and turn body. Stuff smoothly and firmly.

Pin body base in place, turning under edge as you go. Add stuffing to make the skunk stand well. Sew around edge with small sturdy stitches.

ARMS Cut 4 arm pieces from black terry. Right sides together, seam pairs for left and right, leaving tops open. Trim seams and turn. Omit stuffing and sew openings. Pin arms to body, about 4" below top seam and overlapping at front. Sew in place, leaving opening for flower stems.

STRIPE Cut 1 stripe piece from white washcloth, adding seam allowances to edges of outside and of opening. Pin to head about 2½" from nose and continue down to tail, turning under edges. Appliqué to body with small stitches.

EARS Fold and pin black terry with right side in. Mark pattern twice on one surface. First stitch around pairs of ears through two layers, leaving straight edges open. Cut out ears and trim seam allowances; turn. Fold in raw edges, cup ears and sew next to stripe about 1" from its pointed end.

FEATURES For nose, cut a tiny oval about ⅜" long from pink felt; appliqué in place. Chain-stitch a disdainful mouth with pink floss. For downcast eyes, chain-stitch crescents about ¾" long with green floss and stitch a few lashes. For white tufts at top of head, use large-eyed needle to stitch on strands from mop refill. Tie strands in knot and trim to 1½" length.

TAIL Cut 2 pieces from black terry, adding seam allowances. Right sides facing, stitch together, leaving straight end open. Trim seams; turn. To give rigidity to tail, twist together pairs of pipe cleaners, joining pairs to make a strip about 12" long. Lay strip along outline of tail; bend to shape and insert. Sew ends of pipe cleaners to tail.

For furry look, cut strands from white mop refill. With large needle, sew along center of tail, take a small stitch and tie into a knot. Repeat from tip to base; trim ends. Sew 2" loops of black yarn around white band. Turn in terry ends of tail and sew to skunk.

FLOWERS Cut 2 flower shapes and two ¾" disks from yellow felt. Sew a black button to front of each flower. Bend a pipe cleaner and sew to back; cover with disk. Tuck flowers under skunk's arm.

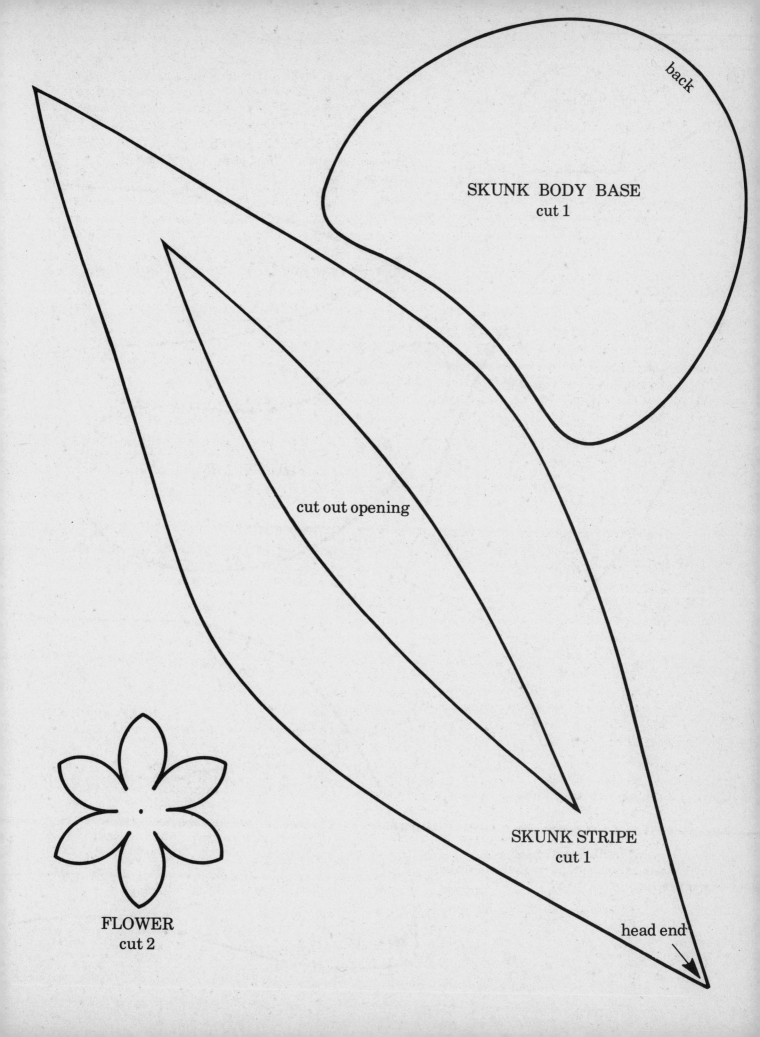

SKUNK BODY BASE
cut 1

back

cut out opening

SKUNK STRIPE
cut 1

head end

FLOWER
cut 2

128

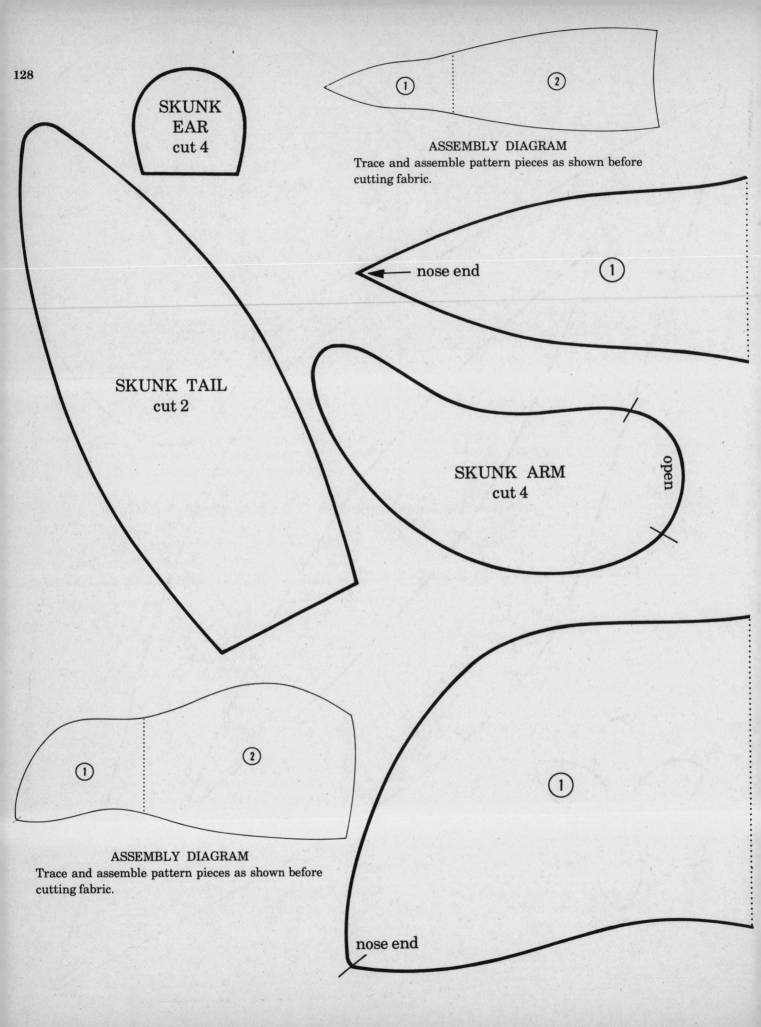

SKUNK
EAR
cut 4

① ②

ASSEMBLY DIAGRAM
Trace and assemble pattern pieces as shown before cutting fabric.

← nose end

①

SKUNK TAIL
cut 2

SKUNK ARM
cut 4

open

① ②

ASSEMBLY DIAGRAM
Trace and assemble pattern pieces as shown before cutting fabric.

①

nose end

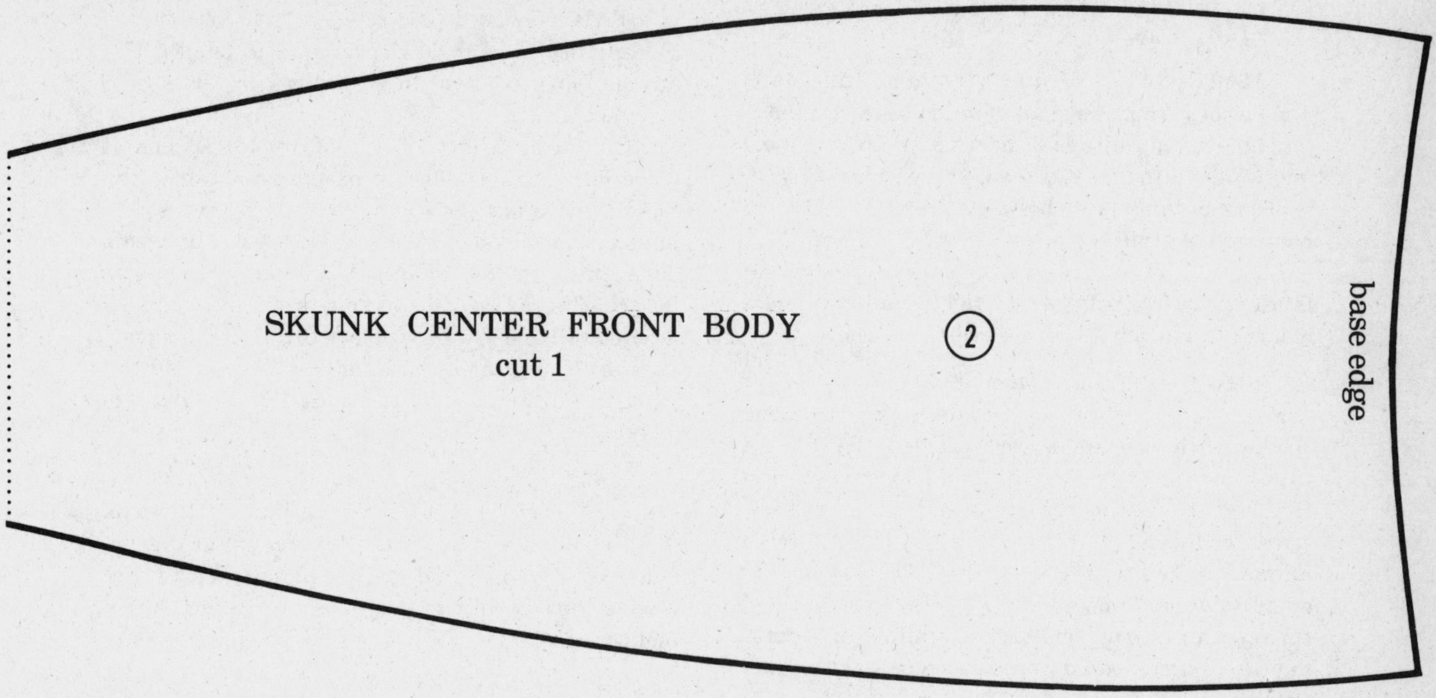

SKUNK CENTER FRONT BODY
cut 1

②

base edge

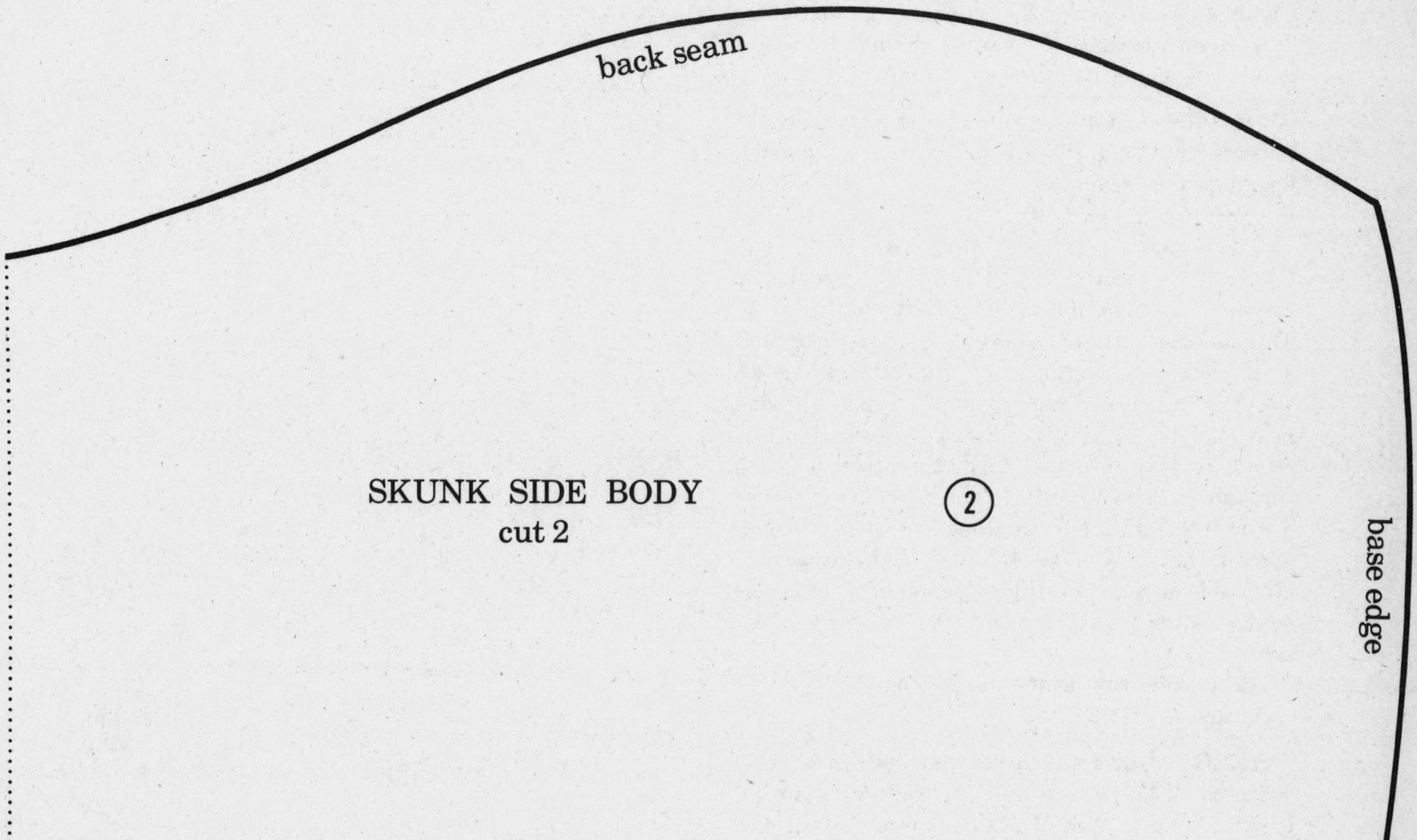

back seam

SKUNK SIDE BODY
cut 2

②

base edge

Squirrel

SIZE 9″ high.

MATERIALS ⅜ yard 36″ orange knit fabric; 4-ply wool yarn in 4 shades of orange; scrap of black felt; brown and white embroidery floss; green sewing and white button twist thread; 4 pipe cleaners; cardboard; 2 buttons; 8″ upholstery needles; Dacron or polyester for stuffing.

Trace 7 pattern outlines on paper. Mark on knit fabric, reversing patterns for right and wrong sides of fabric Add seam allowances when cutting.

BODY Cut 2 side bodies, 1 center body, center head and body base from knit fabric. Pin, baste and sew center head piece between 2 side bodies from A to B. Sew back seam from B down to base edge. Sew the short seam under nose from A to C. Pin and sew center body from C down to base edge. Trim seam allowances and turn. Stuff squirrel with small bits of stuffing until smooth and firm. Pin base to body, turning in raw edge and adding stuffing, if needed, to make squirrel stand well. Sew on base with small stitches.

EARS Cut 4 ear pieces from knit fabric. For each ear, sew together 2 pieces, leaving end open. Trim seam allowance and turn. Turn in end and sew closed. Pleat ears; sew to head 1½″ in front of B.

ARMS Cut 4 knit fabric arms and cardboard for each, as shown on pattern. Seam arms, leaving openings; trim seam allowances, except at openings, and turn. Stuff arms halfway.

To attach movable arms, cut 4 long lengths of button twist and thread 2 lengths on 8″ upholstery needles. Insert needle through body from X to X. Thread other 2 lengths on needle and insert through same holes as in diagram 1; even up all thread ends.

Now insert cardboard into open arm on the side next to body; place button over cardboard. Using a strong needle, rethread 2 lengths of twist; push through arm, cardboard and one hole of button. See diagram 2. Do same with other 2 lengths, through opposite hole of button. Make sure all threads on other side of body are still long enough. Tie threads on first side securely; trim ends. Attach arm at other side.

Complete stuffing of arms; pin together opening edges and sew closed.

LEGS Cut 4 pieces from knit fabric for legs. Seam pairs, leaving openings. Turn; trim seam allowances and stuff firmly. Sew openings closed. Pin legs to body, making sure squirrel will be able to stand when heavy tail is added. Sew on legs.

TAIL Twist 2 pipe cleaners together, then 2 more; twist pairs together, making 8″ length. Cut orange fabric to cover pipe cleaners and hand sew around them.

Cut arm's-length strands from all shades of yarn. For a lighter effect, separate 4-ply into 2-ply. Slowly pull apart the strands until you have a good bunch of the 4 shades. Thread a short strong needle with orange thread, doubled. Using 3 shades of yarn, loop the 3 strands over two fingers of left hand; hold against tail and sew base of loop to tail. See diagram 3. Start at tip and spiral around tail, using the fourth shade every other time. Sew completed tail to body.

FACE See photograph. Cut black felt almond-shaped eyes about ¾″ long. Sew to head. With white floss, chain-stitch around eyes. With brown floss, chain-stitch a nose and smiling mouth. With green sewing thread, stitch five or six whiskers above mouth.

Diagram 1. *Running thread through squirrel*

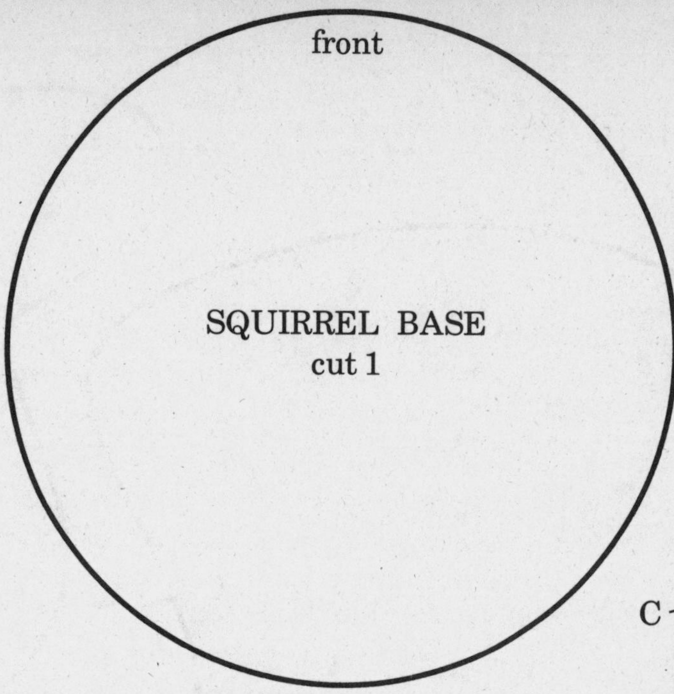

Diagram 2. *Attaching arm with button*

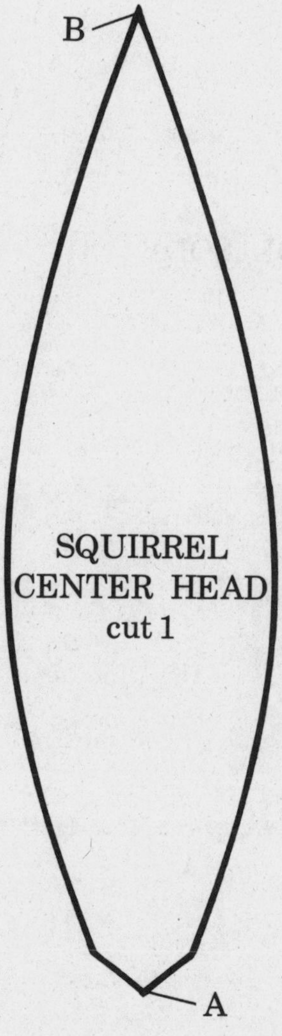

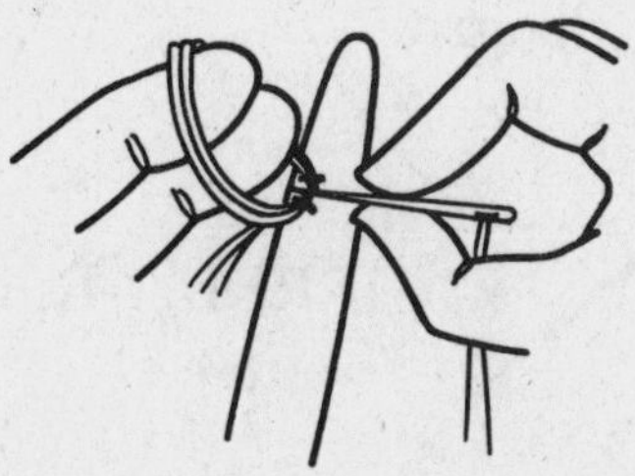

Diagram 3. *Sewing yarn loop to tail*

front

SQUIRREL BASE
cut 1

**SQUIRREL
CENTER HEAD**
cut 1

B

A

C

**SQUIRREL
CENTER BODY**
cut 1

base edge

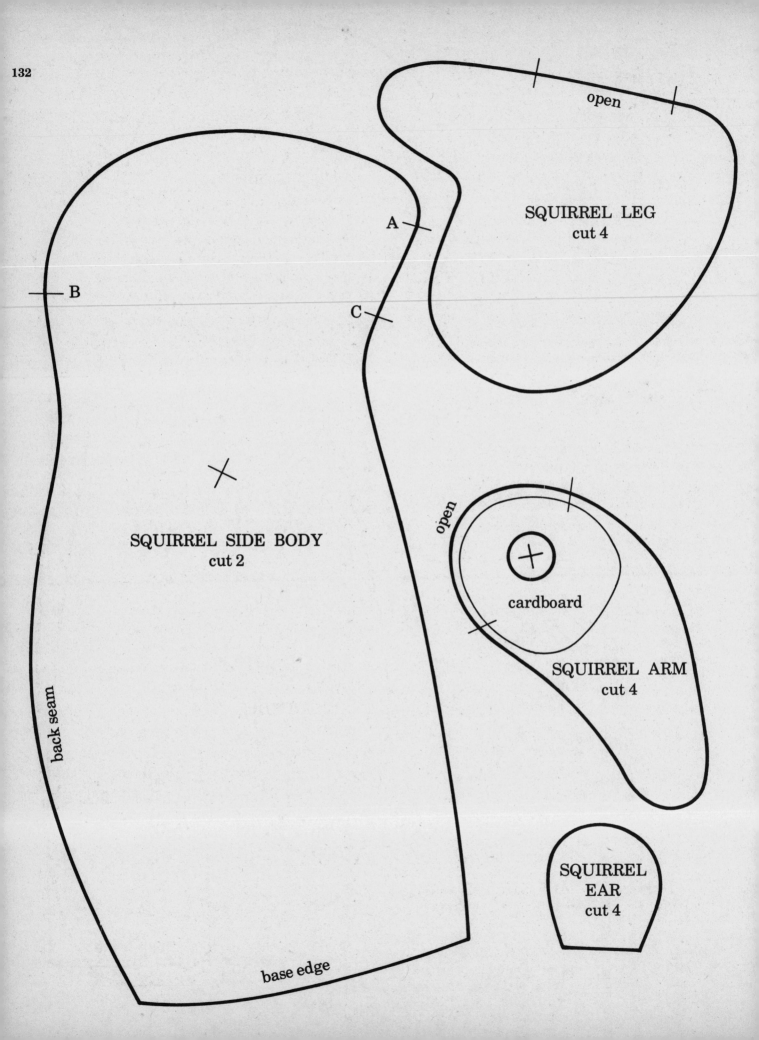

Raccoon

SIZE About 13″ high when seated.

MATERIALS ½ yard 54″-wide herringbone cotton knit fabric; scraps of black felt and black satin; fine white wool yarn for face and heavy black and gray wool yarns for tail; gray embroidery floss; white button thread; two ½″ black buttons with white rims; kapok or Dacron for stuffing.

Trace 9 pattern outlines on paper. Mark on fabrics, reversing patterns for right and wrong sides of material. Add seam allowances when cutting fabrics except for felt mask pieces.

BODY Cut 4 body pieces from herringbone knit, adding seam allowance. With right sides together, pin and sew 2 body pieces along front seam for raccoon front. Pin and sew remaining 2 bodies along back seam for back. Join front and back together along side seams. Trim seam allowance and turn body. Stuff firmly.

HEAD Cut 2 front heads, 2 back heads and 4 ears from herringbone knit. Put ears aside. Pin and sew 2 front heads together along front seam. Pin and sew 2 back heads together along back seam. Join front and back together along side seams. Trim seam allowance and turn head. Stuff firmly and smoothly.

Pin head to neck of body. Turn raw edge under as you go and add stuffing to make neck sturdy. Sew head to body with small, strong stitches.

ARMS AND LEGS Cut 4 arm pieces and 4 legs from herringbone knit. Right sides together, seam pairs for right and left, leaving tops open. Trim seams, turn and stuff almost to tops. Following dotted lines, hand sew divisions for fingers and toes. Sew openings in each arm and leg closed. Sew arms to side seams, about ½″ from neck. Sew legs to body about 2½″ forward of bottom seam to support raccoon.

FEATURES Cut 2 mask pieces from black felt. Pin in place and sew to head with tiny stitches.

Cut nose from black satin, adding ¼″ seam allowance. Turn raw edges in and pin to head. Sew with tiny stitches.

For eyes, try buttons in different places on mask until you get a "Mischief, who me?" effect. Sew in place. (Note: If white-rimmed buttons are hard to find, paint edges white.)

For whiskers, run five strands of white button thread through face, making long whiskers at sides of nose.

For band above nose, use 4 strands of gray floss to work short-and-long stitches along center front seam, from nose to top of head.

For white fringe, thread white yarn in a needle; use short-and-long stitches for white areas above mask. At sides of head, make loops and cut into fringe to give extra width.

EARS With right sides together, seam pairs of pieces, leaving openings. Trim seam allowance and turn. Fold in raw edges and sew closed. Pin ears to head. Sew securely in place along side seams, about 1½″ from top center.

TAIL Cut 2 pieces from herringbone knit. Right sides together, sew seam and turn to right side. Stuff lightly. Starting at tip and using a needle and black wool yarn, make 1½″ loops and sew securely to tail, covering about an inch. Alternating gray and black yarns, make seven stripes in all until tail is covered. Cut loops for bushy effect.

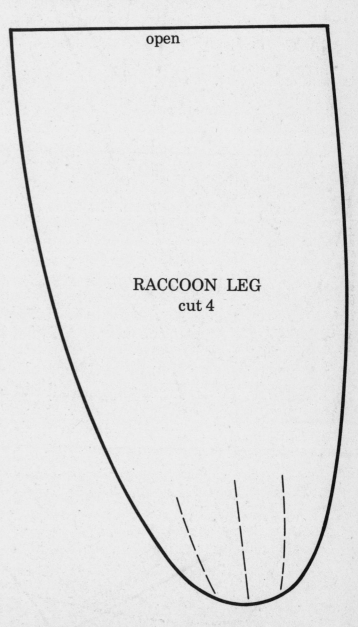

open

RACCOON LEG
cut 4

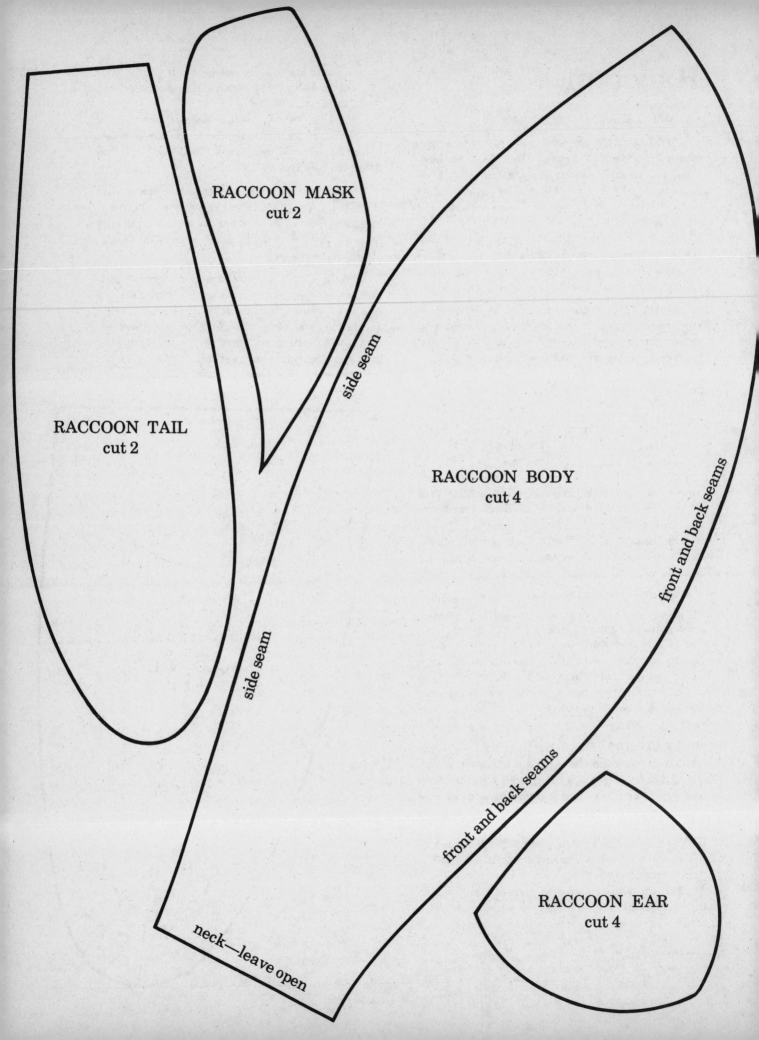

RACCOON MASK
cut 2

RACCOON TAIL
cut 2

side seam

RACCOON BODY
cut 4

front and back seams

side seam

front and back seams

RACCOON EAR
cut 4

neck—leave open

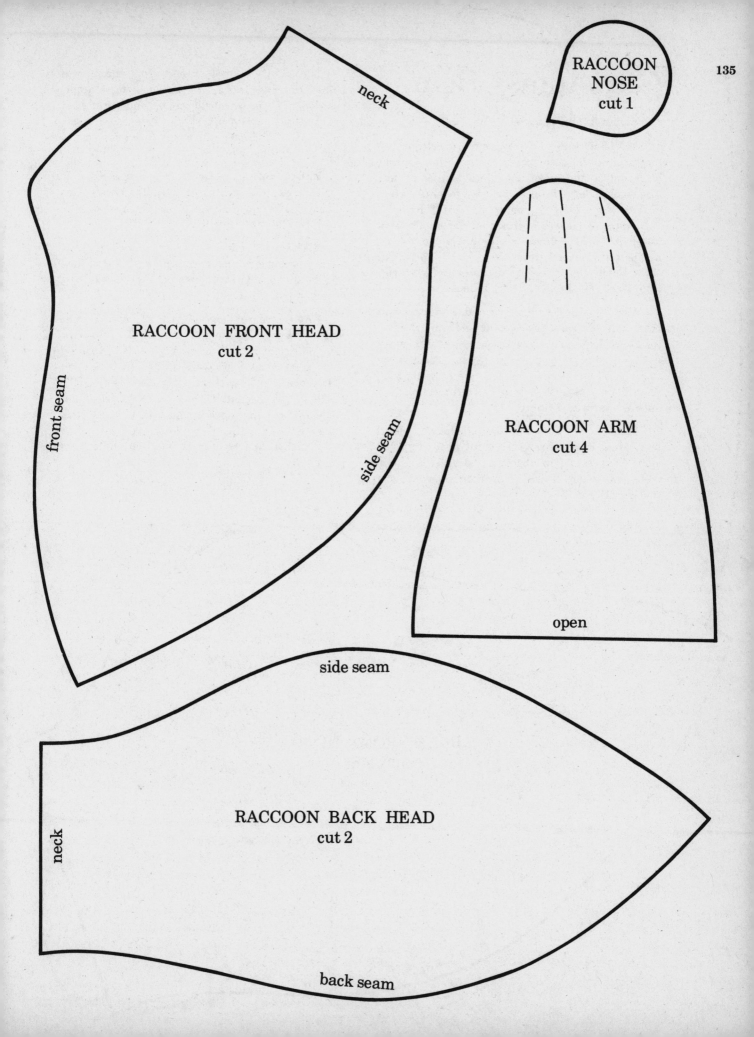

RACCOON NOSE
cut 1

135

neck

RACCOON FRONT HEAD
cut 2

front seam

side seam

RACCOON ARM
cut 4

open

side seam

RACCOON BACK HEAD
cut 2

neck

back seam

Christmasy Bear

SIZE   13″ high, seated.

MATERIALS   16″ x 28″ hand towels, 1 each bright pink and deep orange; scraps of rose fabric, black velvet and green felt; black leather button; rose embroidery floss; ¾ yard green-and-white striped ribbon; Dacron or polyester for stuffing.

Trace 10 pattern outlines on paper. Mark on towels and other fabrics with indelible pen, reversing patterns when fabrics have right and wrong sides. Remember to add seam allowances when cutting. Mark side, front, and back seams.

BODY   Cut 4 pink upper and 4 orange lower body pieces. Pin and sew the pink and orange halves together. Next pin and sew two body pieces together along the front seam, making sure the color-division line matches. Sew the other two pieces along back seam. Join pieces along side seams. Trim seam allowance and turn; stuff firmly.

HEAD   Cut 2 front heads and 2 back heads all from pink. Pin and sew two front heads together along front seam. Sew 2 backs along back seam. Join pieces along side seams. Trim seam allowance and turn; stuff.

Pin head to body, turning raw edges in as you go. Add more stuffing for a sturdy neck. Sew head to body with small stitches.

ARMS   Cut out 4 orange arms and 2 rose palms. Pin and sew arm seams, leaving straight ends open. Trim seam allowances and turn; stuff firmly about three-fourths full. Turn in and sew ends closed. Appliqué palms to arms. Sew arms to body at a slight angle.

LEGS   Cut 4 pink legs and 2 rose soles. Sew and stuff same as arms, with front and back seams at center. Appliqué rose soles. Sew legs to body, forward of the bottom seam line.

EARS   Cut out 2 pink and 2 orange ears. Seam, leaving straight ends open. Trim seam allowances and turn. Turn in ends and sew closed. Sew ears along top head seam.

FACE   See photograph. Cut 2 orange snout pieces; sew together along front seam. Turn to right side; pull tight and pin around bear's face, turning under raw edges. Sew with tiny stitches. Sew on button nose. With rose floss, outline a smiley mouth.

For eyes, cut out 1½″ velvet ovals, which includes ¼″ hem allowance; cut green felt lashes. Tack lashes to face; appliqué velvet ovals in place.

For bow, fit ribbon to bear's neck and sew in place.

BEAR FRONT HEAD
cut 2 pink

front seam

side seam

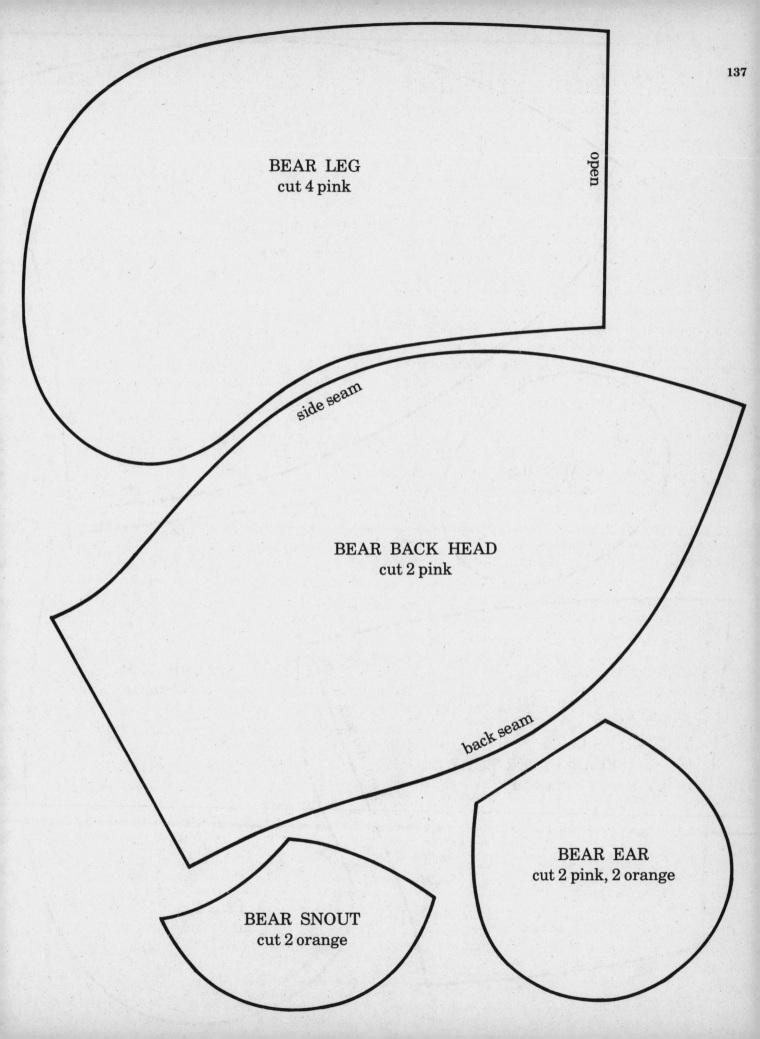

BEAR LEG
cut 4 pink

open

side seam

BEAR BACK HEAD
cut 2 pink

back seam

BEAR EAR
cut 2 pink, 2 orange

BEAR SNOUT
cut 2 orange

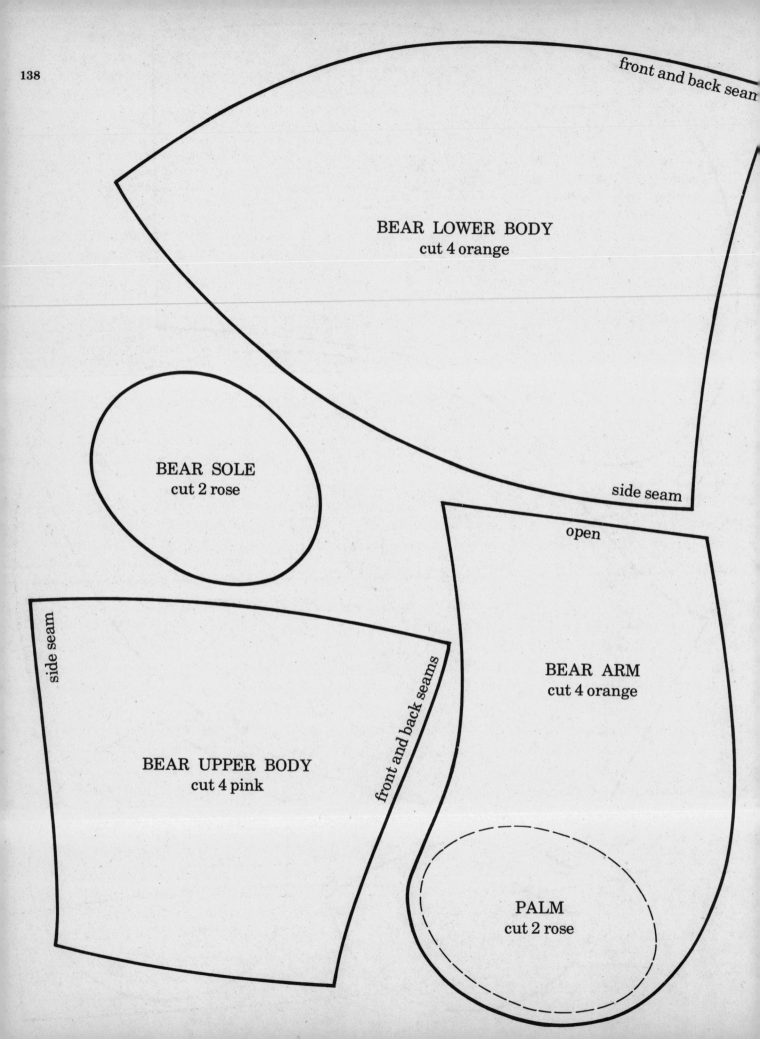

138

front and back seam

BEAR LOWER BODY
cut 4 orange

side seam

open

BEAR SOLE
cut 2 rose

side seam

front and back seams

BEAR ARM
cut 4 orange

BEAR UPPER BODY
cut 4 pink

PALM
cut 2 rose

Frog

SIZE 5"-long body.

MATERIALS ¼ yard of 36" bright green fabric and scrap of yellow print; Dacron or polyester stuffing; brown yarn; two ½" wood ball buttons; marking pens in black, brown and green.

Trace 3 pattern outlines and mark on fabrics, adding seam allowances when cutting.

BODY Cut 1 body each from solid green and yellow print fabrics, adding seam allowances. Make dart on each piece. With right sides facing, seam around body, leaving 2 spaces for stuffing and arms. Trim seam allowance and turn to right side. Stuff the body.

Mark arm patterns on wrong side of folded green fabric. Stitch seams, sewing carefully around fingers and leaving opening at shoulders. Cut out, trim seam allowance and turn to right side, poking fingers with a blunt knitting needle. Stuff the hand firmly. Bend arm at wrist and sew tuck closed with small stitches. Do not stuff past elbow.

Insert arms into body, centering seams on top and bottom. Sew arms and seam line of openings together with small hand stitches.

Mark leg pattern on wrong side of folded green fabric and stitch along seam line, sewing carefully around toes. Cut out, trim seam allowance and turn. This may be tricky, so use a sturdy safety pin to pull the fabric out to the right side and blunt knitting needle to push from the inside out. Stuff lightly. Turn raw ends in, shape into points and sew closed. Sew legs to body with points at under-dart seam, as in frog diagram. Fold legs, pin and sew small tucks at joints.

With marking pens, draw large roundish eyes on buttons. Sew to frog.

To embroider mouth, use two strands of brown yarn to chain-stitch a wide froggy grin.

FROG ARM
cut 4

open

open

FROG BODY
cut 1 green and 1 yellow

open

dart

Attaching legs to frog

FROG LEG
cut 4

open

Mother Rabbit

SIZE   12″ high.

MATERIALS   Pair of men's heavy ribbed brown stretch socks, size 10-13, without printing; scraps of orange and blue felt, print fabric, brown and orange yarn; two ¾″ black buttons; Dacron or polyester for washable stuffing.

See diagrams 1 and 2 for stuffing, sewing and cutting socks. Trace outline of diagram 3 on paper as pattern for hind legs. Add seam allowances when cutting legs and arms from second sock.

HEAD AND BODY   Stuff heel of one sock to form rabbit head. Make 5½″ cut from the toe down to form ears. Turn raw edges to inside and hand sew closed. Cut print ear linings to fit and appliqué to ears. Pinch together base of each ear and sew tightly; tack bases together.

Stuff body from the neck down until it is the height and roundness you like. Turn in cuff to form bottom. With double thread sew around cuff edge, draw thread tight and sew around circle several times.

FACE   See photograph. Sew orange-felt nose to face. Sew on buttons for eyes. Cut 2 blue-felt disks slightly larger than buttons. Cut a slit and small circle from each center and slip under button.

With brown yarn chain-stitch nose and mouth. Sew whiskers with blue thread.

ARMS AND LEGS   From second sock cut 2 arms 4¾″ in from toe, as in diagram 2. Turn in raw edges and hand sew, stuffing lightly as you go. Complete stuffing and sew ends closed. Pin and sew arms to body.

Cut 4 leg pieces from rest of sock, following pattern and slitting open ribbed top and adding small seam allowance. Sew seams and stuff lightly; sew openings. Pin legs to body so they support it and help rabbit sit up. Sew securely.

TAIL   For pompon, wind orange yarn around a 3″ x 5″ cardboard about 100 times. Cut yarn, slide off and tie with yarn. Trim into a 2½″ ball and sew to back.

Baby Rabbit

SIZE   6″ high.

MATERIALS   Pair of child's heavy blue stretch socks, size 6-8½; scrap of orange felt; orange and brown embroidery floss; blue yarn; two ½″ deep-blue buttons; Dacron or polyester for stuffing.

HEAD AND BODY   Stuff the heel section of one sock to form rabbit's head. Make a 4″ cut from the toe down for ears; turn in raw edges and sew. See diagram for Mother Rabbit. Pleat and tack together base of ears. Complete stuffing body. With double thread, sew around cuff edge; draw thread tight into a circle and sew around it several times.

FACE   Follow photograph. Appliqué heart-shaped orange felt nose; chain-stitch cleft lip and mouth with orange floss; stitch brown whiskers. Add button eyes.

From toe of other sock cut 2 arms 3″ long. Seam, stuff and sew to body; tack paws together.

Make a 2¼″ blue yarn pompon for tail, using the same method as for Mother Rabbit.

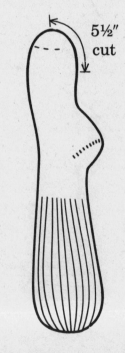

5½″ cut

Diagram 1. Slitting sock for rabbit's ears

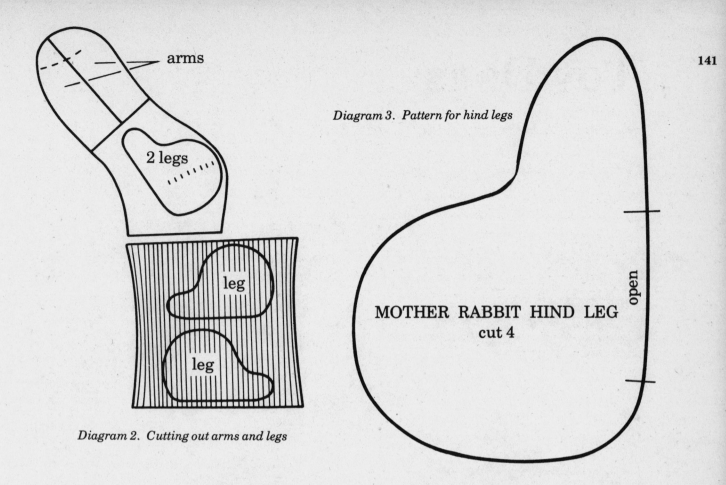

arms

2 legs

Diagram 3. Pattern for hind legs

leg

leg

open

MOTHER RABBIT HIND LEG
cut 4

Diagram 2. Cutting out arms and legs

Woolly Bear Caterpillar

SIZE   About 3½″ long.

MATERIALS   Rust-color and black wool yarn; 1 black and 2 green buttons; black button thread.

BODY   Make one rust-color and two black pompons as follows. For each, wind yarn around the short side of a 3″ x 5″ cardboard 110 times. Cut yarn and slide off cardboard. Tie it very tightly around the middle with a length of yarn. Trim pompons into uniform button shapes.

Thread doubled button thread on a long needle and make a large knot at end. Stick needle through center of one black pompon and anchor thread with a stitch. String on rust and other black pompon. Go back to where you started; sew black button a little below center for nose. With a new thread, sew on green button eyes. Tack on yarn antennae.

Toy Dogs

Any one of these seven sly little charmers will delight a child's heart.

General Directions

PATTERNS AND CUTTING see Construction Techniques, page 11.

SEWING See the directions for individual dogs.

STUFFING Use kapok, which is sold in 1-pound bags, for a smooth, moisture-resistant filling. A pound is enough for two or three of our small dogs; 1¼ pounds is needed for the big basset. Cotton batting also may be used. Stuff all dogs firmly, using a little kapok at a time; poke it into small areas with a pencil. Stuff legs and body areas above them with care so dogs stand upright.

Penelope the Poodle

MATERIALS ½ yard 36″ coral cotton; kapok; 6 yards coral bouclé upholstery fringe; scraps of blue cotton tweed, black grosgrain, yellow felt and red embroidery floss.

From cotton cut body sides, underbody, head front and sides, ears and tail. Pin and sew together two body sides along back seam from neck to A. Sew sides to underbody, matching necks, legs and A's. Fold and sew darts on legs of underbody; trim excess fabric. Trim seams, clip at corners; turn and stuff very firmly.

Pin and sew two head sides along top and back seam, from B to neck. Sew head front to sides, matching B's and necks. Trim seams; turn and stuff.

Pin head to body, turning it to a jaunty angle; add more stuffing if necessary. Turn under neck edge of head and sew firmly to body.

Seam pairs of ears; turn. Pleat and sew to head. Seam tail; turn and stuff; sew to back at A.

To sew on fringe, begin at a point about 1½″ above foot; wind and tack around each leg. Sew rows of fringe across shoulders and chest; continue around face, neck and top of head; add fringe to outside of ears. Sew fringe around hindquarters and to tip of tail.

For features, fit black grosgrain over nose and seam; appliqué in place. For eyes sew on blue ovals about ½″ wide and ⅞″ long; outline-stitch mouth with floss. Tack a tailored bow of yellow felt to poodle's head.

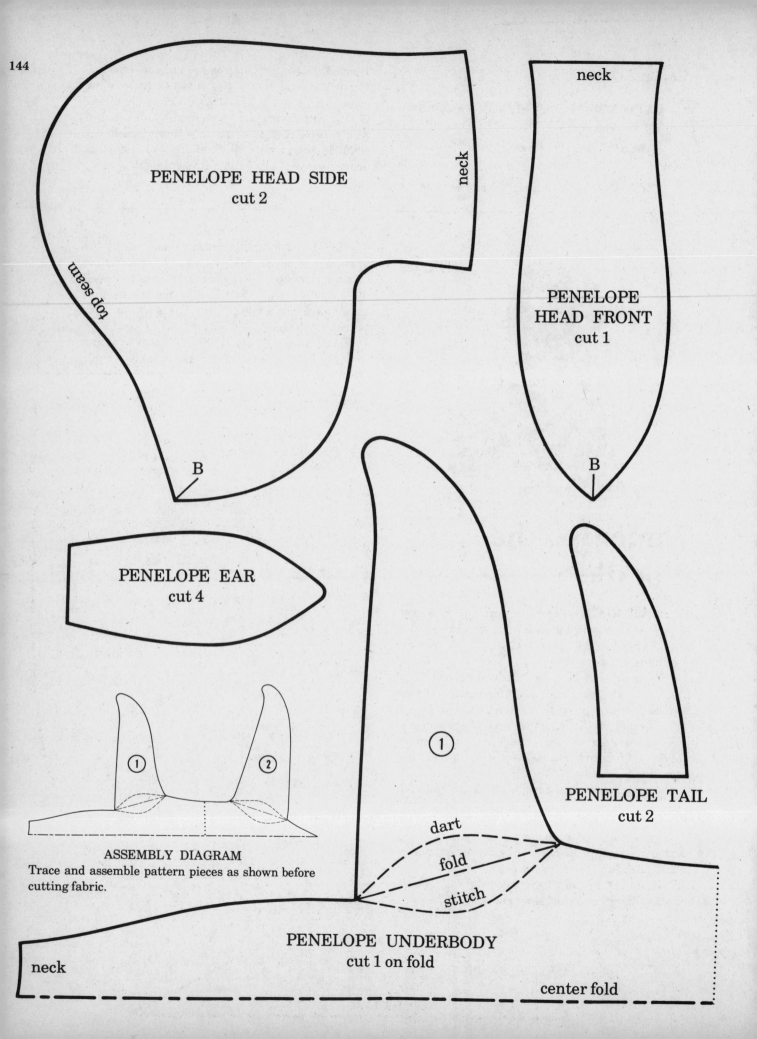

144

PENELOPE HEAD SIDE
cut 2

top seam

B

neck

neck

PENELOPE
HEAD FRONT
cut 1

B

PENELOPE EAR
cut 4

PENELOPE TAIL
cut 2

①

①

②

ASSEMBLY DIAGRAM
Trace and assemble pattern pieces as shown before
cutting fabric.

dart

fold

stitch

PENELOPE UNDERBODY
cut 1 on fold

neck

center fold

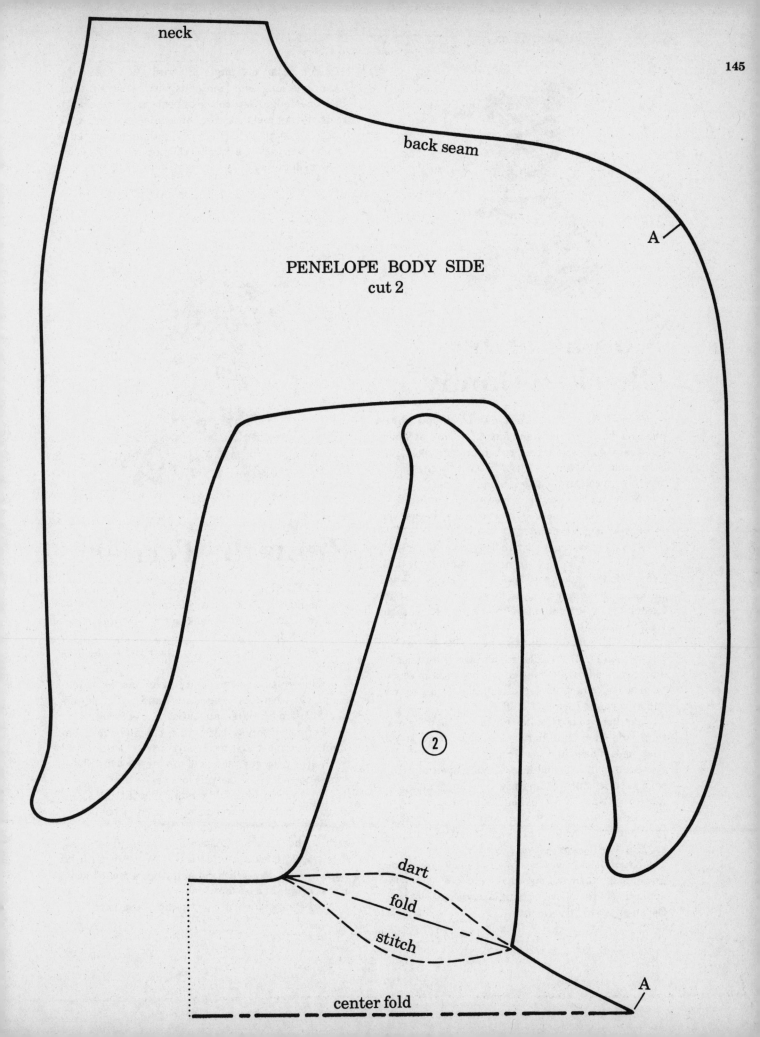

neck

back seam

A

PENELOPE BODY SIDE
cut 2

②

dart

fold

stitch

A

center fold

For collar, cut piqué into two 1½″-wide strips. Seam one long edge and ends with ¼″ seam; turn. Sew open edge. Sew collar to neck seam; turn down ends at front and tack. For boutonniere, cut a 1″ x 20″ red cotton strip. Fold crosswise; gather one long edge tightly and tack to bent pipe cleaner; fringe top edge. Tack to dog.

Montague the Checked Dandy

MATERIALS ½ yard 54″ black-and-white-checked lightweight wool; kapok; scraps of black grosgrain, gold wool fabric, red embroidery floss. *For collar and boutonniere:* 4″ x 12″ strip of white piqué, scrap of red cotton and a green pipe cleaner.

Matching checks on adjoining pattern pieces, cut body sides, underbody, head sides, backs and front, hind legs, ears and tail.

Pin and sew together two body sides along back seam from neck to A, at front seam from neck to B. Seam sides to underbody, matching A's, legs, B's and necks. Fold and sew darts on legs of underbody; trim excess fabric. Trim seams, clip at corners and turn; stuff firmly.

Pin and sew together two head sides from C to D. Sew head front to sides, matching D's and necks. Join two head backs along center back seam; sew to head sides, matching C's and necks. Trim seams, clip at corners; turn and stuff.

Pin head to body, following photograph for position. Add more stuffing if necessary; turn under neck edge of head and sew firmly.

Seam pairs of hind legs, leaving opening. Trim seams, turn, stuff leg and sew opening. Pin legs in place to balance weight of head, then sew.

Seam pairs of ears; trim and turn. Fold under raw edges and sew to head. Seam tail; trim, turn and stuff. Sew to back ½″ above A.

Follow nose pattern to cut black grosgrain. Tuck to fit, turn in raw edges and sew. For eyes, appliqué gold wool ovals about ¾″ wide and 1½″ long. Couch-stitch red floss mouth.

Rufus the Terrier

MATERIALS ½ yard 54″ gold lightweight wool fabric; kapok; 1 ounce gold mohair yarn; scraps of olive and pink felt, black satin and dull green embroidery floss.

Note: Rufus is made from the same pattern as Montague.

Following patterns and directions for Montague, cut wool fabric; sew, stuff and assemble terrier, following photograph for position of head.

For nose, follow pattern to cut olive felt; appliqué; outline-stitch mouth with floss. Follow terrier pattern to cut pink felt tongue; sew in place. Appliqué ⅝″ x ⅞″ satin ovals for eyes.

For tousled coat, fold mohair and thread a long length in a large yarn darning needle; beginning about 2″ above front foot, sew 1½″ loops to leg, hold with a short stitch. Continue covering front legs, chest, neck, back and hind legs. Cover tail with ½″ loops. Sew 2″ loops to head and face, a few 6″ loops across bridge of nose for whiskers.

Bend ears forward, curl tips and tack down.

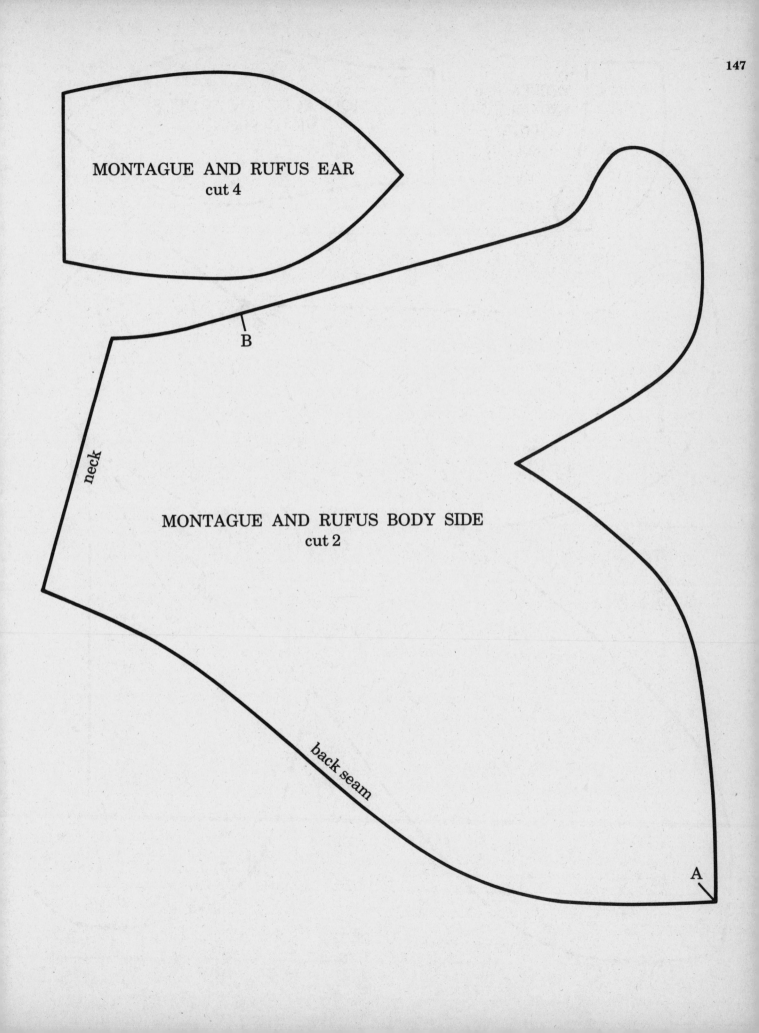

MONTAGUE AND RUFUS EAR
cut 4

B

neck

MONTAGUE AND RUFUS BODY SIDE
cut 2

back seam

A

148

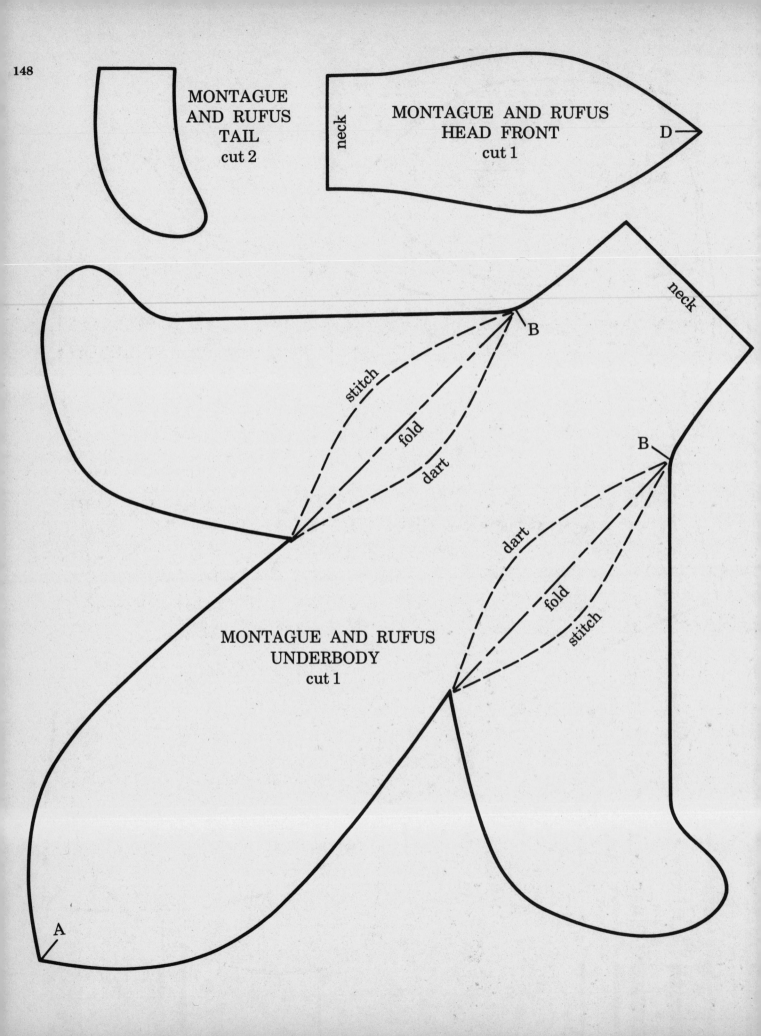

MONTAGUE
AND RUFUS
TAIL
cut 2

MONTAGUE AND RUFUS
HEAD FRONT
cut 1

neck

D

neck

B

stitch

fold

dart

B

dart

fold

stitch

MONTAGUE AND RUFUS
UNDERBODY
cut 1

A

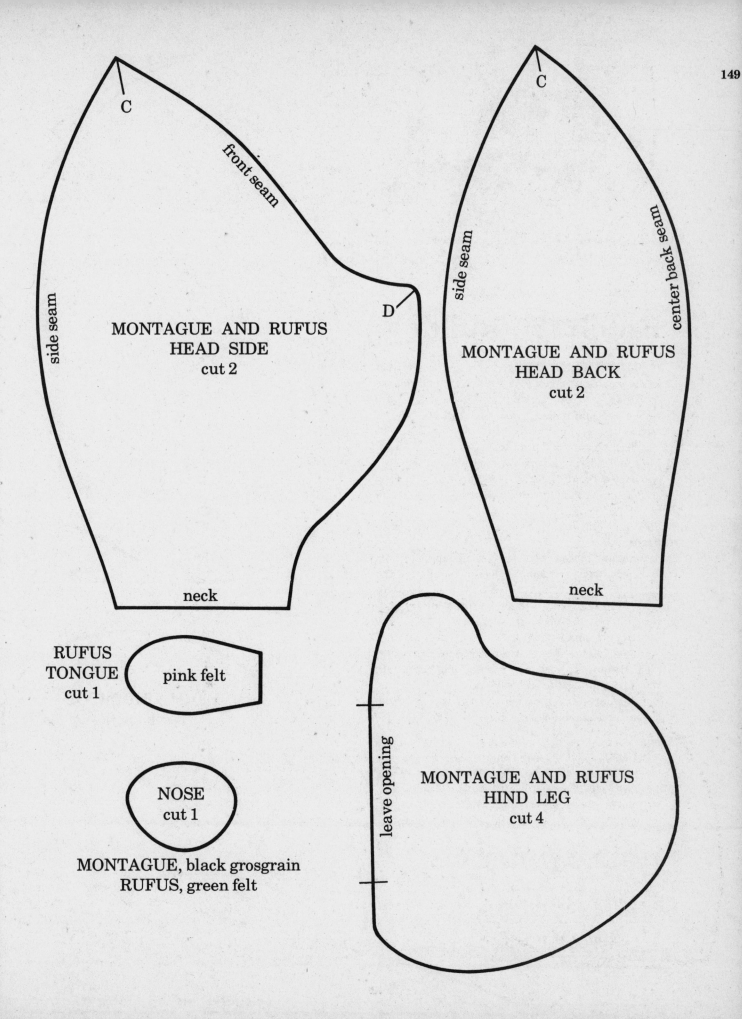

149

RUFUS
TONGUE
cut 1
pink felt

MONTAGUE AND RUFUS
HEAD SIDE
cut 2

front seam

side seam

C

D

neck

MONTAGUE AND RUFUS
HEAD BACK
cut 2

side seam

center back seam

C

neck

NOSE
cut 1

MONTAGUE, black grosgrain
RUFUS, green felt

MONTAGUE AND RUFUS
HIND LEG
cut 4

leave opening

Butch the Bulldog

MATERIALS *Butch:* ⅜ yard 54″ green wool jersey; kapok; scraps of pink felt and red embroidery floss; two ⅜″ gray pearl buttons; ⅜ yard lavender ribbon or seam binding. *Bone:* ¼ yard 36″ printed cotton; kapok.

From jersey cut body sides, underbody, head front and sides, ears and tail. Pin and sew together two body sides along back seam from neck to A. Sew sides to underbody, matching legs and A's. Fold and sew darts on legs of underbody. Trim seam allowance and clip at corners; turn. Stuff firmly with kapok.

Pin and sew two head sides along top seam from B to neck. Sew head front to sides, matching B's and necks. Trim seams; turn and stuff.

Pin head to body, adding more stuffing if necessary. Turn under neck edge of head and sew firmly to body with small stitches.

Seam pairs of ears; turn. Turn in raw edges; pleat and sew to head as in photograph. Seam tail; turn and stuff. Sew to back at A.

Appliqué a ½″ pink felt disk for nose; outline-stitch mouth with floss; sew on buttons for eyes. Tie ribbon around neck.

BONE Cut 2 pieces for bone. Seam pieces, leaving an opening for stuffing. Turn and stuff; sew opening closed.

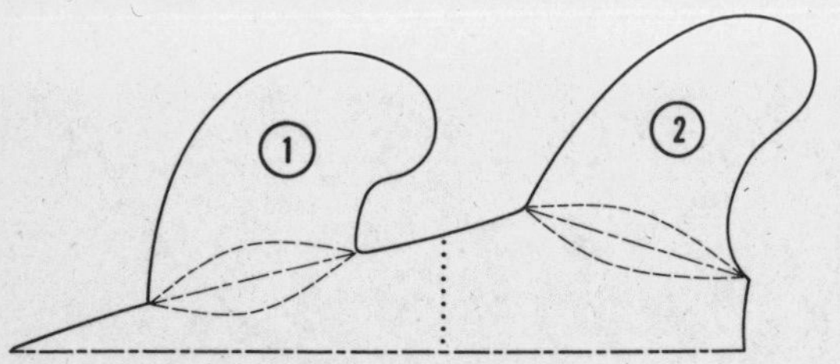

ASSEMBLY DIAGRAM
Trace and assemble pattern pieces as shown before cutting fabric.

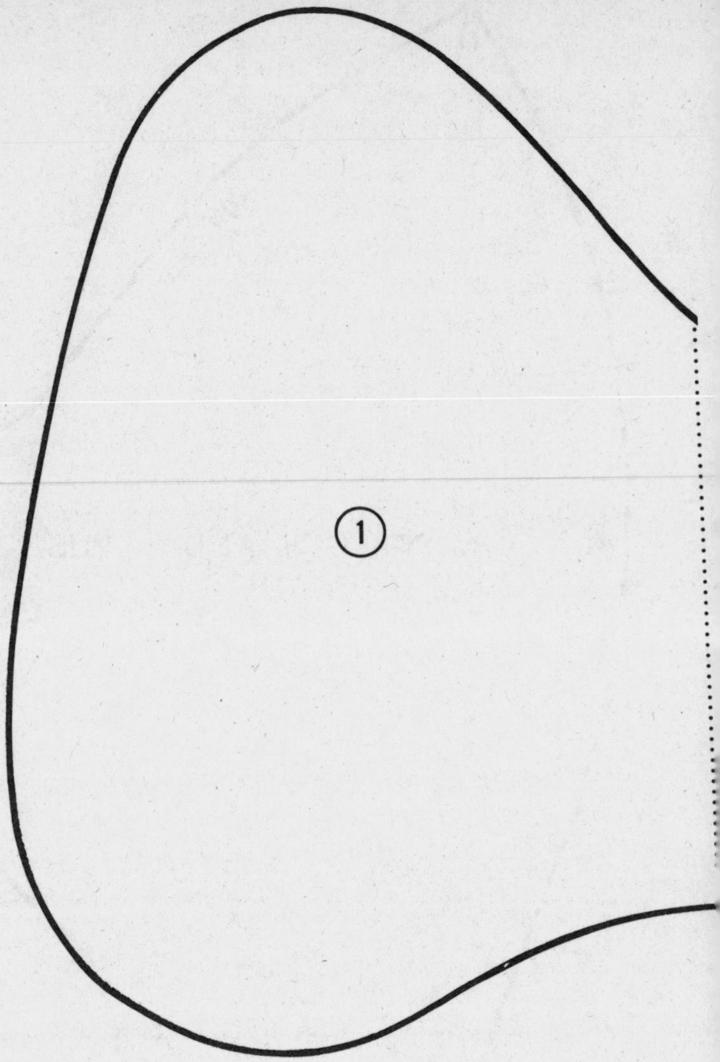

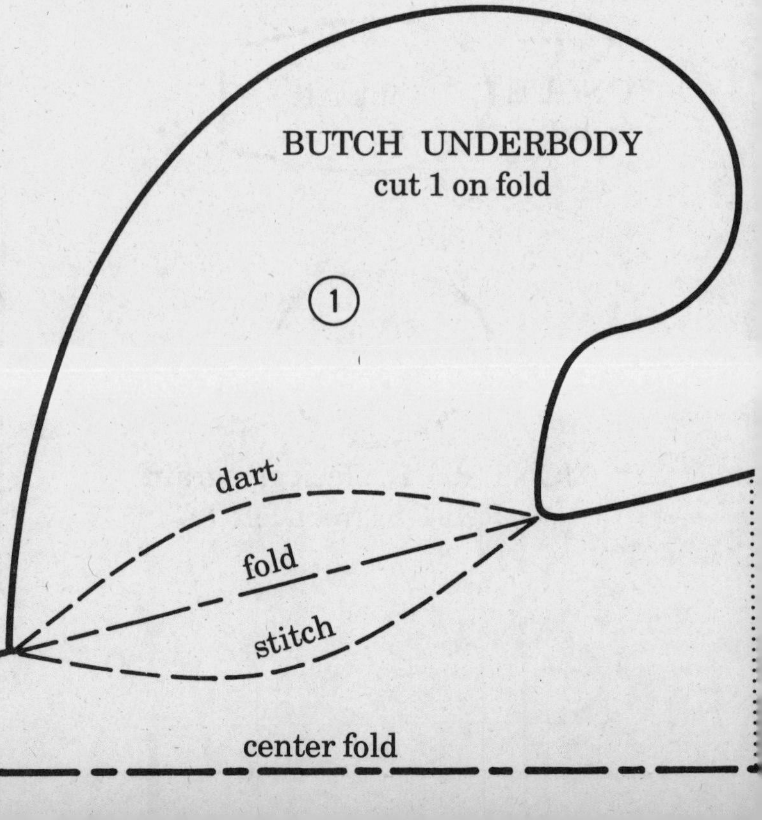

① ②

①

BUTCH UNDERBODY
cut 1 on fold

①

dart

fold

stitch

center fold

A

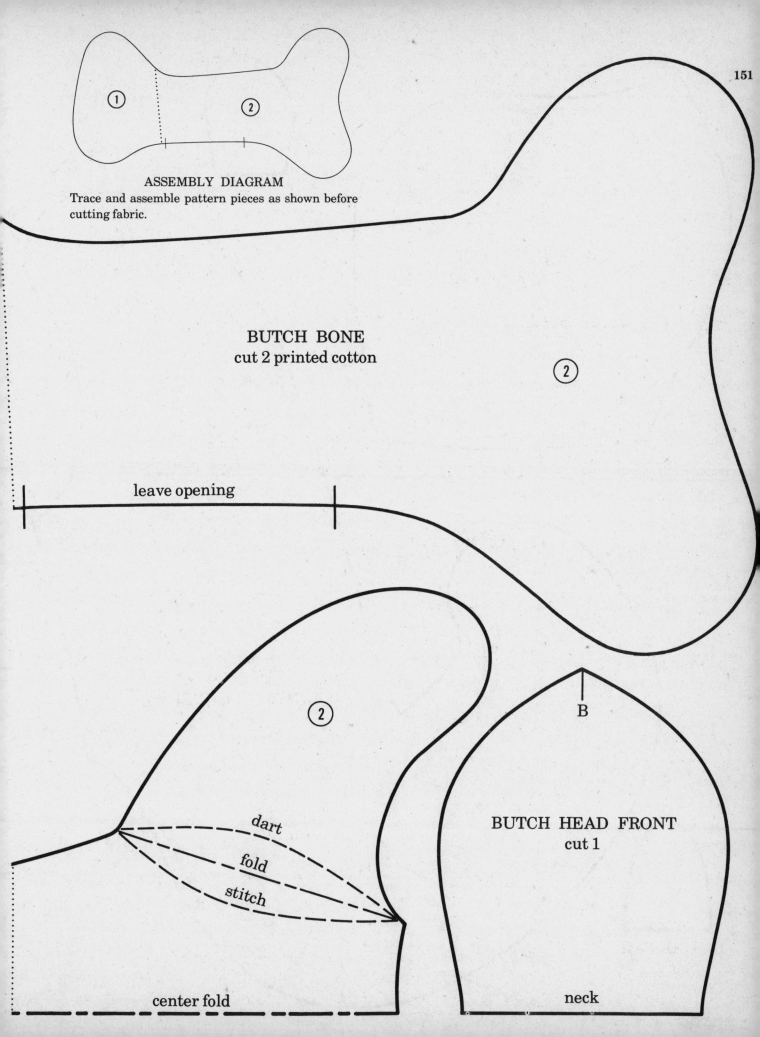

ASSEMBLY DIAGRAM
Trace and assemble pattern pieces as shown before cutting fabric.

① ②

BUTCH BONE
cut 2 printed cotton

②

leave opening

②

dart

fold

stitch

B

BUTCH HEAD FRONT
cut 1

center fold

neck

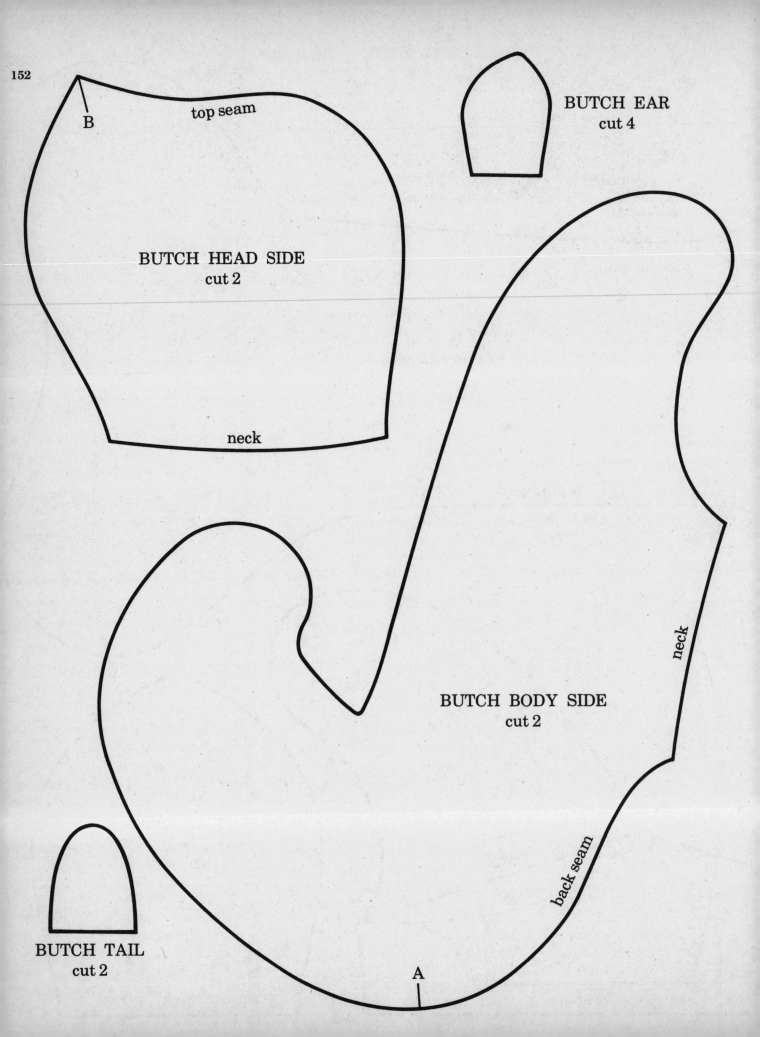

152

B

top seam

BUTCH EAR
cut 4

BUTCH HEAD SIDE
cut 2

neck

neck

BUTCH BODY SIDE
cut 2

back seam

BUTCH TAIL
cut 2

A

Pin and sew together two head sides along top seam from C to D. Sew head front to sides, matching C's and necks. Sew together head backs along center back seam; join to sides at side seams. Trim seam allowance; turn and stuff. Pin head to body, following photograph; turn under neck edges of head and sew securely.

Sew a calico ear to each terry ear; trim seam; turn. Turn under raw edges and pleat; sew to head.

Sew together terry tails; trim seam; turn and stuff lightly. Sew to A and along back seam. Seam calico tip pieces; turn; slip over tail and sew.

For eye patch cut a 3″ calico disk. Turn under edges and appliqué. For nose cut a 2″ grosgrain disk. Fit and seam; turn under edge and sew. For closed eyes cut grosgrain crescents ¾″ deep and 3″ long. Turn under edges; appliqué to each side of top center seam.

Willie the Terry Cloth Pooch

MATERIALS 16″ x 30″ blue terry towel; ⅛ yard blue-and-yellow calico; kapok; scrap of black grosgrain.

From terry cloth cut body sides, underbody, head sides, backs and front, two ears and two tails. From calico cut two ears and two 3″ tips for tail (following pattern).

Pin and sew together two body sides along back seam from A to neck and at front seam from neck to B. Sew sides to underbody, matching A's, legs and B's. Trim seam allowance, clip at B and turn. Stuff body.

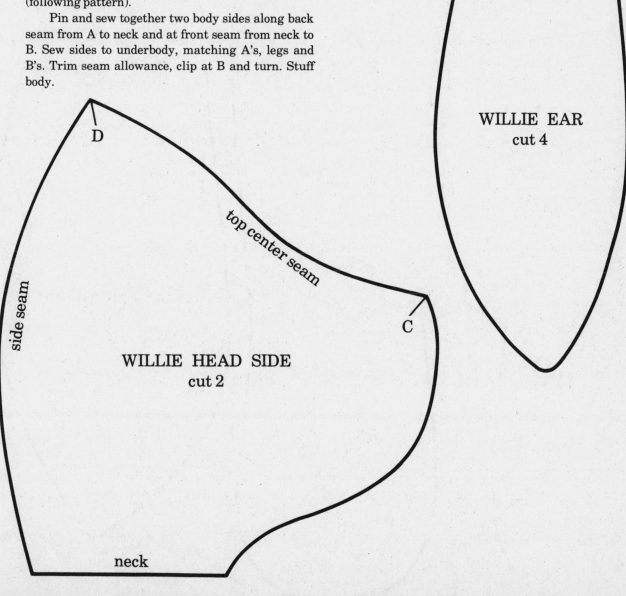

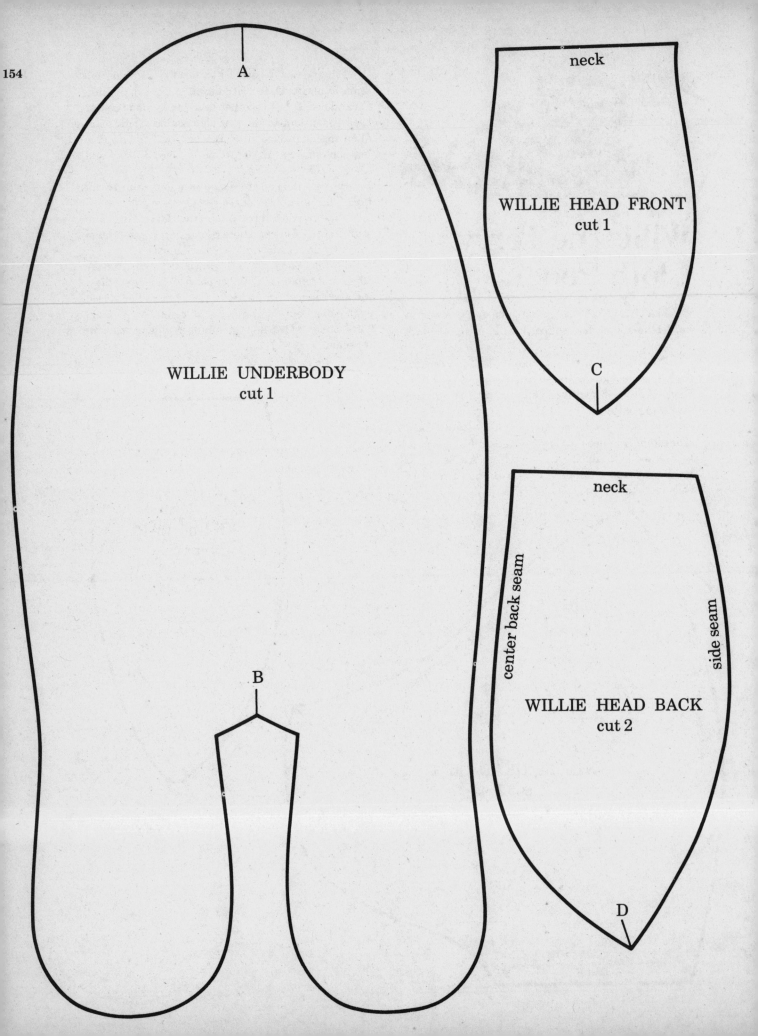

154

WILLIE UNDERBODY
cut 1

A

B

WILLIE HEAD FRONT
cut 1

neck

C

WILLIE HEAD BACK
cut 2

neck

center back seam

side seam

D

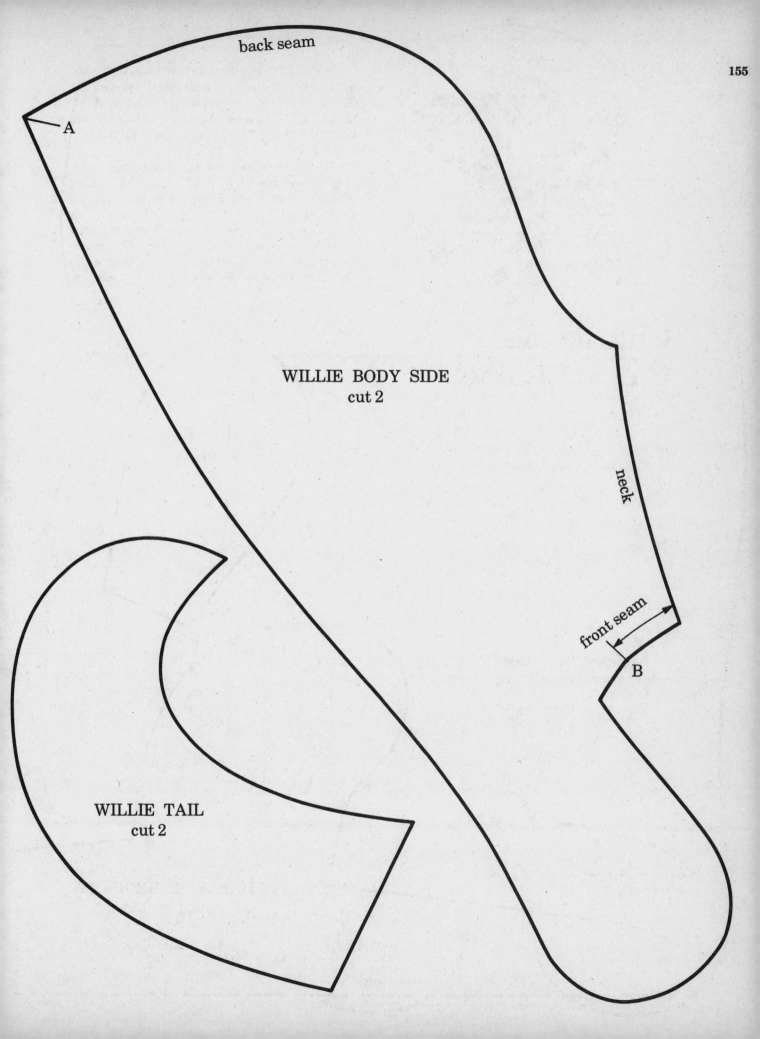

back seam

A

155

WILLIE BODY SIDE
cut 2

neck

front seam

B

WILLIE TAIL
cut 2

back seam

Pin and sew together two sides along back seam from A to B. Sew sides to underbody, matching A's, legs and B's; leave opening on one side from B to C for stuffing. Trim seam allowance, clip corners and turn. Stuff firmly. Turn in edges of opening and overcast.

Seam pairs of ears, leaving straight edges open; turn. Turn in raw edges, pleat ears and sew to head ¼″ from center seam. Seam tail pieces; turn and stuff. Sew to B.

For eyes, appliqué ⅝″ x ¾″ black grosgrain ovals. For nose, sew button to A. For collar, cut ½″ gold felt strip to fit neck; tack in place. Trim with a 1⅛″ scalloped yellow felt flower with a ½″ gold center.

Charlie the Calico Canine

MATERIALS ⅝ yard 36″ red-and-yellow calico; kapok; scraps of black grosgrain, gold and yellow felt; shiny black ½″ button with shank.

From calico cut body sides, underbody, ears and tail.

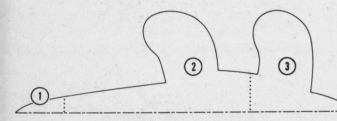

ASSEMBLY DIAGRAM
Trace and assemble pattern pieces as shown before cutting fabric.

CHARLIE EAR
cut 4

A

①

②

CHARLIE UNDERBODY
cut 1 on fold

center fold

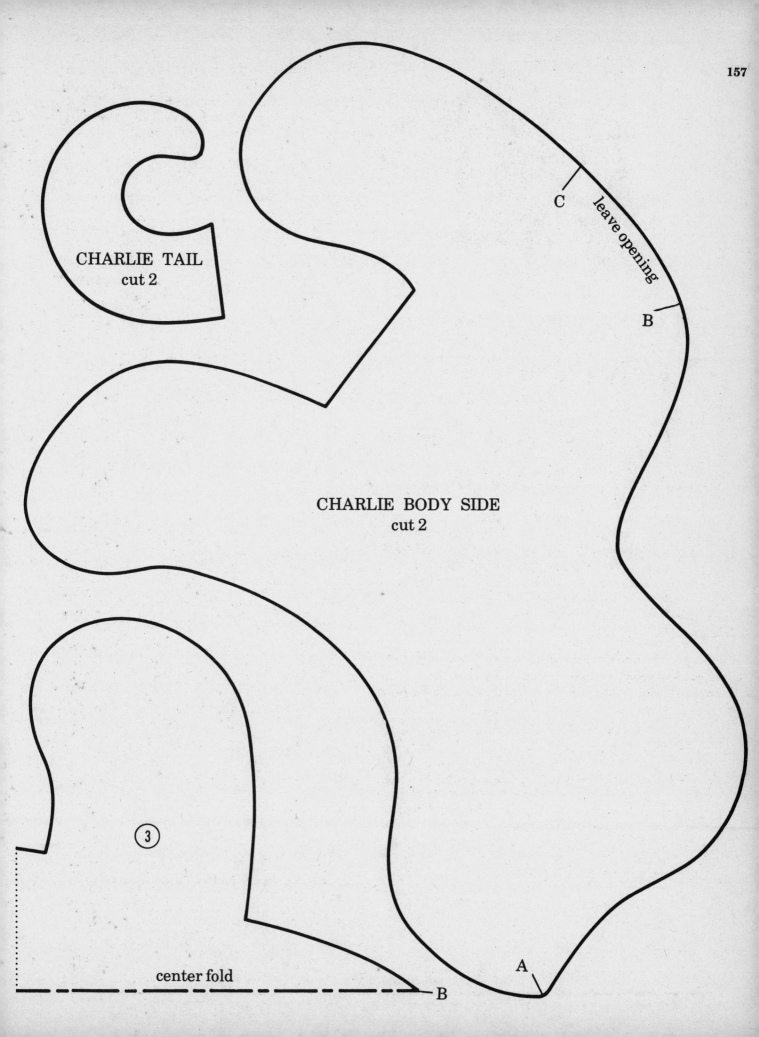

CHARLIE TAIL
cut 2

CHARLIE BODY SIDE
cut 2

leave opening

C

B

③

A

center fold

B

Basil the Basset

MATERIALS 36″ cotton, 1¼ yards blue-green and ¼ yard coral (for coat); kapok; scraps of dark green velvet, orange pin-dotted cotton and red embroidery floss; 1½ yards dark green 1″-wide bias tape; 1 yard dark green rickrack; 1 snap.

From green cotton cut body sides, underbody, legs, ears and tail.

Pin and sew together two body sides along back seam from A to B. Seam sides to underbody from A to B, leaving an opening. Trim seams; turn. Stuff firmly and sew opening closed.

Sew together pairs of legs, leaving an opening. Trim, turn and stuff; sew opening closed. Pin legs to body so they support it; sew securely in place.

Sew together pairs of ears, leaving straight ends open; trim and turn. Fold in raw edges; pleat and sew to head about ¼″ from center seam. Sew together tail pieces; trim and turn. Stuff and sew to B on back.

For nose, cut a dotted oval 2¾″ x 3½″. Fit over nose and seam. Turn under raw edges ¼″ and sew in place. Appliqué 1½″ x 2″ velvet ovals for eyes. Outline-stitch red floss mouth.

COAT From coral cotton cut 4 pieces, following pattern. Pin and stitch pairs together along top seam. Wrong sides together, baste together along outer edge. Bind edge with tape then stitch rickrack around it. For strap under body, cut two 12″ lengths of tape; topstitch together. Sew one end of strap to coat; fasten other with snap.

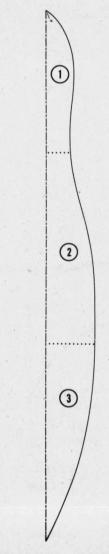

ASSEMBLY DIAGRAM
Trace and assemble pattern pieces as shown before cutting fabric.

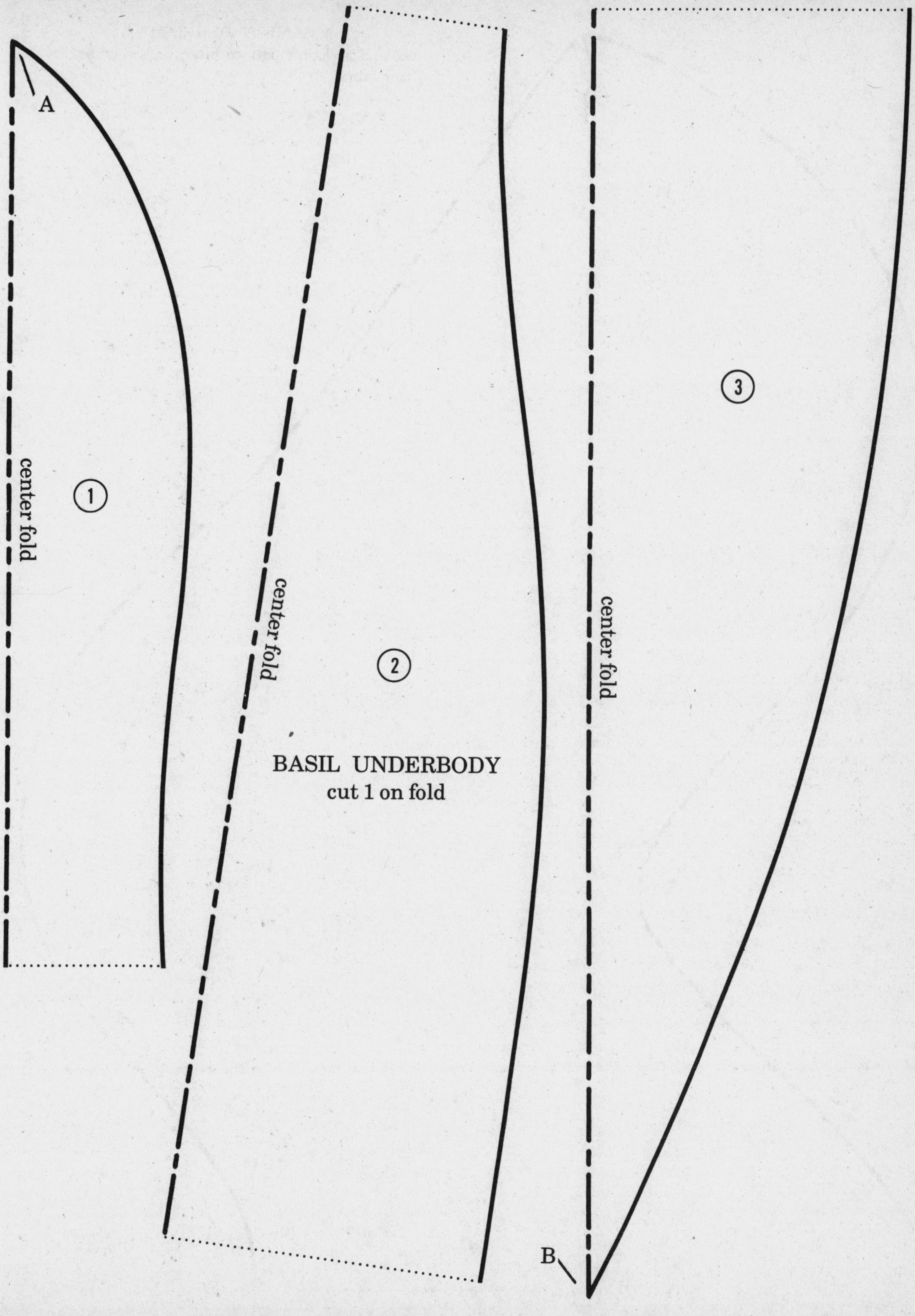

A

center fold

① 1

center fold

② 2

BASIL UNDERBODY
cut 1 on fold

center fold

③ 3

B

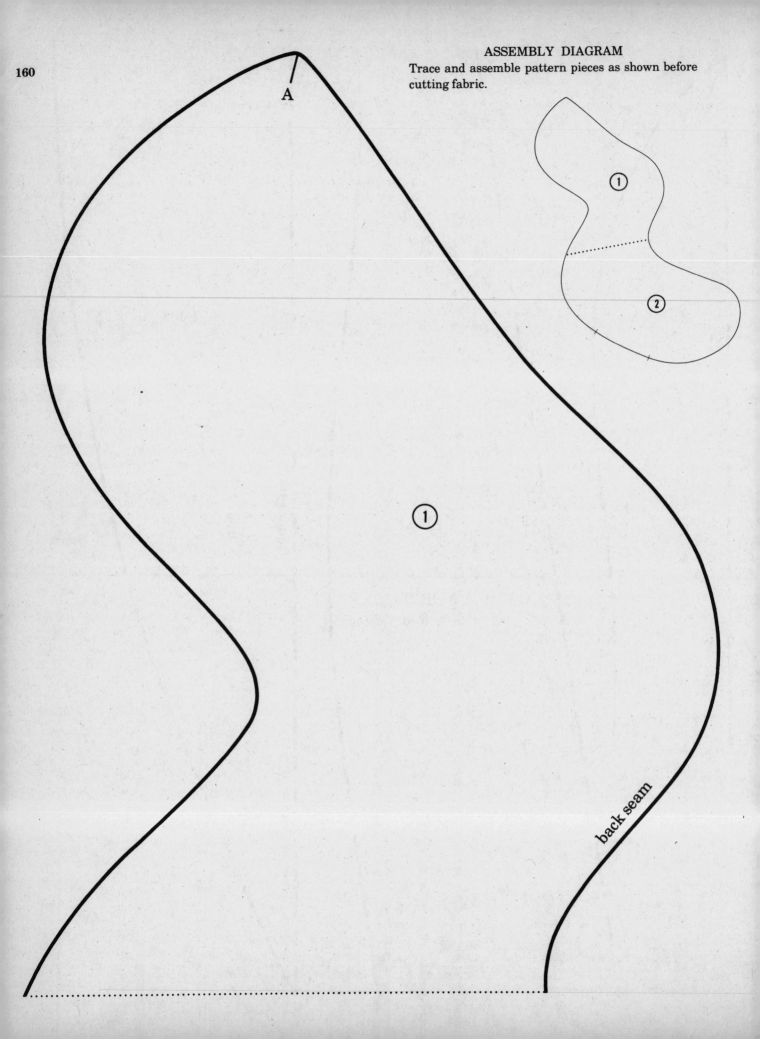

ASSEMBLY DIAGRAM
Trace and assemble pattern pieces as shown before
cutting fabric.

A

①

②

①

back seam

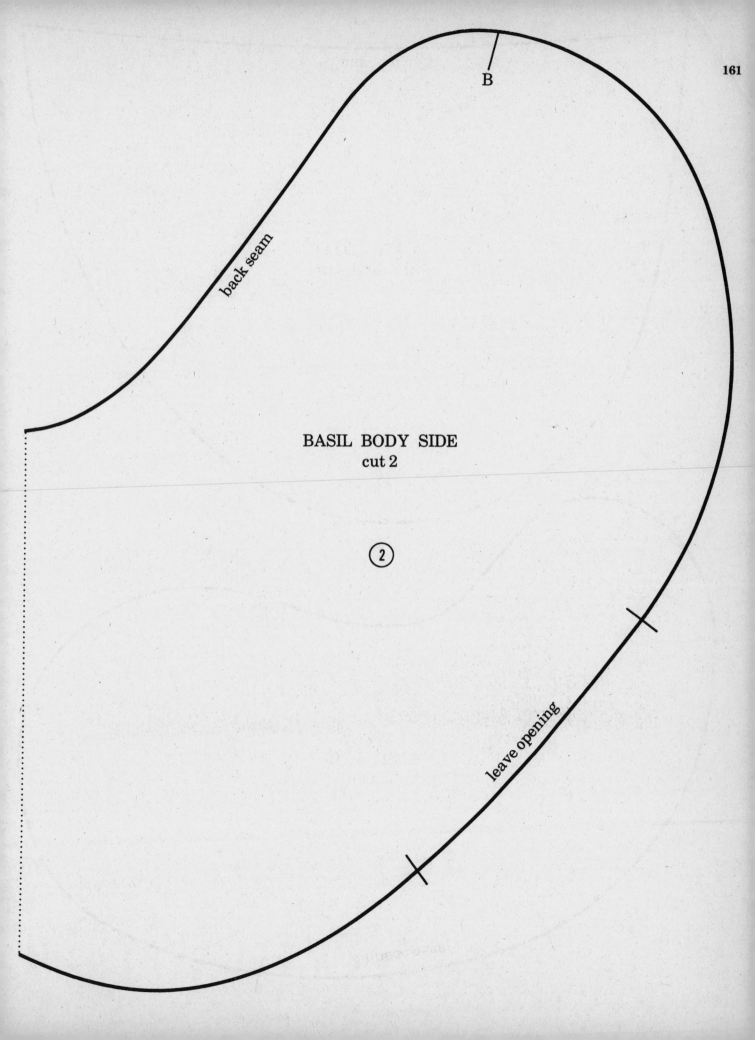

161

B

back seam

BASIL BODY SIDE
cut 2

②

leave opening

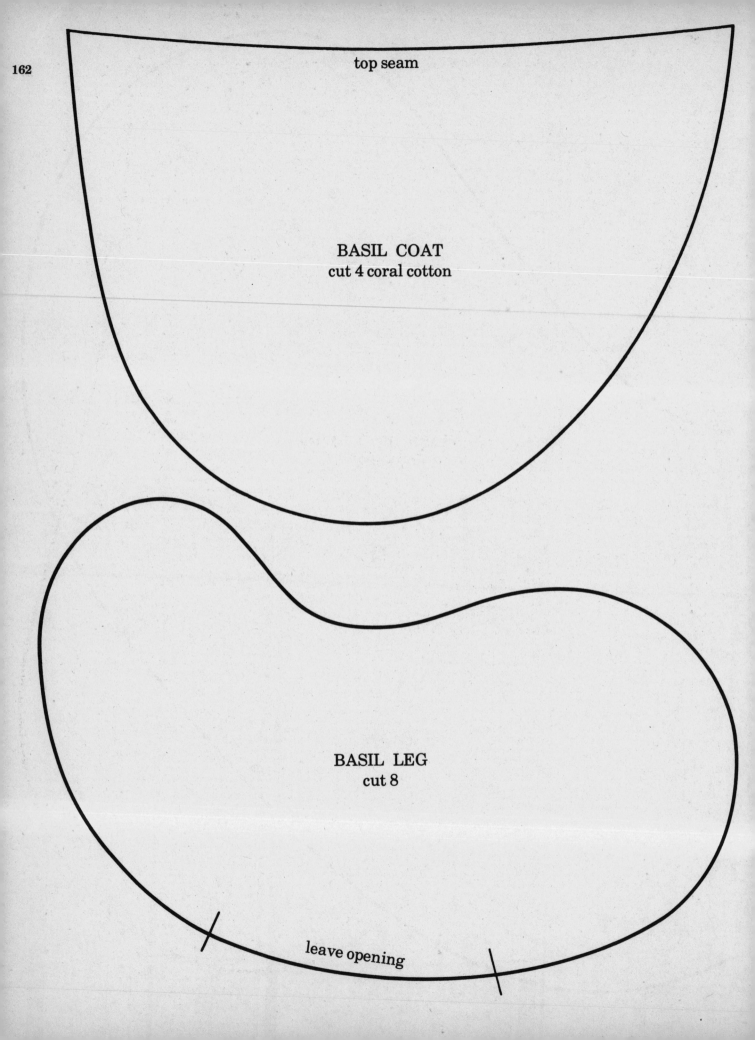

162

top seam

BASIL COAT
cut 4 coral cotton

BASIL LEG
cut 8

leave opening

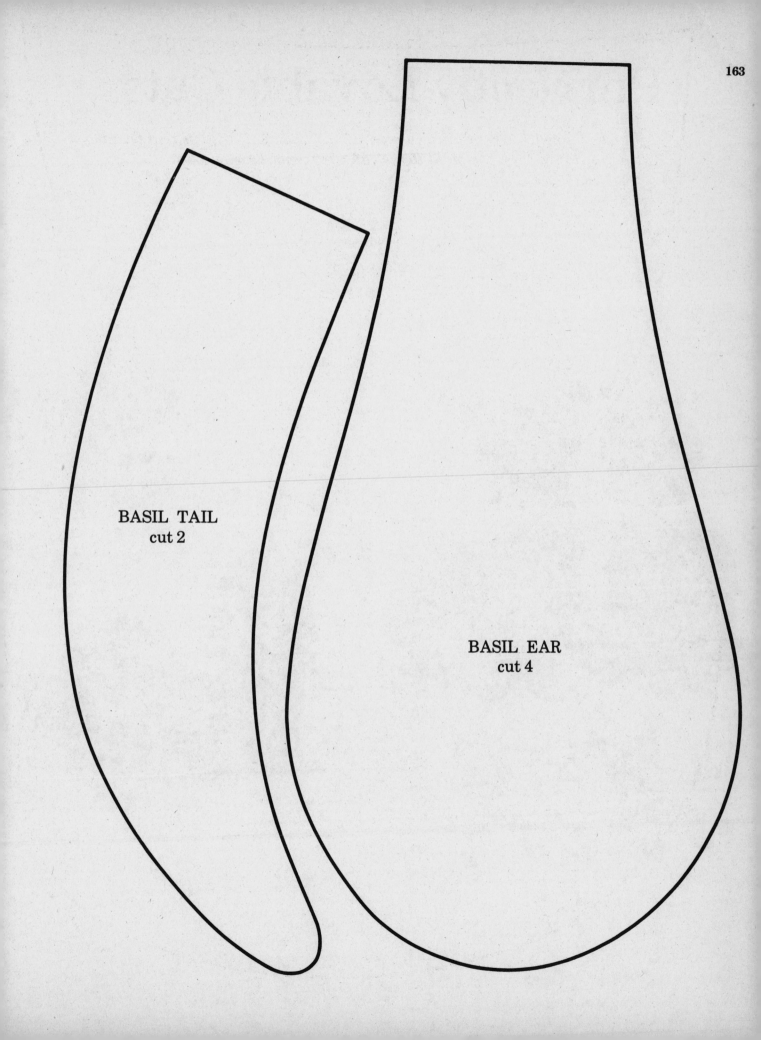

BASIL TAIL
cut 2

BASIL EAR
cut 4

Purrfectly Lovable Cats

Eight new feline friends—Calico Carrie, Ginger Joe, their triplets and Cuddle Kitten are stuffed toys; the plaid twins can also be used as pillows.

Triplet Kittens

Note: One pattern is used to make all three. For a variety of poses, tilt head to right or left.

MATERIALS *For 3 kittens:* 2 pairs child's synthetic blend stretch knee socks, size 9–11; matching polyester thread; polyester fiber stuffing; scraps of felt, blue print fabric, ribbon and embroidery floss; white glue.

Each sock makes one kitten if cut as follows: cut apart down center front; working around ankle, separate foot from leg. Use foot for underbody and ears, leg for other pieces.

Follow 5 patterns and cut kittens from socks, adding ¼″ seam allowance. Following photographs for shapes, cut felt noses and eyes; cut print pieces.

Right sides together, baste, then stitch side pieces along back seam from neck to A. Stitch underbody to sides from neck, along legs and to A. Clip seams and turn; stuff through open neck. Baste and sew together 2 head pieces at center seam for front; sew 2 more pieces at center for back; join at sides. Turn, stuff and pin to neck. Turn under head edges and sew, adding more stuffing if needed.

Seam ears to linings and turn. Pin to head about ¼″ from center seam, cupping ears. Turn in raw edges and sew. Seam tail pieces and stuff. Sew at point A. To bring legs closer to center of underbody, make a tuck along broken lines on underbody.

Glue felt pupils to eyes; sew on eyes and noses. Outline-stitch floss mouths and make 1 long stitch for each whisker. Appliqué blue print heart and tail stripes; add ribbon collars to two kittens.

cutting kitten from sock

cuts

heel

leg

toe

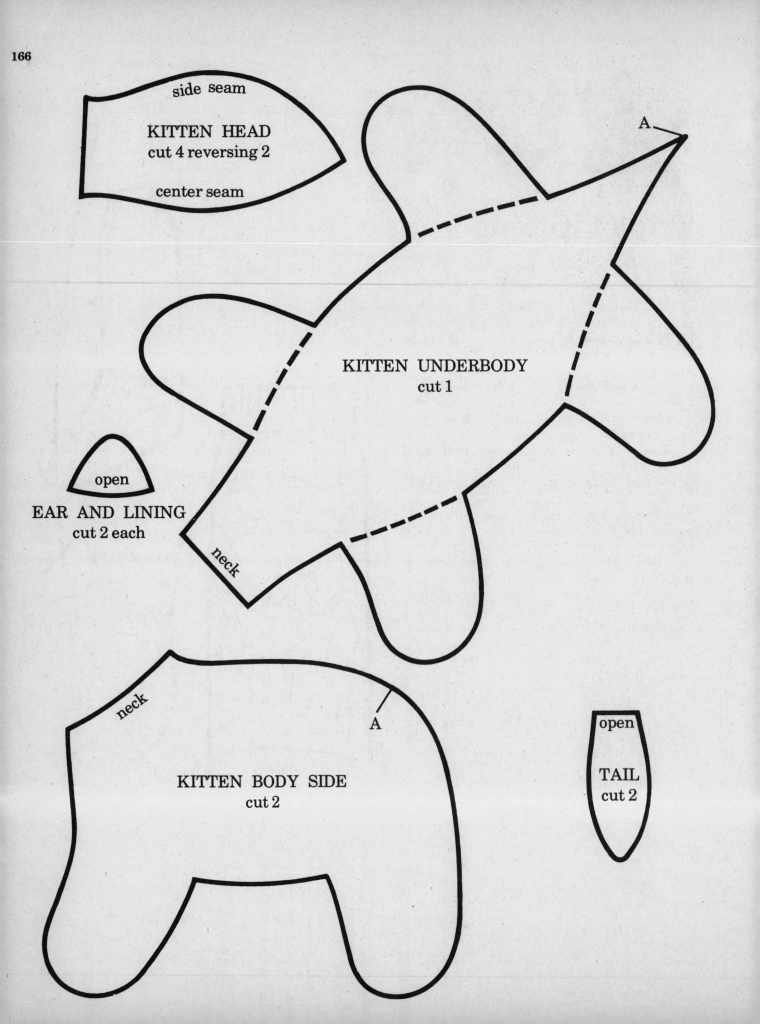

side seam

KITTEN HEAD
cut 4 reversing 2

center seam

A

KITTEN UNDERBODY
cut 1

open

EAR AND LINING
cut 2 each

neck

neck

A

KITTEN BODY SIDE
cut 2

open

TAIL
cut 2

Calico Carrie

Ginger Joe

Ginger Joe

MATERIALS ¾ yard 45″-wide orange stretch terry cloth; matching polyester thread; polyester fiber stuffing; scraps of black, blue and green felt; blue and yellow embroidery floss; yellow 13″ cat collar.

Follow 5 patterns and cut cat from terry, adding ½″ seam allowance. Following photograph, cut felt heart-shaped blue nose and black and green oval eye pieces.

Right sides together, stitch body sides along back seam from neck to A. Stitch center body to sides from neck, along legs, to A. Trim and clip seams. Turn and stuff through open neck.

Seam 2 head pieces at center for front and 2 more for back; join at side seams. Turn and stuff. Pin to body; turn under head edges and sew to neck, adding stuffing if needed. Seam ear pieces, leaving base edges open. Trim and turn. Turn in raw edges and sew to head about 1¼″ from center seam. Stitch tail pieces and turn; stuff and sew at A.

Glue pupils to eyes; sew on eyes and nose (give Ginger a cross-eyed or a straight-eyed look). Outline-stitch blue floss mouth and make 1 long stitch for each yellow whisker. Add collar.

open

GINGER JOE TAIL
cut 2

168

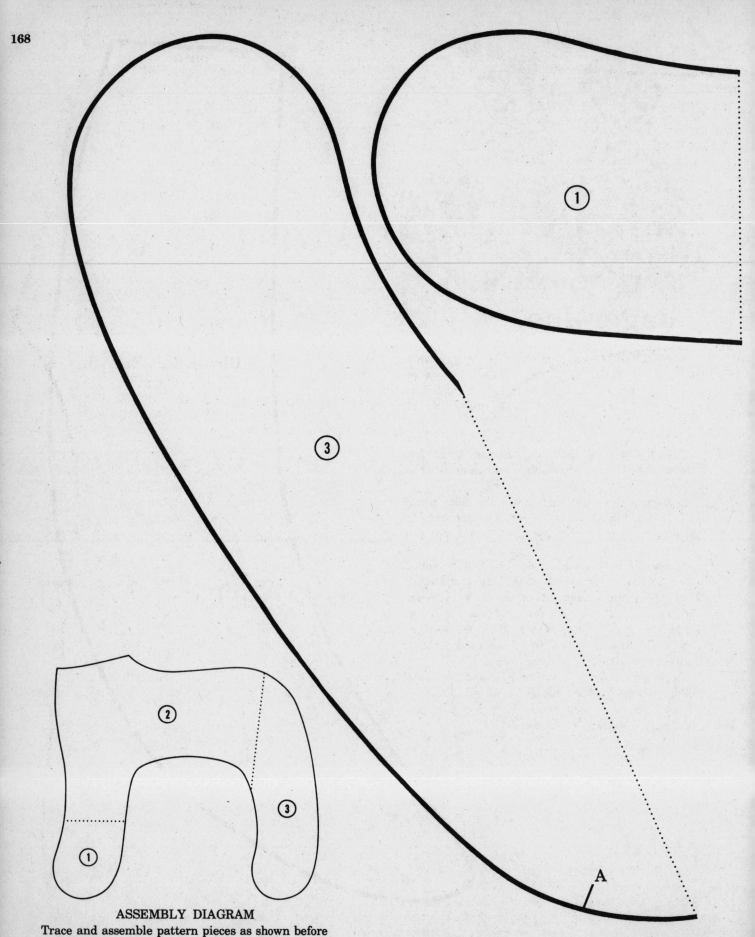

ASSEMBLY DIAGRAM
Trace and assemble pattern pieces as shown before cutting fabric.

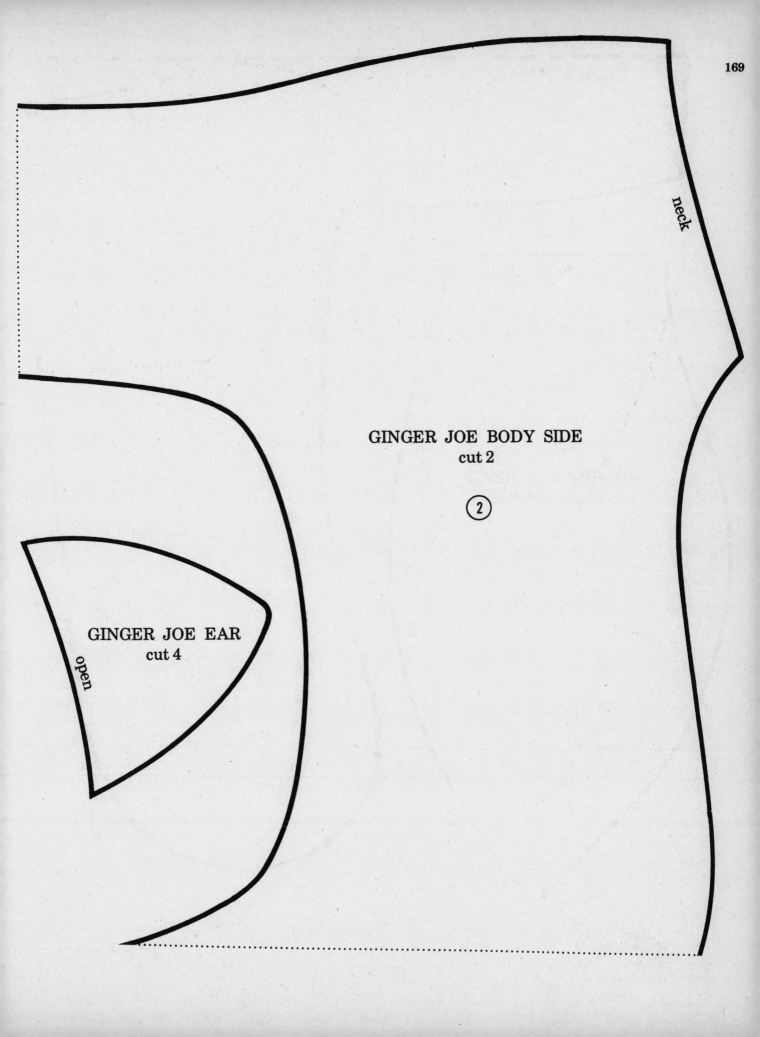

neck

GINGER JOE BODY SIDE
cut 2

②

GINGER JOE EAR
cut 4

open

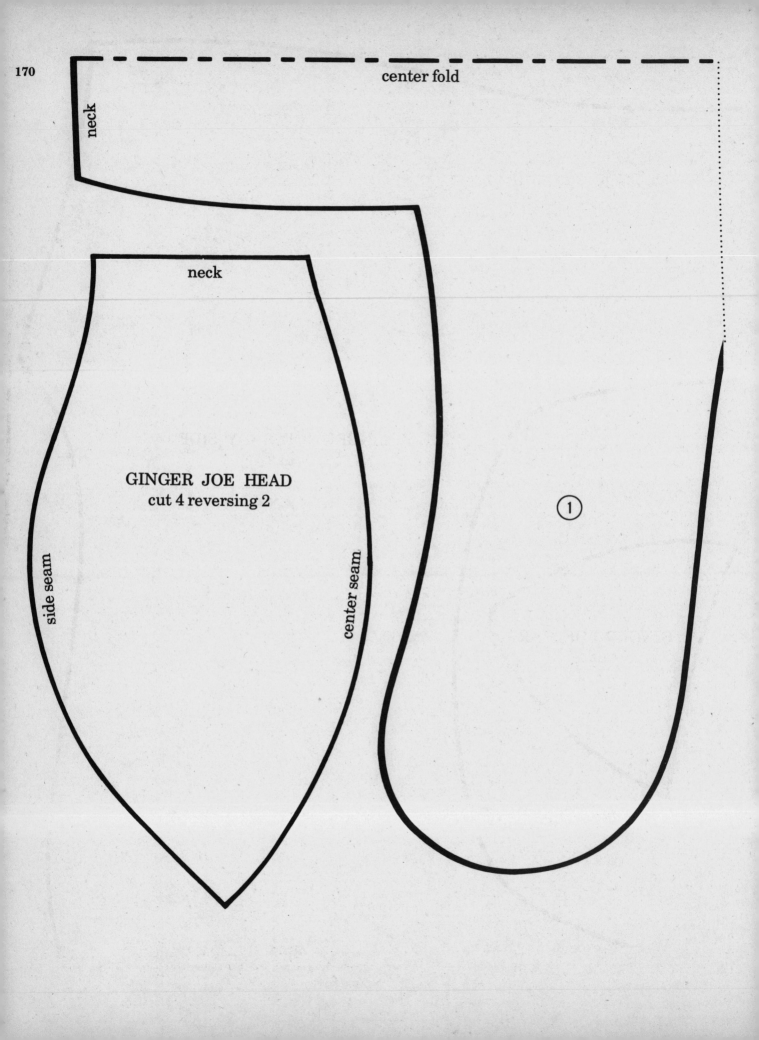

center fold

neck

neck

GINGER JOE HEAD
cut 4 reversing 2

side seam

center seam

① 1

center fold

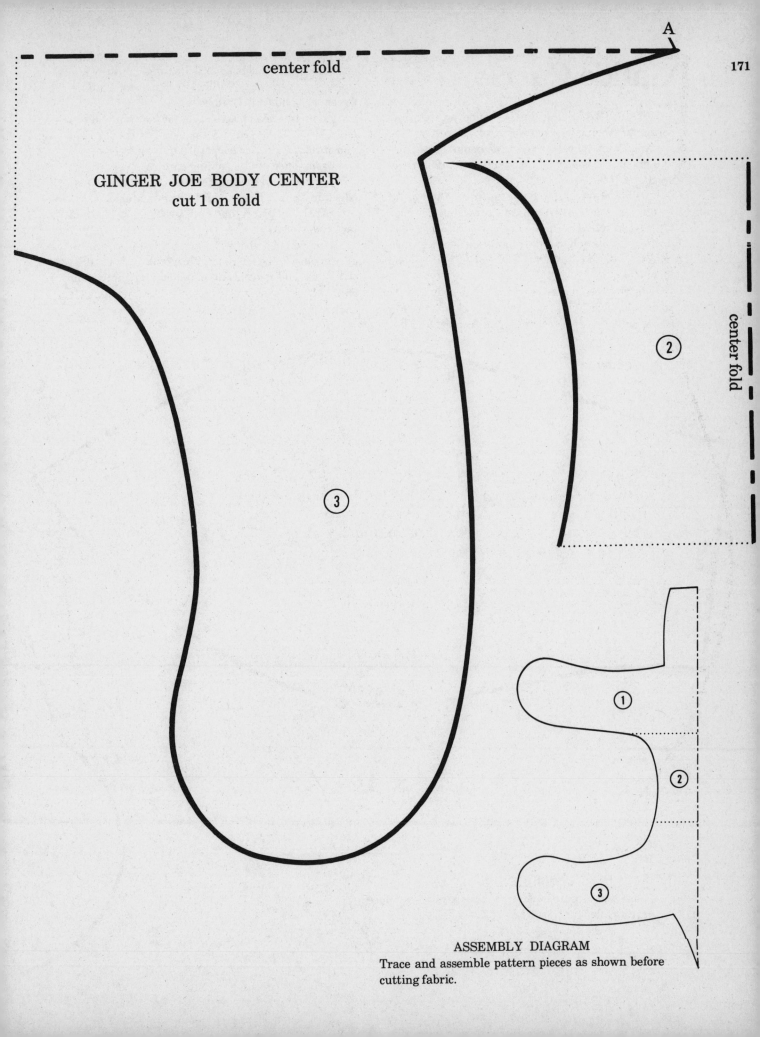

center fold

A

GINGER JOE BODY CENTER
cut 1 on fold

②

③

center fold

①

②

③

ASSEMBLY DIAGRAM
Trace and assemble pattern pieces as shown before cutting fabric.

Calico Carrie

MATERIALS ⅝ yard 44″-wide printed blue cotton; matching polyester thread; polyester fiber stuffing; scraps of yellow fabric; deep pink, turquoise and green felt; deep pink and white floss; 12″ strip of crocheted lace.

Follow 6 patterns and cut cat from cotton print, adding ½″ seam allowance and reversing patterns for corresponding pairs. Cut yellow ear linings. Following photograph, cut deep pink felt heart-shaped nose; cut 1¼″-long teardrop green pieces and ⅞″-long turquoise ovals for eyes.

Right sides together, pin and stitch body back to body sides from neck to B, along back seams. Pin underbody to body sides, matching A's, feet and B's, easing to fit around base. Stitch seams carefully and reinforce seams at top of legs. Trim seams, clip between legs and turn. Stuff body.

Seam two head pieces at center for front and two more for back; join at side seams. Trim seams, turn and stuff. Pin head to body; turn under raw edge and sew around neck twice, adding stuffing if needed.

Seam ears to lining; trim and turn. Turn in raw edges and sew to head about ¾″ from center seam.

Stitch tail pieces, and stuff lightly. Sew to B and tack close to base.

Sew on nose about 3″ down from top seam; sew eyes about 1½″ below seam. With pink floss, outline-stitch a proud mouth and make one long stitch for each white whisker. Add lace collar and tack at back.

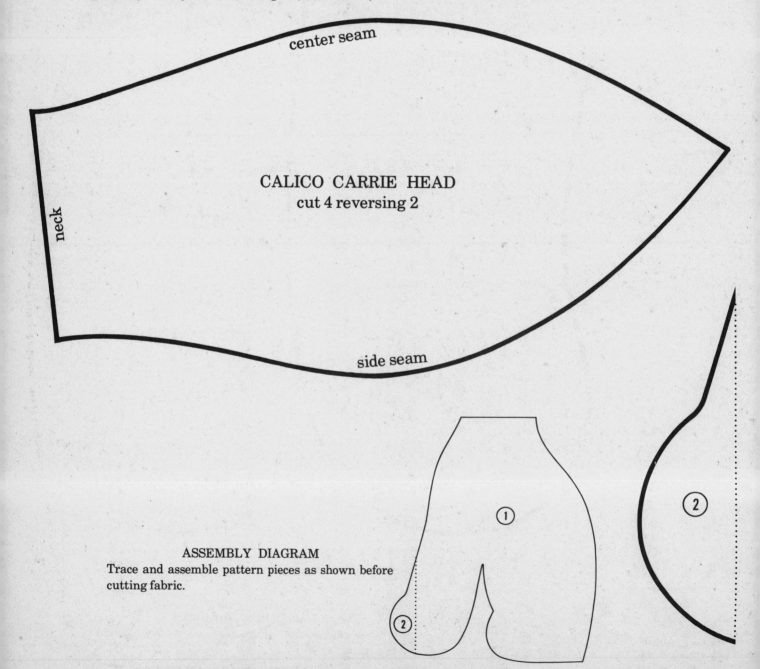

center seam

neck

side seam

CALICO CARRIE HEAD
cut 4 reversing 2

ASSEMBLY DIAGRAM
Trace and assemble pattern pieces as shown before cutting fabric.

① ② ②

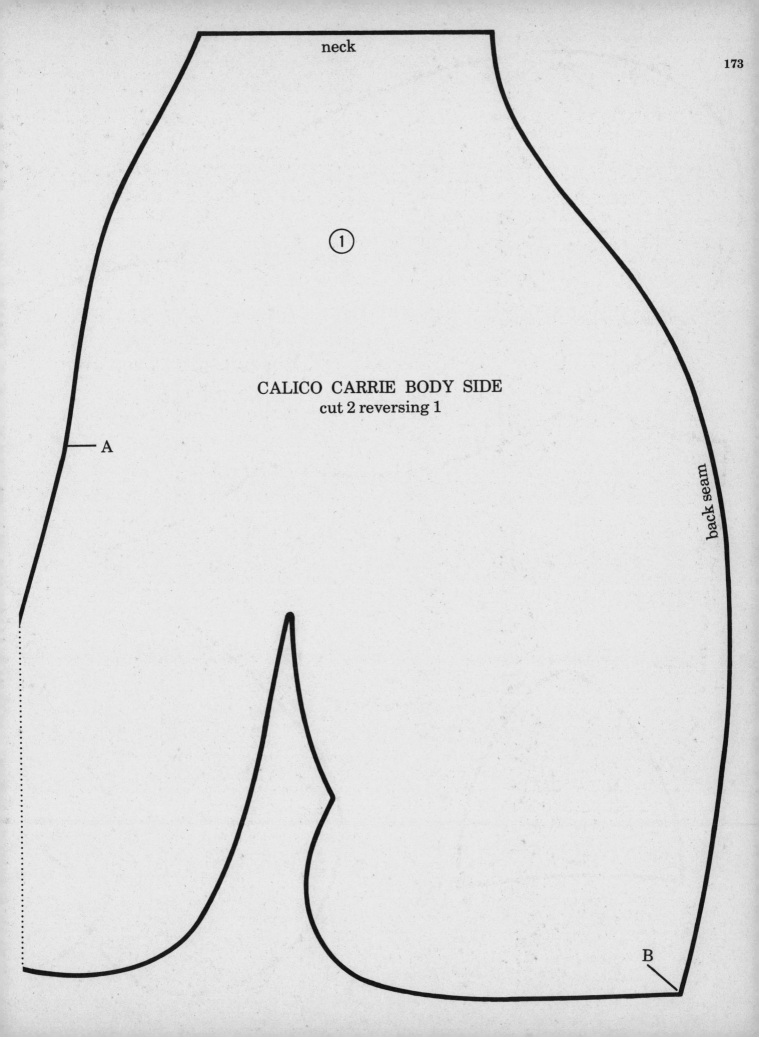

neck

173

①

CALICO CARRIE BODY SIDE
cut 2 reversing 1

A

back seam

B

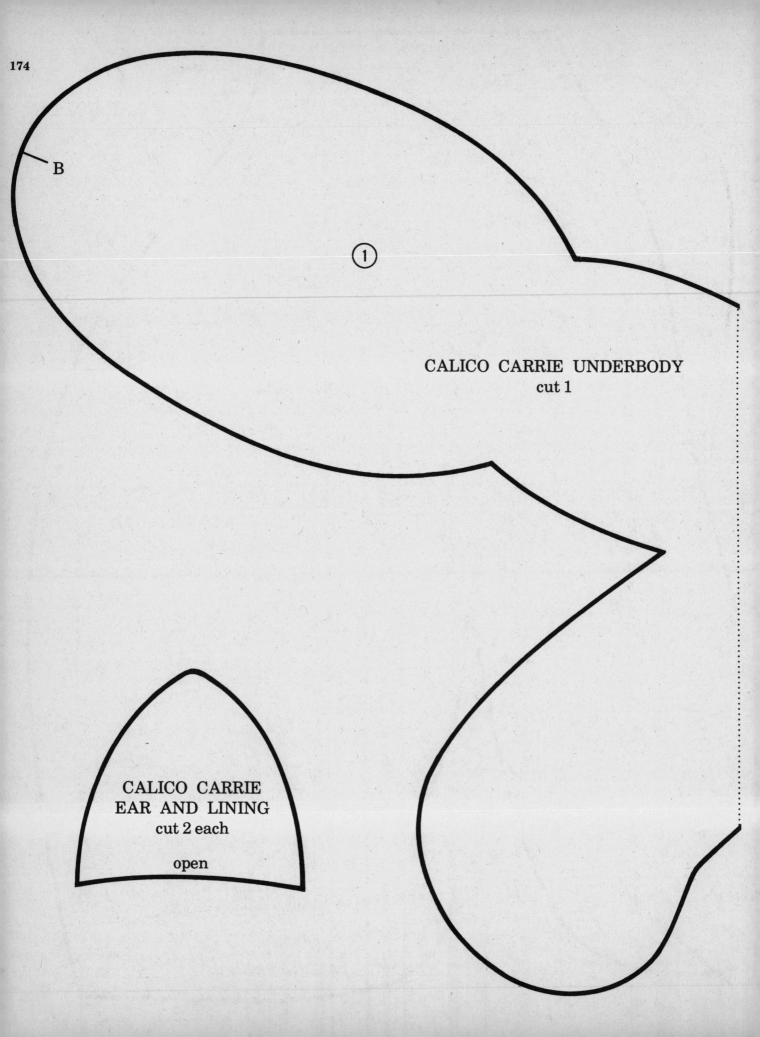

174

B

①

CALICO CARRIE UNDERBODY
cut 1

CALICO CARRIE
EAR AND LINING
cut 2 each

open

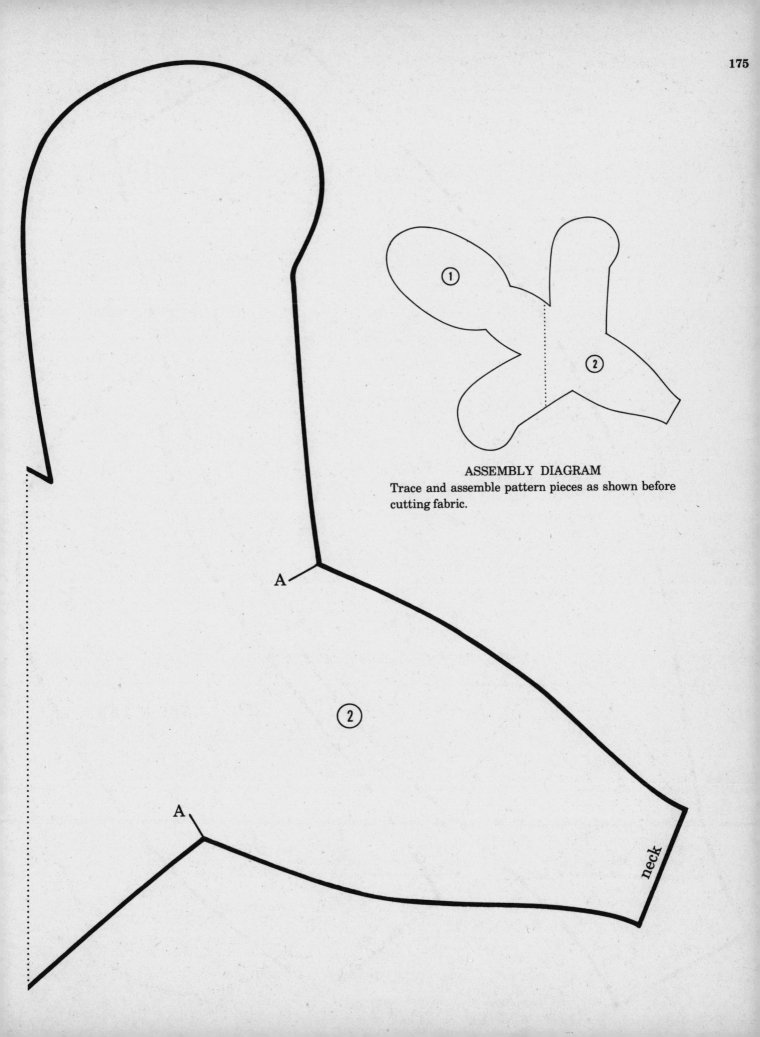

ASSEMBLY DIAGRAM
Trace and assemble pattern pieces as shown before cutting fabric.

A

A

② 2

neck

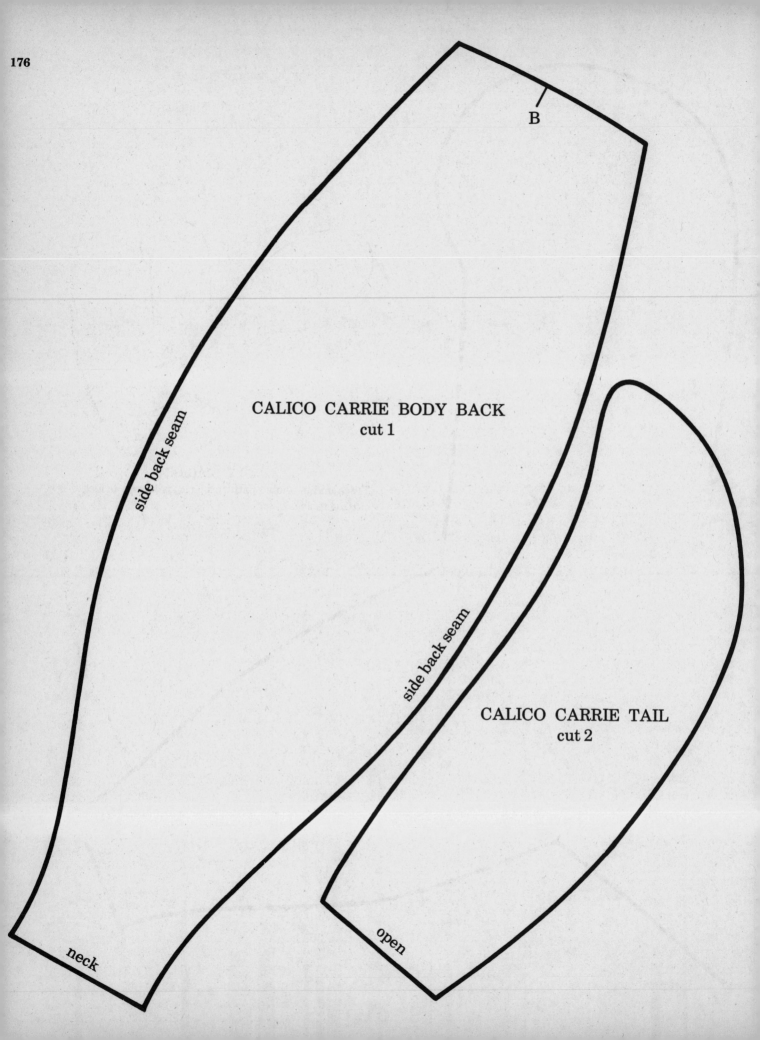

176

CALICO CARRIE BODY BACK
cut 1

side back seam

CALICO CARRIE TAIL
cut 2

side back seam

B

neck

open

Cuddle Kitten

MATERIALS ½ yard 44″-wide gold pile fabric; matching polyester thread; polyester fiber stuffing; scraps of gold sateen, violet-blue and pink felt; pink, orange and gold embroidery floss. Two ½″ navy blue buttons; 1 yard ½″ pink picot ribbon.

Follow 5 patterns and cut cat from pile fabric, adding ½″ seam allowance and reversing patterns for corresponding pairs. Cut sateen ear linings. Following photograph, cut felt heart-shaped pink nose and oval violet eye pieces.

Right sides together, pin and stitch body sides along back seam from neck to B; stitch short front seam from neck to A. Pin and stitch underbody to sides, matching A's and B's. Trim seams. Turn and stuff body.

Seam 2 head pieces at center for front and 2 more for back; join at side seams. Trim seams, turn and stuff. Pin to body, tilting head in a coy manner. Turn under raw edge and sew around neck twice, adding a little more stuffing if needed.

Seam ears to lining; trim and turn. Turn in raw edges and sew to head about 1″ from center seam. Stitch tail pieces, stuff and sew at B.

Sew on nose, felt and button eyes. Outline-stitch pink mouth; make 1 long stitch for each orange whisker and gold toe. Tack a ribbon bow in front of one ear and another around neck as a collar.

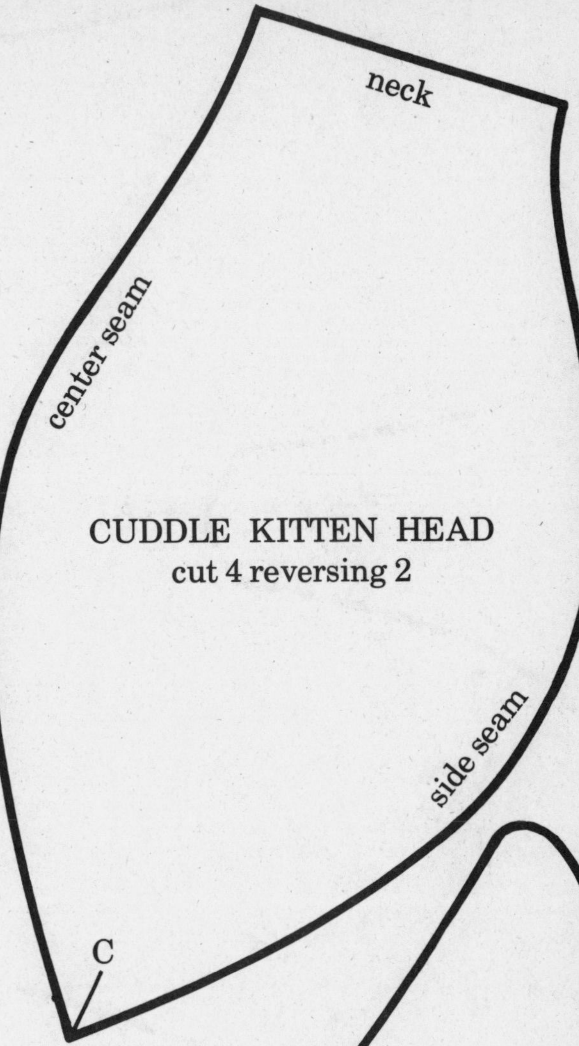

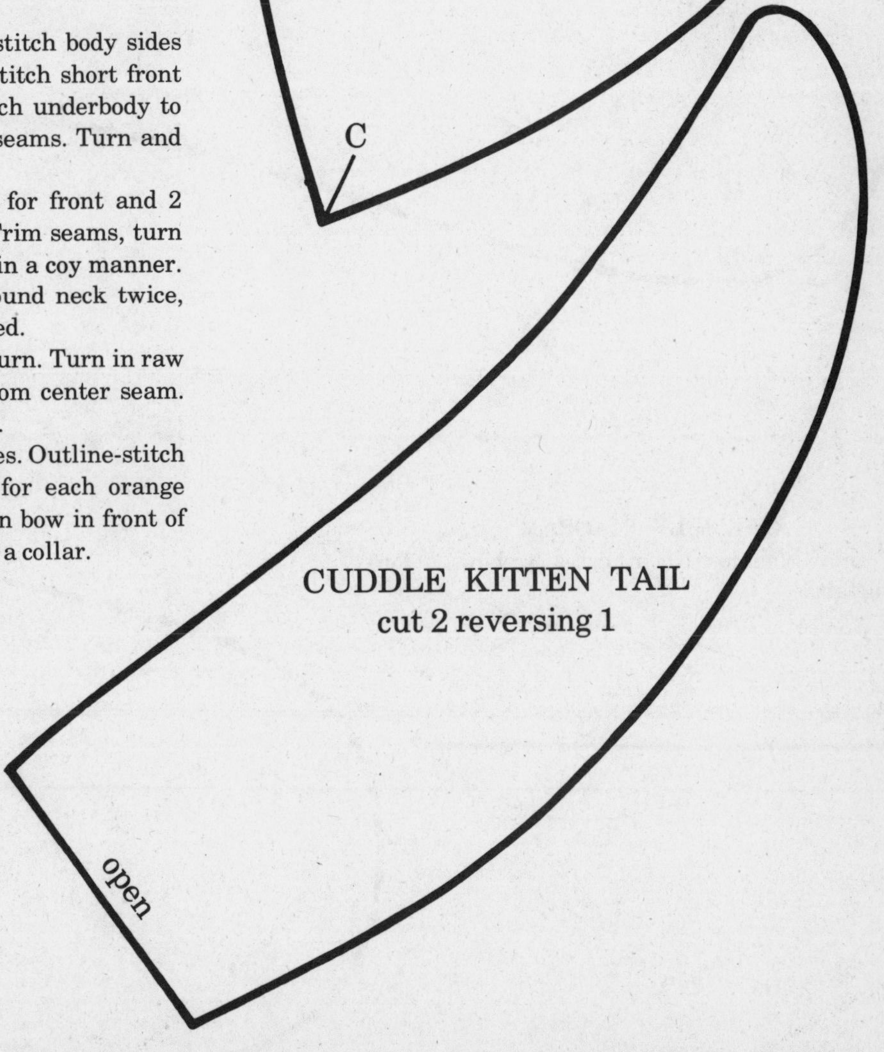

neck

center seam

side seam

CUDDLE KITTEN HEAD
cut 4 reversing 2

C

CUDDLE KITTEN TAIL
cut 2 reversing 1

open

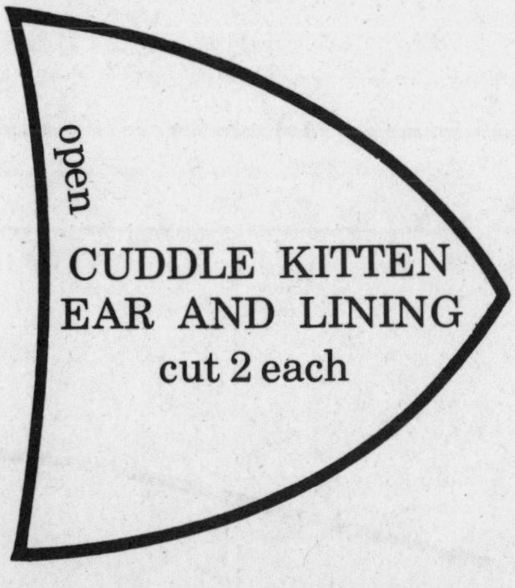

**CUDDLE KITTEN
EAR AND LINING**
cut 2 each

open

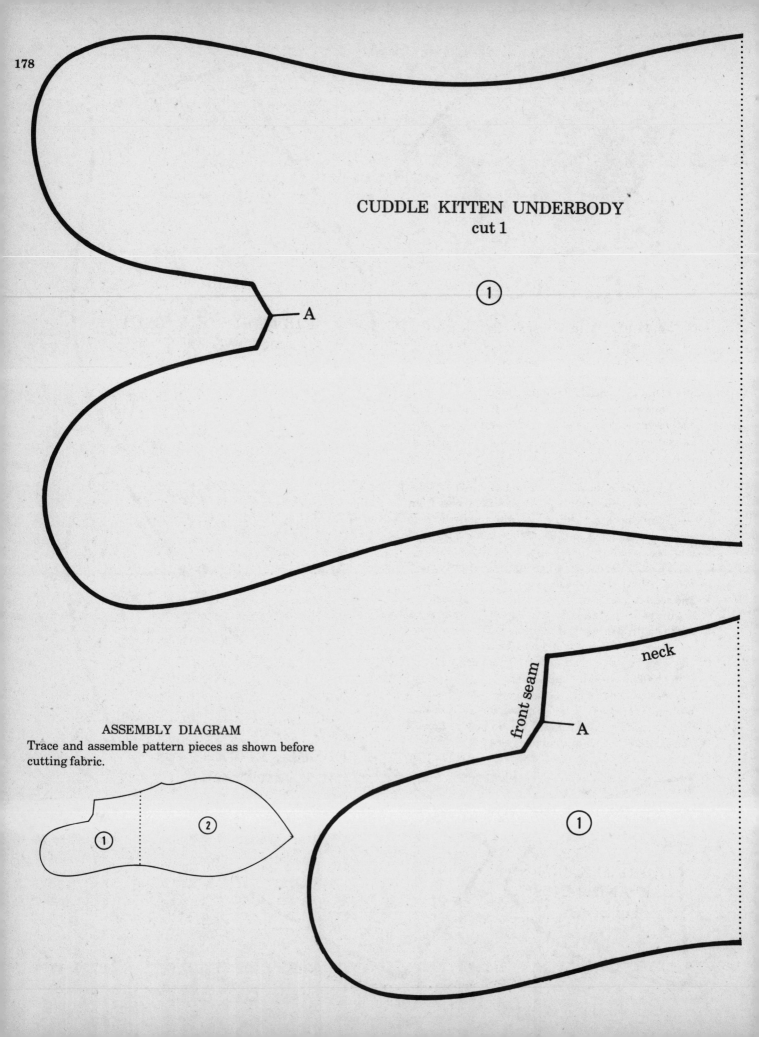

CUDDLE KITTEN UNDERBODY
cut 1

①

A

ASSEMBLY DIAGRAM
Trace and assemble pattern pieces as shown before cutting fabric.

①

②

front seam

neck

A

①

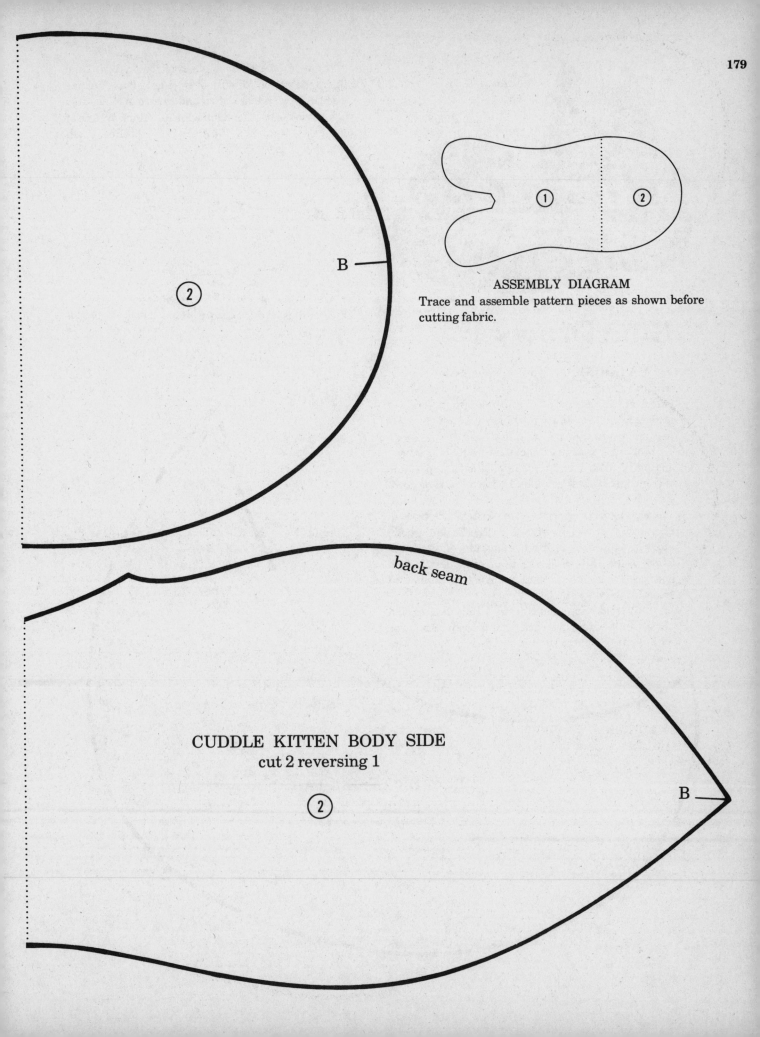

B

②

ASSEMBLY DIAGRAM
Trace and assemble pattern pieces as shown before cutting fabric.

① ②

back seam

CUDDLE KITTEN BODY SIDE
cut 2 reversing 1

②

B

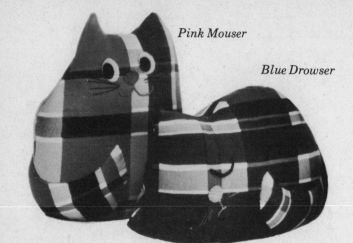

Pink Mouser

Blue Drowser

Sew on orange nose about 4″ below top seam; outline-stitch mouth with orange-gold floss. Outline closed eyes with black yarn and work one long stitch with lavender floss for each whisker. Mark outline of paw to support cat's chin; sew with outline stitch and royal blue yarn.

ASSEMBLY DIAGRAM
Trace and assemble pattern pieces as shown before cutting fabric.

Blue Drowser

MATERIALS ½ yard 44″-wide cotton printed in strong blue-black-and-green plaid; harmonizing polyester thread; polyester fiber stuffing; scrap of orange felt; black and royal blue wool yarn; orange-gold and lavender floss.

Follow 3 patterns and cut cat from plaid fabric, adding ½″ seam allowance. Match plaid at top seams of front and back if you like. Following photograph, cut orange felt nose.

Right sides together, pin and stitch body front to back along top seam from A to B. Pin underbody along under seam of front, matching A's and B's. Stitch seam. Pin under seam of back, leaving an opening for turning. Trim seams, turn and stuff smoothly. Sew opening.

Clip and turn under seam allowance of tail piece; pin to cat with point C at C on body. Appliqué with small stitches, adding a little stuffing as you sew.

C

back seam edge

BLUE DROWSER TAIL
cut 1

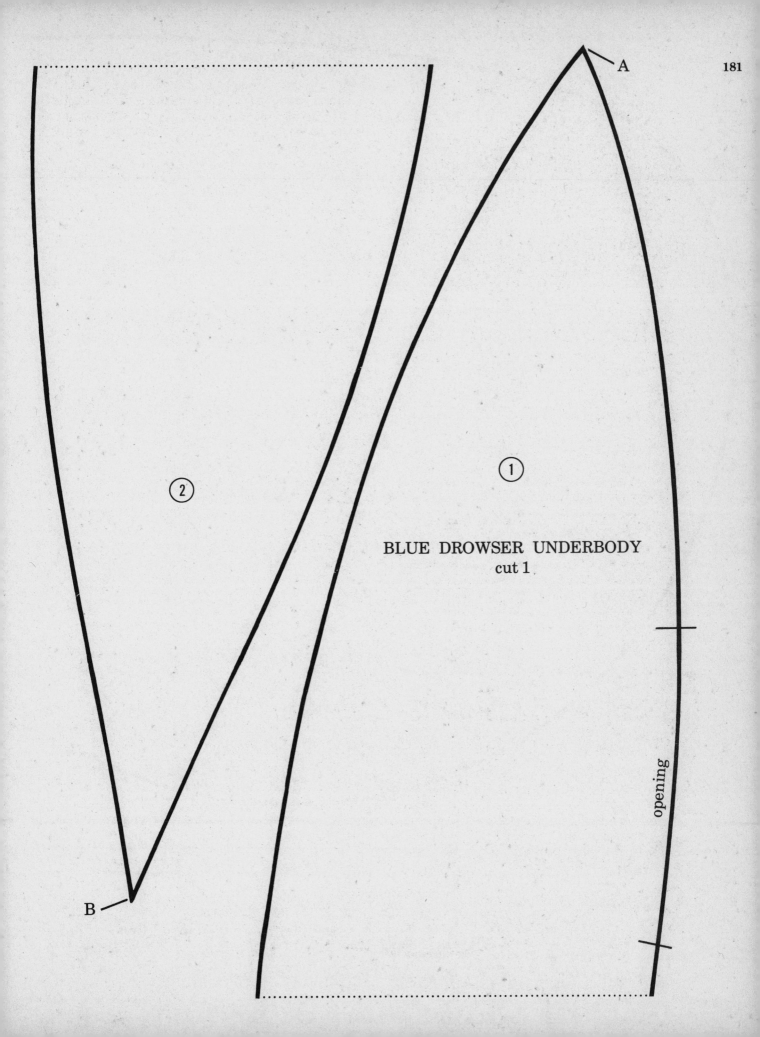

A

181

②

①

BLUE DROWSER UNDERBODY
cut 1

opening

B

182

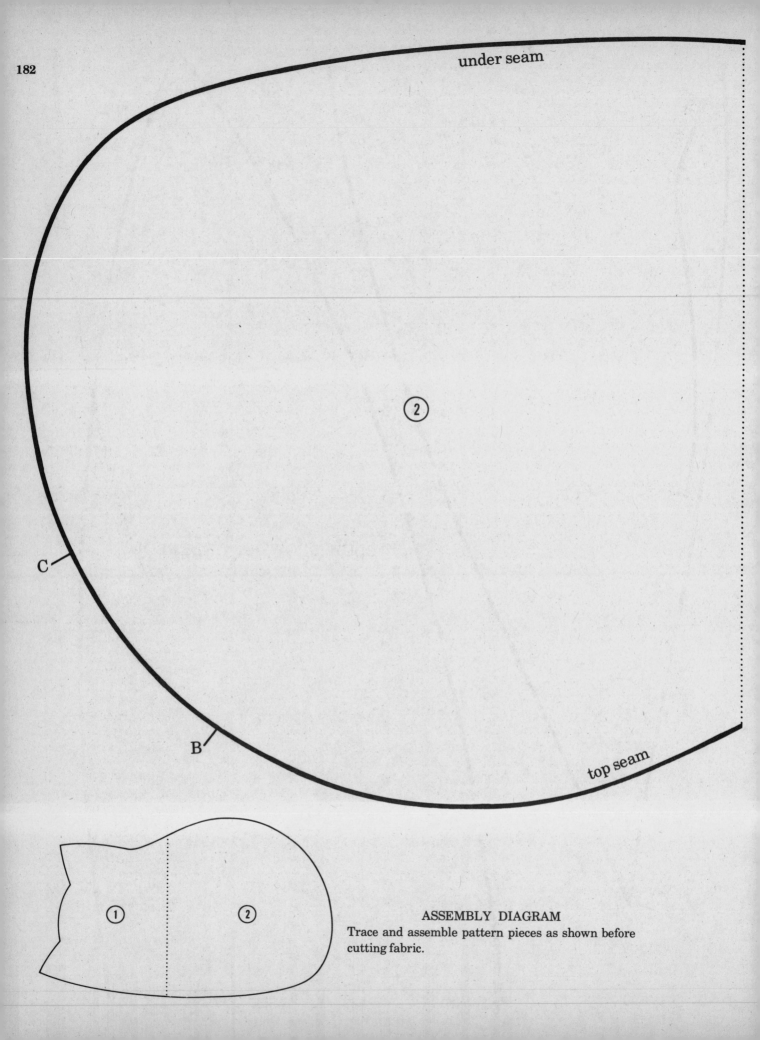

under seam

②

C

B

top seam

① ②

ASSEMBLY DIAGRAM
Trace and assemble pattern pieces as shown before
cutting fabric.

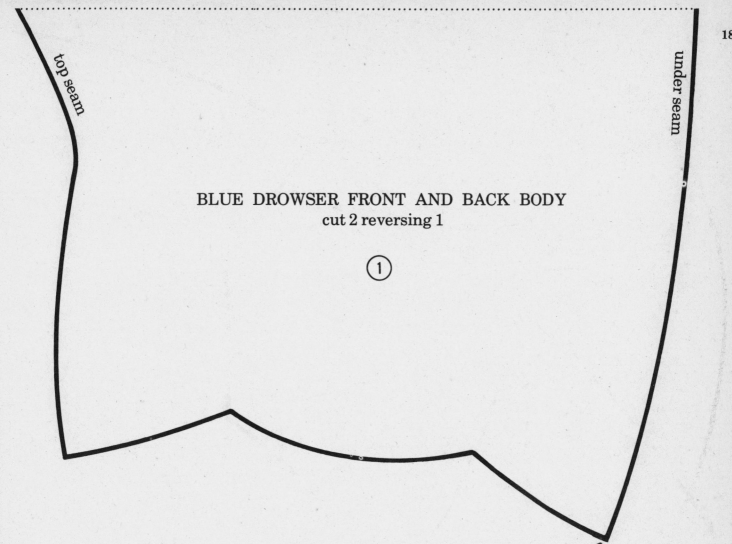

top seam

under seam

BLUE DROWSER FRONT AND BACK BODY
cut 2 reversing 1

① 1

A

Pink Mouser

MATERIALS ½ yard 44″-wide cotton printed in bright pink-yellow-and-green plaid; harmonizing polyester thread; polyester fiber stuffing; scraps of green, yellow and turquoise felt; pink floss and black button thread.

Follow 3 patterns and cut cat from plaid fabric, adding ½″ seam allowance. Match plaid at top and side seams of body if you like. Following photograph, cut green felt nose; cut 1⅛″ yellow ovals and ¾″ turquoise ovals for eyes.

Right sides together, pin and stitch body front to back from A, then along top of head and down back seam to B. Pin underside piece along side seam of front from A to B; stitch seam. Pin side seam of back, leaving an opening for turning. Trim seams, turn and stuff. Sew opening.

Clip and turn under seam allowance of tail piece; pin to cat with back edge of tail on body back, about 1½″ in from back seam. Appliqué tail with small stitches, adding a little stuffing as you sew.

Sew on green felt nose about 2″ below top seam. Add yellow and turquoise ovals for eyes. Outline-stitch pink mouth and make one long stitch for each black whisker.

184

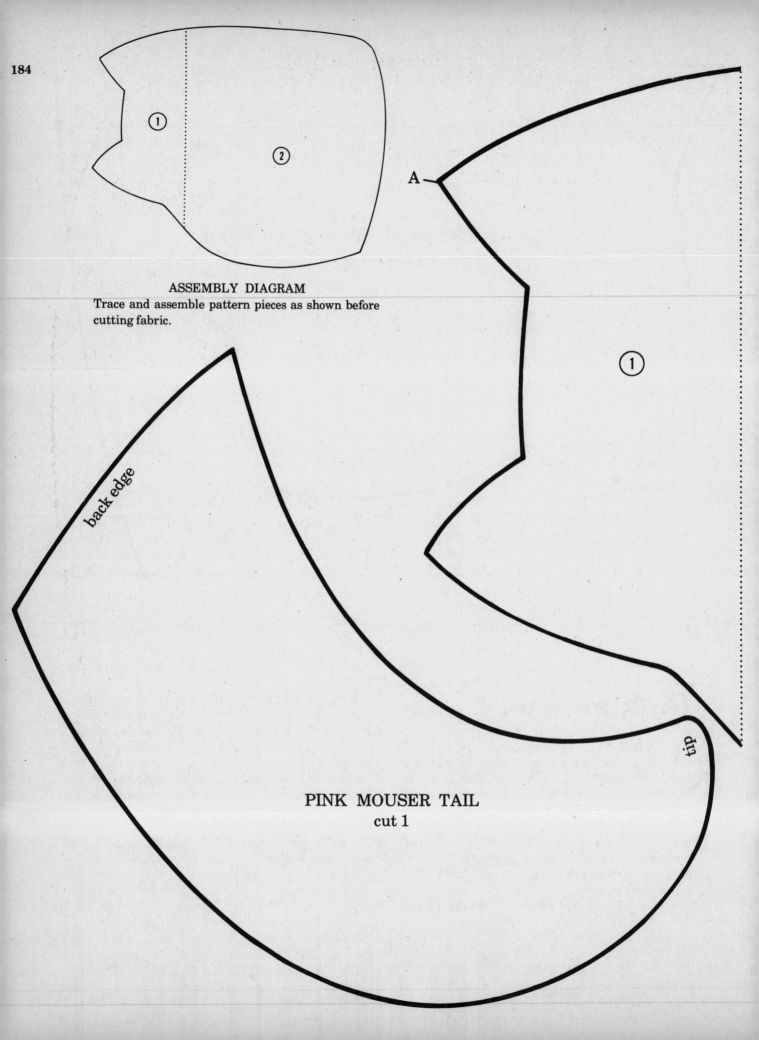

ASSEMBLY DIAGRAM

Trace and assemble pattern pieces as shown before cutting fabric.

① ②

A

①

back edge

tip

PINK MOUSER TAIL
cut 1

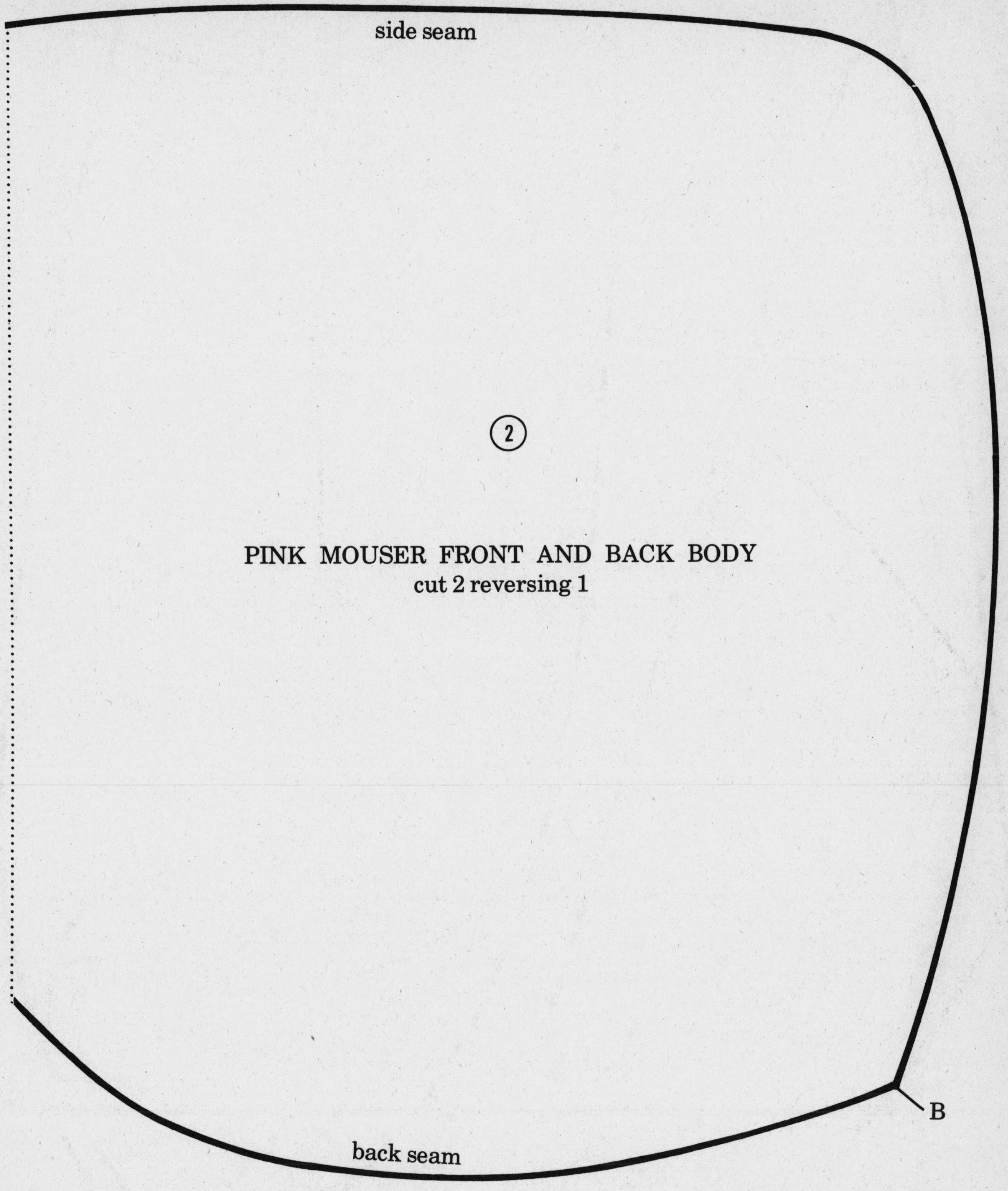

side seam

②

PINK MOUSER FRONT AND BACK BODY
cut 2 reversing 1

B

back seam

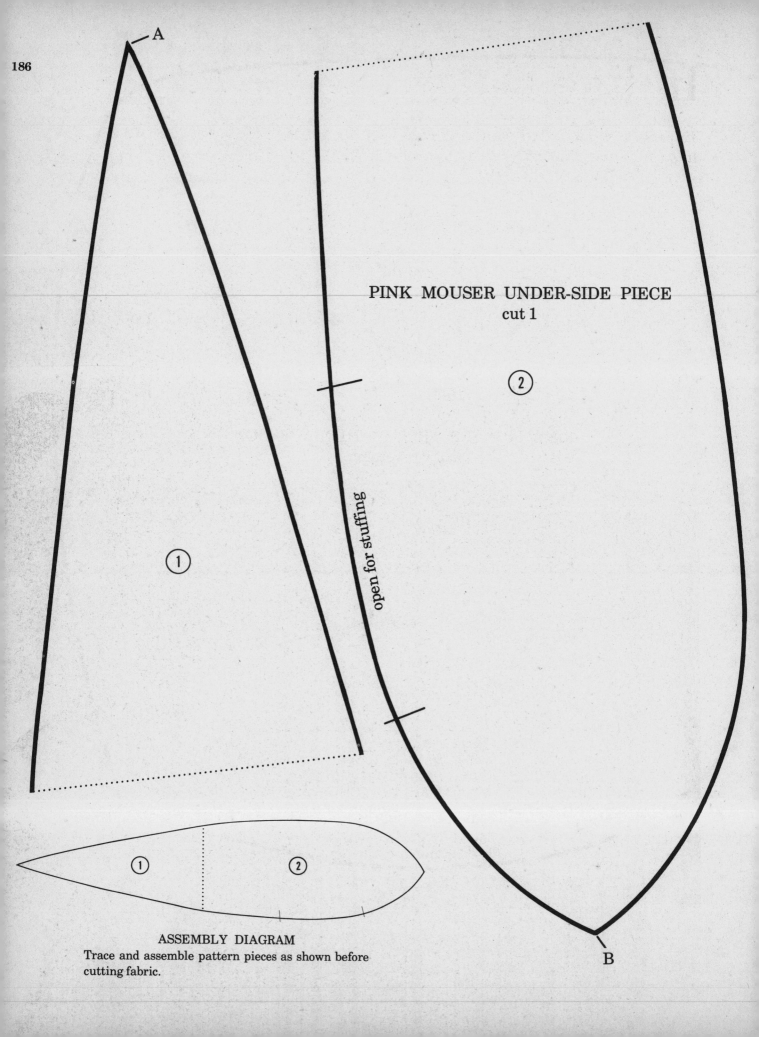

186

A

PINK MOUSER UNDER-SIDE PIECE
cut 1

②

open for stuffing

①

B

ASSEMBLY DIAGRAM
Trace and assemble pattern pieces as shown before
cutting fabric.

Indian Dolls

Six Indian maidens and the slumbering baby. Their costumes and accessories are authentic in every detail, from beaded moccasins to silver necklaces.

General Directions

The six Indian women dolls are made in the same way; the Navajo baby has his own pattern. The dolls' hair arrangements, costumes and jewelry are authentic reproductions of each tribe's manner of dress. If your dolls are to be showpieces rather than toys, fastenings on garments can be omitted.

MATERIALS *For one doll:* ⅜ yard 36″ pinkish tan cotton; kapok for stuffing; black, tan and pink-orange six-strand embroidery floss; fine black wool yarn or embroidery floss for hair.

There are 7 full-size pattern pieces for the doll. Adding ½″ seam allowance, cut out fabric for body, head, arms, legs and soles, reversing pattern to cut second arm, leg and sole if fabric has a right and wrong side.

BODY Pin and sew together two body fronts along front seam from neck to A, stitching seam twice along front neck to reinforce it. Seam two body backs along back seam from neck to A, reinforcing neck. Join back to front at side seams, matching A's. Trim seam allowances and turn to right side. Stuff body firmly.

HEAD Pin head sides to center, easing fabric of center piece at top of head, if necessary. Stitch, following the seam lines of side pieces; sew contours carefully and smoothly. Stitch seam twice along neck to reinforce it. Trim seam allowances and turn. Stuff head firmly.

ARMS Pin and sew two pieces together, stitching a double seam around hand and wrist. Trim seam allowance carefully and turn. Stuff hand lightly; outline fingers with stitching. Stuff arm firmly almost to the top. Turn in raw edges and sew closed.

LEGS Pin and sew two pieces together from top edge to A. Pin sole to foot of front leg piece, matching A's and toe outlines. On back leg, trim fabric close to dotted line to match heel line of sole piece; pin sole carefully to leg and ease it to fit. Sew sole and heel seams. Make a small tuck across front of ankle so sole is at right angle to leg. Trim seam allowances and turn. Stuff firmly almost to top. Turn in raw edges and sew.

ASSEMBLING DOLL Turn in neck edges of head and pin to the body, making it proud and erect. Sew head firmly in place. Sew tip of each arm to shoulder with several long hand stitches; wind thread around stitches to form a shank and fasten off. Sew legs to body front about ½″ from point A.

FEATURES Follow photograph for placement. With black wool, work eyes in vertical satin stitches; use black floss to embroider brows in stem stitch. Take a few small tan stitches for nose and work pink-orange stem stitches for mouth. For rosy cheeks, rub on pink chalk or rouge.

HAIR Follow individual directions to make from black wool yarn or embroidery floss and sew on after completing costume.

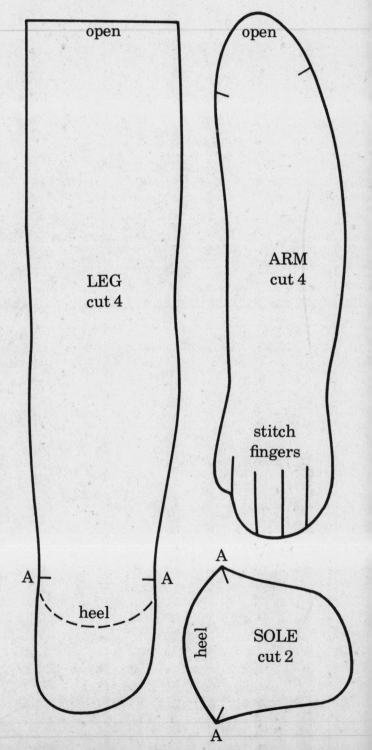

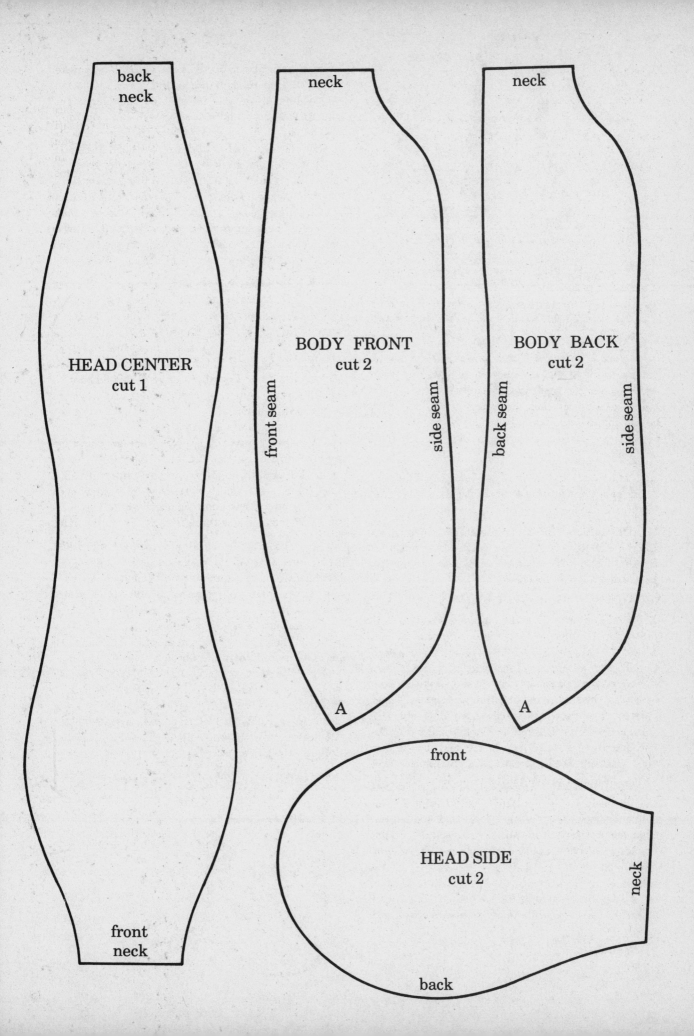

back
neck

HEAD CENTER
cut 1

front
neck

neck

BODY FRONT
cut 2

front seam

side seam

A

neck

BODY BACK
cut 2

back seam

side seam

A

front

HEAD SIDE
cut 2

neck

back

cuffs from yellow calico; slit blouse back only. Also cut ⅜″ x 7″ bias strip to face neck.

Seam back pieces to front at shoulders; trim seam allowances and overcast; hem back opening. Stitch bias strip around neck with right sides together. Turn in and hem down raw edge and ends. Gather top of each sleeve to fit armhole; stitch in place. Right sides together, stitch cuff to sleeve; trim seam allowance. Fold cuff lengthwise; topstitch top and bottom edges.

Try blouse on doll, wrong side out; pin sleeve and side seams. Remove blouse and stitch; trim and overcast seams. Sew 2 snaps to back opening.

WRAPAROUND SKIRT Cut 11″ x 26″ piece from calico, using selvage for one 11″ end; cut 1¼″ x 10″ waistband. Stitch a very narrow hem along one edge of skirt; fold under and hem raw end for back overlap. Run two rows of machine gathering along the other long edge; gather to fit waistband. Stitch right side of band to wrong side of skirt; fold band to outside; turn under raw edge and ends; topstitch along top and bottom.

Try skirt on doll; pin a deep hem about 1″ above soles of feet; remove skirt. Stitch green bias tape along folded edge. Sew a line of basting 2″ above tape. Gather skirt slightly along basting to measure 22″ around; pin another strip of bias tape over gathers and topstitch both edges. Fit and lap waistband around doll; sew snaps to ends.

NECKLACES Dilute red ink with water and dye a few pastinas to make sure color resembles light coral. Then dye enough pastinas to make an 8″ and a 9″ necklace; blot on a paper towel and let dry completely.

Temporarily string pastinas on very thin wire about 11″ long; using tempera paint, color them dark coral. If desired, color a few brown.

For 8″ and 9″ necklaces, use a very fine needle to string light coral pastinas on thread, inserting a brown bead every ½″ if desired. String dark coral beads on thread with a white pastina every ½″. Coat all necklaces with nail polish. Place necklaces on doll, knot thread ends and cut.

HAIRDO See Western Sioux Doll for embroidery-floss hairdo.

Cherokee Doll

This Indian maiden is a member of the eastern Cherokee tribe living in the Smoky Mountains of North Carolina. Her costume is one worn during the 1880's and her feet are bare.

MATERIALS *For hairdo and costume:* 10 or 11 skeins of black 6-strand embroidery floss; 36″ cotton, 18″ x 10″ piece of white and ½ yard of yellow calico; 1½ yards of green bias tape; 4 snaps (optional). *For necklaces:* Thread for stringing, very fine wire, small pastina macaroni shapes with a hole at center; washable red ink; brown (optional) and dark coral tempera paints; colorless nail polish.

Follow General Directions to make the doll. As her feet are bare, stuff them lightly and outline toes with stitching. Stuff legs firmly, and complete.

PETTICOAT Use 18″ x 10″ piece of white cotton. Turn up 1″ along an 18″ edge and stitch hem. Join ends with a narrow seam, leaving 3″ open at top edge; hem opening. Run two rows of machine gathering along top edge; gather to fit doll and tie threads. Sew snap to opening if desired.

BLOUSE Adding ¼″ seam allowance to all edges, follow 3 patterns to cut blouse, sleeves and

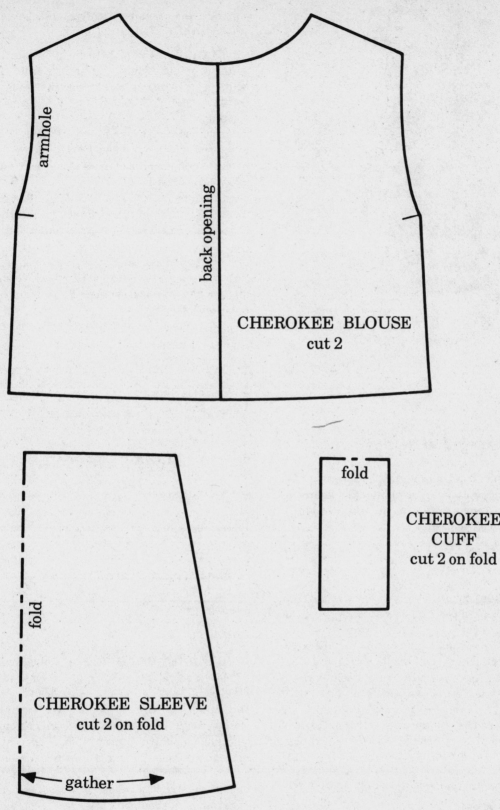

armhole

back opening

CHEROKEE BLOUSE
cut 2

fold

CHEROKEE CUFF
cut 2 on fold

fold

CHEROKEE SLEEVE
cut 2 on fold

gather

top edge and place petticoat on doll; gather to fit and fasten off thread.

BLOUSE Adding ¼″ seam allowance, follow 2 patterns to cut blouse and sleeves from red-and-white print. Also cut ½″ x 7″ bias strip to face neck, two ½″ x 3¾″ cuffs and two ¾″ x 5″ strips to face opening.

Stitch sleeves to armholes and finish each lower edge with a narrow hem. Gather sleeve ½″ from hem. On cuff strip, turn in ⅛″ along each long edge; sew strip over gathers.

Stitch facing strips to back opening, right sides together; turn to inside and hem down. Stitch bias strip around neck, right sides together; turn to inside; sew.

Try blouse on doll, wrong side out; pin sleeve and side seams. Remove blouse; stitch seams; trim and overcast. Hem lower edge. Tack back opening or finish with two snaps.

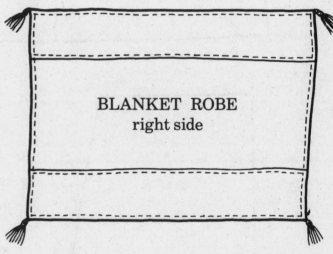

BLANKET ROBE
right side

Pueblo Doll

This Indian maiden from the Southwest lives in an adobe hut in a pueblo, or village. She learns to grind corn on a stone metate and to bake bread in an adobe oven. Her squash-blossom hairdo indicates she is unmarried. After marriage she rearranges her hair so the buns hang to represent the fruit of the squash plant.

MATERIALS *For hairdo and costume:* Black wool yarn; black pipe cleaner; 4¾″ x 13½″ strip of white cotton; ⅜ yard of 2¼″ eyelet-embroidered edging; ¼ yard 36″ red-and-white cotton print; 12″ x 16″ piece of fine, closely woven dark blue wool; 2½″ x 27″ strip of red cotton; ¾ yard of ⅝″ red-and-white woven braid; scrap of tan and 4″ x 20″ strip of white felt; 2 snaps (optional). *For necklaces:* 9″ length of key chain; scrap of heavy aluminum foil from pie tin; small pastina macaroni shapes with hole at center; washable turquoise ink; fine wire; colorless nail polish.

Follow General Directions to make the doll.

PETTICOAT For a petticoat 6½″ long and 13½″ around, join 2¼″ edging to a 4¾″ white cotton strip with a ¼″ seam. Stitch ends together. Gather

BLANKET ROBE Cut dark blue wool fabric 12″ deep and 13″ wide. On both long edges, fold 1½″ of fabric to the right side; turn under ⅛″ along raw edges and hem down by hand. Also sew stitching close to fold line as in drawing. Turn ends to wrong side and hem. Ravel threads from leftover fabric and make four tassels ¾″ long. Sew to robe corners.

Place robe on doll, preferably under her left arm and over her right shoulder; overcast back and front edges for ½″ at shoulder.

SASH Use 2½″ x 27″ strip of red cotton. Fold lengthwise and stitch together the long edges with

¼" seam; turn and center the seam for underside of sash. Run black stitching close to each fold edge. Sew red-and-white ⅝" woven braid to red cotton. (Or substitute wider braid and turn in edges to make it the right width.) At sash ends ravel cotton and braid to make a 1" fringe.

To put sash on doll, place fringed end about 2" above lower edge of robe; fold and wrap once around waist and tack. Wrap again; fold so second end is parallel to first; sew firmly.

HIGH-WRAPPED MOCCASINS Follow 2 patterns (seam allowances included) to cut soles from tan felt and uppers from white felt, reversing patterns for left foot. Also cut 1½" x 12" white felt strips to wrap around legs.

Pin the moccasin upper around the doll's foot then pin the sole over the upper. Sew on sole with small stitches, sew back seam. Beginning at back seam, wind white strip tightly around leg up to knee; sew end.

SILVER NECKLACE Follow drawing to pencil crescent on foil; cut out with scissors. Bend tab over key chain.

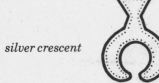

silver crescent

TURQUOISE NECKLACE String pastinas on fine wire about 9" long. Dilute ink with water; dye pastinas and dry on a paper towel. Coat with nail polish. Place on doll's neck, cut wire to fit and twist ends to fasten.

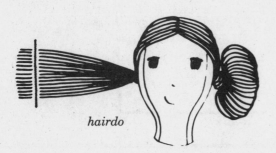

hairdo

HAIRDO Place 28" strands of black yarn across top and back of head. Sew along center, making a part 5" long. Pull strands toward area of ear and tie tightly with yarn; sew to side of head. Cut

yarn ends even. Tack on a few short strands for bangs.

Follow drawing for the squash-blossom buns, which are a bit difficult to make until you get the knack of winding the yarn smoothly. Place half a pipe cleaner over the yarn ends; roll it close to the head, winding yarn over it. Bend cleaner into a circle and fasten ends inside bun. Spread yarn evenly over circle.

PUEBLO MOCCASIN
UPPER
cut 2

heel PUEBLO MOCCASIN
SOLE
cut 2

194

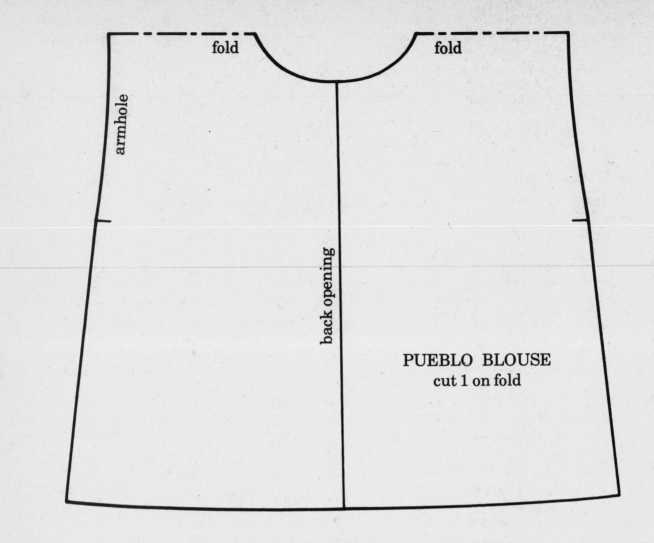

fold

fold

armhole

back opening

PUEBLO BLOUSE
cut 1 on fold

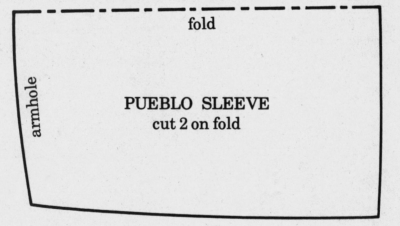

fold

armhole

PUEBLO SLEEVE
cut 2 on fold

Seminole Doll

This Indian maiden lives in the swampy Florida Everglades. Her home has a roof thatched with palmetto leaves, no walls, and is called a chikee. She excels in using the sewing machine to make colorful patchwork skirts and capes; she loves jewelry and wears many necklaces of glass beads.

MATERIALS *For hairdo and costume:* Black wool yarn; 36″ firmly woven cotton, ½ yard of turquoise and ⅛ yard each of purple, red, white and yellow; 36″ batiste, ⅛ yard each of light blue and yellow; narrow rickrack, 1¾ yards of red, 1½ yards each of blue and green, 1⅛ yards each of black and yellow, ⅝ yard of white; ⅝ yard black bias tape; 1 yard narrow lace; 5 snaps (optional). *For jewelry:* Small glass beads in red, blue, green and white; thread; scrap of heavy aluminum foil from pie tin.

Follow General Directions to make the doll. As her feet are bare, stuff them lightly and outline toes with stitching. Stuff legs firmly and complete.

SLIP Adding ¼″ seam allowance, follow pattern to cut bodice from turquoise cotton. Cut ½″-wide bias strips for facings: one 15″ long for neck and back opening edges and two 4½″ long for armholes. Cut slip skirt 9″ x 29″ from turquoise cotton.

On bodice, stitch shoulder seams. Right sides together, stitch bias facing up one back edge, around neck and down second back edge. Turn to inside and hem down. Face armholes in same way. Try bodice on doll; pin side seams and stitch; trim and overcast seams.

On skirt, stitch together 9″ sides, leaving 3″ unstitched for top opening; hem opening. Gather top edge to fit bodice; right sides together, stitch waistline seam. Try slip on doll; pin hem so skirt is 1″ above soles of feet and sew. Tack bodice back or finish with 2 snaps.

PATCHWORK SKIRT The completed skirt measures about 9″ in length and 19″ around. It is made up of 13 bands stitched together with ⅛″ seams (see assembly diagram); two are patchwork and the other bands are solid colors, usually trimmed with rickrack (shown by wavy lines). Here is the Seminole technique for doing patchwork.

Patchwork Pattern 1: Tear (or cut) one ¾″-wide strip each from purple and red fabric. Stitch together with ⅛″ seam as in step 1; press seam. Turn seamed strip; cut as in step 2, following solid lines. Repeat until there are enough units for a 19½″ band. Seam along dotted lines, making pattern shown in step 3.

Patchwork Pattern 2: Tear (or cut) one ¾″-wide strip each from red and turquoise fabric. Stitch together with ⅛″ seam as in step 1; press seam. Following solid lines, cut half of seamed strip with pieces going in one direction, half in the opposite direction; repeat until there are enough units for a 19½″ band. Seam along dotted lines shown in step 2, making pattern shown in step 3. Trim off points at top and bottom of band; follow dotted lines for skirt seams.

Follow skirt assembly diagram for colors and dimensions of solid-color bands; add ⅛″ seam allowances when cutting fabrics. Machine-stitch bands together; stitch rickrack trim to bands and black bias tape to bottom of skirt.

Stitch together 9¼″ skirt edges with ¼″ seam, leaving 3″ opening at top; hem opening. Run gathering stitches along top edge. Cut ¾″ x 8½″ turquoise waistband. Press under ⅛″ along both long edges then press band in half. Gather skirt to fit waistband, insert and topstitch. Tack waistband or fasten with a snap.

CAPE Adding ¼″ seam allowances, follow 2 patterns to cut yoke front and back from turquoise cotton. Cut 4½″ x 32″ piece from blue batiste and 1½″ x 32″ strip from yellow.

Seam two yoke backs to each yoke front, matching A's. Right sides together, stitch the seamed yoke pieces along back opening and neckline; clip corners and turn. Topstitch green rickrack to backs, near lower edges.

Stitch yellow batiste to a long edge of blue batiste, wrong sides together. Turn to right side and hem down. Stitch lace and blue rickrack to yellow batiste. Hem short edges. Gather long raw edge to fit yoke. Right sides facing, stitch to outer layer. Turn in edge of inner layer and sew. Tack back neck or fasten with snap.

NECKLACES With fine needle and thread, string beads for 13 necklaces ranging in length from about 9″ to 11″; make 5 red, 4 blue and 2 each green and white. Tie thread ends together at back of doll's neck.

BRACELET Cut a ½″ x 2″ foil strip; smooth edges with an orange-wood stick. Bend bracelet around doll's wrist.

step 1

step 2

HAIRDO Place 28″ strands of black yarn across top and back of head; sew along center, making a part. Double 14″ strands and sew across forehead as in step 1. Pull up strands smoothly as in step 2; fold under to make pompadour and tack to head.

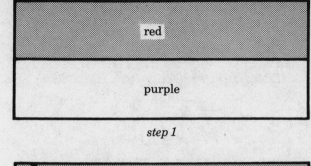

red

purple

step 1

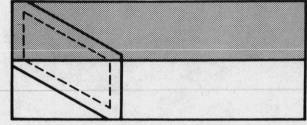

step 2

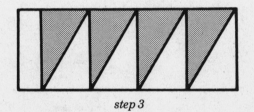

step 3

PATCHWORK PATTERN 1

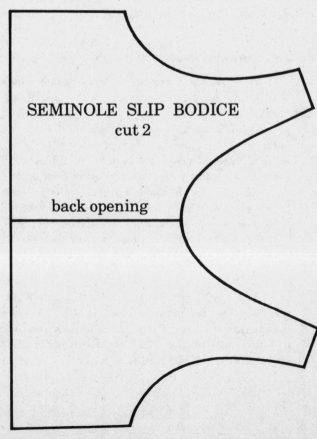

SEMINOLE SLIP BODICE
cut 2

back opening

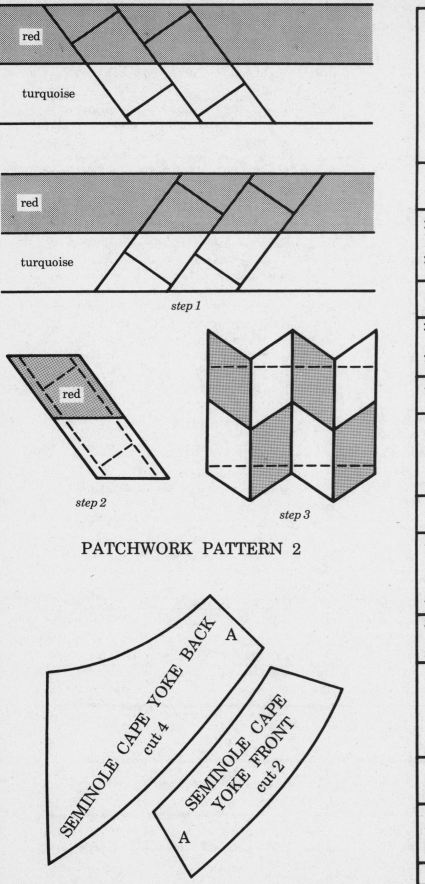

step 1

step 2

step 3

PATCHWORK PATTERN 2

SEMINOLE CAPE YOKE BACK
cut 4

A

SEMINOLE CAPE
YOKE FRONT
cut 2

A

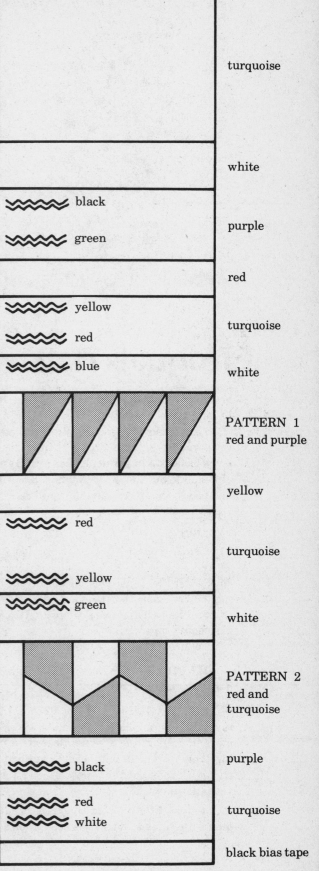

turquoise

white

black

green

purple

red

yellow

turquoise

red

blue

white

PATTERN 1
red and purple

yellow

red

turquoise

yellow

green

white

PATTERN 2
red and
turquoise

black

purple

red

turquoise

white

black bias tape

Iroquois Doll

This maiden is a member of a woodland tribe living in the Northeast. White settlers introduced cloth and beads to her people, so her leggings and wraparound skirt are fabric cut from the same patterns as buckskin garments; her overdress is a copy of a smock worn by white women. The ribbon trim and beadwork are Iroquois designs, the bead edging replacing the buckskin fringe.

MATERIALS *For hairdo and costume:* 11 skeins of black 6-strand embroidery floss; 36″ cotton, ¼ yard black, ¼ yard dark blue with tiny dots; 1 yard ½″ light-blue ribbon; rayon seam binding, ¾ yard rosy red, 1¼ yards dark red; chamois skin; white beads. *For silver pins:* Heavy foil pie tin; sequin pins.

Follow General Directions to make the doll.

HAIRDO See Western Sioux Doll for embroidery-floss hairdo (page 208).

BEADING Use very small beads sold loose in tubes (or, if available, substitute beads on thread or made up into inexpensive necklaces to avoid stringing them). Use one fine needle and long thread to string beads, second fine needle and thread to sew beads down.

Picot-Type Edging For this trim on edges of garments, tie thread around one bead, then slip on 7 or

8 more beads. Sew on first bead parallel to edge; slide next bead close to it and at a right angle as in drawing; sew down third bead parallel to edge. Alternating positions of beads and stringing them as needed, repeat around edge; sew down last bead.

Beading on Skirt Transfer design to fabric. Slip beads on one needle and thread; use second for sewing. Beginning at top scroll, lay beads over line and couch down between every four beads; work two center then bottom scroll, couching at frequent intervals to keep curves. Work vertical motif. Trim edge with diamond motif.

LEGGINGS Adding ¼″ seam allowance to top and side edges, follow pattern to cut two leggings from black cotton. Also cut two ¾″ and 5½″ strips for ties. For each legging, turn under ¼″ at top edge and hem. Stitch front seam, leaving slit at lower end. Fold rosy-red seam binding once to measure ⅛″ along one long edge. With narrow edge on right side, miter corners and sew around slit and bottom of legging; hem down other edge on wrong side. For bead trim, follow instructions for picot-type edging.

For tie, press ¾″ strip lengthwise, turning in ⅛″ on each long edge; press strip in half. Slip leggings on doll; tie below knee with strip.

WRAPAROUND SKIRT Cut 8″ x 12″ skirt from black cotton, omitting seam allowance; also cut ¾″ x 12″ strip for tie.

Fold blue ribbon lengthwise, sew around all skirt edges except 12″ top edge. Copy the bead designs for overlap edge and lower edge on tracing paper; transfer to skirt with dressmaker's carbon paper. Following beading instructions, outline designs with beads. Add picot-type edging as shown in photograph.

On tie strip, press under ⅛″ along each long edge, then press strip in half. Place skirt on doll, wrapping it from left to right; tie at waistline with strip.

OVERDRESS Adding ¼″ seam allowance, follow 4 patterns to cut bodice, sleeves, collar and skirt from dark blue cotton. Also cut ⅜″-wide bias strip to fit neckline and two ½″ x 8″ strips to face front opening.

Seam bodice shoulders. Turn under ¼″ at top edge of skirt pieces; sew machine stitches ¼″ below fold edge and gather to fit bodice. Pin skirt to bodice with fold extending over right side; topstitch.

Sew sleeves to armhole edges of bodice and skirt. Fold dark red seam binding lengthwise; stitch to lower edges of sleeves. Pin sleeve and side seams; stitch. Trim seam allowances and overcast. Sew

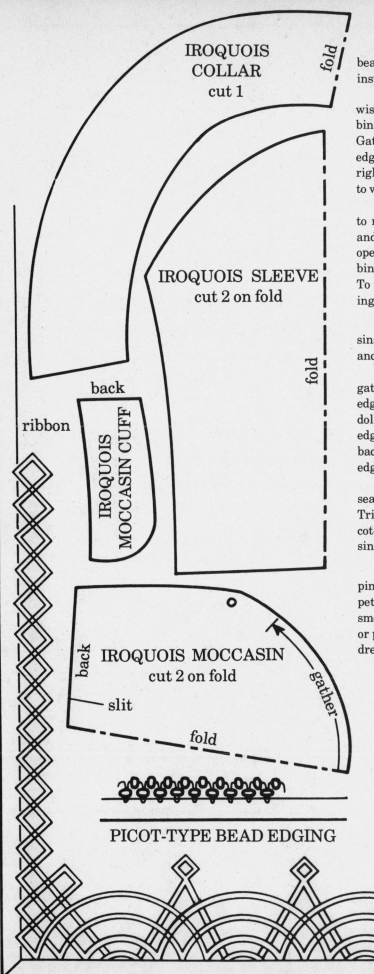

IROQUOIS
COLLAR
cut 1

fold

IROQUOIS SLEEVE
cut 2 on fold

fold

back

ribbon

IROQUOIS
MOCCASIN CUFF

back

IROQUOIS MOCCASIN
cut 2 on fold

slit

gather

fold

PICOT-TYPE BEAD EDGING

BEADING DESIGN FOR WRAPAROUND SKIRT

beads to sleeve binding, following picot-type edging instructions.

For collar, sew dark red seam binding lengthwise; stitch to ends and outer edge. Sew beads to binding, following instructions for picot-type edging. Gather inner edge of collar to fit neckline; with raw edges even, stitch collar to right side of bodice. With right sides facing, stitch ⅜" bias strip to collar. Turn to wrong side, leaving about ¼" standing; hem down.

Along front opening of dress, stitch facing strips to right sides; turn in and sew to wrong side. Fold and stitch dark red seam binding to lower part of opening and around bottom of skirt. Sew beads to binding, following instructions for picot-type edging. To fasten dress, tack at neckline and pin front opening; see directions for silver pins.

MOCCASINS Follow patterns to cut moccasins and cuffs from chamois, adding ⅛" seam allowance. Cut very narrow strips for ties.

Using a fine needle and thread, sew small gathering stitches. Gather tightly and overcast edges for top front seam. Clip at back edge and fit on doll's foot. Fold up section between clips, lap back edges over it and sew back seam. Join cuff pieces at back seam; place inside moccasin and sew to top edge.

String 9 beads; couch down along top front seam, then sew about 25 beads around the nine. Trim cuff with beads, following instructions for picot-type edging. Slip tie through holes, place moccasin on doll and fasten tie.

SILVER PINS Follow patterns to pencil five pin outlines on foil, drawing two each of circular and petal shapes. Cut out with small pointed scissors; smooth and round edges with an orange-wood stick or paint-brush handle. Following photograph, pin to dress in front, or tack in place with thread.

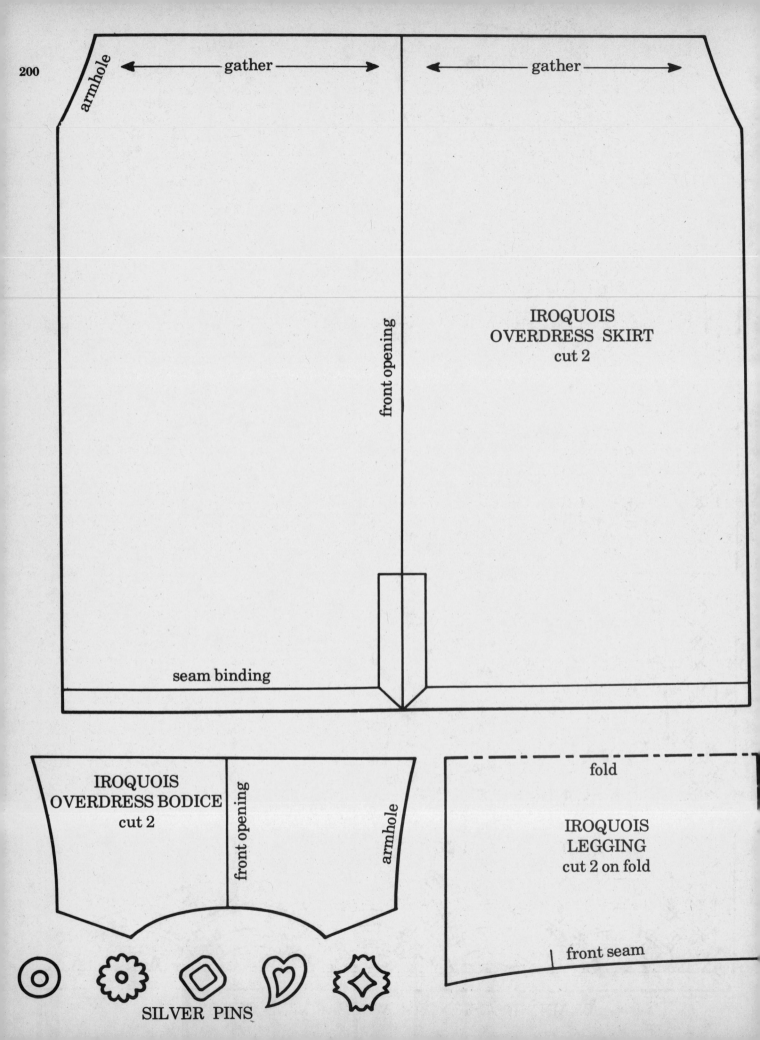

Navajo Doll

This young Indian woman belongs to a Southwest tribe living in Arizona, New Mexico and Utah. Her home is an eight-sided, earth-covered lodge called a hogan. She watches sheep and goats as they graze and is a skillful weaver on an upright loom of bright-colored blankets in beautiful geometric designs.

MATERIALS *For hairdo and costume:* Black wool yarn; white string; 36″ fabric, ¼ yard each of gray-green chambray, bright blue cotton and lightweight red velveteen; 2″ x 7″ red fabric scrap (to line blouse collar); 1¾ yards black bias tape; 1¼ yards red seam binding; scraps of tan and rust-color felt for moccasins; five ⅜″ silver-color buttons. *Silver necklace:* About 12″ length of a silver-color key or stopper chain; heavy foil pie tin; 12 seed beads; fine wire. *Turquoise necklace:* Macaroni shapes, small white pastina with a hole at center and egg bows; washable blue and turquoise inks; colorless nail polish; very fine wire.

Follow General Directions to make the doll.

PETTICOAT Use 9″ x 36″ piece of green chambray. Turn up ½″ along one long edge and stitch hem. Join ends with narrow seam, leaving 3″ open at top edge; hem opening. Run 2 rows of machine gathering along top edge; gather tightly to fit doll and tie threads. Sew snap to opening.

WRAPAROUND SKIRT Cut 8″ x 30″ piece from blue cotton, using selvage for one end. Bind one 30″ edge of skirt with bias tape folded in half lengthwise. Measure 2″ above binding and topstitch a second band of folded tape. Hem cut edge of back overlap. Run 2 rows of machine gathering along top edge; gather to fit doll and overlap about 1½″; tie threads. Sew 2 snaps to waistline.

For broomstick pleats, dampen skirt; wrap tightly around a dowel or broomstick and fasten with rubber bands. Repeat, if necessary, until skirt has a finely creased, worn look.

BLOUSE Adding ¼″ seam allowances to all edges, follow 4 patterns to cut blouse, sleeves, cuffs and one collar piece from red velvet; cut collar lining from matching fabric scrap. Slit blouse front only. (Slit is longer than in authentic Navajo costumes so that blouse can be slipped over doll's head.)

Right sides facing, seam shoulders; overcast seam allowance. On right side of each sleeve, work 4 double rows of stitching from armhole to cuff edge to simulate tucks. Seam cuff to sleeve. Right sides facing, stitch seam binding to lower edge of cuff; turn to wrong side and hem down. Stitch sleeve to blouse armhole; trim and overcast seam allowance.

Seam lining to collar, leaving neck edge open; trim seam then turn. With raw edges even, stitch collar to right side of neckline. With right sides facing, pin and stitch seam binding around collar and front opening. Turn to inside and hem down.

Try blouse on doll wrong side out. Pin sleeve and side seams, leaving slits at lower ends of sides. Remove from doll. Stitch seams, trim and overcast. Finish lower edge of blouse and side slits with binding. Lap front opening about ¼″ at top and taper toward bottom; tack edges; sew on 3 buttons.

MOCCASINS Follow 2 patterns to cut upper from rust-color felt and sole from tan, omitting seam allowances. Patterns are for left moccasin; reverse for right.

Pin upper to doll's foot, overlapping ends at outside; use steam iron to shrink felt to fit. Let dry; trim felt at top. Place sole on foot and attach over upper with pins set close together as in diagram; steam to fit; let dry thoroughly. Remove a few pins, apply white glue to sole and pin again. Repeat around sole edge. Tack button to overlap.

SILVER NECKLACE Using wire cutters, cut chain to 10″ length; save beads in scrap piece.

Follow patterns and sketches to pencil and cut one crescent and make 10 squash blossoms from foil. Cut flaring shape for blossom; bend around a pointed watercolor brush handle or similar object. Remove foil; cut 3 points along lower edge with small scissors; bend points outward. To complete blossom, cut a short length of wire; thread around a seed bead and insert inside blossom; thread wire ends through a bead from scrap of chain.

To assemble necklace, bend crescent tab over center of chain and glue. Wind the wire at top of each blossom around wire of chain, leaving 2 chain beads between blossoms.

TURQUOISE NECKLACE Mix blue and turquoise inks, dilute with water and dye a few pastina to be sure color resembles turquoise.

For necklace center, string *two* long lengths of wire with enough pastinas to cover about 3″ on each wire. Group 3 pastinas at center, slide others down to separate and twist wire gently to hold. Keeping center 3 white, dye pastinas turquoise. Blot on paper towel; let dry; slide beads together and coat with nail polish.

For the 18 irregular pieces, break up egg bows. Smooth edges with emery board so pieces vary in shape and size. Heat point of a corsage pin with a match and punch a hole in center of each piece. Dye, let dry and coat with nail polish.

To assemble necklace, wind two loops of blue pastinas around center of a wire; twist loop ends and cut. On wire at each side of center loops, string 7 white pastinas then one irregular turquoise. Continue until 18 turquoise are used; add pastinas until necklace fits doll; loop wire around last pastina and fasten off.

For silver bracelet, cut ½″ x 2″ foil strip; bend around doll's wrist. For turquoise ring, glue a chip of dyed egg bow macaroni to a pronged rhinestone back; press into finger.

HAIRDO Place 17″ strands of black yarn across head; sew along top, making a center part 1½″ long. Fold pairs of strands and sew along edge of face as in step 1 and to top of head.

Pull yarn to back neck; wind with white string several times, close to head as in step 2. Loop yarn downward then up in a bun as in step 3; wrap center of bun with string and tie as in step 4. Fan out top of bun and fray string ends.

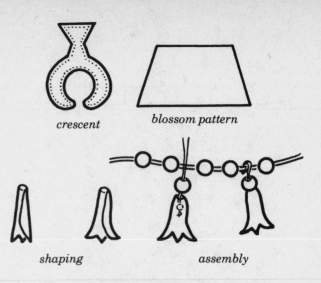

crescent   *blossom pattern*

shaping   *assembly*

SILVER NECKLACE

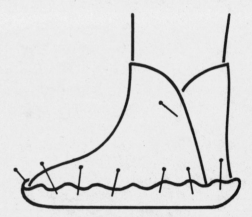

moccasin assembly

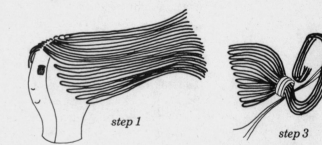

step 1   *step 3*

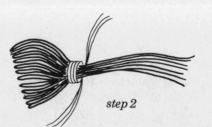

step 2

step 4

HAIRDO

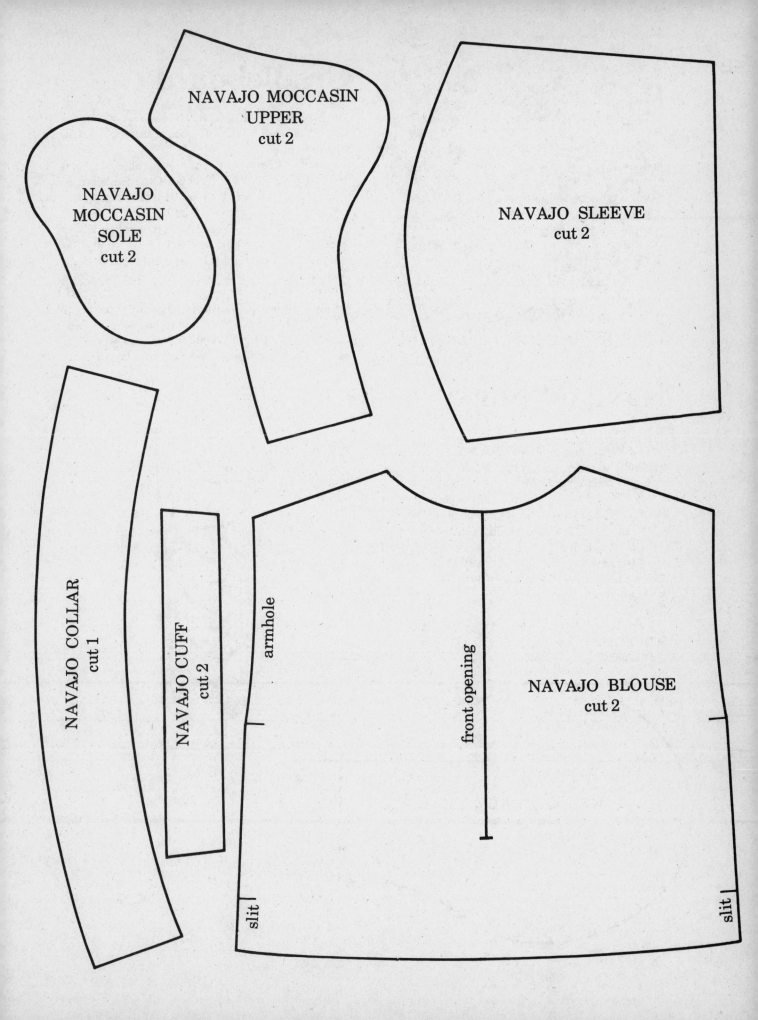

Cradleboard

MATERIALS 3¼″ x 11″ piece of ³⁄₁₆″ balsa wood; 8″ strip of ¾″ flexible wood trim; 1″ x 24″ strip of thin leather.

Follow 2 patterns to cut balsa cradleboard and footboard; mark and drill holes. Glue footboard in place. Cut 7½″ length of wood trim for head protector; drill 2 holes ³⁄₈″ from each end.

Cut four very narrow 2½″ leather strips; insert in holes to tie head protector to board. Cut ⅛″-wide leather strips for lacings. Insert a 4″ length through footboard to make a 2″ loop; trim, if necessary, and knot ends. Following side view, work a 22″ length through 5 holes along each side of board; tie ends.

Place doll on board on remaining flannel folded to fit. Tie a 14″ length of leather to three lower loops; weave through side loops and knot as in top view.

Navajo Baby

MATERIALS *For doll:* Scrap of pinkish tan cotton; kapok; 6-strand embroidery floss, scraps of tan and pink-orange, 1 skein of black; ½ yard white cotton flannel; ¼ yard white muslin.

Adding ½″ seam allowance, follow pattern to cut head pieces from tan cotton. Stitch together, leaving neck end open. Trim seams and turn; stuff firmly with kapok. Using stem stitch, work black closed eyes, tan nose and pink-orange mouth. For hair, cut 5″ lengths of black floss; fold and sew across top of seam and around back of head, covering it thickly. Trim floss.

For body about 2″ wide and 5″ long, fold ¼ yard of flannel and tack to neck; pad with kapok and wind with muslin, folded to fit.

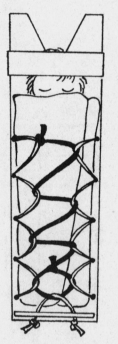

top view

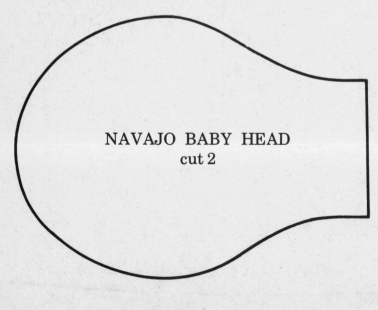

NAVAJO BABY HEAD
cut 2

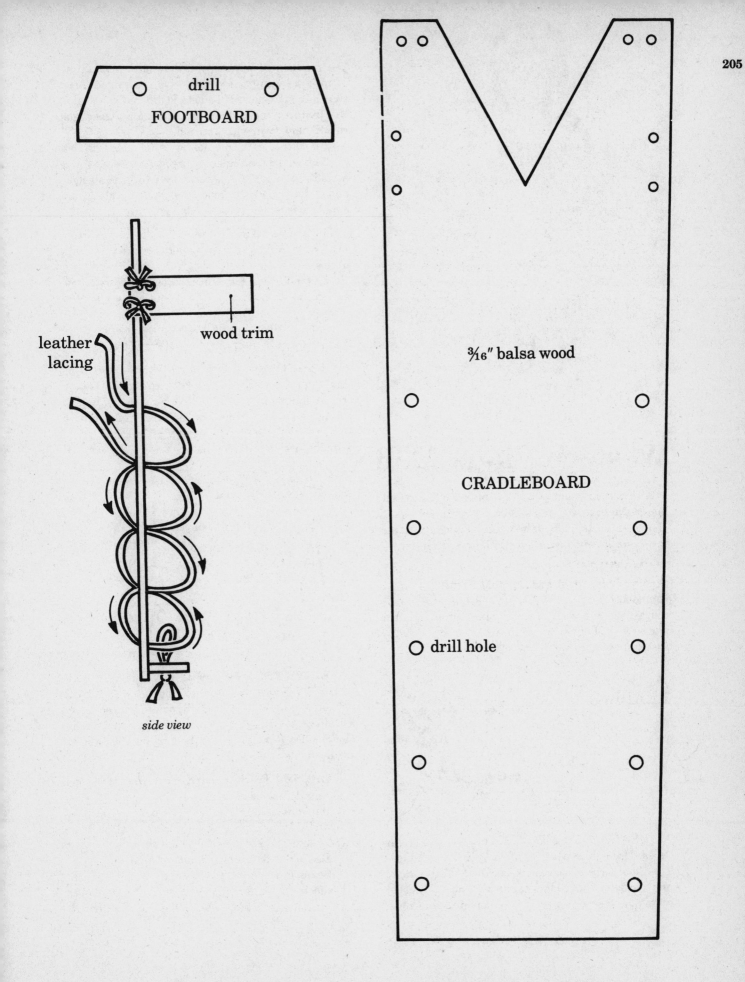

drill
FOOTBOARD

wood trim

leather
lacing

side view

¾₁₆″ balsa wood

CRADLEBOARD

drill hole

Western Sioux Doll

This Sioux maiden from the plains of North and South Dakota lives in a buffalo-skin tipi, or tepee. Her tribe hunts the buffalo, which provides meat for the Sioux as well as skins for clothing and shelter.

MATERIALS *For hairdo and costume:* 11 skeins of black 6-strand embroidery floss; 4 small chamois skins; small beads in light blue, dark blue, red, yellow and white; heavy aluminum foil pie tin and tiny beads for silver baubles.

Follow General Directions to make the doll.

BEADING

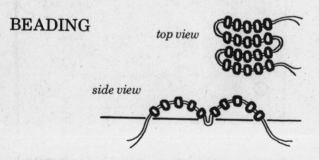

top view

side view

BEADING Use very small beads sold loose in tubes. Use a fine needle and long thread doubled. The Sioux type of beadwork is called "Lazy stitch" and consists of threading a given number of beads, often 5, and sewing them to leather in rows. As the beads are sewed down only at the beginning and end of rows as in top view, they give the ridged effect shown in side view. This method differs from that of the Iroquois, who string beads on one thread and couch them down with a second.

In these patterns, follow solid lines to cut chamois and dotted lines for areas to be beaded. Use actual-size photographs as guides to bead designs and colors. Because moccasins and leggings are small, do beadwork before cutting them out.

MOCCASINS Follow pattern to mark cutting and beaded areas on uppers; cut soles and two ⅛" x 6" ties.

Sew on beads, following photograph. Slit moccasin upper at center, making cuff; cut holes in cuff for ties.

To assemble, sew back seam; sew sole to upper. Turn down cuff; insert strip in holes and tie.

LEGGINGS Follow pattern to mark cutting and beaded areas; cut two ¼" x 6½" ties. Sew on beads, following photograph, which shows half of design; work second half to correspond. Seam each legging from lower edge to top of beading. Make baubles as below and sew on.

SILVER BAUBLE

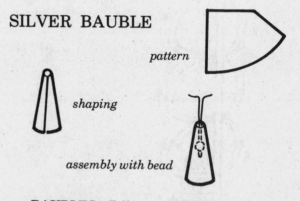

pattern

shaping

assembly with bead

BAUBLES Follow pattern to cut 10 aluminum-foil baubles for each legging; to shape, bend around a pointed paintbrush handle. To attach, slip a bead on thread, run it in and out of bauble as in sketch; sew to legging. Slip legging on doll; knot a tie around leg.

DRESS Follow pattern to cut dress front and back; mark beaded area on front only. Cut 7 pairs of slits in front and back with razor blade or pointed scissors. Cut opening about 3" long in center back. Cut 14 strips ⅛" x 4" to run through slits.

Sew on beads, following photograph.

Seam dress front to back at shoulders, right sides facing; turn. Fringe all unseamed edges. With fine running stitches, seam sides close to fringe,

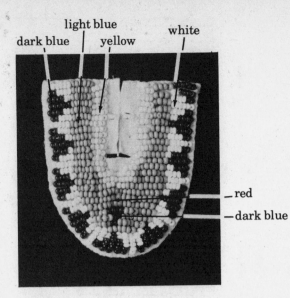

dark blue
light blue
yellow
white

red
dark blue

MOCCASIN BEADING

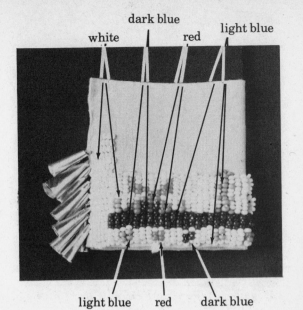

white
dark blue
red
light blue

light blue
red
dark blue

LEGGING BEADING
(half of design)

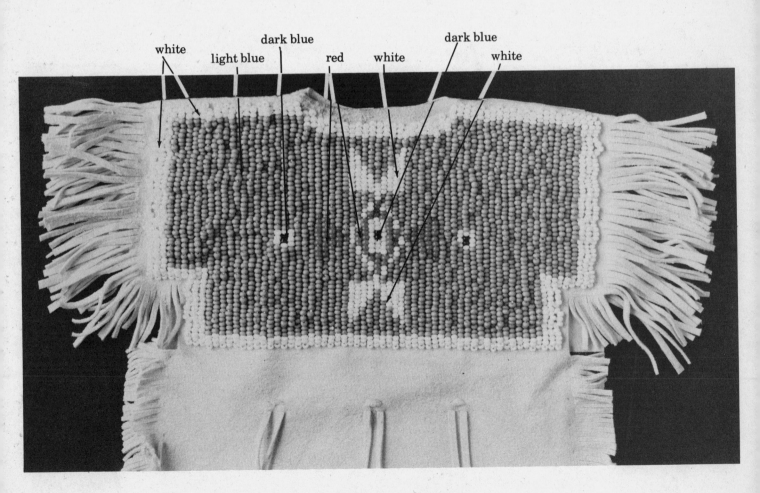

white
light blue
dark blue
red
white
dark blue
white

DRESS BEADING

208

from lower edges to within 2″ of beading. Run strips through slits. Tack back neck or sew on strips and tie.

hairdo

HAIRDO Place 28″ strands of embroidery floss across top and back of head. Sew along center, making a part 4¾″ long, as in drawing. Pull strands toward sides and divide into 3 equal sections; sew down middle section at area of ear. Make braids and wind ends with floss.

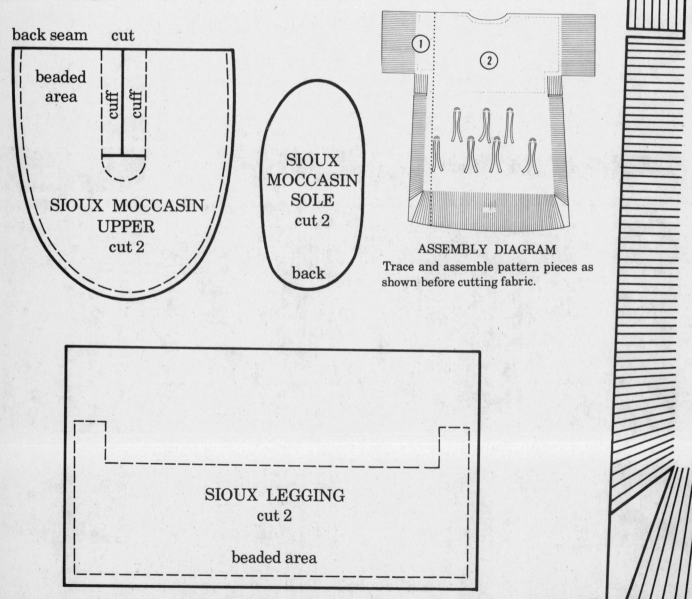

back seam   cut

beaded area   cuff cuff

SIOUX MOCCASIN UPPER
cut 2

SIOUX MOCCASIN SOLE
cut 2

back

ASSEMBLY DIAGRAM
Trace and assemble pattern pieces as shown before cutting fabric.

SIOUX LEGGING
cut 2

beaded area

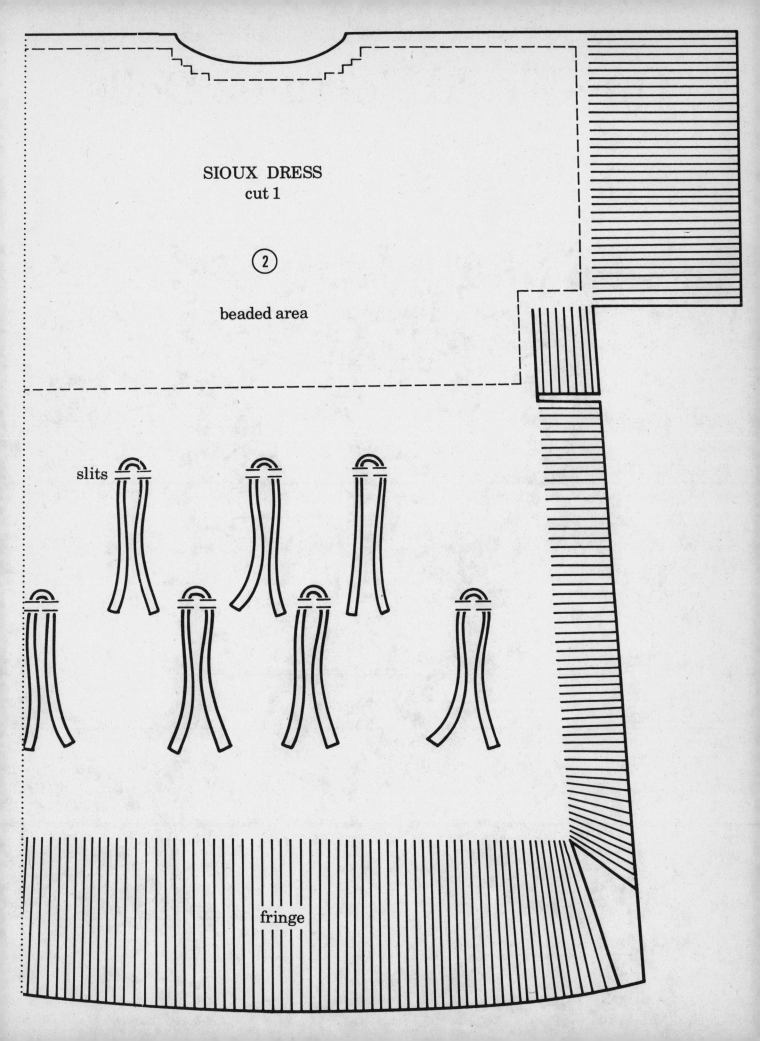

SIOUX DRESS
cut 1

②

beaded area

slits

fringe

One-World Costume Dolls

Six smiling friends from faraway places.

General Directions

MATERIALS *For each doll:* ⅜ yard of firm cotton and polyester blend 44" wide; matching thread; polyester fiber filling to stuff doll; one skein of yarn specified for hair; six-strand floss for features.

Follow 7 patterns for each doll. Pin and cut out all pieces from fabric specified, adding ½" seam allowance to each piece (see Construction Techniques, page 11).

BODY Pin and sew two body fronts together along the front seam. Pin and sew the center back to the two side backs along back seams. With right sides together, pin and sew front and back together along side seams. Stitch neck seams twice to reinforce them. Trim seam allowance and turn through open neck to right side.

HEAD Pin and sew side heads to center head, working with each side head toward you. Sew the seam carefully along curves of face. Every odd bump will show after you turn and stuff head, so it's better to check and correct each seam line now. Trim seam allowance and turn through open neck to right side.

ARMS Pin and sew two arm pieces together, stitching twice around thumb and finger edges. Leave top of arm open for stuffing. Trim seam allowance and clip at wrist and thumb. Turn to right side, pulling the thumb and fingers to the right side with a pin if necessary.

LEGS Pin and sew two leg pieces together, leaving top open for stuffing. Trim seam allowance and turn to right side.

STUFFING AND SEWING Stuff body and head with small pieces of polyester fiber filling until they are firm and smooth. Place the head on neck firmly. Keeping neck short, turn lower edge of head under and pin to body. Add more stuffing if needed. Sew head to neck with double thread, using small stitches.

Arms Stuff each firmly to just past the elbow; stuff upper arm slightly to within 1" of top. Turn top edges in and sew to make a rounded top. Pin arm to shoulder and sew securely.

Legs Stuff legs firmly almost to top. Turn in raw edges and sew closed. Pin legs to body and sew securely to front, about ½" from bottom seam.

FEATURES AND HAIR See individual dolls.

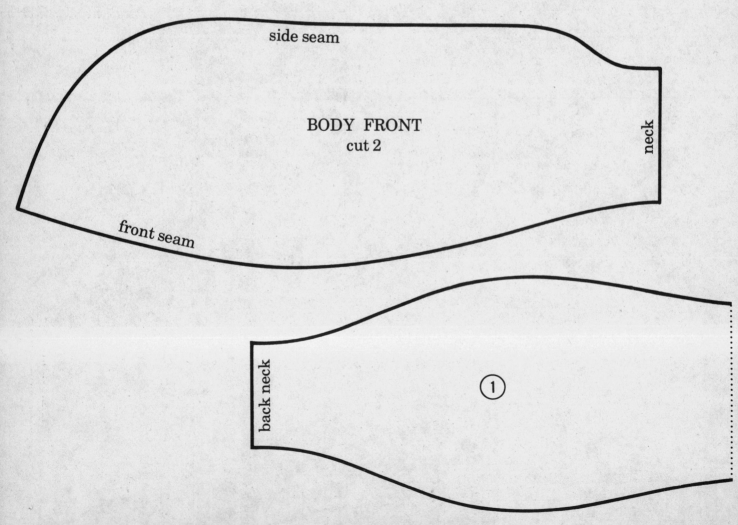

side seam

BODY FRONT
cut 2

neck

front seam

back neck

①

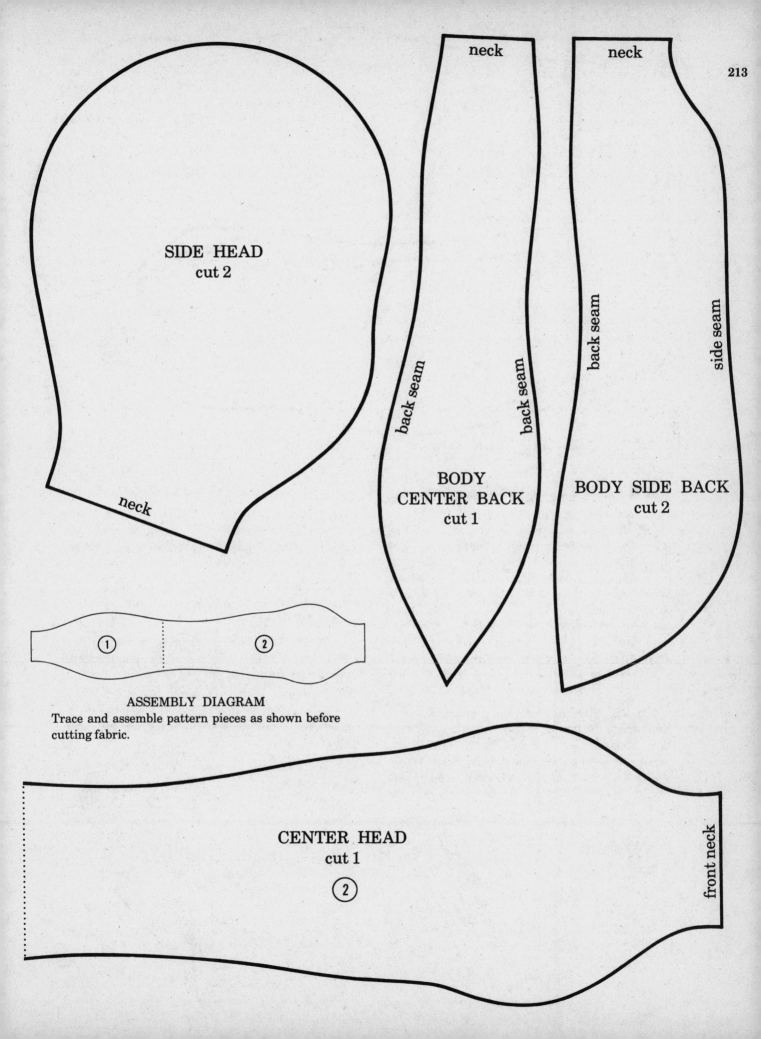

SIDE HEAD
cut 2

neck

neck

neck

back seam

back seam

BODY
CENTER BACK
cut 1

back seam

side seam

BODY SIDE BACK
cut 2

① ②

ASSEMBLY DIAGRAM
Trace and assemble pattern pieces as shown before
cutting fabric.

CENTER HEAD
cut 1

②

front neck

213

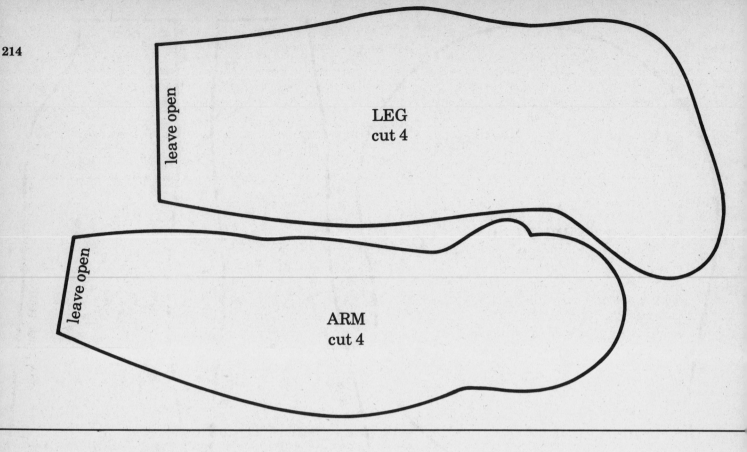

leave open

LEG
cut 4

leave open

ARM
cut 4

Soo-Ni from Korea

MATERIALS *For doll:* ⅜ yard 44″ rosy tan cotton; polyester fiber filling; 1 skein shiny black yarn; six-strand floss in black, deep beige and pink. *For costume:* ¼ yard 44″ white cotton fabric; ¼ yard 44″ red silk organza; ¼ yard 44″ yellow silk faille; scrap of white cotton knit; scraps of red and white felt; satin ribbon as follows: ¼″ wide, 1 yard red and ½ yard rose; ½″ wide, ½ yard each royal blue, yellow, green and 1 yard each red and white; 1½″ wide, 1 yard yellow for hair ribbons.

Follow General Directions to make doll.

HAIR Following sketches 1 and 2, use long, large-eyed needle to sew loops of yarn over doll's head. Make center part and have yarn ends reach to ear level, sewing ends smoothly to head. Fill in spaces between loops with 40″ lengths for braids; sew on 3″ loops for bangs. Divide strands in three

and sew center sections to head. Make braids, tie ends and trim. Loop back and tack ends to ear areas. Sew on yellow ribbon bows.

FACE Using black floss, satin-stitch almond eyes and outline-stitch brows. Outline-stitch beige nose and pink mouth.

COSTUME Follow 2 drawings and 8 patterns to cut garments, adding seam allowance unless specified otherwise.

Baggy Pants Following dimensions on drawings, cut 2 rectangles for pants legs and square center section from white cotton. Cut two 2″ x 6″ cuffs and 2″ x 11″ waistband.

3. *Seam A edges of leg pieces to A's of triangle.*

2. *Tack long strands between for braids.*

1. *Loop and sew yarn hair along center.*

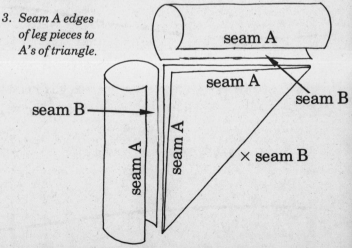

seam A

seam A

seam B

seam B

seam A

seam A

× seam B

Following sketch 3, fold triangle and seam A edges of leg pieces to A of triangle. Repeat with B edges. Gather ankle ends of pants to fit cuffs; pin and sew cuffs to right sides. Turn to wrong side and hem down.

Pin waistband to right side of waistline edge, gathering it to fit; stitch seam. Turn band in and hem down. Pants fit the doll loosely; they can be held up by skirt or a ribbon.

Skirt Cut red organza 9″ x 44″ and white cotton 1½″ x 10″ for waistband; cut two 8″ lengths of ¼″ white ribbon for ties.

Sew narrow hems on one long and two short edges of skirt. Sew 2 rows of gathering stitches along raw edge. Gather to fit doll and check length of skirt. Fold waistband and sew over gathers. Turn in waistband ends, insert ribbons and sew securely as ties.

Socks Follow pattern to cut white cotton knit, adding small seam allowance. Seam pieces, hem top edges and turn.

Shoes Follow 4 patterns to cut red felt uppers, white felt soles and back trim plus cardboard soles, adding seam allowance to uppers. With seams on outside, sew instep, sole and back seams. Rubber-cement cardboard soles inside shoes; cement back trim and white soles to outside.

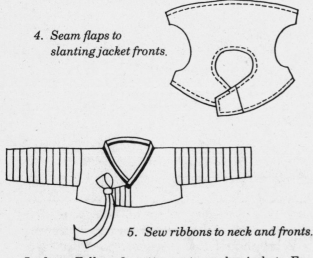

4. Seam flaps to slanting jacket fronts.

5. Sew ribbons to neck and fronts.

Jacket Follow 3 patterns to make jacket. For striped sleeves, first make two 5″ x 7″ rectangles from ribbon. Arrange so narrow ribbons are sewed over wide ones and wide ones overlap, making all stripes appear about ¼″ wide. Make one flap piece from ribbons also, with seam line at right. Cut sleeves by pattern, adding seam allowance. Cut 2 jackets and 3 flaps from faille.

Pin and sew flaps to front opening edges, with ribbon flap at left side. With right sides together, pin and seam jacket pieces at lower front, opening and

neckline edges; seam at lower back. See sketch 4. Trim seam allowance and turn to right side. Hem sleeve ends; sew sleeves to jacket armholes.

Try jacket on doll; pin side and sleeve seams. Remove and stitch. Fold ½″ red ribbon over neckline and sew; stitch narrow white ribbon over red. Fold ½″ red ribbon lengthwise and sew on 8″ strips for ties. See sketch 5.

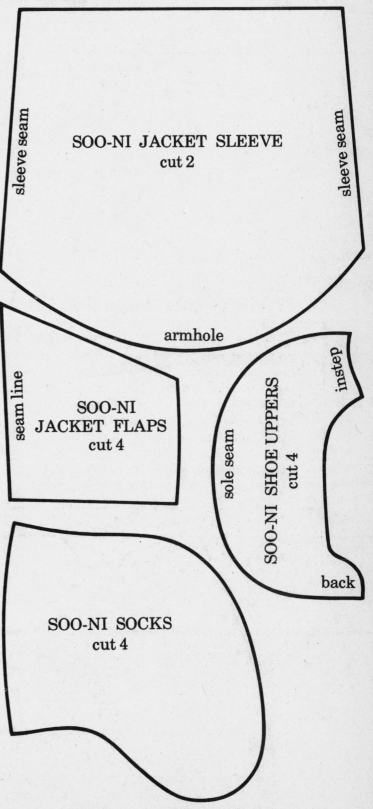

SOO-NI JACKET SLEEVE
cut 2

sleeve seam

sleeve seam

armhole

SOO-NI JACKET FLAPS
cut 4

seam line

SOO-NI SHOE UPPERS
cut 4

instep

sole seam

back

SOO-NI SOCKS
cut 4

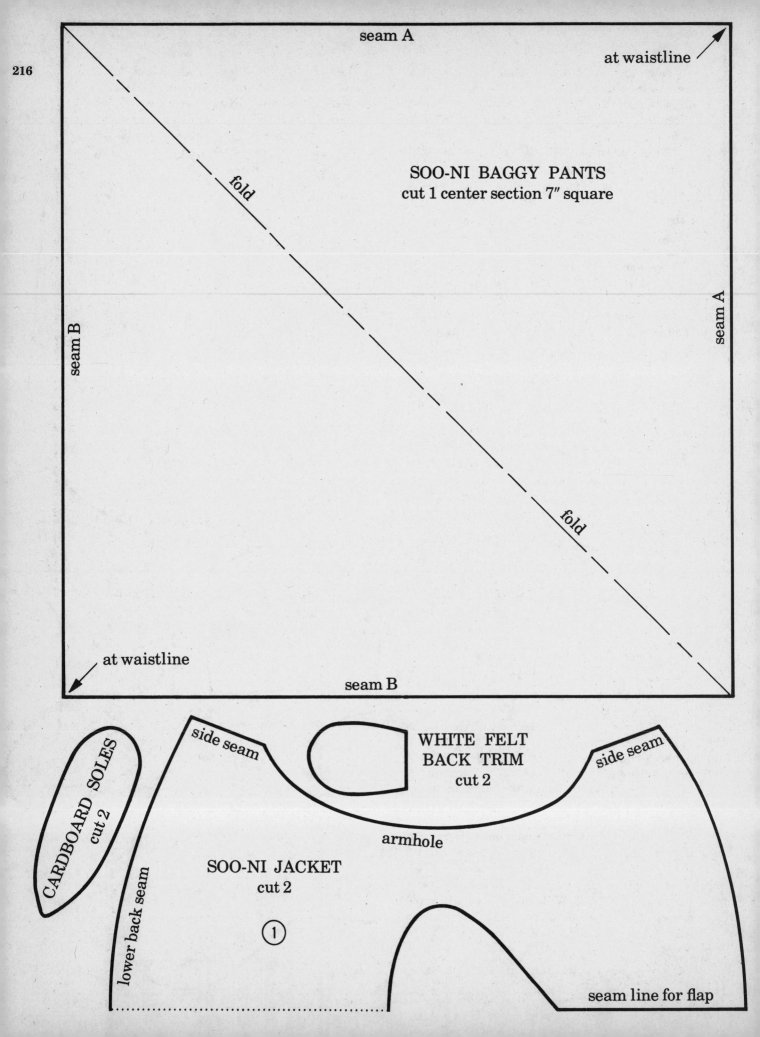

seam A

at waistline

fold

seam B

SOO-NI BAGGY PANTS
cut 1 center section 7″ square

seam A

fold

at waistline

seam B

CARDBOARD SOLES
cut 2

side seam

lower back seam

SOO-NI JACKET
cut 2

①

armhole

**WHITE FELT
BACK TRIM**
cut 2

side seam

seam line for flap

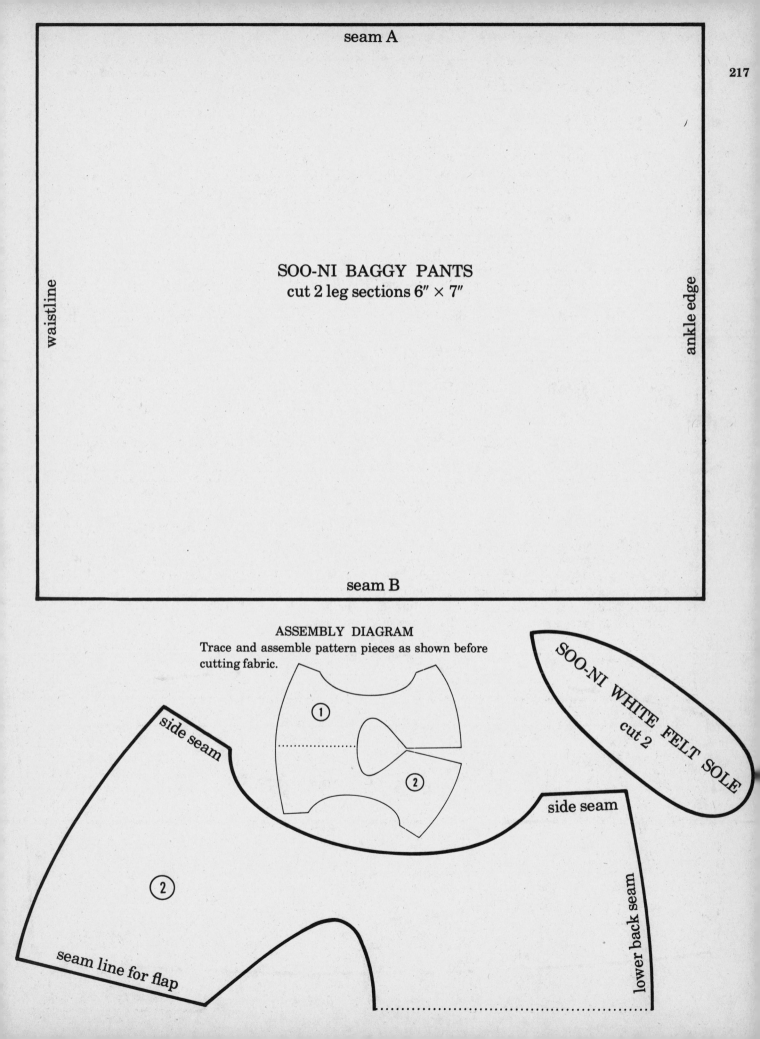

seam A

217

waistline

ankle edge

SOO-NI BAGGY PANTS
cut 2 leg sections 6″ × 7″

seam B

ASSEMBLY DIAGRAM
Trace and assemble pattern pieces as shown before
cutting fabric.

side seam

① ②

side seam

②

SOO-NI WHITE FELT SOLE
cut 2

lower back seam

seam line for flap

Howya from Alaska

MATERIALS *For doll:* ⅜ yard rosy tan 44″ cotton; polyester fiber filling; 1 skein black sport-weight knitting yarn; six-strand floss in black, orange and bright pink. *For costume:* ¼ yard 44″ imitation fur fabric; 4½″ x 36″ piece of suede cloth; ⅝ yard 44″ red and yellow calico; 1 skein off-white, heavy weight Orlon rug yarn; ⅝ yard each of bright green and yellow seam binding; ⅝ yard white tape; three 1½-yard lengths each of orange, yellow and green yarn.

Follow General Directions to make doll.

1. *Sew yarn hair near neck.*   2. *Cover head with stitches and loops.*   3. *For furry edging, stitch zigzag yarn to tape.*

HAIR Thread black yarn in a long, large-eyed needle and sew short-and-long stitches as in sketches 1 and 2. Beginning about an inch from crown, make 2″ stitches toward back neck. Continue around head, making strands shorter in ear areas and about 2″ in length for front bangs. Sew a row of loops over first strands then a third row from top of head. Cut a few loops for a shaggy effect.

FACE Cut out 1″ crescents of black fabric or felt in the approximate shape of the eyes. Try on doll's face until the effect is just right. Using a red pencil, make small dots on face around fabric eyes and take off shapes. Using black floss, satin-stitch "smiling" black eyes. Outline-stitch fine black eyebrows.

Using outline stitch, embroider orange nose and grinning pink mouth. Stroke cheeks with orange chalk.

COSTUME Follow 7 patterns to cut garments, adding ½″ seam allowance unless specified otherwise. Reverse patterns when back of fabric differs from front.

Fur Jacket and Pants Following 2 patterns and adding seam allowance, cut jacket and pants from fur fabric. With fur sides of jacket together, pin and sew side and shoulder seams. Omit hems on raw edges. Cut 4 narrow strips of imitation leather or suede cloth; sew as ties to top and middle of front opening. On pants, sew side and crotch seams; omit hems. Pull pants on doll.

Boots Following 2 patterns, cut soles and uppers from suede cloth. Do *not* add seam allowance. With double thread, sew line of running stitches around each sole. Place on doll's foot, gather to fit snugly and tie thread ends.

With right sides together, pin upper over gathered sole, matching toe and heel centers. Hand sew to sole, using backstitch and double thread. Sew back and turn boot. Turn under top edge; hem, if necessary.

crotch seam

HOWYA FUR PANTS
cut 2 on fold

waistline

side seam

Mittens Following pattern, cut 4 pieces from suede cloth, adding small seam allowance and reversing 2 pieces. Right sides together, sew seams, trim and turn. Tuck wrist edges under fur sleeves or hem.

Calico Parka Follow 2 patterns and cut parka section, folding calico at shoulder line and center; cut 4 hood pieces for outer hood and lining. Add seam allowance. Cut front opening on parka. To face opening, cut a ¾″ x 9″ bias strip; for ruffle, cut straight 4″ x 40″ strip.

With right sides together, pin and stitch facing to front opening. Turn to inside and hem raw edge.

Turn under each sleeve on fold line and sew 2 rows of gathering stitches. Try parka on doll over fur outfit; gather to fit arm, allowing fabric for seam; tie thread. Pin sleeve and side seams; remove and stitch. Trim seam allowance and finish with zigzag

stitch or as desired. Turn up ½″ of parka bottom to right side.

For ruffle, fold 4″-wide strip in half lengthwise and iron. Run 2 rows of gathering stitches along raw edges. Gather ruffle to fit parka bottom; pin over turned up edge and stitch. Trim excess above seam line. Topstitch green seam binding over seam. Fold yellow binding lengthwise, center on green and stitch.

For hood and lining, pin and stitch 2 pieces at center top and center back, with right sides together. Stitch front of lining to hood at front edges, right sides together. Turn; press front edge. Run stitching ½″ and ⅜″ from edge of casing.

With right sides together, pin outer hood to neck edge of parka jacket; stitch seam. Turn hood upward, fold in raw edge of lining and hem to neck.

For furry edging, cut white tape 1″ longer than hood front. Lay white yarn across tape in 5″ loops, zigzagging it. Stitch down tape center, pushing loops together as you sew. Be sure yarn is firmly attached. Cut loops and comb yarn. Sew tape around hood, avoiding casing.

Make a 36″ braid from yellow, green and orange yarn. With bobby pin, pull through hood casing for ties.

shoulder seam

side seam

HOWYA FUR JACKET
cut 2 on fold

cut front opening only   center fold

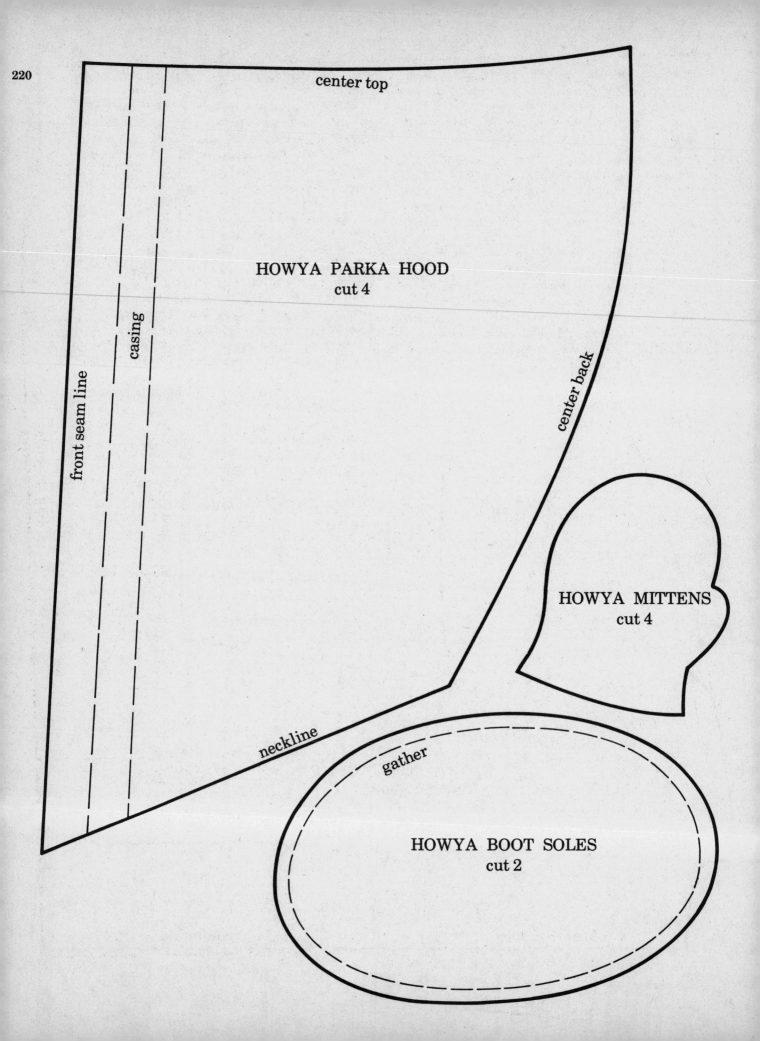

220

center top

HOWYA PARKA HOOD
cut 4

front seam line

casing

center back

neckline

gather

HOWYA MITTENS
cut 4

HOWYA BOOT SOLES
cut 2

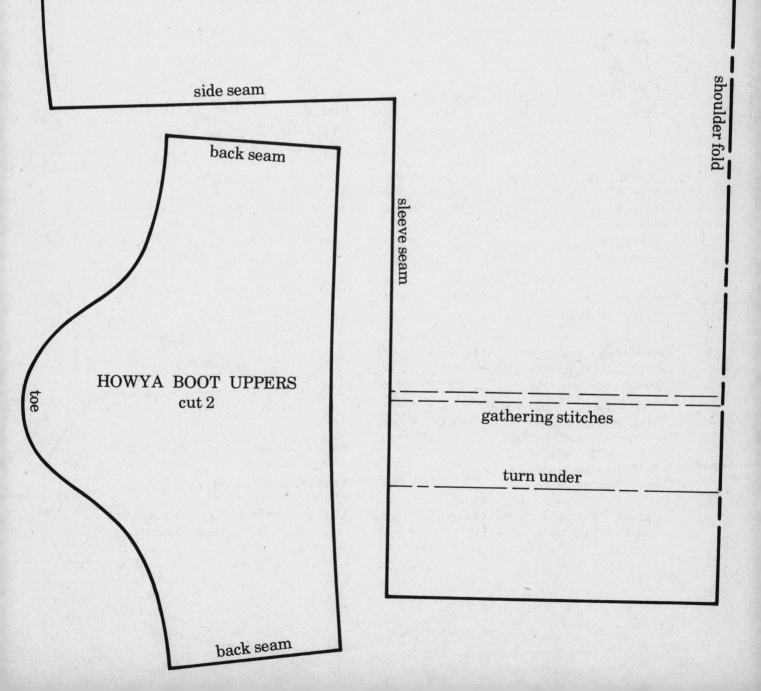

cut front opening to A

A

neckline

HOWYA PARKA JACKET
cut 1 on folds

shoulder fold

side seam

back seam

sleeve seam

HOWYA BOOT UPPERS
cut 2

toe

gathering stitches

turn under

back seam

222

Manuelo from Mexico

MATERIALS *For doll:* ⅜ yard rosy tan cotton; polyester fiber filling; 1 skein black sportweight yarn; six-strand floss in black, orange and deep orange. *For costume:* 12″ x 22″ piece of white cotton fabric; 2″ x 18″ strip of red silk (necktie); ¼ yard of 44″ navy velveteen; 9″ x 12″ piece of blue lining fabric; ⅜ yard cream-colored felt; scrap of deep brown felt; silver sequins; small silver chain or string of silver beads; ½″ x 18″ strip of brown suede cloth; buckle from a watch band; ½ yard narrow cream-colored ribbon; 2 silver buttons, 3 pearl buttons and 4 snaps.

Follow General Directions to make doll.

1. Stitch row of yarn hair around neck and ear areas; then add two rows above.

HAIR Thread black yarn in a long, large-eyed needle and sew to head in short and long stitches as in Sketch 1. Take inch-long stitches above back of neck and continue around head, making sideburns and short bangs. Work 2 more rows of longer stitches around, leaving some strands loose for tousled effect.

FACE Using black floss, satin-stitch black eyes and outline eyebrows. Work light orange nose and deep orange mouth.

COSTUME Follow 9 patterns to cut garments, adding seam allowance unless specified otherwise. When cutting velveteen pants and jacket, be sure nap runs in same direction.

Shirt Follow 3 patterns and cut white cotton, folding fabric to cut shirt in one piece and adding seam allowances throughout. Cut ¾″ x 16″ bias facing. Cut front opening.

Seam collar pieces, leaving inner edge open. Trim seams and corners, turn and press. Pin collar to right side of shirt neckline, with raw edges even; stitch seam. Pin facing to opening edges and around neckline, to right side of shirt and over collar. Sew ⅛″ from edge and turn facing to inside. Hem down raw edge.

Sew gathering stitches along sleeves and gather to fit cuffs. With right side of cuffs facing wrong side of sleeves, stitch seams. Turn cuffs to right side and hem down raw edges.

Try shirt on doll; pin sleeve and side seams to fit. Stitch seams, trim and overcast seam allowance. Hem bottom edge. Sew 3 buttons to opening with snaps underneath.

Necktie Turn under and hem 2″ x 18″ strip of red silk or other fabric. Place under collar and tie in bow.

Pants Follow pattern and cut 2 pieces from velveteen, adding seam allowance. Hand hem pants waistline and bottom edges. Try on doll and pin ⅛″ tuck down side of each leg, making flap for sequins. Allow room in pants legs for doll's feet. Stitch tucks. With right sides together, pin and stitch pants along back seam and front seam from A

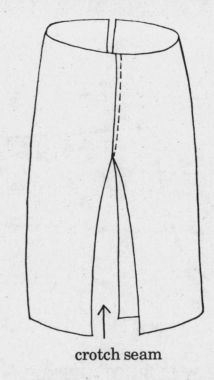

crotch seam

2. Seam pants from A up at back and front.

upward, leaving opening at top back. See sketch 2. Then pin and stitch inner leg seams and crotch. Sew waistline tucks if snug fit is desired; hem back opening and add snap. Sew sequins to legs.

Jacket Follow 3 patterns to cut velveteen and jacket lining, adding seam allowance. With right sides together, pin and seam collar pieces. Trim seam, turn and press lightly. Pin collar to right side of jacket from A to A, with raw edges even; stitch seam. Pin lining to right side of jacket and on top of collar; stitch front and neckline seams from B to B; stitch lower back seam from C to C. See Sketch 3.

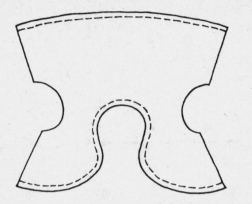

3. Seam lining to jacket along broken lines

Clip seam allowance at curves and turn lining to inside through open sides.

With right sides together, pin and stitch sleeves to armholes. Fit to doll and hem sleeve ends. Again try jacket on doll, over shirt and pants; pin sleeve and side seams. Stitch seams. Hem lining to armholes. Sew 2 silver buttons to front and add silver chain.

Belt Cut suede cloth ½″ wide to fit doll's waist plus 1″; cut ½″ x 1½″ belt keeper. Stitch belt and keeper edges for leather look. Punch belt and sew on buckle with prong. Fit belt, loop keeper around it and tack. Punch prong holes.

Boots Following 2 patterns, cut 4 uppers and 2 soles from brown felt, adding small seam allowance. Seam pairs of uppers from A, up front to top; turn. With right sides together, pin and hand sew uppers around soles; sew back seams and turn.

Sombrero Hat For crown, cut 9″ square of cream-colored felt. For brim, cut two 8″ diameter felt circles, using plate as a guide.

To shape crown, steam it over a large plastic-foam Easter egg, using a steam iron. Pull felt down and secure with straight pins; continue steaming, stretching and moving pins until crown is desired shape. Trim off excess.

Rubber-cement brims together and let dry. Use bottom of a ½-gallon 4¾″-diameter wine bottle or other object to curve up brim edge, steaming and pulling felt. Let dry. Cut out a small center circle in brim and slash opening edges to fit doll's head and crown. Turn up resulting brim tabs and place crown over them; sew together. Cement ribbon band over seam.

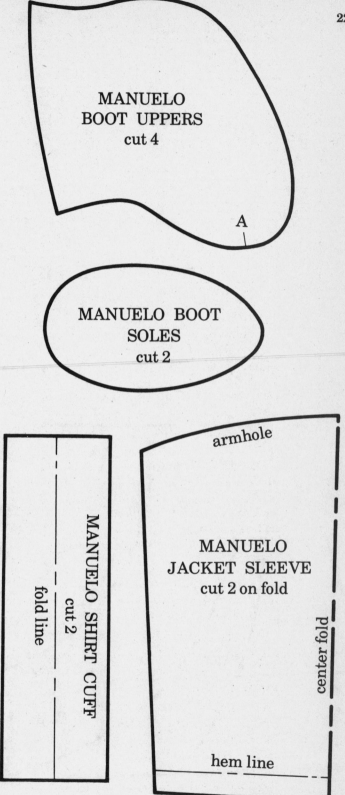

MANUELO
BOOT UPPERS
cut 4

A

MANUELO BOOT
SOLES
cut 2

MANUELO SHIRT CUFF
cut 2
fold line

armhole

MANUELO
JACKET SLEEVE
cut 2 on fold

center fold

hem line

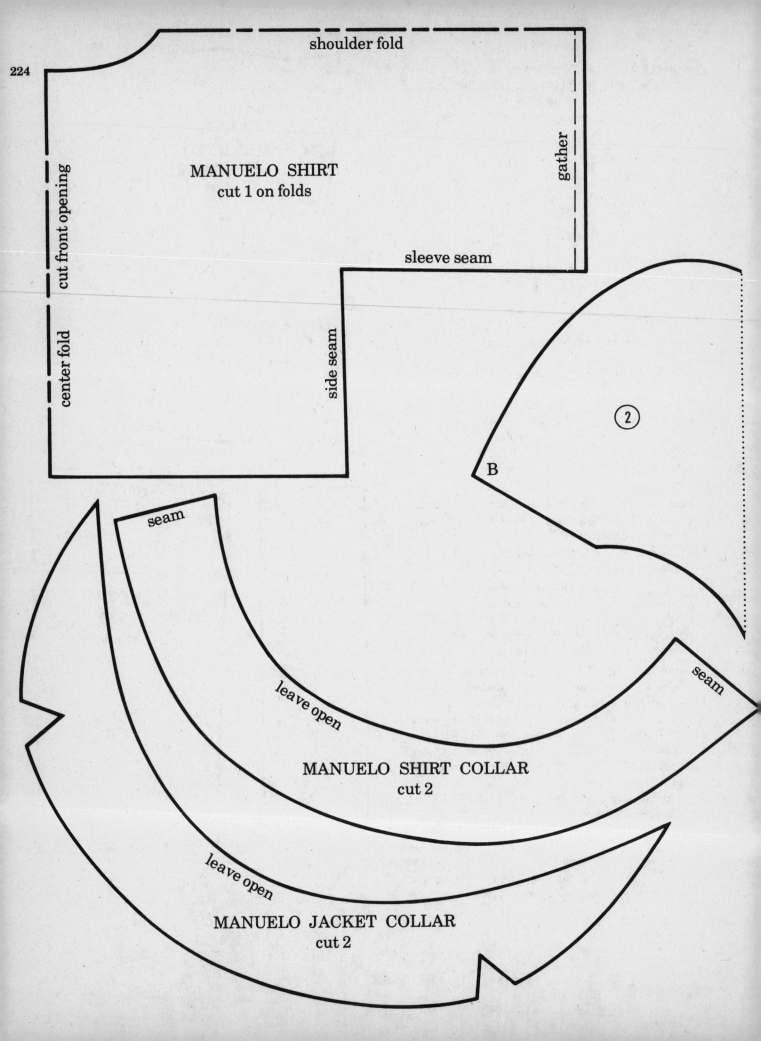

shoulder fold

224

cut front opening

gather

MANUELO SHIRT
cut 1 on folds

sleeve seam

center fold

side seam

②

B

seam

leave open

seam

MANUELO SHIRT COLLAR
cut 2

leave open

MANUELO JACKET COLLAR
cut 2

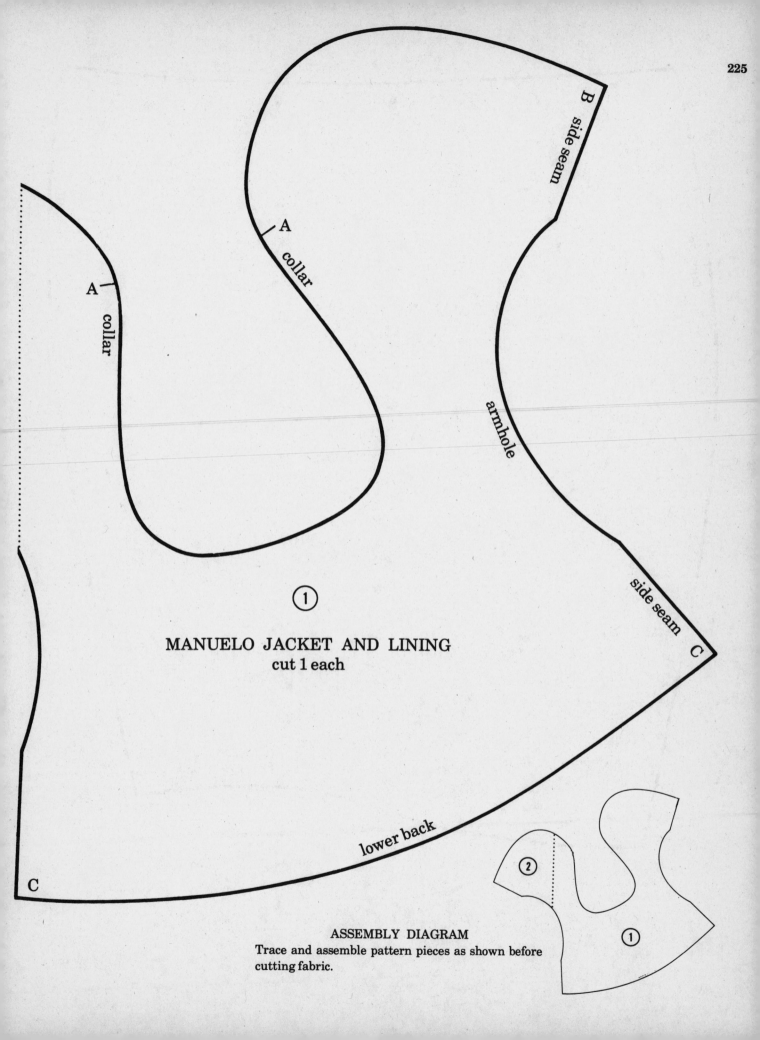

B

side seam

A

collar

A

collar

armhole

side seam

C

①

MANUELO JACKET AND LINING
cut 1 each

②

①

C

lower back

ASSEMBLY DIAGRAM
Trace and assemble pattern pieces as shown before
cutting fabric.

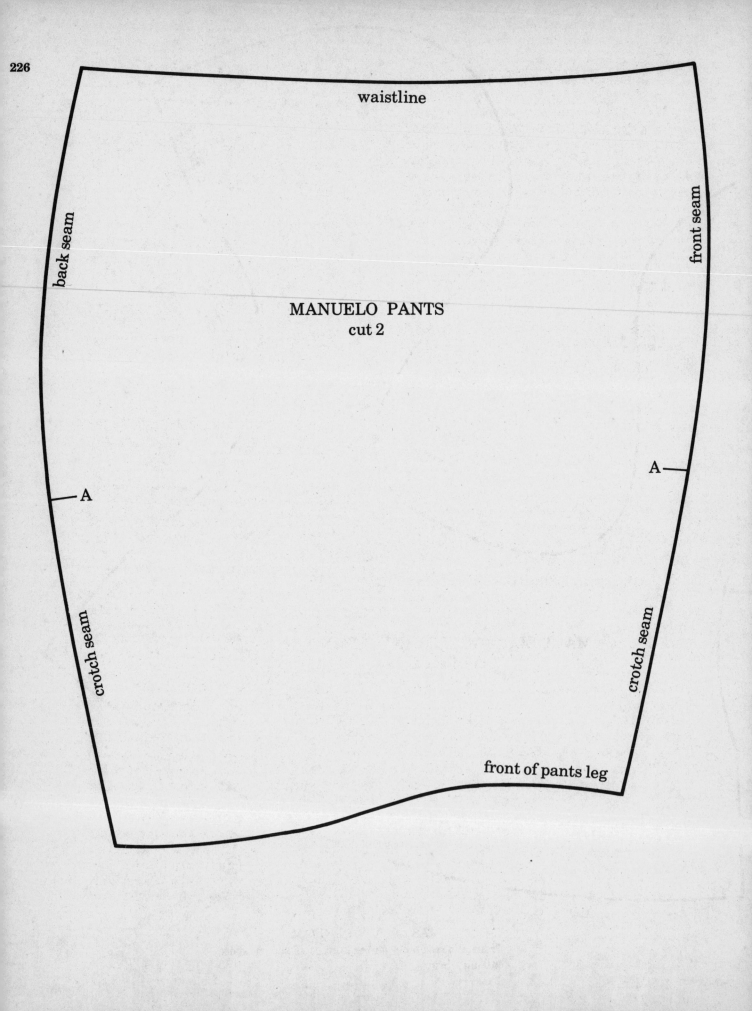

waistline

back seam

front seam

MANUELO PANTS
cut 2

A

A

crotch seam

crotch seam

front of pants leg

Ari from Greece

MATERIALS *For doll:* ⅜ yard 44″ beige cotton; polyester fiber filling; 1 skein sport-weight brown yarn; six-strand floss in brown, beige and orange-pink. *For costume:* ¾ yard 44″ white cotton fabric; 11″ x 15″ piece of white cotton knit fabric; 4″ x 20″ strip of lightweight tan fabric; ¼ yard 44″ turquoise fabric; scrap of brown felt; 6″ x 16″ piece of medium-weight red knit fabric; 1 ball of black crochet cotton; 10″ length each of black soutache braid and cord; ¾ yard each of gold braid and cord; ½″ button to cover with fabric; 6 small pearl buttons; 3 snaps.

Follow General Directions to make doll.

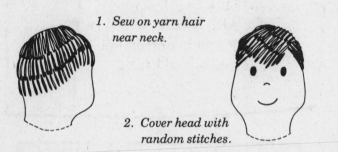

1. Sew on yarn hair near neck.

2. Cover head with random stitches.

HAIR Thread brown yarn in a long, large-eyed needle and sew to head in long and short stitches as in sketches 1 and 2. Beginning at back of neck, work 1″ stitches around head. Mark side part and work 2 more rows at random, making lock on brow.

FEATURES Using brown floss, satin-stitch oval eyes. Outline-stitch beige nose and orange-pink mouth.

COSTUME Follow 9 patterns to cut garments, adding seam allowance unless specified otherwise.

Shirt Follow 2 patterns and cut white cotton, folding fabric to cut shirt in one piece and adding seam allowances throughout. Cut ¾″ x 17″ bias facing. Cut front opening.

Seam collar pieces, leaving inner edge open. Trim seam and corners, turn and press. Pin collar to right side of shirt neckline, with raw edges even and collar ends about ¼″ from opening. Stitch seam. Pin facing to opening edges and around neckline, to right side of shirt and over collar. Sew facing with narrow seam and turn to inside; hem down raw edge.

Try shirt on doll. Pin under sleeve ends and hem them. Sew 2 snaps at top and middle of front opening; trim with 6 tiny buttons. Again try shirt on doll; pin sides and very full sleeves to fit. Remove; stitch seams and trim allowance. Hem lower edge.

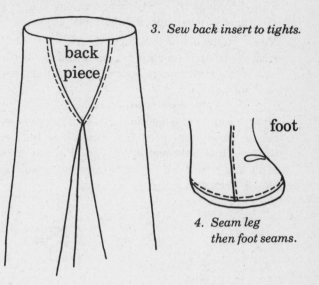

3. Sew back insert to tights.

4. Seam leg then foot seams.

Tights Follow 2 patterns to cut white knit fabric, with grain of fabric running up and down. Pin and sew back insert to both back seam edges of main piece. See sketch 3. Cut opening for legs. Fit fabric to doll and pin inside leg seams. Remove and stitch. Pin and sew feet seams; hem waistline. See sketch 4.

Garters Tack black soutache braid and cord below each knee. For tassel, wind black crochet cotton around 1¼″ cardboard. Tie, remove and wind with cotton. Tack to back of leg.

Shoes Following 3 patterns, cut brown felt, adding small seam allowance. Cut cardboard soles. Sew each pointed instep to upper, joining edge A–A to B–B with ¹⁄₁₆″ seams. Keeping all seams on the outside, sew upper to sole, gathering toe to fit; sew back seam. Glue cardboard inside.

For pompons, wind black crochet cotton over 2″ cardboard. Tie, remove cotton and trim into balls. Tack to insteps.

Skirt Cut 8″ x 36″ skirt and 1½″ x 10½″ waistband from white cotton. Fold skirt in half the long way and iron; hem ends. Make tiny pleats by folding fabric and basting down pleats as you go; or sew on machine, using a long stitch. Machine-baste one row along folded edge, which is bottom of skirt; baste another row halfway up to hold pleats. Press pleats with iron. Pin the raw edges of still-basted skirt to waistband, right side of waistband to underside of skirt. Stitch seam. Turn waistband to outer side, turn raw edge under and topstitch over first seam.

Turn in waistband ends and sew closed. Fit around doll and add snap. Take out basting.

Sash Cut lightweight tan fabric about 4″ x 20″. Pull threads to make 1½″ fringe on one long edge. Pleating top, wind around waistline; lap and pin.

Vest Following 2 overlapping patterns, cut 1 back, 2 fronts and lining from turquoise cotton, adding seam allowance. Seam 2 fronts to each back at shoulders.

 With right sides together, seam lining to vest along lower front edges and around neckline; seam across lower back. Trim seam allowance and turn lining to inside through open edges. Pin side seams to fit and sew. Turn in armhole edges ⅛″ and sew closed. Trim vest with braid and cord.

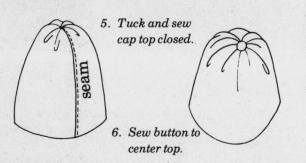

5. *Tuck and sew cap top closed.*

6. *Sew button to center top.*

Cap Cut 6″ x 14½″ piece of red knit fabric. Seam 6″ edges and turn. To close top end of cap, fold in tucks and sew together tightly by hand. Cover a ½″ button with fabric and sew to center top; fold under bottom edge. See sketches 5 and 6.

 For tassel, wind black crochet cotton around 3¼″ cardboard. Tie loops at top and fasten to button. Wind around loops tightly and cut lower ends.

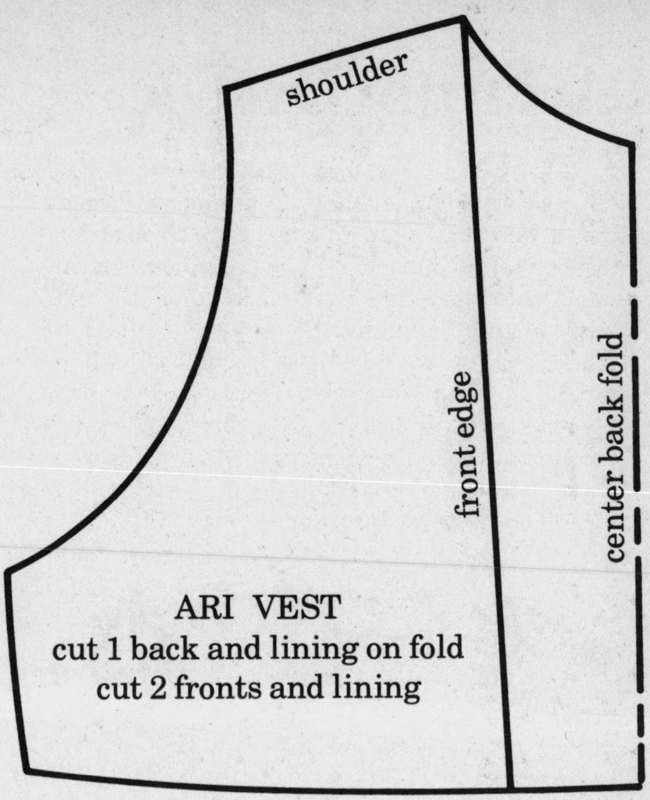

shoulder

front edge

center back fold

ARI VEST
cut 1 back and lining on fold
cut 2 fronts and lining

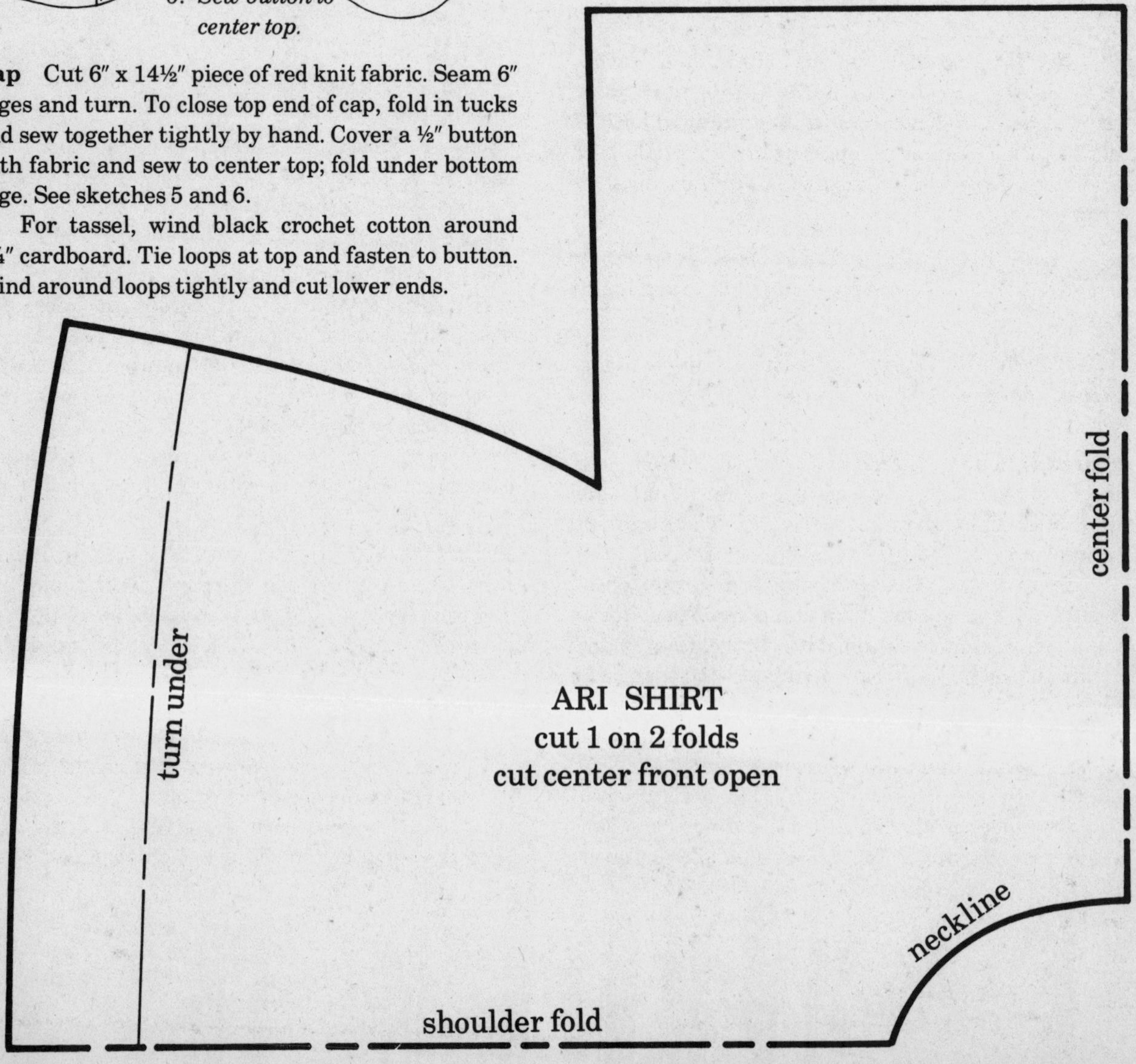

center fold

turn under

ARI SHIRT
cut 1 on 2 folds
cut center front open

neckline

shoulder fold

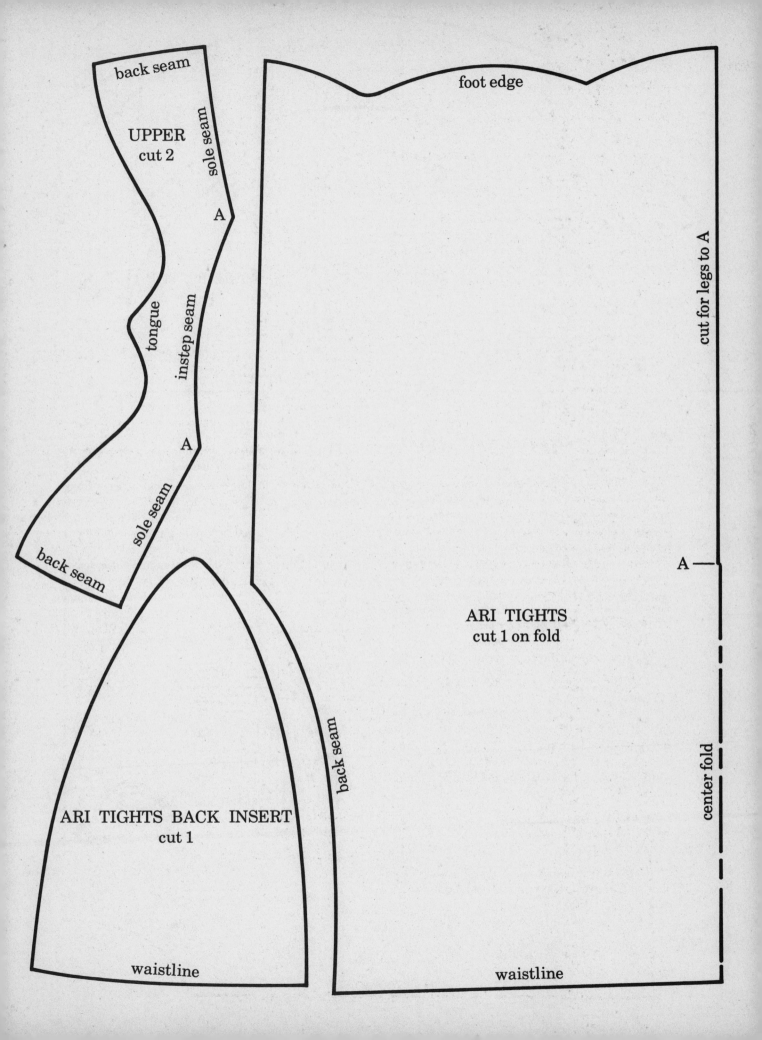

back seam

UPPER
cut 2

sole seam

A

tongue

instep seam

A

sole seam

back seam

foot edge

cut for legs to A

A —

ARI TIGHTS
cut 1 on fold

back seam

ARI TIGHTS BACK INSERT
cut 1

center fold

waistline

waistline

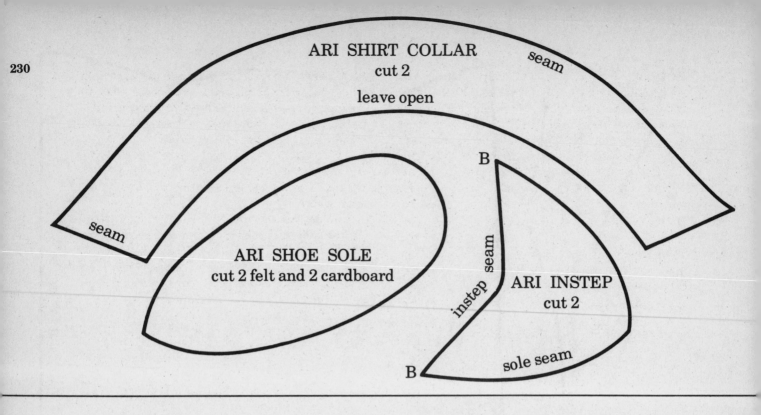

ARI SHIRT COLLAR
cut 2
leave open

seam

seam

B

ARI SHOE SOLE
cut 2 felt and 2 cardboard

instep seam

ARI INSTEP
cut 2

B

sole seam

Caitlin from Wales

MATERIALS *For doll:* ⅜ yard light pink cotton; polyester fiber filling; 1 skein orange sportweight yarn; six-strand floss in deep green, pink-orange and pink. *For costume:* ½ yard 44″ white cotton fabric; ¼ yard each of bright red cotton and green-and-white gingham; 8″ square of homespun-style striped fabric; ½ yard eyelet embroidery edging; ¾ yard 1½″ gathered lace (cap); 1 yard 1″ white satin ribbon; pair of child's white cotton socks; 9″ x 12″ pieces of felt—3 black and 1 orange-red; 9″ x 30″ iron-on interfacing; 4 snaps; 2 buttons.

Follow General Directions to make doll.

HAIR Following sketches 1 and 2, sew long strands of orange yarn over top of doll's head, making a side part. Fold strands and sew loops across back of head. Pull hair to one side, making a dip across forehead. Sew in place. Take several strands of yarn and curl over fingers. Place curl against head and sew in place. Repeat all around head at different levels.

FACE Using green floss, satin-stitch oval eyes. Outline-stitch orange brows and nose, pink mouth.

COSTUME Follow 7 patterns to cut garments, adding seam allowance unless specified otherwise.

Note: Before cutting white cotton fabric, carefully plan placement of garments to be made from it: underpants, petticoat, blouse and cap.

Underpants Follow pattern and cut 2 pieces from white cotton, adding seam allowance. Cut waistband 1¼″ x about 14″. Pin and sew crotch seam. Fold up legs and hem. Fit pants to doll, pinning side seams and making tucks at waist. Open one side seam at top and remove pants. Stitch tucks and sides, leaving generous opening. Hem edges of opening.

Pin and stitch right side of waistband to wrong side of pants. Turn waistband to right side. Fold under raw edge and stitch over first seam. Turn in and sew ends; add snap.

1. *Sew yarn across head making side part.*

2. *Curl yarn around fingers and sew to head.*

Petticoat Cut 7½" x 18" skirt from white cotton and waistband 1¼" x about 15". Stitch 1" hem on one long edge of skirt; sew eyelet edging over hem. Pin and sew one or two narrow tucks above hem. Sew 2 rows of gathering stitches along top edge. Fit waistband to doll, gather skirt to fit band and attach band as in underpants. Stitch back seam, leaving upper third of seam open. Hem edges and add snap.

Blouse Following 2 patterns, cut blouse and cuffs from white cotton, adding seam allowance; cut 1¼" x 15" neck ruffle. Cut back opening in blouse. Fold and press ruffle strip lengthwise. Run 2 rows of gathering stitches along raw edges; gather to fit blouse neck and tie thread ends. With raw edges even, pin and stitch to right side of neck; trim seams and overcast. Turn up ruffle; hem back opening.

Sew gathering stitches along sleeve ends; gather to fit cuffs. Right sides together, pin and stitch cuffs to sleeves. Turn in cuffs and sew to inside.

Try blouse on doll over underwear; pin sleeve and side seams to fit. Remove blouse. Stitch seams, trim and overcast edges. Hem bottom edge. Add 2 snaps to opening and buttons to cuffs.

Skirt Cut 7" x 19" skirt from red cotton and 1¼" x 15" waistband. Following method for petticoat, hem lower edge of skirt and gather upper. Add waistband and fasten with snap.

Apron Cut 6" x 12" skirt, 1¼" x 15" waistband, 3½"-square pocket and two 1" x 8" ties, all from green gingham. Turn in pocket edges and topstitch to skirt. Fold ties lengthwise and topstitch.

As for petticoat, hem lower edge of skirt and gather upper. Add waistband, inserting ties in ends.

Socks Pin a child's white sock to fit around each doll leg. Remove sock and cut, seam leg and foot on wrong side, overcast seam and turn to right side.

Shoes Follow 2 patterns to cut soles and uppers from orange-red felt, adding small seam allowance. Cut two ⅜" x 3" straps. Cut cardboard soles. Sew uppers to soles, stitching back seams twice. Trim seams and turn shoes. Glue cardboard soles inside. Sew on straps.

Shawl Pull threads in 8" square of striped fabric for fringed edges. Fold into triangle and pin to doll or tuck ends inside apron.

White Cap Cut 8"-diameter circle from white cotton. Hem edge and trim with 1½"-wide gathered lace. Sew gathering stitches around circle, gather to fit doll's head and fasten thread ends. For ties, sew on ½-yard lengths of white ribbon.

Black Hat Following 2 patterns, cut crown on fold and crown top from black felt, adding seam allowances; cut stiffening for pieces from iron-on interfacing. Cut two 7½"-diameter felt brims and 1 interfacing brim. Iron interfacing to all pieces.

With right sides together, sew crown side seam. Outline seam allowance on crown top with light pencil; pin to crown wall and sew with narrow seam. Trim seam allowance.

Rubber-cement brims together with interfacing between and cut out small center circle. See sketch 3. Slash cutout's edge and fit to doll's head and crown. Stay-stitch inner brim. Turn up brim tabs; cement, then sew to crown edge. Let dry; turn to right side.

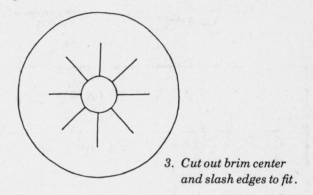

3. Cut out brim center and slash edges to fit.

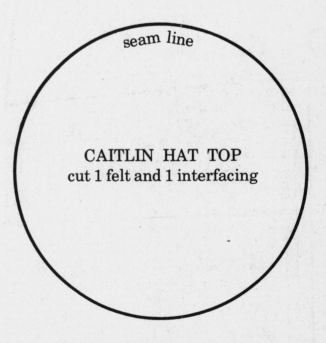

seam line

CAITLIN HAT TOP
cut 1 felt and 1 interfacing

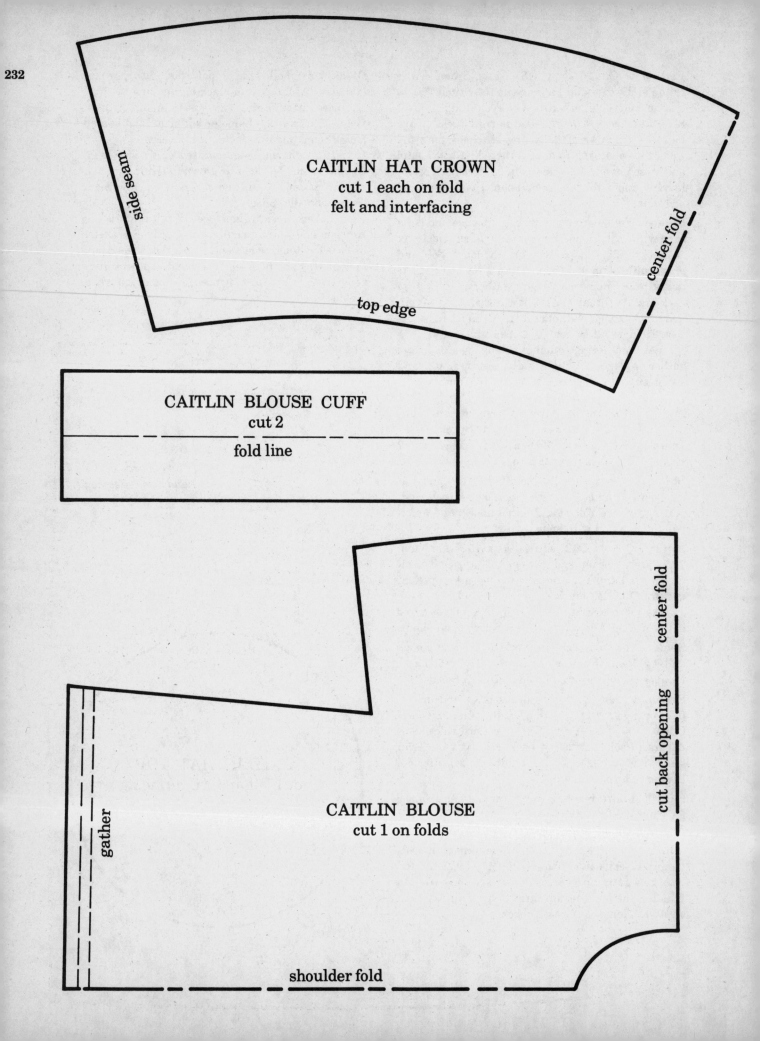

232

CAITLIN HAT CROWN
cut 1 each on fold
felt and interfacing

side seam

center fold

top edge

CAITLIN BLOUSE CUFF
cut 2

fold line

center fold

cut back opening

gather

CAITLIN BLOUSE
cut 1 on folds

shoulder fold

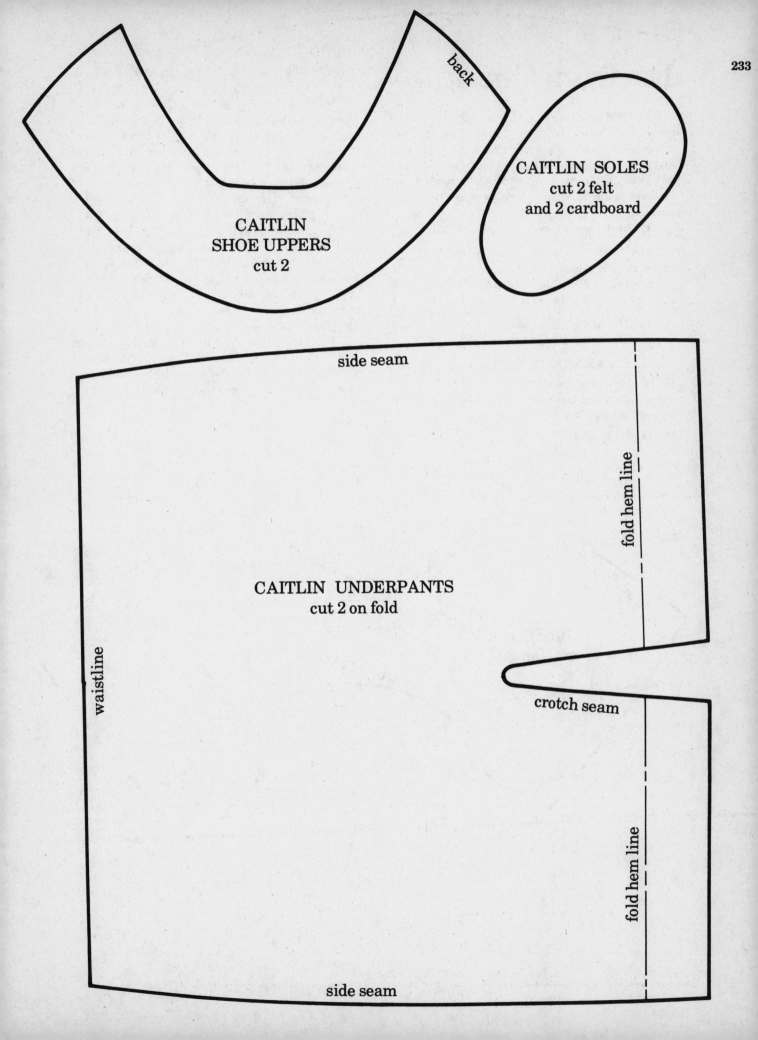

CAITLIN SOLES
cut 2 felt
and 2 cardboard

back

**CAITLIN
SHOE UPPERS**
cut 2

side seam

fold hem line

CAITLIN UNDERPANTS
cut 2 on fold

waistline

crotch seam

fold hem line

side seam

Esi from Ghana

MATERIALS *For doll:* ⅝ yard of chocolate brown 44″ cotton; polyester fiber filling; 1 skein black mohair yarn; six-strand floss in black, orange and deep pink. *For costume:* ⅜ yard blue and white 44″ cotton print; ⅜ yard matching narrow ribbon; 2 snaps; pair of small earrings; seed beads for necklace.

Follow General Directions to make doll.

HAIR Wind black yarn around index finger 3 times; place loop on doll's head and sew in place with needle and doubled thread. Continue making curls in rows around doll's head until it is thickly covered.

FACE Using floss, satin-stitch round black eyes; outline-stitch orange nose and pink mouth.

COSTUME

Underskirt Cut print fabric 8″ x 16″. Turn raw edges under and hem along all sides. Wrap skirt around doll and tie with ribbon at waist.

Dress Following pattern, cut 2 bodices on front folds, adding seam allowance. Cut 4½″ x 20″ top skirt.

With right sides together, pin and seam bodices along back openings and neckline. Trim seam allowance. Turn to right side and press. Turn raw edges of armholes in ⅛″ and sew. Try bodice on doll, pinning back opening closed and side seams to fit. Remove bodice and sew side seams.

On skirt strip, turn ½″ of one long edge to wrong side and hem. Also hem two ends of skirt. Sew 2 rows of gathering stitches along upper raw edge. Pull threads to fit waistline edge of bodice. With right sides together, pin skirt to outer bodice, making sure gathers are evenly spaced. Sew seam and trim seam allowance. Turn bodice upward, fold in raw edge of inner bodice and hem to skirt. Sew snaps along back opening.

For necklace, thread a very slim needle with strong thread and string beads to fit. Tie around neck or attach to clasp. For earrings, buy a tiny pair or make from beads; sew to doll's head.

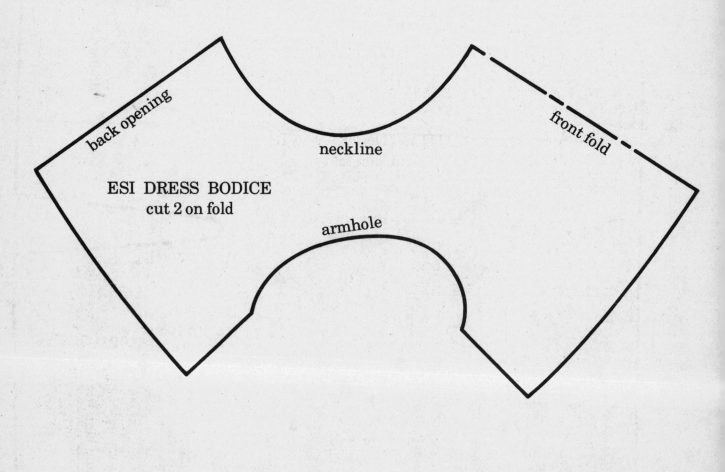

back opening
neckline
front fold

ESI DRESS BODICE
cut 2 on fold

armhole

This Is Amy.
She's a Doll!

Amy is a charming 14-inch edition of Joan Russell's youngest child. This large doll has five colorful outfits in her sensational wardrobe and a small doll of her own.

Amy Doll

MATERIALS ¼ yard of 42″ pink cotton fabric; scrap of blue fabric for eyes; polyester fiber filling; brown wool yarn for hair; embroidery floss in blue, light pink and orange-pink; thread to match skin fabric and brown yarn; ½ yard ⅞″ striped ribbon for bow.

Following 7 patterns, cut doll from pink cotton, *adding seam allowance*. Note that center head is to be cut on the bias.

BODY Pin two front bodies together, right sides facing, along the front seam. Stitch seam from neck to A, reinforcing neck by sewing seam twice. Pin center back to one side back along back seam. Stitch seam from neck to A. Pin center back to other side back and seam. Pin and join front and back pieces along side seams, with right sides facing. Trim seam allowance, clipping it carefully along neck edge. Turn to right side.

HEAD Pin one side head to center head, holding the side piece so it faces you and easing the center piece to fit. Baste and sew the seam carefully, especially around cheeks and forehead. Any irregularities will be especially prominent after the head is stuffed. Pin, baste and sew the other side head to the center head. Check seams and do them again if they are at all crooked or uneven. Trim seam allowance and turn to right side.

ARMS Pin two arm pieces together, with right sides facing. Stitch seam, leaving a part of two upper edges open for stuffing. Sew seam twice around hand, from wrist to wrist. Trim seam allowance and turn to right side. Repeat for other arm.

LEGS Pin two leg pieces together and stitch seam around leg, leaving top open for stuffing. Trim seam allowance and turn to right side. Repeat for other leg.

ASSEMBLY Stuff body, head, arms and legs, using small bits of polyester fiber. Stuff firmly but leave about ¼″ space at top of each arm and leg so they can be sewed on easily.

Pin head to body, turning under raw edge of head's neckline; add stuffing if needed. Sew with double thread and use tiny stitches. Turn in raw edges of top of each arm, following pattern shape. Sew opening closed by hand. Fold over top of arm and pin to body, with fold at shoulder and end B at underarm. Sew arms to body with double thread. Using dotted lines on hands as guide, sew lines to indicate fingers. Turn in raw edges of top of each leg so foot points forward; sew opening closed by hand. Pin legs to front body about 1″ in front of point A and sew securely in place.

HAIR For bangs, lay loops of wool yarn 2″ to 2¼″ long on doll's forehead, with loop ends about an inch above eyes. Sew tops of loops to head. Lay yarn loops about 9″ to 10″ long across top and back of head; sew along middle, making a center part. Fill in with loops sewed to sides and lower back to head.

FACE Follow pattern guide or draw the face you wish with chalk or pink pencil. Embroider blue eyes in satin stitch, backing eyes with small dots of matching fabric. Outline-stitch light pink nose and orange-pink mouth.

HAIR RIBBON Make a 3½″ tailored bow, wrap center and tack to head.

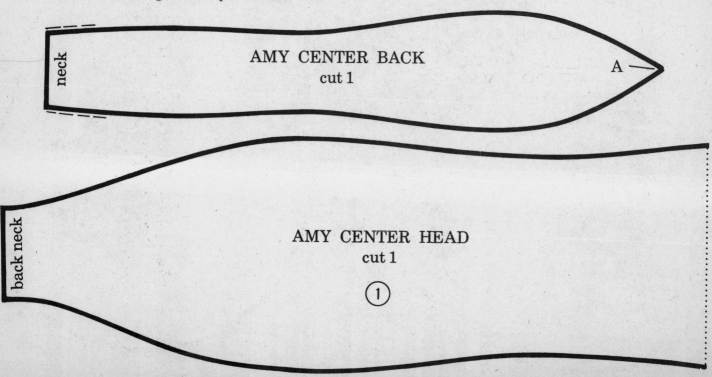

AMY CENTER BACK
cut 1

neck

A

AMY CENTER HEAD
cut 1

back neck

①

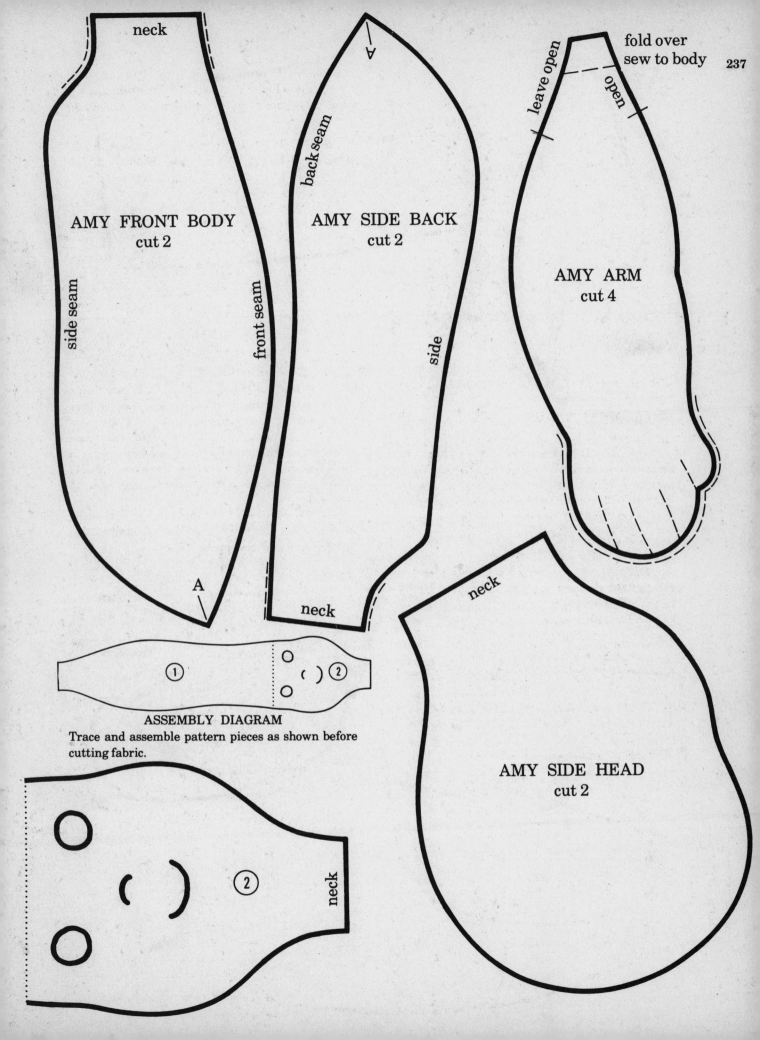

neck

AMY FRONT BODY
cut 2

side seam

front seam

A

back seam

AMY SIDE BACK
cut 2

side

neck

leave open

**fold over
sew to body**

open

AMY ARM
cut 4

neck

AMY SIDE HEAD
cut 2

① ②

ASSEMBLY DIAGRAM
Trace and assemble pattern pieces as shown before
cutting fabric.

②

neck

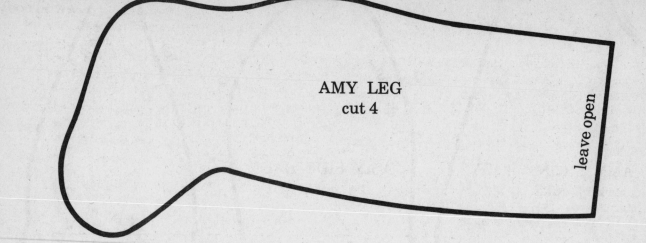

AMY LEG
cut 4

leave open

Amy's Socks and Shoes

MATERIALS *For socks:* Ribbed white cotton socks or knit fabric. *For gold shoes:* scrap of gold felt; matching thread. *For orange shoes:* Scrap of orange felt; white thread and embroidery floss; white glue.

SOCKS Follow doll's leg pattern from foot to within 2″ of top edge. Place fold of each sock front or fold of knit fabric at each leg front then cut foot and back edges, adding small seam allowance. Pin and sew seam on wrong side. Turn and place on doll, folding over 1″ cuff.

GOLD SHOES Trace pattern on one piece of gold felt; pin to a second piece of felt. Stitch the two layers together along seam lines; sew seam twice. Cut out shoe, leaving narrow seam allowance. Turn to right side. Repeat for second shoe.

Cut ⅝″ x 2⅜″ bow and ¼″ x 1½″ knot strip from felt for each shoe. Shape bows, wrap with strips and tack in place.

ORANGE SHOES Mark shoe pattern on felt with two outlines facing left and two facing right. Before cutting out, use white thread to stitch trim along light dotted lines. Cut apart shoe outlines. Pin a left to a right with right sides facing and stitched trim matching. Sew seams twice and cut out shoes, leaving a narrow seam allowance. Turn to right side. Cut out tongue shapes and sew to underside.

Punch holes for laces, dab glue on each hole and remake when half dry. Cut a double length of floss for each shoe and lace through holes.

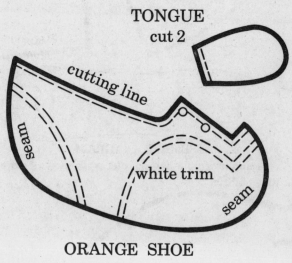

TONGUE
cut 2

cutting line

seam

white trim

seam

ORANGE SHOE
cut 4

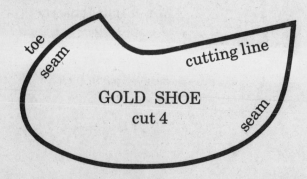

toe

seam

cutting line

GOLD SHOE
cut 4

seam

Amy's Petticoat

MATERIALS ¼ yard or 5" x 21" piece of white cotton fabric; ⅝ yard of 1¼"-deep eyelet-embroidered edging with insertion area for ¼" ribbon; ¾ yard of ¼" Nile green ribbon; 10" length of ¼" elastic.

Use 5" x 21" piece of fabric. At one long edge, make an ⅛" fold then a second ⅛" fold to wrong side. Stitch along fold edge for skirt hem. On right side, pin and then stitch eyelet embroidery to hem, running stitches at top and bottom of insert area. Use a small safety pin to pull ribbon through.

At opposite long edge, fold under ⅛" then ⅜" to wrong side for waistline casing. Stitch along lower fold. With right sides together, pin and stitch petticoat ends for back seam, catching ribbon in seam and leaving casing open. Cut elastic to fit doll's waist plus ¾" for joining. Pull through casing with safety pin and tack together elastic ends. Now stitch casing ends, going over elastic to reinforce joining. Make a small tailored ribbon bow and tack to front of petticoat.

Amy's Play Outfit

This three-piece outfit is made up of a sun dress, matching hat and polka dot bloomers.

MATERIALS *For sun dress:* ¼ yard or 9" x 14" piece each of bright pink and orange cotton fabric; a scrap each of dotted yellow and dotted green cotton; pink, orange and green thread; two ⁵⁄₁₆" pearl buttons. *For sun hat:* 7" x 12" piece each of bright pink and orange cotton; 4" length of ¼" elastic; matching thread. *For polka dot bloomers:* ¼ yard or 7" x 20" piece of dotted green cotton; 10" length of ¼" elastic; 12" length of round elastic.

SUN DRESS Following dress pattern, cut pink dress and orange lining, *adding seam allowance.* Cut yellow tulip with lining and green leaf for pocket and appliqué. Seam lining to tulip and turn. Lightly mark lower seam line on dress for placement and pin tulip and leaf in place. Sew with machine zigzag or hand buttonhole stitch, leaving top of tulip free. Outline tulip with orange thread, leaf and stem with green.

Right sides together, pin lining to dress. Stitch around edges, leaving an opening for turning. Trim and clip seams at armholes and corners; turn and press. Sew opening closed. Try on doll; mark location of buttons and buttonholes. Make buttonholes and sew on buttons.

SUN HAT Following pattern, cut pink hat and orange lining, *adding seam allowance.* Cut a 1" x 3" strip each from pink and orange to hold hat at back.

Right sides together, seam lining to hat, leaving inner curved edge open. Trim seam allowance and clip curved edge; turn. Seam pink strip to orange along both 3" edges, making ⁵⁄₁₆"-wide tube. Trim seam allowance; attach safety pin to one end and pull tube to right side. Insert 2" elastic and stitch ends closed.

Pin elasticized strip between pink and orange fabrics on inner curve at A. Turn in raw edges and topstitch, securing strip ends.

POLKA DOT BLOOMERS Following panty –bloomer pattern cut 2 pieces from green cotton, *adding seam allowance* at back, front and crotch seam edges.

Following panty directions, fold ⅛" then ½" to wrong side at each lower panty edge. Run one row of stitches along top fold edge then a second row ⅜" below first, to make casing for elastic.

Right sides together, stitch front seam and back seam. Matching seams, stitch crotch. Sew casing at waistline; insert ¼" elastic; run round elastic at legs.

Amy's Panties

MATERIALS ¼ yard or 7" x 20" piece of yellow miniature-print cotton or fabric desired; ¾ yard of 1¼"-deep eyelet-embroidered edging with insertion area for ¼" ribbon; ¾ yard of ¼" Nile green ribbon; 10" length of ¼" elastic.

Following panty–bloomer pattern, cut 2 pieces from cotton print, *adding seam allowance* at front, back and crotch seam edges.

At each lower leg edge, fold ⅛" then ½" to wrong

side; stitch along top fold edge for hem. On right side, pin and then stitch eyelet embroidery to hem, running stitches at top and bottom of insert area. Use small safety pin to pull ribbon through.

Right sides together, pin and stitch panties along front seams and back seams. Match seams at crotch, then stitch. Trim seams and overcast.

At waistline, fold ⅛″ then ½″ to wrong side for casing. Stitch along lower fold, leaving openings for elastic. Cut elastic to fit doll's waist plus ¾″ for joining. Pull through casing with small safety pin and tack together elastic ends. Stitch openings, catching elastic ends.

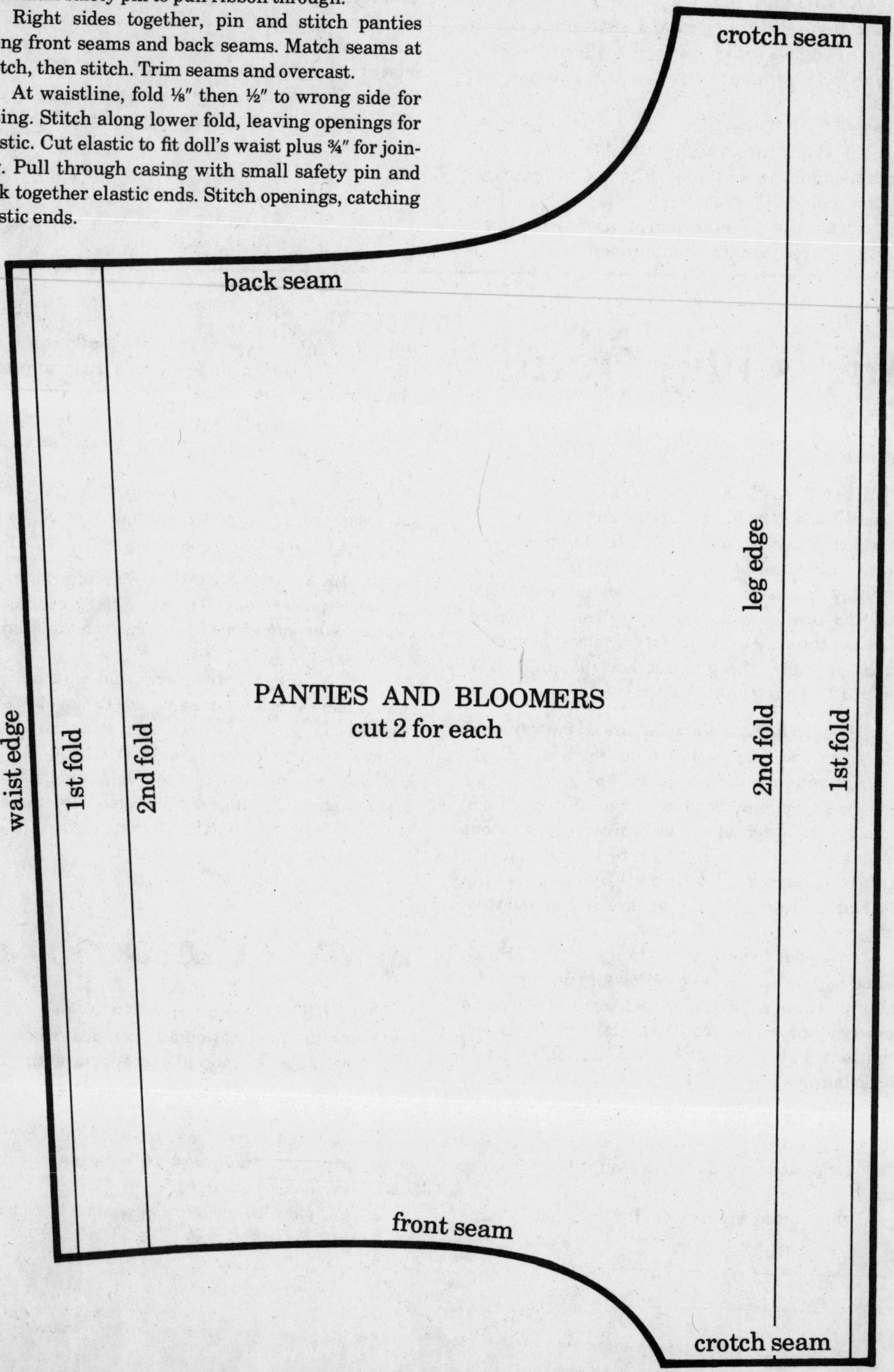

crotch seam

back seam

leg edge

waist edge

1st fold

2nd fold

PANTIES AND BLOOMERS
cut 2 for each

2nd fold

1st fold

front seam

crotch seam

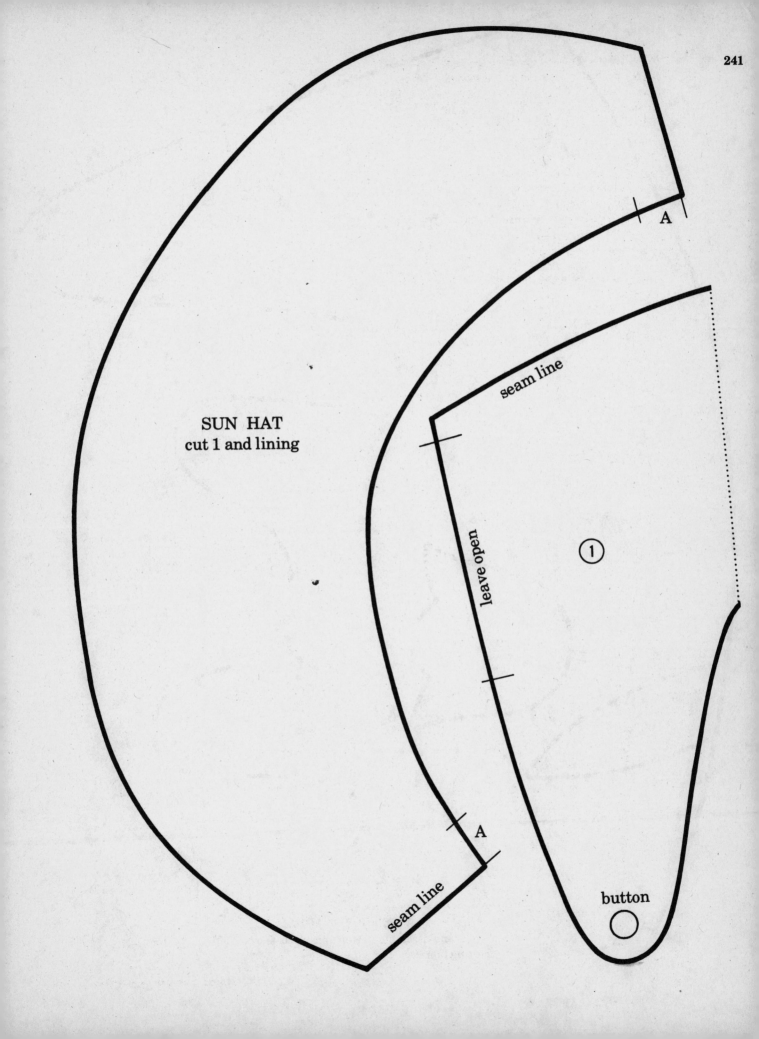

SUN HAT
cut 1 and lining

A

seam line

leave open

①

A

seam line

button

241

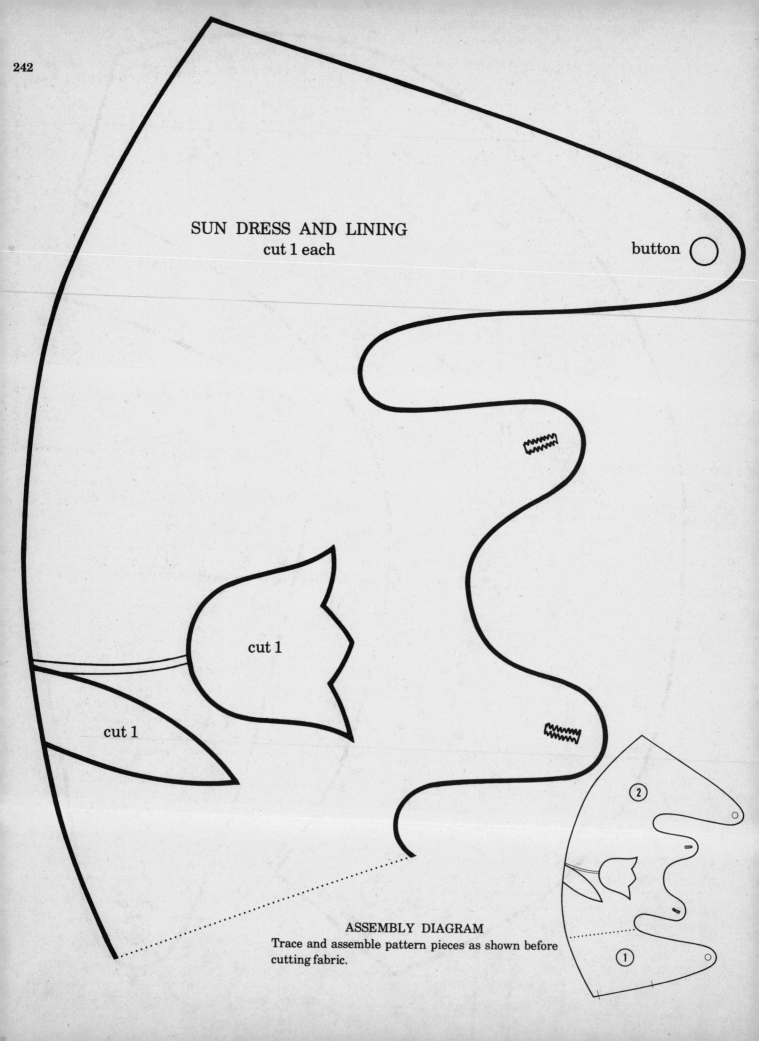

242

SUN DRESS AND LINING
cut 1 each

button

cut 1

cut 1

②

①

ASSEMBLY DIAGRAM
Trace and assemble pattern pieces as shown before
cutting fabric.

SHIRT SLEEVE
cut 2

armhole

side sleeve seam

Amy's Blue Jump Suit and Striped Shirt

MATERIALS *For blue jump suit:* ⅜ yard of 42″ blue stretch knit fabric and scrap of red; 7″ nylon zipper to match suit. *For green-striped shirt:* Long sleeves from a child's size 6X knit shirt; 2 snaps to fasten back.

BLUE JUMP SUIT Following 3 patterns, cut blue jump suit front and back, red pocket and lining; *add ¼″ seam allowance* all around, including neckline, armholes and lower edges of legs.

Pin and sew together two back pieces along back seam; pin and sew front along short front seam. Fold in zipper seam allowances of front; pin and baste zipper in place, putting top of zipper ¼″ below raw neckline and letting surplus hang down until zipper is stitched. With zipper foot, stitch along zipper, sewing across bottom of front opening several times. Turn to wrong side and cut off surplus zipper.

Pin and seam jump suit at shoulders, inner leg seams and sides. Turn in raw edges of neckline, armholes and legs; topstitch. Turn in edges at top of zipper and sew.

Seam heart pocket to its lining with right sides together; turn and sew opening. Pin pocket to suit and sew in place by hand.

GREEN-STRIPED SHIRT Amy's shirt is made from the sleeves of a child's knit shirt. The body of the doll shirt is fitted and cut without a pattern, sleeves are cut with a pattern. Note: If you buy ¼ yard of knit fabric and prefer using a pattern throughout, cut shirt body by Amy's pajama top patterns.

Measure your Amy first and cut off 9″, including ribbed cuff, from lower part of each sleeve on child's shirt. Cut open the sleeve sections along seams; front body will be cut from one piece, two backs from the other and ribbed cuffs will make turtleneck collar. Cut off cuffs and pin body pieces to fit along neck, shoulders and sides; overlap backs and allow for ¼″ turn unders. Unpin and remove; cut body, shaping armholes to fit sleeve pattern. From child's upper sleeves, cut doll sleeves by pattern, *adding small seam allowance.*

Stitch shoulder seams; seam ribbed cuffs together and to neckline, right sides together. Hem back opening. Fold ribbed section in half, right sides together, and seam ends; turn to right side. Fold in raw edge and slip-stitch to neckline.

Pin sleeves to armholes and sew; hem wrist edges. Stitch sleeve and side seams; hem lower shirt edge. Sew snaps to back.

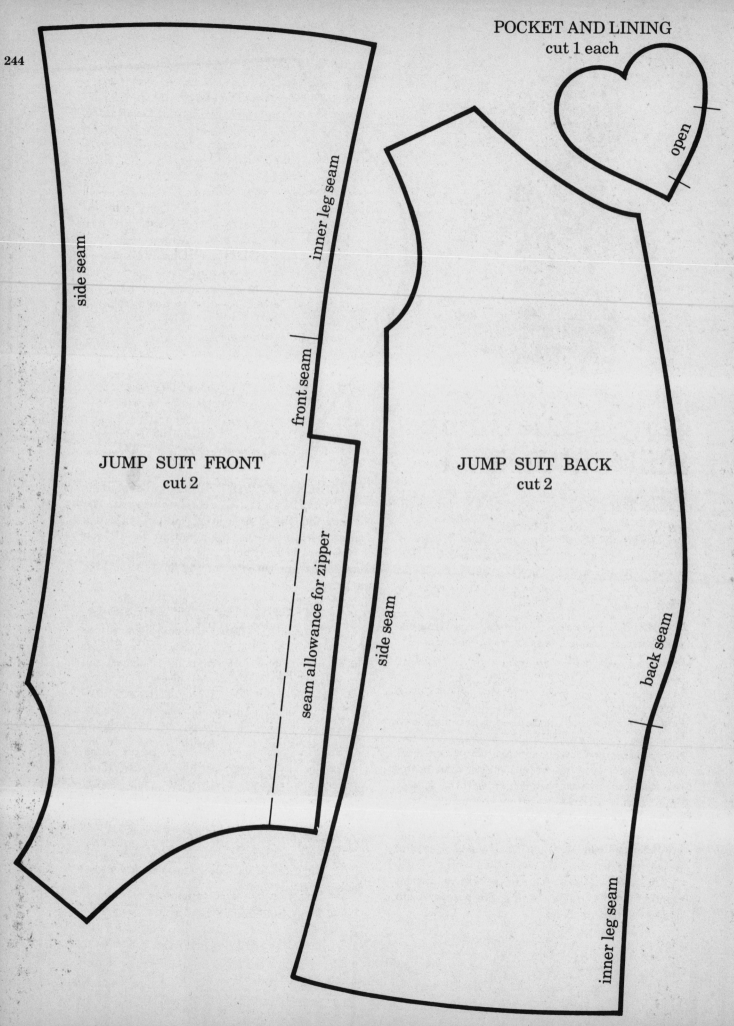

244

POCKET AND LINING
cut 1 each

open

inner leg seam

side seam

front seam

seam allowance for zipper

JUMP SUIT FRONT
cut 2

JUMP SUIT BACK
cut 2

side seam

back seam

inner leg seam

On each sleeve fold ⅛″ then ½″ to wrong side at wrist edge. Stitch along top of ½″ fold; stitch again ¼″ below to make casing for elastic. At top edge, sew 2 rows of long machine stitches; gather slightly to fit armhole. With right sides together, pin sleeve to armhole; sew with ¼″ seam. Check that curve of armhole is even and that stray stitches are covered; seam again if necessary. Trim seam allowance.

Try bodice, wrong side out, on doll. Pin back opening closed; pin side and sleeve seams to fit easily. Unpin back and remove bodice. Stitch side and sleeve seams; trim seam allowance and overcast.

Cut elastic to fit doll's wrist plus ½″. Remove a few stitches where sleeve seam crosses casing. Pull elastic through casing with a small pin, leaving ¼″ of elastic ends extending; restitch seam, catching elastic.

Skirt Along skirt's 7½″ edges, fold ⅛″ then another ⅛″ to wrong side; stitch along folded edges. At one long skirt edge, fold ⅛″ then 1¼″ to wrong side for hem; stitch along top fold. At opposite long edge, sew 2 rows of long machine stitches; gather to fit bodice waistline. Pin skirt to bodice, right sides together, and space gathers. Stitch seam ¼″ from edge; check that gathering stitches are covered. Overcast seam allowance.

Place dress on doll and mark for snaps or buttons and loops; sew in place.

GREEN GINGHAM PINAFORE *Note:* Bodice, ruffles and skirt are all self lined.

Following 3 patterns, cut bodice, shoulder ruffles and pockets, *adding seam allowance.* Cut a piece for skirt 9½″ x 20″.

Bodice Pin and sew together bodice backs at shoulder seams. Pin and sew together left bodice fronts at shoulder; repeat for right fronts. Turn seamed pieces.

With right sides together, pin and seam the two layers of bodice along neckline and center front opening, leaving armholes, sides and lower edges open. Trim seam allowance and turn to right side. Bodice now is identical on inside and outside.

Stitch together pairs of ruffle pieces along curved outer edge; turn to right side. Run long machine stitches along straight edge; gather to fit. With right sides together, pin ruffle to outside of bodice from A to A along armhole; have raw edges of ruffle match raw edge of armhole. Sew seam. Turn under raw edge of *inside* bodice along ruffle-armhole seam line and pin. Slip-stitch by hand. Repeat for other ruffle.

Fit bodice on doll over underwear and dress, pinning front opening closed and side seams to-

Amy's Calico Dress and Gingham Pinafore

MATERIALS *For brown calico dress:* ⅜ yard of 44″ brown cotton print; ¼ yard ⅛″ elastic; 3 snaps or buttons, thread for button loops (optional). *For green gingham pinafore:* ⅜ yard 44″ green-and-white gingham; 4 small buttons; white thread.

BROWN CALICO DRESS Following 2 patterns and *adding seam allowance,* cut bodice and sleeves from print, using light lines for bodice backs and reversing pattern for one back. Cut 1″ x 11″ strip for neck ruffle and 7½″ x 21″ piece for dress skirt.

Bodice For bodice, pin and seam pieces at shoulders. At back opening edges, fold ⅛″ then ¼″ to wrong side. Stitch along both long edges of ¼″ fold.

Fold ruffle strip lengthwise with wrong side inside; press. Sew 2 rows of long machine stitches along raw edges and turn in strip ends; gather threads so ruffle fits neckline. Pin ruffle to right side of neckline with raw edges even; stitch seam ¼″ from edge and check that curve is even. Overcast seam allowance. Turn ruffle upright and topstitch on right side.

246

gether. Remove bodice. Open up sides and repin from interior; sew side seams, joining inside and outside.

Skirt For double skirt, fold fabric in half to measure 4¾" x 20" with right side inside. Stitch short ends with ¼" seam. Clip corners and turn. Run 2 rows of long machine stitches along raw 20" edges, gather to fit bodice waistline. With right sides together, pin and sew to outside bodice. Trim seam allowance if needed and turn to inside. Turn under and pin raw edge of inside bodice; hand sew.

Pockets For pockets, sew ⅛" hem on one edge of each; turn under ¼" on remaining edges and press. Sew to skirt by hand with hemmed edges at top.

Sew 4 buttons to right side of bodice (as you face it) and make 4 thread loops on left side.

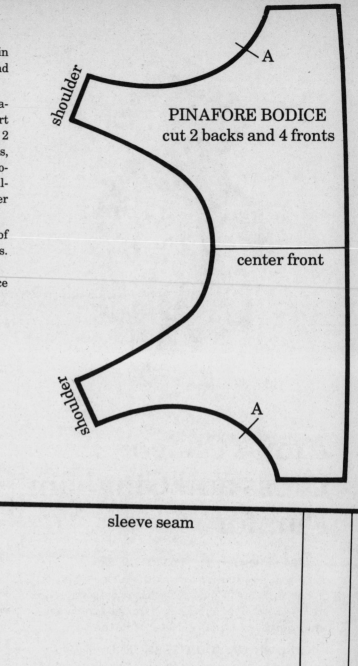

PINAFORE BODICE
cut 2 backs and 4 fronts

shoulder

A

center front

shoulder

A

PINAFORE POCKET
cut 2

bias

PINAFORE SHOULDER RUFFLE
cut 4

seam line

seam line

gather

gather

CALICO DRESS SLEEVE
cut 2

sleeve seam

sleeve seam

2nd fold

1st fold

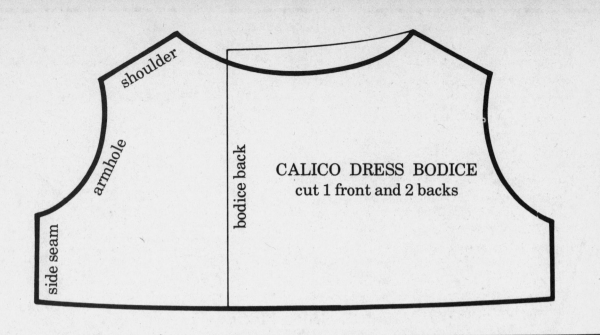

shoulder

armhole

side seam

bodice back

CALICO DRESS BODICE
cut 1 front and 2 backs

Amy's Red Wool Cape and Cap

MATERIALS For cape and cap: ⅝ yard of 42″ red knit fabric; ¼ yard bias tape for neck and ¾ yard for armholes (optional); hook and eye; scrap of red yarn for pompon on cap.

CAPE Following 2 patterns and *adding seam allowance,* except at armholes, cut large and small cape pieces.

Beginning with large cape, pin and stitch pairs along back seam. Right sides together, pin seamed pieces to one another and stitch along front and outer edges. Clip seam allowance at corners and turn; press. To finish armholes, clip seam allowance and turn in edges of outer and inner layers; pin and topstitch. For an easier finish, trim seam allowance and sew bias tape around armholes.

Next pin and stitch small cape pieces along front and outer edges. Clip at corners and turn.

Pin small cape to large cape around neckline, pinning only to outside layer. Stitch seam around neck. Spread capes on a work surface. Fold raw inner edge of large cape over seam and seam allowance; slipstitch in place. If desired, bind neckline with bias tape. Sew on hook and eye.

POMPON CAP Following diagram, cut 7½″ x 13″ piece of knit fabric. Seam two 7½″ edges from A to B. Clip seam allowance at B. Turn cap inside out and pin seam; stitch from B to C. Turn cap upside down and fold up C to B for cuff; stitch cuff. Gather top of cap and sew securely. Make a 1¼″ yarn pompon and sew to top.

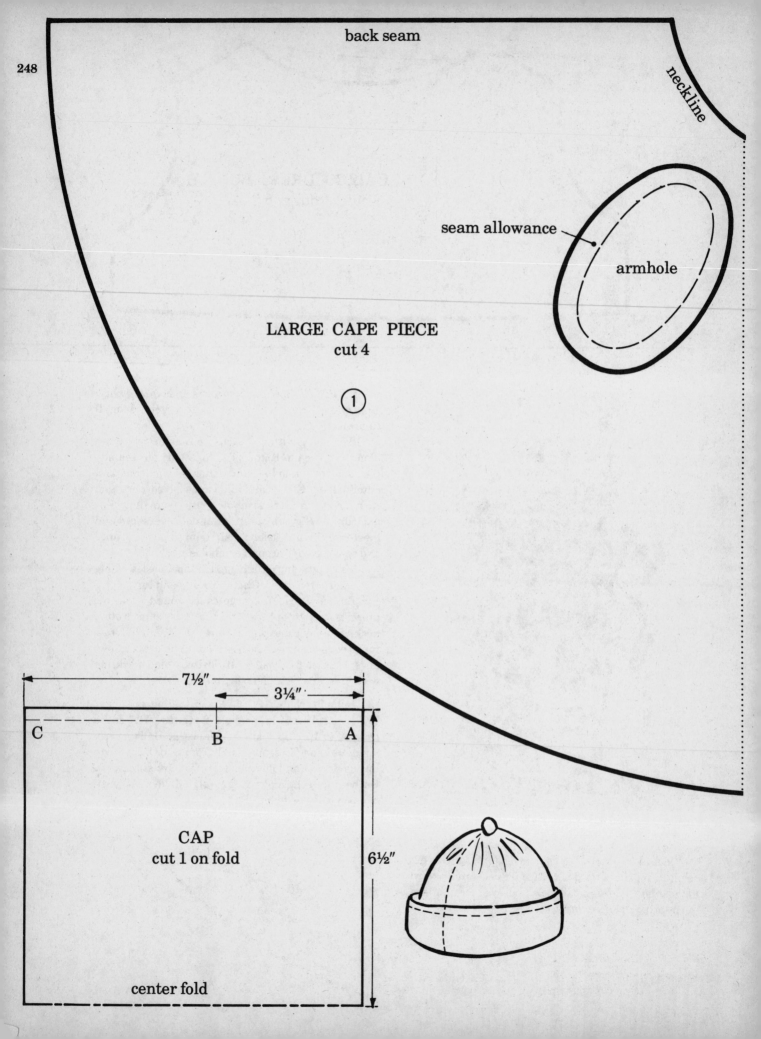

back seam

neckline

seam allowance

armhole

LARGE CAPE PIECE
cut 4

① 1

7½"

3¼"

C   B   A

6½"

CAP
cut 1 on fold

center fold

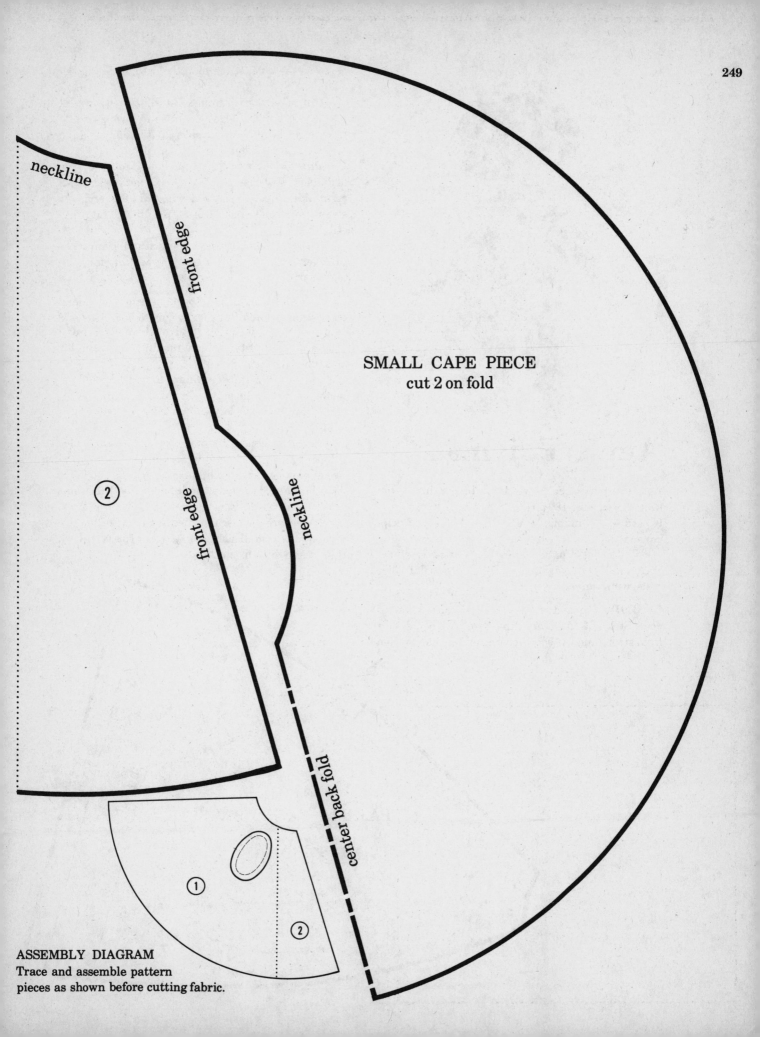

neckline

front edge

SMALL CAPE PIECE
cut 2 on fold

②

front edge

neckline

center back fold

①

②

ASSEMBLY DIAGRAM
Trace and assemble pattern
pieces as shown before cutting fabric.

Amy's Pajamas

MATERIALS ⅜ yard 42″ blue print cotton knit fabric; 4″ x 18″ piece of solid blue knit fabric; ½ yard seam binding; 5″ length of ¼″ elastic; 7 gripper snaps.

Following 8 patterns and *adding seam allowance,* cut print pajama top and pants, solid color cuffs, vamps and soles.

TOP Pin and stitch backs to front at shoulders. Stitch ⅛″ from neckline edge to prevent knit from stretching. At back opening edges, fold ¼″ then ½″ to wrong side; stitch along fold edges and outer edges.

Cut ¾″ x 9″ strip from solid color knit for neck facing. Right sides together, pin in place; seam ¼″ from edge. Turn to wrong side. Fold in ends and pin under ⅛″ at long edge; slip-stitch in place.

Pin sleeves, with right sides together, to armholes; sew seams. Stitch cuffs in place, with right sides together; turn down cuffs. Pin and sew sleeve and side seams; turn cuffs to inside and slip-stitch in place.

Turn up hem at lower edges. Stitch seam binding over hem inside pajama top as backing for gripper snaps.

PANTS Pin and sew back piece to pants along back seams. Stitch front leg seams to back legs and along crotch. At waistline, fold ⅛″ then ½″ to wrong side; stitch along two edges, making ½″ casing for back and hem for rest of waist.

For feet, pin and sew vamps to pants legs along instep seams, with right sides together. Pin soles to vamps and back of legs; stitch around soles. Turn pants to right side.

Try top and pants on doll and mark location for gripper snaps, using two to fasten back of top and five at pants waistline. Omit from pants back casing. Attach snaps, following manufacturer's directions.

To insert elastic in back casing, remove a few stitches where back seams meet casing. Pull elastic through with small safety pin to fit doll snugly. Tack then stitch ends in place.

PAJAMA PANTS BACK
cut 1

back seam

crotch

back seam

2nd fold

1st fold

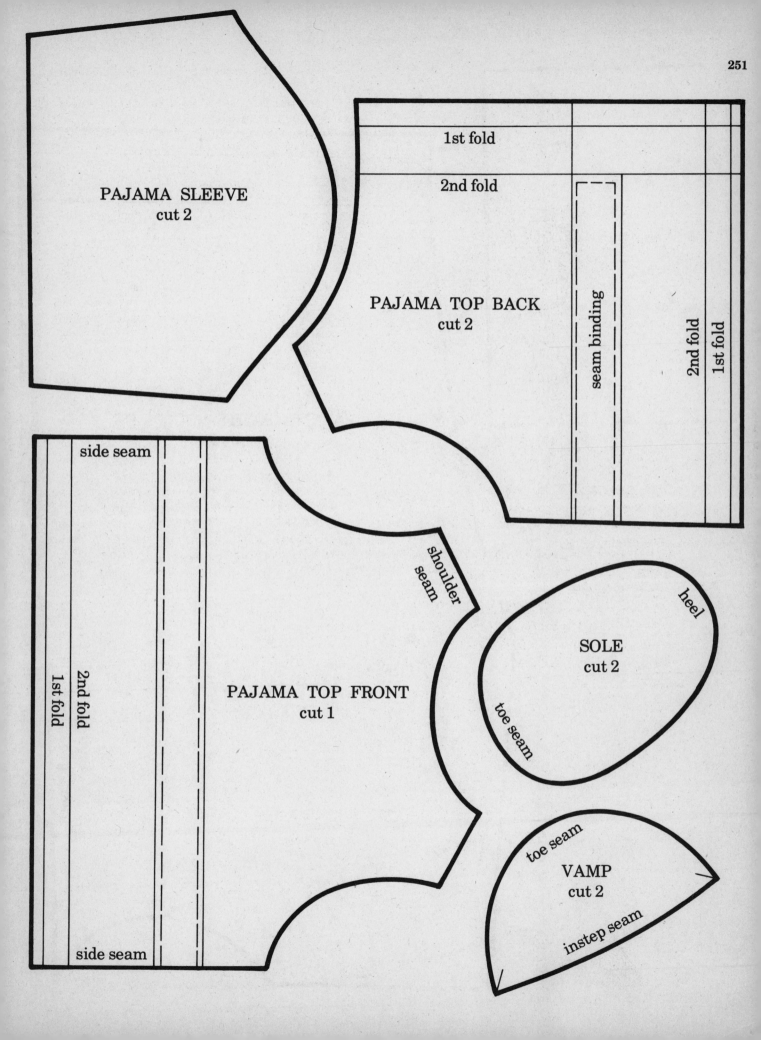

PAJAMA SLEEVE
cut 2

1st fold

2nd fold

PAJAMA TOP BACK
cut 2

seam binding

2nd fold

1st fold

side seam

2nd fold

1st fold

shoulder
seam

PAJAMA TOP FRONT
cut 1

side seam

heel

SOLE
cut 2

toe seam

toe seam

VAMP
cut 2

instep seam

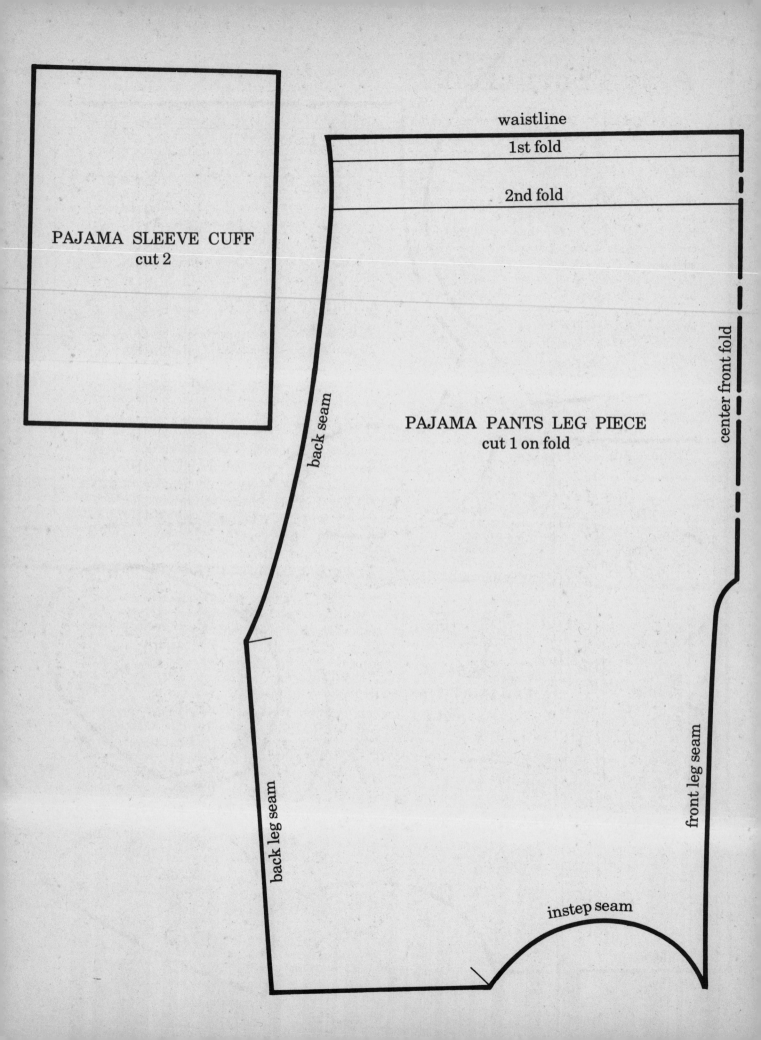

PAJAMA SLEEVE CUFF
cut 2

waistline

1st fold

2nd fold

center front fold

back seam

PAJAMA PANTS LEG PIECE
cut 1 on fold

back leg seam

front leg seam

instep seam

Amy's Small Doll

MATERIALS 8″ x 14″ piece of pink cotton fabric; orange wool yarn; blue, pink and orange embroidery floss; black thread; polyester fiber filling; pink and orange waterproof felt marking pens.

Following pattern, cut body pieces from pink cotton, *adding seam allowance*. Pin pieces together and stitch seams, leaving openings at head and side. Reinforce seams at neck, thumb, underarm and crotch; trim seam allowance and clip at reinforced edges.

Turn doll to right side, which is rather tricky because of its small size. Slowly push with a blunt crochet hook or pull with a pin to turn legs and arms.

Next stuff doll, using small bits of filling and beginning with legs. Stuff them almost to top and stitch across dotted lines so legs move easily. Stuff arm opposite side opening, leaving space at top; stitch along dotted line so arm can flap. Stuff and sew second arm, then body center, making it pleasingly plump. Sew side opening. Stuff neck and head through top of head and sew opening.

HAIR Lay strands of orange yarn about 8″ long across and in back of head; sew in place, making a center part. Divide strands into 3 groups and tack center group to each side of head. Make braids, tie thread at ends and trim.

FACE Using embroidery floss, outline-stitch pink nose, orange mouth and satin-stitch blue eyes; work lashes with black thread. With pink marking pen, draw rosy cheeks.

SLIPPERS Color with orange marking pen. The doll will never lose them!

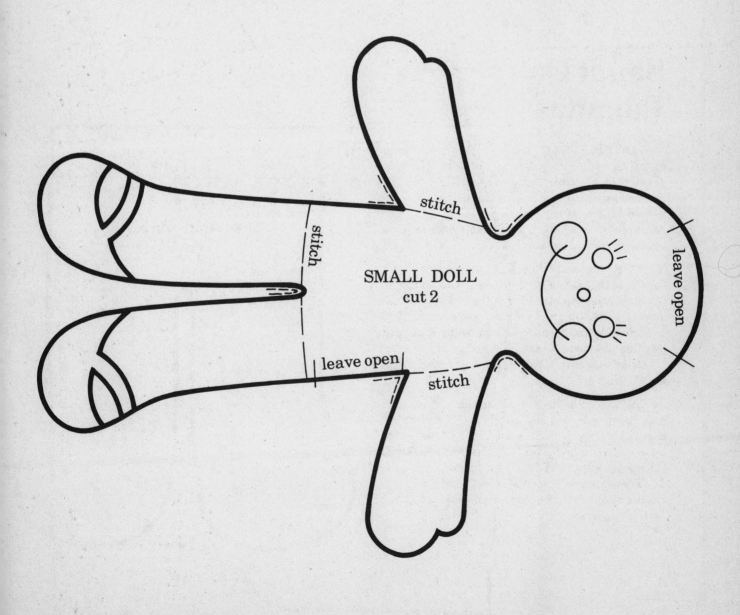

stitch

stitch

leave open

SMALL DOLL
cut 2

leave open

stitch

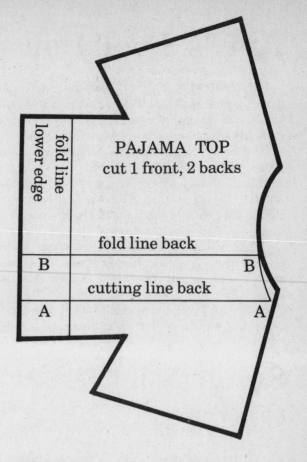

PAJAMA TOP
cut 1 front, 2 backs

fold line
lower edge

fold line back

B   B

cutting line back

A   A

Small Doll's Pajamas

MATERIALS 6″ x 20″ piece of blue print cotton knit fabric; 1″ x 12″ strip of solid blue knit; 4″ length of ⅛″ elastic; 3 gripper snaps.

Following two patterns and adding ¼″ seam allowance, cut print pajama top and pants, using line A-A to cut top backs. Cut ¾″ x 4″ solid color strips to bind neckline and sleeves.

TOP Pin and stitch backs to front at shoulders. Fold the back opening to wrong side on line B-B; stitch down. Right sides together, pin and stitch binding to neckline and sleeves. Leave narrow fold on right side and turn binding to wrong side; hem neckline ends and slip-stitch all binding in place.

Stitch side seams. Fold up lower edge and stitch. Turn to right side.

PANTS Pin and stitch together front and back along side, leg and crotch seam. Fold in ½″ along waistline; stitch close to fold and ⅜″ below it to make casing. Snip side seam stitches and run elastic through back casing. Trim seams and turn.

Try pants and top on doll; mark location for one gripper at center back of top, two at front waistline. Attach grippers.

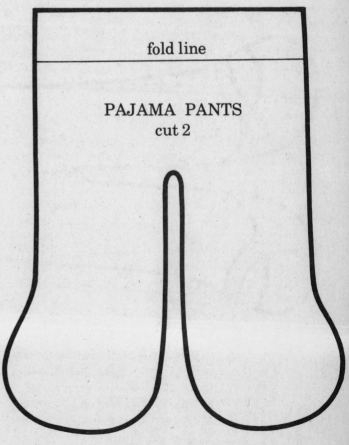

fold line

PAJAMA PANTS
cut 2

making a casing. With right sides together, stitch one side seam. Make casing at waistline. Seam open side and crotch.

Cut elastic to fit legs and waist plus ½″ for ends. Where seams interfere with casings remove a few stitches. Insert elastic with tiny safety pin; sew ends and restitch seams.

Small Doll's Play Outfit

This two-piece outfit is made up of sun dress and polka dot bloomers.

MATERIALS *For sun dress:* 5″ x 7″ piece each of bright pink and orange cotton; scrap each of dotted yellow and dotted green cotton; yellow and green thread; two small snaps and two pearl buttons. *For polka dot bloomers:* 4″ x 9″ piece of dotted orange cotton; 12″ length of round elastic.

SUN DRESS Following dress pattern, cut pink dress and orange lining, adding seam allowance. Cut yellow tulip for pocket and green leaf for appliqué.

Right sides together, pin lining to dress. Stitch around edges, leaving an opening for turning. Trim and clip seams at armholes and corners; turn and press. Sew opening. Hem pocket top. Pin tulip and leaf to dress; sew in place with machine zigzag or hand buttonhole stitch, using yellow thread for pocket, green for leaf and stem.

Try dress on doll and mark location of snaps; sew in place and top with buttons in front.

POLKA DOT BLOOMERS Following pattern, cut 2 pieces from orange cotton, *adding seam allowance* only at side and crotch seam edges.

At each lower leg edge, fold ⅛″ then ¼″ to wrong side; stitch along top fold edge and near lower edge,

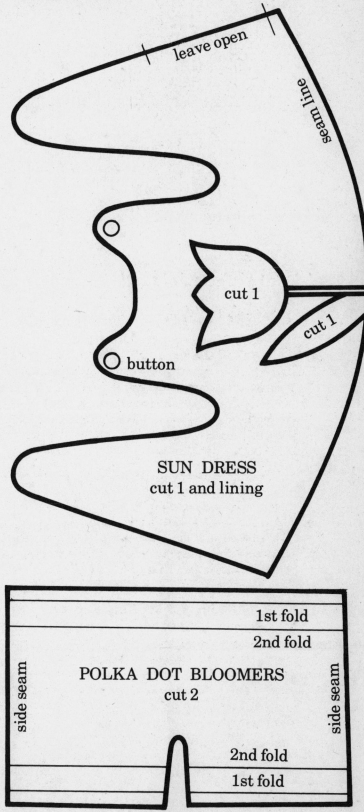

leave open

seam line

cut 1

cut 1

button

SUN DRESS
cut 1 and lining

POLKA DOT BLOOMERS
cut 2

1st fold

2nd fold

side seam

side seam

2nd fold

1st fold